Monkeys with TYPEWRITERS

HOW TO WRITE FICTION AND UNLOCK THE SECRET POWER OF STORIES

SCARLETT THOMAS

CANONGATE

Edinburgh · London

Published in Great Britain in 2012 by Canongate Books Ltd,
14 High Street, Edinburgh EH1 1TE

1

Copyright © Scarlett Thomas, 2012

The moral right of the author has been asserted

www.canongate.tv

British Library Cataloguing-in-Publication Data
A catalogue record for this book is available on
request from the British Library

ISBN 978 0 85786 378 2

'Plato's Cave' image © Norah Perkins

Typeset in Plantin Light by Palimpsest Book Production Ltd,
Falkirk, Stirlingshire

Printed and bound in Great Britain by CPI Group (UK) Ltd, Croydon, CR0 4YY

CONTENTS

I think it is not for writers to solve such questions as the existence of God, pessimism etc. The writer's function is only to describe by whom, how and under what conditions the questions of God and pessimism were discussed. The artist must be only an impartial witness of his characters and what they said, not their judge.

Anton Chekhov[1]

INTRODUCTION

It was a rainy Tuesday in Canterbury, Kent. I'd been teaching 'The Death of the Author' by Roland Barthes to my third-year students, which was probably unwise. One of my senior colleagues had recently found out that I'd been teaching literary theory to creative writing students, and she wasn't happy about it. 'What do you think you're doing?' she'd said, after a group of them had tried to 'borrow' a sofa they needed for their seminar presentation on structuralism. 'Just teach them the difference between first person and third person and let them *write*, for God's sake.'

After that, no one was allowed to use furniture in a presentation.

This was during my first year of teaching. It wasn't how I'd thought it would be. I'd imagined turning up and finding groups of terrifyingly well-read students who all wanted to be Raymond Carver or Sylvia Plath. What I found were, mostly, quite modest people who hadn't even heard of Carver and Plath. They had some great ideas, and were often fascinating and charismatic in person. But when they wrote, their easy, natural voices often turned into formal, wordy, lumpen prose. 'Are you writing to your great-aunt?'

I'd ask them. I'd started setting essay questions like 'What is the point of metafiction?' just to shake things up a bit. It wasn't working. So I was willing to try anything, even Barthes. My theory at the time was that if the students could read better, they'd write better. But more than that, I thought it would be useful to get away from the idea of 'author as genius' and the sorts of biographical readings that made my students think that you could only write fiction if you were rich or beautiful or had a complicated personal history. I wanted the students to see how much the words on the page matter.

Teaching 'The Death of the Author' hadn't actually gone that well. In the seminar I'd introduced the students to the Infinite Monkey Theorem. This theorem states that a monkey hitting typewriter keys randomly will eventually, given enough time, produce the works of Shakespeare. I asked the students to imagine a monkey writing *Hamlet* completely by accident. If *Hamlet* had been written by a monkey with a typewriter, would it still mean something? Yes. Of course it would, we'd decided, after a lot of frowning and thinking. Or maybe it was just me that decided. Anyway, the Infinite Monkey Theorem, I said, proved that it is the text that matters, not the author. It didn't really matter who'd written *Hamlet*: it was a deep, moving and mysterious play because of the words on the page and nothing more.

I ended up with the odd feeling I often had in those days that I'd taught something important and interesting, but that it hadn't had quite the effect I wanted. I half wondered if my colleague had been right, and I should just let the students write. After all, her students were doing OK, and writing some pretty decent short stories. My students all seemed to be beginning vast, peculiar novels about the afterlife.

Then there was a knock at my office door. It was an American student who always called me Professor Thomas, even though at the time I was a junior lecturer. I invited him to come in and sit down.

'Professor Thomas,' he said sadly, 'I just don't understand "The Death of the Author", however hard I try. Especially this stuff about monkeys.'

'Yes, well,' I said. 'Sorry. That was a weird example. But don't blame Barthes for that – it was my idea. I thought it would help. Anyway, just focus on his essay.'

'But why are the monkeys typing in space?'

'Not space. Infinity. Although I guess it might amount to the same thing . . .'

'But why?' he said.

I thought back to the class. There *was* something a bit, well, wrong about the monkeys with typewriters thing, but I couldn't put my finger on what it was. We probably all knew intuitively, even if we couldn't do the mathematics, how unlikely it would be that the exact combination of typewriter characters that made *Hamlet* would ever just 'randomly' occur in nature. In fact, mathematically, you'd need millions of universes and millions of monkeys for this to happen. There is only a one in fifteen billion chance that a monkey would even write the word 'banana' randomly. But we'd persisted in persuading ourselves that this thought experiment meant that the author doesn't matter, and that Shakespeare doesn't matter, even though we were all trying to be authors, or, at least, writers. Mathematically and philosophically, Shakespeare shouldn't matter. But I think we sensed that he did. Shakespeare himself was a random fact of nature, with almost the same genetic sequence as a monkey, and he produced *Hamlet* in less than a year.

But anyway, most of us had agreed that it was the words and sentences on the page that meant something, not the thoughts of the author (which you could never know anyway). But this student hadn't agreed with anything. He'd just looked lost.

'OK,' I said to him. 'Let's think about Bret Easton Ellis's *Lunar Park*. We know from studying it that it's all about fictionalisation, the limits of reality, father–son relationships and so on. Now, imagine that Bret Easton Ellis walks in here now and says that the novel is actually all about goldfish, or clothes-pegs. Can he change the book by saying that? Just because he's the author? It's impossible, right? So we can't really take the author's intentions into account when reading, because they might change, or because the author may not even know what they are, or may have forgotten. We don't want the text closed, but opened . . . '

I noticed that the student had begun to look a little quivery and was no longer concentrating on what I was saying.

'Are you OK?' I said.

He looked at me. 'Professor Thomas?' he said. 'Honestly? If Bret walked in here now, like the *real* Bret? I just don't know what I'd do. I love him.'

That was the moment I realised.

We love writers.

However suspicious of language we might (rightly) be, we still love writers.

Why? Why do we love them more than random word generators, or immortals with nothing better to do than randomly strike typewriter keys for all eternity? Why would no one in their right mind want to read a computer-generated novel, even if it were possible to create one? I realised that we love our favourite writers because they are *human*, and they have made an effort to communicate something important to us. In knowing they are human we understand that they feel just as much as we do. We know that they understand what it means to want something you can't have, to love the wrong person, to be misunderstood, in pain, embarrassed and alone. Writers are important to us because they look at the world and see something interesting, and they manage to write it down in a way that makes our brief lives more substantial. We know that writers appreciate beauty, whatever we think that is, just as we do, because they are human. Humans are not able to sit around writing randomly until the end of time. We are fragile, finite and afraid. We suffer.

I realised that *this* was what I needed to teach my students.

We are part of the great ape family, *Hominidae*, just like gorillas, chimpanzees and orang-utans. Our animalistic desires – for sex, food, a nest, some kind of wealth or status – form the basis of much fiction. We won't live for ever, but at least we've learned to use our typewriters. And we have something to say. We might not be able to know the true intentions of authors, and we might not consider these intentions important when we are reading, but by God we'd better have some when we are writing. And our intentions, as we will see over the course of this book, must be both ambitious and modest: they must be about asking big questions, rather than providing small answers.

We shouldn't be afraid of big questions. Anyone who has looked at the sky has wondered what's out there. Everyone wonders who they really are. Everyone thinks about death, aging, love, sadness, delight and all the ideas we encounter in the best writing. These questions aren't just for 'special' people, or even just for people on creative writing courses. They are for everyone. But it is very hard to write in such a way that someone else can feel what you felt, or think what you thought. Language has limitations, for a start. How do we say something if there's no word for it? And structure is tricky too. How do we have enough structure so that what we are doing is recognisable as, say, a novel, but not so much that it becomes completely formulaic? Perhaps most importantly, how do we decide what to write about, given all the amazing things we have seen and experienced? And how do we begin to turn this into fiction?

In the end I gave up trying to teach 'The Death of the Author'. But I still thought we could do more for the students than tell them to 'just write'. It's particularly useful to teach people what to do *before* they 'just write'. Over the years I have encountered a surprising number of people who simply can't recognise what is most interesting about them or identify the 'special knowledge' that they have (and everyone does have something). I now begin every fiction writing class by getting the students to make some kind of inventory of what they know, what dramatic things have happened to them, what their 'special skills' are, what unique knowledge they have and so on. One of the ways I do this is with a matrix that I have included here in Appendix One. You might want to fill this out now and just leave it for a while. Later on I'll show you how to use it to start plotting a novel, short story, screenplay or some other kind of fiction. There's no obligation for you to then write this, of course. But it is an interesting process even for non-writers, working out what you could write if you wanted to. Of course, to you, your matrix will probably look a bit boring and familiar. Most people say this. I have had students not notice exciting things like beekeeping, archery, grade seven piano, profes-sional gardening experience and advanced mathematics lurking on their matrixes. So often, in class, a student says something about what they know and everyone else says, 'Wow, that's so interesting. I'd love to read a book about that.'

I was beginning to establish some idea of what could be 'taught' in creative writing, and so much of it was about the preparatory stages of writing. *What will you write about and how will you do it?* Most people are OK once they know this stuff, but not enough time is spent on it. At the time that I began doing it, creative writing teaching – even sometimes my own – often involved little more than passing around postcards and asking students to describe them, or giving them three incongruous objects and asking them to put them in a story. This sort of creative writing was some-thing any intelligent person could easily do on their own, or with some friends, or with one of the creative writing books available at that time. Why come to university to do it? I spent a lot of time trying to imagine Tolstoy or Chekhov on a university writing course and not being able to do it. Sylvia Plath, I reminded myself, actually got rejected from a writing course. A great writing course should, like a great novel, be a life-changing experience.

I realised that there was a whole set of things that everyone knew about creative writing ('show don't tell', 'write what you know', 'never use a cliché', 'delete all your adverbs' and so on). People even 'knew' that it was a bad idea to read great fiction while you were trying to write it. One of my MA students once asked me what he should do about this. 'I want to read Hemingway,' he said. 'But I'm scared that I'll, you know, pick up too much of his voice.' Of course, if it was this easy to pick up a writing voice, the world would be full of great (if derivative) writers. 'Don't worry,' I said to this student. 'Read what you like. You're definitely *not* going to turn into Hemingway.' At the time we all laughed. But he went ahead, and guess what? He didn't turn into Hemingway, just from reading him: he turned a bit more into himself.

Some other quite simple truths were being overlooked as well, for example that fiction is all about suffering, conflict and drama – all the things that make us humans from the family *Hominidae*. How do you teach that? The existing 'rules' were being thrown around without any explanation about why they exist, and why they might even be wrong sometimes. Why should we show rather than tell? How do we write what we know without becoming too autobiographical? And what is actually wrong with clichés and adverbs? In *The Bell Jar*, Esther Greenwood says at one point, 'My drink was wet and depressing.' This is 'bad writing' by normal creative writing standards, because it is abstract rather than specific, but in context it's a brilliant line, just right for the character and the situation. I sensed it was important in creative writing teaching not just to recognise that something works, but to analyse how and why. I also wanted to encourage new writers to take risks and be ambitious. I wanted them to understand writing as a profound act of communication, not just an exercise in technique.

But I also wanted them to have fun, and to develop a lightness of touch. We have a short-fiction course at Kent where students read Anton Chekhov, Katherine Mansfield and Raymond Carver and then write their own short stories. Last time I taught it, almost everyone's favourite story was Raymond Carver's 'Feathers'. In the story a young couple, Jack and Fran, go to visit a married couple, Bud and Olla, who live in the countryside with their baby and a pet peacock. When Olla wants to let the peacock come in Bud says, 'We got company in case you hadn't noticed. These people don't want a goddamn old bird in the house. That dirty bird [. . .] What're people going to think?' Olla's response implies that Bud has never called the peacock 'dirty' before and is doing so now only to impress the guests. Eventually, the peacock is allowed to come in, and he plays with the baby. We realise that this is a very happy, if eccentric, family. However, the scene where Olla brings the baby out to show Jack and Fran is the one that the students always remember.

The baby stood in Olla's lap, looking around the table at us. Olla had moved her hands down to its middle so that the baby could rock back and forth on its fat legs. Bar none, it was the ugliest baby I'd ever seen. It was so ugly I couldn't say anything. No words would come out of my mouth. I don't mean it was diseased or disfigured. Nothing like that. It was just ugly. It had a big red face, pop eyes, a broad forehead, and these big fat lips. It had no neck to speak of, and it had three or four fat chins. Its chins rolled right up under its ears, and its ears stuck out from its bald head. Fat hung over its wrists. Its arms and fingers were fat. Even calling it ugly does it credit.[2]

All the students I have ever taught have been absolutely delighted by this passage. Afterwards, weeks or months later, you only have to say 'ugly baby' to them and they collapse into fits of laughter. Why? Well, for one thing they seem to love it that a serious writer like Carver takes such obvious pleasure in describing a really ugly baby, which is something no one, if they wanted to be polite, grown-up and sophisticated, would ever contemplate doing. It's as if there's a Venn diagram in which the set of 'things you find in serious literature' and the set of 'things that are very funny in real life' overlap. It's silly and freakish, but it's somehow serious as well.

I started to notice similar responses to other texts from our reading lists. There's the wonderful George Saunders story 'Sea Oak', in which the protagonist's aunt dies, becomes a zombie and yells 'show your cock' at him (he works in a male topless bar but knows he can get more money if he does 'extras'). There's Magnus Mills's book *The Restraint of Beasts*, in which some high-tensile fencers keep accidentally killing people and then burying them under gateposts. There's Nicola Barker's novel *Five Miles from Outer Hope*, in which a teenage girl, Medve, falls in love with a guy who smells of antiseptic but then frightens him off with a prank that goes wrong involving pulling a plastic centipede out of her vagina. There's Chekhov's story 'Rothschild's Fiddle', which begins, 'It was a tiny town, worse than a village, inhabited chiefly by old people who so seldom died that it was really vexatious.'

When I remind students of the ugly baby, their conversation goes something like this:

'Oh my God, the ugly baby. The *ugly baby*!'

'I loved that story.'

'It's harsh, though.'

'Yeah, but it's totally hilarious.'

'I *love* the ugly baby.'

'Me too. It's so sweet.'

'And what are the names of those people? Fran and . . . '

'Jack?'

'Yeah. Don't they end up having a really mean, horrible baby?'

'That's right. After that evening she's like, "Fill me up with your seed!".'

'It's so gross.'

'And then their baby ends up with a "conniving streak".'

'And Fran cuts her hair and gets fat.'

'Yeah, and then they're really miserable.'

'What happens to the peacock?'

'Doesn't it fly into a tree one night and not come down?'
And so on.

'Feathers' is one of Carver's more sentimental stories,
but it does ask serious questions about the domestic choices
people make, and the role of beauty in life. The students
think about these questions as a result of reading it. They
think about how one dinner party can change your life,
and how people are influenced to do things by watching
other people. The ugly baby is where they start, though.
Everyone loves the ugly baby. The ugly baby is defamiliarising and somehow earthy. It's real. It shocks us a little bit,
wakes us up, makes us pay more attention to the rest of
the story. Playful, irreverent moments like this are one of
the great pleasures of fiction. They don't just occur in
contemporary writing, and they don't always feature sex
and death (although it's very common that they do). Who
hasn't laughed at the Dormouse in *Alice in Wonderland*, Mr
Wemmick in *Great Expectations*, Jane Austen's parody of
Gothic fiction in *Northanger Abbey*, or Baby Kochamma's
'armfat' in Arundhati Roy's *The God of Small Things*? ('Baby
Kochamma was holding on to the back of the front seat
with her arms. When the car moved, her armfat swung like
heavy washing in the wind.'[3]) Indeed, there is no such thing
as a great novel with nothing funny in it. So anyone learning
how to write must also consider how to work with playful-
ness and humour.

No one, it seemed, had written a contemporary writing
book that covered everything. There were plenty of books
out there, though. Some focused on 'giving yourself permis-
sion to write'. Some suggested automatic writing. Some

had exercises in perspective and general technique. Some of them were even very good. I encouraged all my students to read *On Writing* by Stephen King, *How Fiction Works* by James Wood and *Eats, Shoots and Leaves* by Lynne Truss. But there was no single book I could give my students to read that covered everything I thought they should know. So I gave them Plato and Aristotle on plotting, Stanislavski on characterisation, Nietzsche on tragedy, Chekhov on sentence-level writing, and worked around it that way. We read Viktor Shklovsky's classic essay on defamiliarisation, and many other things. But all these texts needed explanation, and I always had a lot of my own material to add as well, especially contemporary examples that made sense of old or difficult ideas.

So I started giving lectures, which was a very unusual thing to do on a creative writing programme. It was an exciting process for me, working out ways of explaining how and why *The Matrix* told the same story as Plato's Simile of the Cave, and how the death of Princess Diana followed the rules of tragedy in the same way that *Oedipus the King* does. I analysed pop culture alongside classics not just to make the lectures more accessible, but because I wanted the students to get used to seeing plot, structure and writing techniques in the world around them. *Toy Story*, while not being as deep and complex as *Pride and Prejudice* or *Great Expectations*, really does follow many of the same structural 'rules'. *The Da Vinci Code*, while being a pacy novel that does ask big questions and is structurally sound in many ways, is very predictably (and even badly) written. Tabloid newspapers, while not good at offering deep analysis, are full of tight, evocative prose. There are a limited number of plots that we use to tell stories (I think there are eight, but other people argue for one, two, three, five or seven), but an almost unlimited supply of nouns and verbs we can use to create the characters and imagery that make our stories mean something to people.

The lectures ended up showing that good writing is always that which is the most human, and therefore the most, well, *animal*. A machine can easily be programmed to say 'She was very sad'. But a machine can't create an original image that explores sadness. It can't look at the world, see something sad, and write that instead of the usual old adjective. A machine could use an algorithm to create the structure of a tragedy, but not its crucial details. It would take a machine far longer to write *Hamlet* than it would take a monkey with a typewriter. It would just never happen. You have to be human to write *Hamlet*. A machine could write something like 'Once upon a time there was a man who went to visit his friend and realised his friend was happier than he was'. But a machine could never create an ugly baby.

I sometimes received emails from people outside the university who had enjoyed my books, asking if they could sit in on my lectures. I sent the written versions of the lectures to them instead. After a while it became clear that this was the best way for the lectures to be experienced anyway. They were, after all, written documents rather than a list of bullet points. And they'd become so long that I always ended up frantically editing as I read them out, cutting whole paragraphs so I could keep within the 50 minutes. Then the third-year students started asking to have copies of their first-year lectures so they could re-read them. Our MA students had often done no formal creative writing before, or none at Kent, so I started giving each student a bundle of these documents. Then I started to re-write them and add a few more examples and explanation to each one. They became essays rather than lectures. I realised that these essays were beginning to come together in one big document, and as I refined this document further, I finally noticed that I was writing a book. The whole process has taken seven years.

I feel passionate about all the material in this book. It is not just for students; it is for anyone who wants to study fiction in order to become a better writer or a better reader. The main focus is on novel-writing, but you don't have to want to write a novel, or any kind of fiction, to get something out of it. But once you have read it, you will, I hope, know how to construct a good sentence, a good metaphor, a good scene, a good plot and a good character. At no point in this book do I pretend that writing a novel (or even reading one deeply) is easy. It isn't easy. But it is a lot easier when you know how to work with your own special material, and when you have considered how other novels are constructed. It's also useful to realise how much of a novel's construction can be accidental, and everyone learns that when they begin writing one.

My mother recently got her PhD at the age of 63. She decided that she wanted to turn her research into a popular history book. She realised that she needed to tell a story, just like a novelist would, but also that she didn't know how to do this. Despite reading thousands of novels in her life (she is the type of person who reads the heaviest book first on holiday so she can leave it behind), she did not know the basic things about storytelling – even that you have a choice between (among other things) first and third person, past and present tense. So this book is partly for her. Both my father, Gordian, and my stepfather, Couze, have expressed an interest in writing novels, and this book is partly for them, too. It's also for Hari, Nia, Sam, Jo, Daisy, Sheila, Vybarr, David S and everyone I know who half-secretly plans to write a novel one day. This book is for anyone who wants to find a way of putting their thoughts and feelings down in words. It's for everyone on a creative writing course, and for everyone who'd love to do a creative writing course but is too poor, shy, busy or scared. It's for all the people who have ever asked me, 'Where do you get your ideas?'

Lots of people have helped with this book. Most thanks must go to Rod Edmond, whose love, support and, of course, thoughtful and insightful comments on the manuscript have been invaluable. Thanks too to my mother, Francesca Ashurst, who created my bibliography. I am also very grateful to my wonderful editor, Francis Bickmore, and my fantastic agents Simon Trewin and Dan Mandel. Suzi Feay has been a good friend and commissioning editor over the years. I'd also like to thank everyone at Canongate, particularly Norah Perkins, and my copy editor Lorraine McCann. A book like this can only come together as a result of many seminars, lectures and conversations in corridors, where ideas get kicked about, thrown around and sometimes dropped altogether. In some cases I have tried many different ways of teaching something before stumbling on the thing that works. Therefore, I would like to thank all my students and colleagues – past and present – at the University of Kent. In particular, thanks are due to Sam Russell, Gonzalo Cerón Garcia, Karen Donaghay, Amy Lilwall, Alice Furse, Simon Smith, Patricia Debney, Amy Sackville, David Flusfeder, David Herd, Ariane Mildenberg, Jennie Batchelor, Sarah Moss, Abdulrazak Gurnah, Jan Montefiore, David Ayers, Caroline Rooney, Donna Landry, Anna Katharina Schaffner and David Stirrup.

Scarlett Thomas

Kent, 2012

PART I

THEORY

INSIDE PLATO'S CAVE

All the great story lines are great practical jokes that people fall for over and over again . . . Somebody gets into trouble and then gets out again; somebody loses something and gets it back; somebody is wronged and gets revenge; Cinderella; somebody hits the skids and just goes down, down, down; people fall in love with each other, and a lot of other people get in the way; a virtuous person is falsely accused of sin; a sinful person is believed to be virtuous; a person faces a challenge bravely, and succeeds or fails; a person lies, a person steals, a person kills, a person commits fornication.

Kurt Vonnegut[4]

Either follow tradition, or develop something that is consistent within itself, writer.

Horace[5]

HAVE YOU EVER had your heart broken, or broken someone else's heart? Have you ever won an argument but later realised you were wrong? Have you ever tripped over in public, or spilled wine on someone else's carpet? Have you ever tried to help someone who didn't want to be helped (or even someone who did)? Have you ever been in trouble, big or small? Have you ever felt trapped? Have you ever gossiped, felt bad about it, and then found that you've been the subject of gossip yourself? And have you, as the result of any of these situations, found yourself thinking and thinking about what *really* happened, and what it meant? Have you edited your life in your head and wondered what would have happened if you'd said or done something else, or if someone else had? Do you drive yourself half mad sometimes thinking about life, and how you and other people live it?

If the answer to these questions is yes, then you almost certainly have what it takes to be a writer, or to understand how and why other people write. Why? You know what drama is, you have suffered, and, most importantly, you've started to analyse these things.

At the moment, though, your life experiences are probably a bit like a pile of steel, with, perhaps, a few nuts and bolts scattered around. If someone told you to go and build a bridge with these components, I'm guessing you wouldn't be able to do it. It certainly wouldn't be easy. This is what I think it is like when you try to write your first novel, short story or screenplay. You have all this *stuff*, but you don't know what to do with it, or even which way up it all goes. You probably don't know how bridges are built, even if you have gone over thousands of them. Of course, one way of learning how to build bridges is to go out and examine some examples, and see how they work. This is how most people who write good fiction learn to do it. We will be doing that too, in this book. We will start by taking apart all kinds of different narratives, from Tolstoy to *Toy Story*, in order to see how they are put together. Only after we know exactly how narrative works will we start to think about how it looks and feels and how it could potentially change us. We will also spend a good deal of time later on considering how to write with depth, humour and originality.

I am assuming you are reading this because you want to become a better writer, or a more informed reader. But I hope you don't mind that I am going to pretend, in this book, that you *do* want to be a writer, and that you want to be a writer for some reason other than just making money. This won't necessarily be true, I know. I do hope that you will write fiction, and that you'll become the kind of storyteller who changes people's lives in some way. But in fact you might want to write commercial fiction (and there are far worse things to do). You might want to be a screenwriter. You might want to know how to apply fictional techniques to narrative non-fiction. You might want to become an English teacher, a book reviewer or a journalist, or gain a greater understanding of how fiction works for another reason, or just for fun. This book will help you do all those things – I hope. But for simplicity's sake, I am going to address you as if you want to write fiction. And the first thing you need to do if you want to write good fiction (or do any of the things I've just mentioned) is to understand the basics of how narrative works. That's what this chapter is about.

I will define 'narrative' for now as 'the way we tell stories'.

Narrative *tells* a story, which means that narrative is different
from story. Plato says in Part III of *The Republic* that stories
– in Greek the word *pseudos*: a 'fiction' or a 'lie' – '. . . are
of two kinds: true stories and fiction'.[6] This is quite a
profound idea to begin with. We all know the fictional story
of *Cinderella*, of course. But we also spend our days being
told stories with varying degrees of fictionality. There might
be news stories, gossip, the story of how Arsenal did last
night, a story about how we can become more relaxed using
meditation techniques. And those are just what you get in
newspapers. As we drive to work, we might listen to a story
on the radio about someone trying to climb a mountain,
and this might really have happened, or it might not have.
We might be told, though billboards, stories that suggest
how happy our family would be if only we would buy this
apartment, or that breakfast cereal. Other billboards might
subtly (or not so subtly) suggest parts of familiar stories:
the princess in beautiful clothes; the hero in a fast car. *Story*,
clearly, does not necessarily mean 'something that is made
up'. Or maybe it does, if you realise that 'made up' means
'put together' or 'constructed', not just 'fictional'. 'Making
up' can of course refer to creating a dress from a pattern,
or a meal from a recipe, both of which are not that different
from the way fiction is constructed, as we will see.

Something happens, and then because of that, something
else happens. That's a story. When we tell it, it becomes a
narrative. Although we could spend many hours talking
about terminology, and how to break down all the parts of
narrative, we can say for now that basic narrative comprises
a story, often arranged into a plot. Very basic narrative may

not have imagery, theme, characterisation and all the other elements we'll be looking at in this book, and the story and the plot might be the same thing. So what is the most basic possible narrative? 'The cat sat on the mat' is not a narrative, because it tells no story: nothing happens and no change occurs. It is a statement. 'The cat sat on the mat and then went outside to look at birds' is two statements, and although something happens, it doesn't happen because of something that has happened before. In other words, it doesn't work according to cause and effect. 'The cat was shooed off the mat and so decided to go outside and look at birds' *is* a narrative because it tells a story based on cause and effect. The cat is outside now partly because she was on the mat before. This narrative is a simple chronological story that has not been plotted. 'The cat was outside watching birds. She had been comfortable on her mat before Rachel came and shooed her away' is now a plotted narrative, because it is not simply chronological. In the narration, the past happens after the present, not before. Other writers and theorists will look at these distinctions differently.[7] But I think this is the most useful way for writers to look at narrative.

We'll be looking at motivation much later, but note for now that in our most basic story the cat has some motivation to get off the mat, and so *change* occurs. Change is one of the most important aspects of fiction. And it helps us to understand what distinguishes a basic chronological story from a sequence of statements. Change occurs *because* of something. And because of that something else happens, and then something else. So let's begin by properly exploring the difference between this kind of chronological *story* (which Russian formalists call 'fabula'), where change happens on a simple timeline, and *plot* (which you might come across as 'sujet' or 'sjužet'). As Boris Tomashevsky says, 'Plot is distinct from story. Both include the same events, but in the plot the events *are arranged*.'[8]

A simple example of how story and plot differ from one another can be found in the Harry Potter series of novels. The chronological story being narrated begins before Harry is born, with the rise of Voldemort and the Death Eaters, or even before that, with the birth of Dumbledore and the founding of Hogwarts School. However, the first scene in *Harry Potter and the Philosopher's Stone* is set much later than this, and we meet Harry as an older child living with his uncle and aunt. The plot begins when Harry finds he is going to attend Hogwarts school, and elements from the chronological story are revealed later. Most narratives do not begin at 'the beginning', as we will see. While most narratives begin with some kind of question about the future of the main character (Will he/she fall in love? Save the world? Escape?), complex plotted narrative usually at some point asks questions about a past, or 'backstory', which has been concealed. One of the key skills of writing is knowing what to conceal and when to reveal it.

The dramatic effect of *Pride and Prejudice* relies on parts of its backstory being concealed from its protagonist Elizabeth Bennett (and from the reader). There is a 'true' story concerning the past actions of Mr Darcy and Mr Wickham that she must discover if she is to truly love Darcy. Who betrayed whom? First she believes that Darcy is the betrayer, but she later discovers that it was Wickham after all. In a narrative like this, there is a 'true story' that is not fully known until the end of the novel. The plot is made up of several competing stories – Elizabeth Bennett's story about Darcy, Wickham's story about Darcy, and Darcy's story about Wickham, among others – and in this competition there is drama. We would not find the novel anywhere near as compelling if Jane Austen simply just told us chronologically 'what happened', beginning with Darcy as a sweet child being kind to the servants, then with him and Wickham at Cambridge, then Wickham's descent as it really happened, then the meeting with Elizabeth Bennett.

Plot gives a story drama. In the crime genre, each narrative has a plot arranged in such a way as to conceal an entire chronological story from the protagonist and usually from the reader as well, until the final chapter, where the plot reveals the story hidden within it all along. The story may be, in chronological order: Mr White's colleague does something awful to him; then it begins to snow;[9] then Mr White kills his colleague, exits through a window and leaves footprints in the snow; then a detective comes, sees the footprints and arrests Mr White. In a plotted detective narrative we'd get the detective's investigation first, *then* the seeing of the footprints, *then* the apprehension of Mr White, and only then the reason for the murder. We'd need to wait for the end of the story to know the beginning. The whole of this story arguably contains the births of all the characters and all their motivations for doing everything they do. Some parts of the entire chronological story will be left out of any narrative. In *Pride and Prejudice*, we don't learn very much about Elizabeth's childhood, because it has no effect on the story: nothing is caused by it. Darcy's childhood is important, however, and so we do learn something of that.

To help think more about this relationship between chronological story and plot, we could use some analogies. The relationship between the story and the plot in narrative is similar to the relationship between the material and the pattern in sewing, the ingredients and the recipe in cooking, and the construction materials and the architectural drawings in house-construction. In each of these a basic material is cut and shaped according to some plan, and the result is a whole new thing. As I said before, it's all to do with 'making things up', although it helps to remember that this doesn't necessarily mean (and will actually hardly ever mean) fabricating things entirely from your imagination. We'll see why later. For now, it is important to realise that when you write fiction you will work with familiar patterns, even if you plan to be very original. Great fashion designers still make dresses that we recognise as such, even though we have perhaps never seen this dress, in this material, before. In fashion, no one would actually present a roll of material as a dress, but the equivalent does sometimes happen when we begin to write fiction – we forget to shape our story. Patterns and shapes are not the point of story-telling. But it is very important that we understand them, and learn how to work with them.

We already work confidently with patterns and shapes in our everyday narratives, although we might not always realise this. Looking at some of these structures will help us begin to understand more about how narrative works.

Those funny anecdotes that you might tell your friends about your life will all have a similar structure. Something unexpected or problematic will happen. There'll be a 'narrative question' that will later be resolved. ('How did he get home with no clothes?' 'Did everyone really overhear what she said about her colleague?' 'Does the fact that he blushed mean that he is attracted to her?') Often these anecdotes are little tragedies, and in the resolution we are embarrassed – we seem to like telling each other stories of our embarrassment. One of my friends' favourite anecdotes is about the time her puppy ate one of her library books. She tells it the same way every time: taking a phone call in the other room and leaving the puppy alone with the book, then returning to discover the book partially in shreds and partially digested by the dog. It was a shame, she always says, because she hadn't even finished it. The problem of how to return the book to the library was resolved when she decided to buy a new copy to give them. Most people have been in a social situation with a couple who want to tell a shared anecdote and say things like, 'No, you tell it. You tell it best.' In these cases at least, we can see that there are obviously better or worse ways of constructing a narrative (or it wouldn't matter who tells it).

In *The Poetics of Prose*, Tzvetan Todorov attempts to uncover a 'grammar' of narrative and suggests that all narrative has the same basic 'rules'. He says:

> An 'ideal' narrative begins with a stable situation which is disturbed by some power or force. There results a state of disequilibrium; by the action of a force directed in the

opposite direction, the equilibrium is re-established; the second equilibrium is similar to the first, but the two are never identical.[10]

My friend's anecdote fits this pattern exactly. The puppy eating the book is the disequilibrium, and the final return of the book to the library is the re-establishment of equilibrium. If you look closely at the stories you tell, you'll often find the same structure. Indeed, if you look at the way you understand your life so far, you will probably find several stories fitting this pattern. You will also find it in 'factual' news stories, gossip columns, conversations and in all sorts of other places too. Even our fears – perhaps especially our fears – often take on a familiar narrative structure. It's very common to fear that something bad is going to happen because something good just has. Being in an exciting new relationship makes us all anxious, because we know what happens in any story that has a good beginning. Usually, things soon start to go wrong, and there is no such thing as equilibrium that lasts (unless it's at the end of a story).

We can express the basic act of storytelling, therefore, as follows: taking a character in a state of equilibrium, messing it all up to create disequilibrium, and then resolving this into a new state of equilibrium. The character travels through these states in what is commonly called an arc. We may begin our narrative at any point on this arc – remember that narrative has a plotted story, not just a chronological story. In *The Odyssey*, for example, we meet Odysseus when he is already in a state of disequilibrium, but understand that there was some equilibrium before he left for Troy. Hamlet is already in the midst of trouble and complication when he sees the ghost. That's not to say that all narratives must begin in the way the ancient Roman writer Horace, in *The Art of Poetry,* describes as *in media res* (into the middle of things). Sometimes narratives do begin *ab ovo* (from the egg).[11] *Great Expectations* wouldn't be as moving and compelling if Pip's childhood were told via flashback; it has to begin virtually *ab ovo* or we would have no idea what Pip has to lose by dedicating himself to becoming a gentleman. Perhaps the most basic, but important, observation we can make about stories is this: they always involve change. And narrative makes sense of that change.

If a narrative is well-structured it will have effects on us, the audience. Plato writes a lot about this in *The Republic*, and has Socrates, his narrator,[12] suggesting that stories are so powerful that they need to be controlled by the state.[13] The first thing Socrates identifies as a real problem in fiction is the representation of the behaviour of the gods in the myths of the time. For Socrates, gods must be perfect beings (otherwise what is the point of them?) and perfect beings surely would not do harm, or get into dramatic emotional tangles, as most of the gods often do in the most popular myths. Socrates says:

> Nor can we permit stories of wars and plots and battles among the gods; they are quite untrue, and if we want our prospective guardians to believe that quarrelsomeness is one of the worst of evils, we must certainly not let them be told

the story of the Battle of the Giants or embroider it on
robes . . . On the contrary, if we are to persuade them that
no citizen has ever quarrelled with any other, because it is
sinful, our old men and women must tell children stories
with this end in view from the first, and we must compel
our poets to tell them similar stories when they grow up.
But we can admit to our state no stories about Hera being
tied up by her son, or Hephaestus being flung out of Heaven
by his father for trying to help his mother when she was
getting a beating, nor any of Homer's Battles of the Gods,
whether their intention is allegorical or not.[14]

On telling the myth of Cronos, in which Cronos castrates
and kills his father and eats his own babies, Socrates suggests
that it should be avoided, or at least restricted:

It would be best to say nothing about it, or if it must be
told, tell it to a select few under oath of secrecy, at a rite
which required, to restrict it still further, the sacrifice not
of a mere pig but of something large and difficult to get.[15]

Socrates continues talking about the way the gods are
depicted in myths, condemning stories of them creating
evil out of jars, shape-shifting and appearing in disguises,
among other things. He then talks about a moral weakness
that can be created by frightening stories.

It looks, then, as if we shall have to control story-tellers
on this topic too. We must ask the poets to stop giving
their present gloomy account of the after-life, which is

both untrue and unsuitable to produce a fighting spirit, and make them speak more favourably of it.[16]

Today we'd probably talk about this as propaganda – the act of presenting persuasive narratives to achieve a political outcome. We may recall the news reports that emerged after 11 September 2001, that told of stories narrated to the plane hijackers in which, after their deaths, they would be rewarded in a heavenly paradise. Who knows if these stories ever really existed, but they certainly sound compelling.[17] It is no doubt intentionally ironic that *The Republic*, itself a fictional work, contains arguments that the state should control other fictional works, as well as, in Part X, warning against storytelling altogether.

It's quite clear that this is because stories have *effects* on people. They do not just depict change, they change *us*. They make us change our minds and even our feelings. Throughout *The Republic*, Plato explicitly or implicitly identifies the different functions of narratives (some of which are deemed desirable in the republic, some the reverse). Crudely summarised, he says narrative may function:

1. As representation[18] (of reality) – to encourage us to BELIEVE and RECOGNISE[19]
2. As persuasion – to encourage us to ACT[20]
3. As philosophy – to encourage us to THINK[21]
4. As approximation (of fact) – to encourage us to KNOW[22]
5. As drama – to encourage us to FEEL (pleasure)[23]

We can see that in the ideal state proposed by Socrates, citizens must not be persuaded that death is awful, or see representations of gods being un-godlike, because their actions will be affected (they may not want to go to war, or revere the gods highly enough). But there is drama and pleasure in all the stories Socrates condemns. And stories do give pleasure. All that disequilibrium being neatly resolved into equilibrium keeps us locked in a cycle of pain and pleasure that usually ends in pleasure (even when the outcome of the fiction is tragic, as we'll see).[24]

All stories – true and fictional – will include one or more of Plato's functions, and they will therefore change us. We will believe, do, think, know or feel something we didn't before. Let's now compare two surprisingly similar narratives, Plato's The Cave[25] and the Wachowski brothers' film *The Matrix* (1999) in order to see how plot has an effect on the function of the story, and therefore on us. I'll give summaries of both stories first and then we'll try to apply some of the terms and ideas introduced in this chapter to each of them.

*

The Cave is probably best introduced via an image that can show its elaborate set-up.

Plato's myth tells of a group of people trapped from birth inside a cave. Their legs and necks are fastened so that they cannot move, and they can only look straight ahead. An arrangement of a fire and a well-used road behind the prisoners creates shadows that are projected onto the

wall in front of them. The shadows are not even of the
people travelling along the road, but of the carved figurines
they carry. Since they do not know any better, the prisoners
believe that the shadows depict the 'whole truth' – i.e. the
highest level of reality – and deduce that the voices they
hear must belong to the shadows. If one of these prisoners
were forced to become free, Socrates asks in this dialogue,
what would his experience be like? He would begin by
being too dazzled to properly comprehend the truth he can
now see – that the shadows belong to three-dimensional
objects carried by three-dimensional beings, and that outside
the cave there is an upper world lit by bright sunlight. But
eventually, after being dragged into the sunlight, he would

comprehend the truth. Now there would be a conflict, however, between his old life and his new one. How can he possibly explain his experience to the other prisoners who have never left the cave? How can he explain the poverty of their mental life? How can he ever be one of them again? The man would probably make a fool of himself, garbling about 'other worlds' and unable to believe in the shadows any more. And if he tried to free his fellow prisoners, they would probably wish him dead.

The Matrix tells of another set of prisoners. Set in the future, it depicts a society of humans who believe themselves to be living in the 'real world' of the late twentieth century but who are actually living inside the Matrix – a vast computer simulation that keeps the minds of the humans happy while, unknown to them, intelligent machines farm their bodies for their energy. The people trapped inside this simulation do not know it is a simulation and believe it to be reality. The protagonist of the story, Thomas A. Anderson, aka 'Neo', is a computer hacker looking for the meaning of the Matrix. He cannot understand it from the inside, and needs the hackers Trinity and Morpheus to come and show him the truth. They give him a pill that enables his mind to disconnect from its 'chains', and now, after the simulation dissolves, he can comprehend the reality of his situation: that his body is actually confined in a pod in something like a post-apocalyptic battery farm. Once freed from his pod, Neo will return to the Matrix several times (in this and the subsequent films in the trilogy) with the purpose of saving a world that doesn't know it needs saving, and perhaps doesn't want to be saved at all. In the first film we meet the character Cypher, who wishes he had never seen the truth and has made a deal with the machines that he will go back to a state of ignorance and re-enter the Matrix if he helps them to kill Neo.

★

Although these two narratives appear to be very different, I hope it is clear that they tell roughly the same story. In each narrative, one member of a society comprising people who don't know they are prisoners, and who see images that they think are reality but are not, escapes and finds the truth. So there's certainly in both cases a state of equilibrium, which dissolves into disequilibrium, just as Todorov says. In both narratives there is a truth that is not known by, and cannot be easily told to, the remaining members of the society, who would have to consent to experience the truth for themselves. In each case the hero of the story is left with an amount of responsibility. Now he knows the truth he needs to know what to do with it. The state of disequilibrium continues as the hero battles to restore a new state of equilibrium – where everyone knows the truth and no one is a prisoner.

We can see that in these examples the same basic story structure has been made very different by its narrative treatment. The Cave is part of a philosophical dialogue. In it the nameless hero doesn't even leave the cave; we are simply invited to imagine what would happen if he did. *The Matrix* is a Hollywood film that tells this story with a fully realised and named character, Neo, who has helpers and enemies, and who leaves his fictional prison in high dramatic style. In this version of the story we meet Trinity and Morpheus, the helpers who lead Neo out of his illusion, while in the Cave, the entity who unchains the prisoner is never revealed. The Cave implies antagonists (bad guys), although we never find out who has chained up the prisoners. The thematic implication seems to be that it is an abstract force such as 'ignorance' and that the prisoners may, symbolically at least, be their own captors. *The Matrix* keeps the implied thematic link between the prisoners and their captors (the chronological story actually begins with humans creating the artificial intelligence that will end up enslaving them) but dramatises the captors as the enemy machines and their black-suited 'agents'.

In both narratives there is a metaphorical depiction of the real world: in one, there is a simple cave set up to show a society that sees two dimensions instead of three; in the other a 'Matrix' that actually does look like our world (and that is part of the power of the film), but is also revealed to be a world of too few dimensions. The computer simulation is the same thing as the shadows on the wall of Plato's cave. In both scenarios the prisoners think they are having meaningful experiences that lose their meaning when the absolute reality outside the simulation is grasped.

Both narratives follow a plot that begins (more or less) with the release of the hero and his ascent into the metaphorical sunlight of the truth. Neo initially rejects the truth: he is as 'dazzled' as the protagonist of the Cave. Plato's story is left tantalisingly open, and we are left to read it as an allegory about the experience of education, or a cautionary tale about the wrongful execution of Socrates, or an inspirational story of transcendental enlightenment, or a warning of the dangers of thinking you can ever see the whole truth. *The Matrix* fills in enough details and backstory to enable us to articulate readings that may emphasise the problems surrounding artificial intelligence,[26] or may dwell on specific problems posed by the media in our society. However, it is also possible to read *The Matrix* as a narrative that attempts to wake us up in the same way that Plato's narrative does: the implication in both is that *we* are in the cave *now*. Many commentators, including the Wachowski brothers, have suggested that *The Matrix* offers a metaphorical exploration of what Buddhist enlightenment may be like, or how to escape from hyperreality.[27]

Although both the Cave and *The Matrix* offer us a 'What if?' situation in which a fictional character escapes from a metaphorical prison that implies a position of ignorance, both narratives also suggest that to attain absolute truth is not something that's likely to happen to many of us. Indeed, it could be argued that both narratives are actually about the experience of being trapped in a cave or a matrix, or any kind of prison, in which you can't possibly know what is outside. And of course, this is the essence of the human condition: none of us knows what is outside our universe, or our own finite life. Some people do claim to have ascended to the sunlight and come back, but we tend not to believe them.

The Cave as a 'basic story' can lead to many different narratives. We see it in the story of the Buddha's awakening, in narratives like *Buffy the Vampire Slayer* and often in science fiction. *The Truman Show* has an interesting treatment of this story in which only one man, Truman Burbank, is trapped in the 'cave', and everyone else already knows the truth (that his life is a cruel soap opera complete with scripts, other actors and an audience of millions). When you find this basic story within fictional narratives, it always tends to come with very big themes, usually about our perception of reality. But they are not always exactly the same themes. We can see, also, that the same story plotted in different ways can have very different functions. *The Matrix*, with its high-resolution visuals, soundtrack, fight scenes and love-interest certainly gives this story more drama than the Cave. It could be argued that we therefore get more pleasure from this narrative. However, perhaps because it is so pleasurable, and so emphasises the dramatic function, we more readily recognise it as fiction and this may lead us to reject some of its philosophical and thematic elements. Both of these narratives have some sort of persuasive function ('we must try to leave the cave') and their philosophical functions tend to concern the opposition of ignorance and knowledge. Each represents a world we recognise, although usually in heavily metaphorical set-ups (we live in societies; these societies trap us in some way; if we learn more than our neighbours we may become outcasts and so on), and each approximates a historical period, with its own concerns about what our apparent 'reality' may be hiding.

Why do we tell the same stories again and again? Most authors will tell you that they do not sit down to deliberately re-write the Simile of Cave, or *Cinderella*, or *The Odyssey*, or any other basic stories, but it is possible to identify basic stories (and basic plots, which are different) in almost every narrative. One perhaps obvious point is that we enjoy familiar stories. When we curl up on the sofa to watch a romantic comedy we know how it's going to end (with a nice wedding, literal or symbolic). If the central characters died suddenly five minutes before the end we'd be very unhappy and shocked. It is impossible that Elizabeth Bennett will die in a coach accident on her way back from Pemberley, because it's not that sort of story. When we see a fictional character escaping from 'reality' we damn well want him or her to discover some mind-boggling truth, because . . . Why? Just because that's how the old story goes and we like hearing it repeated? Or because these basic stories actually acknowledge our basic anxieties? Is story-telling something that simply comforts us, or is it something we want to keep doing until those thorny questions of reality and identity and truth are resolved once and for all?

One thing that is certain is that story is not the centre of narrative. It is not where we will find new, exciting ideas. But well-known stories provide frames, with edges and boundaries. If random things happened in fiction, it would be indistinguishable from life. Crafting a narrative that references a well-known story – whether this is through re-writing, adaptation, metafiction or intertextuality – means you have put a frame around your ideas. You are telling your reader that they don't need to worry too much about what is going to happen. Good storytellers make readers worry instead about *how* it's going to happen, which is different, as we shall see. Giving your narrative a familiar frame means you have separated it from the world. You have made a space for art.

The Matrix may repeat plenty of what is in the Cave but it creates a whole new narrative situation that gives us more access to the hero and his world, as well as asking questions about technology and the media that clearly could not have been asked this way in any previous generation. It has a different palette of imagery, which underlines these questions. There are more ideas than there are stories to go with them, and that isn't necessarily a bad thing. It's far better to have a new idea than a new story. So how will you do it? What 'realities' will you use your stories to represent or uncover? What acts will you use your fiction to encourage? What questions will you use these stories to ask? What feelings will your fiction inspire? With fiction, we can make people think about important things – these can be huge, *Matrix*-style questions, or subtle questions of the sort we would expect to find in short fiction. Fundamentally, we use fiction to encourage people to imagine that they are in a situation, and to try to figure out what they would do in the hero's place. And 'doing' in this sense is not just action, but *thinking*. Of course, not everyone uses fiction to ask important questions. But you should. There are already enough Mills & Boon books; and life is short, after all.

My first piece of advice to you, then, is this: learn to understand stories, but realise that they are well-used frames. You are not going to be very original when it comes to story. You can be much more original in the way you plot, the characters you create, the little details you use and, of course, the way you use story to explore themes. You can become a very original writer. But you probably won't create a completely new story. That's OK, because just plotting is hard enough, as we'll see over the next three chapters.

GOING TO BED WITH ARISTOTLE

Tragedy is not an imitation of persons, but of actions and of life. Well-being and ill-being reside in action.

Aristotle[28]

'The real fucking world. First of all, you write a screenplay without conflict or crisis, you'll bore your audience to tears. Secondly, nothing happens in the world . . . Are you out of your fucking mind?'

Adaptation[29]

Aristotle's *Poetics*, written around 335 BCE, is probably the most useful practical writing book available, especially if you want to learn about plotting. And it's only about 45 pages long. This is why you should go to bed with it. Get under the covers and read it again and again. Read it by torchlight in secret when you're supposed to be doing something else. Underline things in the dark. It will improve your plotting more than anything else, once you understand it.

Remember Plato's assertion that certain types of story are not suitable for children? Well, the *Poetics* instructs you in exactly how to tell *those* stories: the comedies and tragedies that were the Ancient Greek equivalent of musical comedy and opera. These are highly emotional narratives that included dramatic reversals of fortune, big 'Aha!' moments and, of course, catharsis: a process by which a story *changes* you, not in a rational, persuasive, thoughtful way (although it will ideally do this too), but on the level of feelings and emotions. You come out of the theatre, or put down the book, feeling drained but happy; purged and satisfied. You find you are able to understand something better because you have examined it in a fictional form. When Aristotle talks about poetry, he means narrative poetry, by the way. The book is called *Poetics*, but it is all about fiction.

Many people (including various Hollywood screen-writers[30]) believe that Aristotle simply tells us how to write Hollywood blockbusters. On one level he does. He tells us exactly how to plot stories so that the audience can wring the most pleasure from them. He tells us how to check our plots for errors, and how not to 'disgust' our audience by showing a bad guy getting away with murder, or a decent person suffering through no fault of their own. But in the end, I believe Aristotle comes out against the simple pleasures of formula and in favour of something deeper. True pleasure is all about understanding, as we shall see.

I'm now going to summarise what I think are the key moments from the first pages of *Poetics*, and show you how they relate to the Sophocles play *Oedipus the King*, the Pixar film *Toy Story*, and an episode of the Channel 4 reality TV programme *Supernanny*. At the end of the chapter I am going to analyse two classic Hollywood musicals, *Gentlemen Prefer Blondes,* which works perfectly (if eccentrically) according to Aristotle's rules, and *There's No Business Like Showbusiness*, which breaks them all (and is a far worse film for it). Below, there is a table that shows you just the beginnings, middles and endings of *Oedipus the King*, *Toy Story* and *Supernanny*. We will see later why every story should have three parts or 'acts', with a complication, a setback and a resolution.

	ACT 1	ACT 2	ACT 3
Toy Story	Woody is threatened by the arrival of a more powerful toy.	In trying to remove his rival, Woody puts both himself and his rival in jeopardy – they are lost and must be found before Andy's family moves house.	The toys resolve their problems, work together and get home in the nick of time.
Oedipus the King	Oedipus learns that Thebes is cursed because a murder has gone unsolved.	In trying to solve the murder, Oedipus discovers more and more disturbing facts about his life.	Oedipus discovers that he is the murderer he seeks and the plot resolves with his exile.
Supernanny	The Bixleys have a son, Brandon, who will not eat.	In trying to solve their problem, the Bixleys make it worse by arguing and trying to force-feed their son.	The Bixleys learn to create more harmony at home by not arguing and not force-feeding their son.

Of these three stories one is obviously fictional, one is based on a myth and one is true, although the truth has been edited to fit a pattern. In some ways they could not be more different. However, we can probably already see from the table that they have many things in common, and most of these are things that Aristotle has pointed to as features of all good plots.

IMITATION

According to Aristotle, poets (i.e. storytellers) 'imitate people doing things', which creates drama.[31] So what, then, is an imitation? Aristotle opens his text by defining an imitation (the Greek is *mimêsis*), and explaining that storytelling is no different from the visual arts in the respect that both provide imitations of life. This concept of imitation may seem obvious – it says that fiction is not real or, to be more specific, not a real account of something that actually happened – but it is actually crucial to our understanding of stories. *Toy Story* is obviously not real. It depicts conscious toys: an impossibility. The scenery in *Toy Story* is created entirely by CGI animation. There's not a 'real' thing in it. However, we may want to agree that *Toy Story* does 'imitate' a recognisable, familiar world. It depicts houses and streets and parents and cars and birthday parties. Andy is not a real, specific little boy from the world we know. But he *could* be. Toys obviously can't walk and talk, but these ones look like humans and in some sense they could therefore be imagined to be alive and animate in a way that, say, an earplug or a courgette could not (unless Pixar decided to put eyes on them, in which case anything would be possible – note the animated lamp sequence at the beginning of *Toy Story*). In a sense, every fictional imitation (and there are non-fictional imitations, too, for example news stories, but we won't go into that here) is a thought experiment: a sequence of 'What if?'s that show not what did happen to a real person, but what could happen in a particular set of circumstances. So a fictional imitation is always of something that doesn't exist. Aristotle says that:

> . . . the function of the poet is not to say what *has* happened, but to say the kind of thing that *would* happen, i.e. what is possible in accordance with probability or necessity.[32]

Aristotle is saying that the whole point of imitation isn't to simply copy the real, but to make stories out of that which is *realistic* or believable. So when you take something out of the world and fictionalise it, you are somehow going beyond the real into a parallel universe full of events that didn't happen but could have. Toys can't talk, but if they could, we imagine that they would probably talk a bit like the ones in *Toy Story*, and that they'd fall in love, bicker and experience drama the way we do. The imitation isn't of speaking toys, but of us.

Fiction therefore has a *metaphorical* relationship with reality: it is not it, but it is similar to it. So what are we doing when we engage with (or create) fictionalisations of a recognisable world? Aristotle says that:

> . . . we take delight in viewing the most accurate possible images of objects which in themselves cause distress when we see them (e.g. the shapes of the lowest species of animal, and corpses). The reason for this is that under-standing is extremely pleasant, not just for philosophers but for others too in the same way, despite their limited capacity for it.[33]

So we can gain philosophical pleasure from understanding, and we imitate things so we can understand them better. Narrative, in some sense then, is a form of philosophical thought experiment where we work out how we feel about things by playing-through simulations – or, indeed, imitations – of them. And Aristotle is not just being superior when he says that not all people are philosophers. It's true that some people want to spend their whole working lives thinking about deep questions and other people only want to do it when they are reading (or experiencing in some other way) a fictional narrative. Still, if Aristotle is right then the best fiction should speak to the philosopher in all of us. Truly satisfying fiction changes our understanding in some way.

PLOT

So what kinds of imitations work, and what kinds don't work? First, and most importantly, the kinds of imitations Aristotle is concerned with in the *Poetics* – the epic, the tragedy and the comedy – must have *plots*. Aristotle defines a 'plot' as 'the organisation of events'.[34] The events are what make up the chronological story, and the plot is how this story is related (in exactly the way we saw in the first chapter). Aristotle identifies two main kinds of plot in the *Poetics*: tragedy and comedy. Tragedy deals with the downfall, or sometimes near-downfall, of 'admirable' people; comedy with the happy resolution of problems faced by what Aristotle calls 'inferior' people, in other words, ordinary people like you and me (and Elizabeth Bennett), with neither fame nor fortune. Tragedy ends in the death of the hero (and often others); comedy usually ends with one or more weddings. We'll look in more detail later at the difference between a simple plot, which more or less tells a chronological story, and a complex plot, which mixes things up much more.

Any good story (and a plot may be made up of a number of such stories, although there will usually be a main one) will tell of an agent going from good fortune to bad fortune or the reverse. Imagine two graphs. One is the shape of a bowl higher on the right side than the left; the other the shape of a hill lower on the descent. The bowl-shaped graph represents comedy (which in this book means a romantic story, not a funny story), in which an unhappy protagonist's fortunes get worse before getting much better. The hill-shaped graph represents tragedy, where a successful protagonist's fortunes become better before getting much, much worse. We know intuitively that this is how plots should work, and if a story begins well we somehow know it must end badly, and the reverse. This works not just in fiction, of course, but in the narratives we create around celebrities, and even, if we're not careful, our friends and acquaintances. Many celebrities don't understand why people like to read about their awful affairs, their drug habits and anorexia. Aristotle does. We want them to move from good fortune to bad fortune not because we are bad people, but because this is what we expect from narrative. We always expect change.

Plots deal with changes in fortune. All plots. Try it out on TV programmes and films and you'll see that it holds true. In our three examples we can see that *Toy Story* and *Supernanny* deal with changes of fortune from bad to good, and *Oedipus the King* the reverse. *Toy Story* and

Supernanny are simple plots; *Oedipus* is complex.

Aristotle argues that everything in a narrative, from changes of fortune to characterisation, must be demonstrated through action as far as possible. He says that, therefore, the *plot* is the most important part of telling stories, not character: 'Tragedy is not an imitation of persons, but of actions and of life. Well-being and ill-being reside in action.'[35] If you hear someone say 'show don't tell' in writing, this is what they mean. If I decided to tell you about someone you don't know, I would probably bore you to death if I simply told you her height, hair colour, eye colour, job, family background and so on. You'd probably be more interested if I told you about that time she fell out of a window while trying to escape from a spider. We learn about a character best by hearing about the actions of that character. We put them in a little plot that tells a little story – and this is one of the reasons we may want to agree that plot is more important than character: it's through plots that we experience characters, not the other way around. In Camus's *The Outsider*, we learn something significant about Meursault when he drinks a cup of coffee while viewing his dead mother's body. We see from his action that he is unconventional; or perhaps we deduce that he did not care for his mother very much. Because other characters also see his action (no one can see something as abstract as pure 'character'; character is only known to other characters through action) the plot moves on. He is judged and, later, punished for his unconventionality. In *The Bell Jar*, Esther Greenwood doesn't need to tell us that she is descending into depression. We *see* her wearing the same clothes for days and being unable to even make a phone call.

But even if we take this on board and get our characters right by showing them through their actions, we need to know how to plot a sequence of these actions that take our characters from good to bad fortune or the reverse. Taking someone from bad fortune to good fortune (or the reverse) is not as easy as it sounds, especially not if we want the resulting story to be satisfying. Imagine a character: a rich, perfect young woman striding out of an exclusive department store wearing expensive clothes and giggling into a mobile phone. She's a stereotype, of course, but she'll do for illustration. When we come across this character our narrative antennae tell us that there must be something bad about her, and we start anticipating her downfall. As storytellers, we could ruin her life by having her fall down a hole, quite randomly. There she is, walking along, and she falls down a hole. Is that a satisfying story? Or would it be more satisfying if she had dug a hole herself, intending to hide the evidence of the murder of her rival, and then fell in it? It's not a very interesting story either way, but you should be able to see that a hole dug by the character who is due to fall into it is much, much more compelling than a random hole. If we re-imagine this character as Carrie Bradshaw in *Sex and the City*, we may realise that although this character does have beauty, money, a great writing job and a stylish apartment, and could appear as stereotypically perfect at first, we know that she is going to have many romantic 'downfalls'. Indeed, the opening sequence of *Sex and the City* foreshadows this by showing Carrie walking along in a high-fashion white tutu before being splashed by a passing car. Good fortune always turns to bad in fiction (and bad to good, of course).

★

Aristotle says that:

> Tragedy is an *imitation* of *an action* that is *admirable, complete*
> and *possesses magnitude*; in *language made pleasurable* [. . .]
> *performed by actors, not through narration*; effecting through
> *pity and fear* the purification of such emotions.[36]

This is almost as complete an account of what a piece of fiction should contain as you're likely to find, and it doesn't just apply to tragedy in the sense that we understand the term, but to most fictional plots. So let's go through these italicised terms one by one.

THE SINGLE ACTION

We've already looked at imitation. An imitation, or story, will contain a single, central *action* (or, in other words, *storyline*) whereby, for example, a lost toy tries to get home (and therefore retain his power), a man tries to solve a murder or a family tries to make their son eat. Narratives can seem complex, but most of the time you can reduce their central story to a one-line summary (like TV guides sometimes do). This one-line summary will contain the single action on which the plot is based. *The Wizard of Oz* is about a lost girl trying to get home. The Harry Potter novels are about Harry trying to overcome Lord Voldemort. George Eliot's *Middlemarch* is about many things, but the focus is on whether Dorothea will be able to marry Will Ladislaw. The film

Memento, which has a complex plot that makes the story run backwards, is actually just about a man trying to get revenge for the murder of his wife. *Pride and Prejudice* is about sisters trying to make favourable marriages. Most actions will involve a character trying to do something. As I mentioned in the first chapter, I like to phrase this single action in the form of a question, which I call a 'narrative question' (there must be thematic questions, too, but more on these later). Will Dorothy get home? Will Harry Potter defeat Lord Voldemort? Will Elizabeth Bennett marry Darcy? Will Pip ever win Estella's affections? Will Neo save the world?

THE ADMIRABLE ACTION

That this single action should always be admirable is at first hard to comprehend. Tragic heroes in particular do not, after all, perform admirable actions. Or do they? Oedipus's motivation is certainly admirable at first. He wants to find out who murdered Laius. (Laius's own motivation was to keep himself and his family safe.) Hamlet also has an admirable motivation when he decides to find out who killed his father. In Thackeray's *Vanity Fair* Becky Sharp wants to elevate her social position. In Tolstoy's novel *Anna Karenina*, Anna wants to feel passionate love. Aristotle is quite clear that tragic heroes should be particularly admirable in themselves, or certainly a bit better than us, so that we feel pity when they meet their downfall. We don't care about stupid or weak characters. We care about people who are trying to do something we understand to be important, who overcome many obstacles and succeed or fail. We particularly like stories about people more beautiful, rich or talented than us who try to do something amazing and succeed for a while but ultimately meet their downfall. We like Meursault because of his extreme honesty. We like and admire Anna Karenina because she gives in to feelings that we may suppress, or may never even have.

But we also like stories of more ordinary people struggling with things that we recognise. There will be admiration here too, or at least approval. We like Bridget Jones perhaps especially because of her flaws (she's constantly trying to give up smoking and drinking and lose weight; and she always gets into embarrassing situations) and therefore want her to fall in love and experience a change for the better. We like Lorelei Lee in *Gentlemen Prefer Blondes*, despite her being a gold-digger, because she is honest and naive. And why shouldn't she try to improve her life? Note that while admirable characters are usually flawed, they are also usually honest and desire things that we understand, and approve of. Non-admirable characters include, for example, Cruella De Vil (in *One Hundred and One Dalmatians*), Orlick (in *Great Expectations*), Claudius (in *Hamlet*) and Wickham (in *Pride and Prejudice*). Some writers, notably Anton Chekhov, argue that all characters must be admirable, because once we've looked at anyone deeply enough and understood their motivation we must identify with them rather than judge them. We will explore this in more detail later.

THE COMPLETE PLOT

Aristotle's conceptualisation of the 'complete' plot is probably the most familiar of his ideas. 'A *whole* is that which has a beginning, a middle and an end.'[37] That's easy enough to understand. It's the basic three-act structure that begins with a complication (*desis* – literally 'tying') and ends with a resolution (*lusis* – literally 'untying'). Todorov's idea of equilibrium-disequilibrium-equilibrium that we encountered earlier is clearly very similar to this. In Act 1 the problem is revealed; in Act 2 the protagonist tries to solve it with more or less success; in Act 3 the protagonist succeeds or fails, and faces the consequences.

We can see from our three examples (see table on p.46) that each one has a plot that tells a story with a clear three-act structure: a beginning, a middle and an end. Each one begins with a problem: a powerful stranger has 'come to town' and threatened its hierarchy; a murder has been committed; a child will not eat. Note that in each plot there is a symmetry, and the *exact* complication stated is resolved. You could state the beginnings of these plots inexactly as: Woody is unhappy; the Thebans are unhappy; the Bixleys are unhappy. But unless the story addresses and resolves the exact cause of the unhappiness, it will not be successful. So, for example, the Bixleys could win the Lottery halfway through the programme, and this would make them happy, but the exact problem about Brandon's eating habits will not have been resolved, and the narrative will not be satisfying. Oedipus is destined for a bad end; we know that. But it must be as a result of finding out about this murder. A rock falling on his head at the end of Act 3 will have almost exactly the same effect as his discovery, but it will not be satisfying. He could fall over and blind himself – but instead he chooses to blind himself with his wife/mother's brooch.

Note how each column is so similar, even for three such different plots, and how problems tend to get worse before they get better (in the case of *Toy Story* and *Supernanny*) and better before they get worse (*Oedipus*). Even though Oedipus's arc is different from Woody's or the Bixleys', note how symmetrical the structures are. As we have already noticed, each plot begins with the discovery of a problem and the characters trying to solve it. The only thing that is different for Oedipus is that his attempts to solve his problem seem to be going well, and we sense he will suffer as a result. For the others, their attempts to solve the problem go wrong, which causes them to learn something. Then all can be resolved. This analysis is not intended to reduce *Oedipus the King* to mere plot, incidentally. But it is interesting that even one of the most profound pieces of fiction in existence can be seen to have a similar structural logic (when one accounts for some mirror-reversals) to *Toy Story*.

To properly be complete, the plot must also have a determinate structure. In other words, it must work according to the laws of cause and effect. In a good story, the events in the beginning *cause* the middle to happen, and the events in the middle *cause* the end to happen. This will also apply to the plot, sometimes in a very complicated way, since story and plot will not always be the same thing. For example, the plot of *Oedipus* can be untangled to reveal two stories (or, if you like, one long one): Oedipus's past, and his present. The plot of *Oedipus the King* takes place over less than 24 hours, but the whole story has taken years. One story (the present) is used to reveal the other (the past). Although in chronological terms the past has obviously happened before the present, in this plot we get the present before we learn the past. However, you will notice that both the past and the present stories are structured via cause and effect. *Because* the prophet warns Laius that his son will kill him, Laius arranges for the murder of his son. *Because* of this they don't know one another years later, and so on. Every single part of this story builds on something that happened before, apart from the very first incident (the first prophecy). Why is Oedipus ruler of Thebes? Because he overcame the Sphinx. How did he come to meet the Sphinx? He was on his way to Thebes after escaping Corinth to try to avoid a prophecy coming true. Why did Thebes need a new ruler? Because Oedipus killed the previous one.

Also note the way that Act 2 of each of our plots begins with 'In trying to . . .' In *Toy Story* it is Woody's desire to get rid of Buzz Lightyear that *causes* Buzz to fall out of the window and for them to end up together in the car on the way to Pizza Planet. In narrative when people try to solve problems they more often than not end up making them worse, leaving them with more problems to solve. And as we'll see much later, in the chapter on characterisation, people are motivated to act through their desire for things to be better, however problematic their desire is, and whatever they imagine 'better' will be.

I'm sure you already know how to use cause and effect, and just how difficult it can be to get right. You'll know, for example, how hard it can be to maintain a chain of cause and effect over a really complex lie. (One of the great rules of lying is also one of the great rules of storytelling.

Only ever have one cause per effect and vice versa. You can't go over to your friend's house not because you're ill *and* the car has broken down, but because of one of those things.) You'll also use cause and effect when you're merely stretching the truth, or even telling the truth, but you want to make sure you are believed, or not blamed for something. When we want to excuse our behaviour, we often have to come up with a narrative that makes sense of it. 'I was feeling ill, which is why I ran out of the room crying' leads us to wonder if that is the whole reason or not, but it still makes narrative sense. 'I ran out of the room crying randomly, for no reason' makes sense to no one.

Aristotle warns against the 'episodic' plot, in which several things happen, one after the other, but do so without each thing being caused by the one before. He even tells you how to check a plot to make sure this has not happened: 'So the structure of the various sections of the events must be such that the transposition or removal of any one section dislocates and changes the whole.'[38] In other words, if you can lift a part of your narrative out (a scene, a chapter or even a whole character) and you don't see the plot collapse, then that part has no place in the whole. There is no part of *Oedipus* that can be removed, for example. Try it and see. The end of *Toy Story* is satisfying because the toys use a firework rocket (attached to Buzz by Sid in a previous scene) to escape. If some new character just happened to be walking past and helped them, this would 'feel' wrong. So the scene where Sid attaches the rocket can't be removed or the end would not make sense; this in itself means it is a good scene. Beware of those childish stories that are

driven by 'And then . . . and then . . . and then . . .' What
works better is 'And because of that . . . and because of
that . . . and because of that . . .' Incidentally, it is very easy
to make up episodic stories, and very hard to make up
determinate stories (and then plot them satisfactorily),
which is why the great majority of people who want to
make their fortune through telling stories actually fail.

MAGNITUDE

Aristotle says that 'beauty consists in magnitude as well as
order.'[39] So your story has to be the right size. Not length
– that's not what Aristotle's talking about here. You could
have written a 100,000-word novel or a one-paragraph story
and it wouldn't matter. It's the *story* that matters here, not
the actual text. 'An animal a thousand miles long' is no
good, he argues, because you can't see it all at once. You
also can't see things if they are too tiny. A good plot, he
says, should be 'readily taken in at one view'.[40] In other
words you should be able to tell a friend a synopsis of the
film you've seen or the book you've read fairly easily (and
it should inspire pity and fear in them – more on this later).
You can usually do this because films and published books
have one main focus, the single action, which can be easily
summarised, although much will be lost in the summary,
of course. But the single action should have the correct
magnitude. 'A man tries to get revenge for the murder of
his son' can be taken in one view. 'Four hundred people
go on different fairground rides' cannot. The main action
of the narrative should take place over as short a time-period

as possible, Aristotle says, with backstory filled in as required. Correct magnitude leads to greater unity, which is the next term on the list.

Aristotle warns against thinking that a plot is unified simply because it is 'concerned with a single person.'[41] A single person and a single action are different. The man who sets out to get revenge for the murder of his son will, presumably, have had a childhood full of incidents, and will have grown up, fallen in love, perhaps been fired from a telesales job, perhaps got lost once on the way back from a festival, perhaps seen a bank robbery. Putting all these things in a plot does not make it unified just because they all happened to one person. When someone sits down to tell you their 'whole life story' are you interested? But what about if they tell you in detail about one really bad relationship they've had, or the time they accidentally took magic mushrooms? What about history lessons where you learn about an entire war from start to end? Surely it's more interesting to explore war through one dramatic episode, as Kurt Vonnegut does in *Slaughterhouse 5*?[42] The whole chronological story of Oedipus's life does not provide the structure for *Oedipus the King*, and it's useful to think about why this is. A good plot should have a definite shape, even if this is concealed to some extent, and there should be one main problem and one main resolution. *Great Expectations* is not Pip's unstructured life story, but is focused on the question of whether or not he will ever win the affections of Estella. Of course many other things are important in the novel – much more important, and this is part of the point – but the focus is on Pip's love for Estella. Interestingly, several endings were written for *Great Expectations*, and they all concern what happens between Pip and Estella even though by that stage Pip has learned enough that it should hardly matter any more.

PLEASURABLE LANGUAGE

When you write you should use pleasurable language. For Aristotle, this primarily includes the use of metaphor, which we will learn much more about later. The key thing about metaphor, though, is that it usually tries to explore something abstract (love, power, delight or whatever) using specific language and imagery that we can visualise, and that somehow make sense of the abstract idea. Remember that *pleasure* in this context implies a feeling of understanding, and the satisfaction that comes from that. So you should use the type of language that will aid understanding not just of your plot and your characters, but your themes. On the whole remember that pleasurable language is anything apart from abstract. Business-report language and jargon give no one pleasure, and help no one understand anything.

Aristotle says that these stories, with their pleasurable language, should be 'performed by actors, not through narration.'[43] He is emphasising again this principle of 'show, don't tell'. He's not really saying that everything should be dramatised on an actual stage, but rather that as much as possible in a story should be learnt by the actions of the characters, not through the author or narrator telling us what is happening. If you like, this is an ancient argument against voice-over. I could begin a story with the words, 'Paul was a very greedy little boy', or I could begin with a scene where Paul steals sweets from his sister. Paul is the 'actor' performing this action, and we learn more about his character from this scene than from the simple narration. Of course, when Aristotle was writing there were no such things as novels or mass-market paperbacks. People watched fiction being performed. But the structures of stories have not changed very much in the last 2,000 years, and it was just as easy for a lazy playwright to have a narrator tell the audience that a character is jealous or mean as it is for us now to chuck in an abstract word and think that we are done with that bit of characterisation. Note, though, the way that 'show, don't tell' relates mainly to characterisation. Sometimes in fiction it makes more sense to tell something rather than show it, otherwise you'd end up showing everything and lose all sense of unity.[44]

PITY AND FEAR

Every good plot contains what the Greeks called *pathos*: where the audience experiences the suffering of the characters in some way, and identifies with it. Think about this, and test it out on stories you're familiar with. You'll find – perhaps to your surprise – that narrative is all about suffering. Our three examples are full of it: Woody's jealousy; Buzz's identity crisis; Oedipus's horrible recognition; the Bixleys' terrible mealtimes. Everyone in these stories is suffering almost all the time. Aristotle says that we enjoy seeing fictional characters suffer. Indeed, we have to feel 'pity and fear' (the Greek words are *eleos* and *phobos*) in order for a story to be interesting to us, and for us to feel 'involved' with it. Pity is when we feel sorry for someone who does not deserve their misfortune. Fear is when we think that something similar could happen to us. We will feel pity and fear to some extent during both tragedy and comedy; in fact, you could summarise most classic comedy plots as 'lots of suffering and then a wedding'. With tragedy the suffering comes later.

In the next chapter we'll be looking in more detail at tragedy. But for now we can learn from Aristotle how to begin plotting the kind of story that people want to read, and that, through its mode of imitation, will give them pleasure. Later we will look at forms of narrative that deliberately withhold this kind of pleasure, and wonder whether they work as well as Aristotelian plots do. In the meantime it's worth considering just how many Aristotelian plots there are in the world around you: in advertising, sport, on packaging, as well as in books and films. Look particularly for stories that tend to be about one thing (the unified action), driven by cause and effect, and which take an agent from good to bad fortune or the reverse. Next time you watch a film, try to break down the three-act structure as well. You'll often find narratives that include more than one story, each with its three acts, especially long novels like *Anna Karenina* or *Great Expectations*. Part of the skill of good novelists is in this kind of multiple-plotting.

And remember when you are writing that while most successful writers use (consciously or unconsciously) all the techniques Aristotle describes, the greatest writers do it so that there is no sense of formula. Great stories never have stereotypical characters doing predictable things. Instead, you'll find complex characters struggling with life in all sorts of ways and undergoing sometimes very subtle changes of fortune. You'll find humour, too, usually, innovative language and all sorts of other things. So it's not enough to follow Aristotle's rules with any old characters and any old actions in any old language. But using his suggestions will make your plots enjoyable, and they will also help you focus on your themes.

★

Let's look now at two Marilyn Monroe films and consider the extent to which they have Aristotelian structures. *Gentlemen Prefer Blondes* (1953) is a quirky romantic comedy in which Lorelei Lee, a loveable blonde showgirl, sets out to find true happiness by getting a rich man to give her diamonds. Although our cultural conventions may make us disapprove of this as an aim in life (and surely we know that the love interest in a romantic comedy should ultimately be the man and not the diamonds), we nevertheless recognise an element of satire here, which makes the aim more interesting. Haven't so many romantic comedies in the past been about women securing rich men, after all? And is it really more shallow for a woman to want a rich man than it is for men to want a pretty girl? The whole film is somehow about the management of economies, particularly economies in relationships, where wealth may be traded for beauty. Somehow, we sense these themes, and we admire Lorelei despite her materialism. We also approve of her honesty – she never pretends to be something she is not – and we therefore want her to succeed. At the beginning of the film she becomes engaged to a rich but weak man, Gus Esmond Jr, who has planned a romantic trip to Paris for the two of them. His father, Gus Esmond Sr, disapproves of the relationship, however, and so Lorelei makes the trip to Paris with her friend Dorothy Shaw, a more down-to-earth showgirl who wants to marry for love, not money. Gus Esmond Sr has sent a private detective, Ernie Malone, to travel on the same boat to Paris and see what Lorelei gets up to. On the boat, Lorelei soon meets Lord Beekman, aka 'Piggy', an elderly, married, diamond-mine owner. A table probably best shows what happens next so that we can examine it, although the table will make a lot more sense if you can see the film first. If you watch the film, you'll see just how intricately it is constructed in order that these three acts can work together coherently. Let's look again at Aristotle's summary of many of the elements a good plot should contain:

> Tragedy is an *imitation of an action* that is *admirable, complete* and *possesses magnitude*; in *language made pleasurable* [. . .] *performed by actors, not through narration*; effecting through *pity and fear* the purification of such emotions.[45]

	Act 1	Act 2	Act 3
Lorelei	Wants to secure wealth by marrying Gus, but once on the boat finds she can't resist the diamond tiara owned by Piggy's wife.	In trying to get the tiara by charming Piggy, Lorelei ends up caught in incriminating photographs with him. She and Dorothy trick Ernie out of the photos and then she exchanges them with Piggy for the tiara. Unfortunately, when Lorelei gets to Paris, Gus has found out about her indiscretion. Her letter of credit is withdrawn. All seems lost.	Has to work as a showgirl in Paris and is successful, except she is soon picked up by the police for the 'theft' of the tiara. Dorothy tells her to give it back, but she can't because she no longer has it. The tiara has been stolen. Lorelei now must marry Gus, or at least get the money from him to buy a replacement tiara. The engagement is soon back on. While Dorothy pretends to be Lorelei in court, Lorelei charms Gus Sr with her honesty ('I don't want to marry him for his money; I want to marry him for *your* money') and he consents to let her marry his son.
Dorothy	Wants to keep Lorelei out of trouble (and is also falling in love with Ernie).	Fails to keep Lorelei out of trouble. Finds out that Ernie is a detective. She thinks he never really loved her; he was just interested in Lorelei all along. All seems lost.	Buys time for Lorelei to get the money for the tiara by posing as her in the courtroom. It becomes clear that Piggy has stolen the tiara back and has set up Lorelei so he can claim the insurance for it. Dorothy persuades Ernie to track down Piggy at the airport. She realises his love for her and they are married.
Ernie	Wants to get incriminating pictures of Lorelei (and is also falling in love with Dorothy).	Gets the photos he needs, but loses them again. Dorothy doesn't seem to love him now that she knows he's a detective. She thinks he was just stringing her along. Gets the photos back again. He has been successful on his case, but all still seems lost.	Wants to prove his love for Dorothy so helps solve the mystery of the tiara. Marries Dorothy.

Here we see that this is a plausible fiction (an imitation) with one action at the centre of it: Lorelei wants to be secure, and for her, security is based on wealth. She must marry a rich man, or at least convince one to give her diamonds. Note that although this is the main action in the narrative, and the structure of the whole is based around her becoming engaged to Gus, losing him (because she is tempted by what seem to be greater riches) and finally marrying him, we have secondary characters whose actions support those of Lorelei. Dorothy wants to help Lorelei, but she also wants to marry for love. Ernie wants to do the right thing, which involves betraying Lorelei, but he also wants to marry Dorothy. There are many conflicts in the plot, which lead to drama. As we can see from the table above, the plot is neatly constructed, with a clear beginning, middle and end. The problem posed at the beginning (how can Lorelei marry Gus?) is the one solved at the end. Secondary problems are structured in a similar way. All characters are in crisis at the end of the second act. In trying to get what they want, they have actually succeeded in losing it. Their fortunes are always changing, and at this point it looks as if things have got worse for everyone. The determinate structure of the plot means, however, that things will change again, for the better, in Act 3. It is *because* of Lorelei's unwavering honesty that she ends up in the fix with the tiara, and then also because of this that she ends up meeting Gus Sr and convincing him she is the right woman for his son. It is *because* Ernie and Dorothy have fallen in love that they are able to solve the problem of the tiara. Ernie is set in opposition to Lorelei, and will only help her because he believes he is helping Dorothy. There are lots of other crucial little moments of cause-and-effect running through the whole plot, but these are the main elements that hold it together. Note that the plot is all the more 'whole' and unified because of Ernie's role in it. If a random policeman had solved the mystery of what had happened to the tiara the plot would not be as satisfying. There is a good reversal here (we'll be looking at reversal more closely in the next chapter). Ernie is the one who got Lorelei into trouble (with the photographs) and he is now the person who will get her out of it.

The plot possesses magnitude. It does not begin with the births of Dorothy and Lorelei in Little Rock, show their childhoods, explore the reasons for their different motivations in life, show the childhood of Ernie, Piggy in his diamond mines and so on. We also don't see what happens after the couples are married at the end. The plot focuses on one main thing – the missing tiara, and how this problem can be resolved – and what is at stake is one clear thing: marriage.

Because this is not a book (it is adapted from the novel by Anita Loos, but it is simpler to focus on the film here), it should be difficult to talk about pleasurable language. But the film certainly has style, and a pleasurable language of its own. Pleasurable language should always highlight themes, or, in Aristotle's terms, allow us to examine something so we can understand it better.

The themes in this film are of course not as complex as themes in a great novel, but they are there. As we have already noted, one of the main thematic questions is about women and wealth. How can women obtain wealth in a world where they are expected to be submissive and do domestic work for free? Do younger women have more power because of their 'charms', and if so, should they use this power to accumulate wealth as an insurance for their old age? It's worth remembering that this is a society in which people are expected to use their charms to succeed. In Arthur Miller's 1949 play *Death of a Salesman,* protagonist Willy Loman attributes success in business to being 'well liked'. Women, mostly excluded from business in '50s America, perhaps have no option other than using what charms they have on the men who can make money from business. If this leads to excessive materialism in women, then what does that mean? Youth and beauty and female 'charms' are (often ironically, or satirically) celebrated in the film through its own 'language': the beautiful costume design is a part of this. Lorelei's great number towards the end of the film, 'Diamonds are a Girl's Best Friend', uses imagery, metaphor and authentic language to reinforce the themes of the whole film. 'There may come a time / When a hard-boiled employer / Thinks you're awful nice, / But get that ice or else no dice. / He's your guy / When stocks are high, / But beware when they start to descend. / It's then that those louses / Go back to their spouses. / Diamonds are a girl's best friend.' Here we see the youthful charms of a woman being compared with high stocks. The metaphor might be a slight cliché, but it certainly emphasises the theme of economy, and allows us to ask questions about the validity of trading in what you have at just the right time, if what you have is beauty.

There is very little narration in this film, and certainly nothing formalised like voice-over. Everything is shown through action and dialogue. It is very useful for writers to examine films, as most of them have no narration. No one needs to tell us what Lorelei is like – we see it for ourselves. There is considerable humour in the scene when Lorelei meets Piggy, because we already know how she feels about diamonds, and how she is likely to react to a man who owns diamond mines. The fact that Dorothy tries to prevent the meeting only highlights its humorous inevitability.

Because we admire Lorelei and Dorothy, or at least feel them to be in some way like us, we can feel pity and fear for them. This is not a great tragedy, of course, where there would be more intense pity and fear. But we do feel sorry for Lorelei's predicament. When she suffers misfortune in the film – for example, becoming stuck in a porthole while trying to escape from Ernie's cabin – we want her to be OK. We don't desire her to be discovered and humiliated. We have identified with her, and we feel pity for her (mixed with embarrassment and humour). Fear is an extension of the identification process. We fear that she will be discovered (and this fear gets mixed up with our own anxiety about being discovered doing something embarrassing); we fear that she will be too disgraced to marry Gus (and by extension we fear our own disgrace); we fear that she will be wrongly imprisoned for stealing the tiara (just as we fear injustice in our own lives) and so on. Pity and fear let us share the characters' suffering, and, according to Aristotle, we get considerable pleasure, and a kind of emotional release (catharsis), from this.

There's No Business Like Show Business (1954, hereafter known as *TNBLSB*) also has a part for Marilyn Monroe. She plays another showgirl, Vicky Hoffman (later Vicky Parker – a stage name), who goes from cloakroom attendant to megastar over the course of the film. However, her rise is not the focus of the film. The main narrative focuses on the Five Donahues, a family vaudeville act made up of Molly, Terence, and their three children: Tim, Steve and Katy. Summarising this film[46] is easy but very boring, as one thing happens after the other for no clear reason. There is also no point in trying to draw up a three-act table for this narrative. It is a rambling story of the life of a whole family (plus Marilyn Monroe), with no central action apart from Tim's disappearance halfway through, which is connected to his relationship with Vicky. The problem with this being the central action is that it revolves around Tim, who is not an admirable character. It is possible to be drunk and admirable, or at least likeable (look at how we hope that Withnail's life will improve in *Withnail and I*, and how much we like Grace Kelly's character in *High Society* once she loosens up and drinks too much champagne), but Tim is neither admirable nor likeable. He is not struggling with anything in any way we can understand. As Vicky points out to him, he hasn't even become a performer through hard work and merit, but because of his family. He has no obvious qualities as a character apart from his drunkenness, and so we can't identify with him. Vicky also has no discernible features, apart from her ambition. We partly admire this, but wonder why she gets mixed up with such an unappealing family. What has Tim got to offer her?

There is also a clear lack of a determinate structure. Although an argument with his father provides a reason for Tim to disappear, there is no clear reason for him to come back. The plot is broadly episodic: one thing happens after another – far too many things – but the events aren't strongly connected. Symmetries that should be there simply collapse; Tim has argued with his father, but makes up with Vicky, for example. We don't feel for these characters, and it is not clear what is at stake for them, beyond being a happy family. As a result, although there is action in the story, the plot itself is very weak and there is very little real drama. It is actually a boring film to watch – try it and see. In contrast, there is no boredom in *Gentlemen Prefer Blondes*. Although both films are thematically light (they are Hollywood musicals, after all), there is, as we have noted, some interesting material in *Gentlemen Prefer Blondes* about economics, and the American concept of trading on personal charm. There's something to go away and think about afterwards, even if we don't agree with the film in the end, or can't apply it to the early twenty-first century very easily. The structure of the film supports its themes. Honesty (and the charming effects of it) is seen to be such an important quality that it gives a character licence to be as materialistic as she likes. It is only when Lorelei attempts something deceitful (her deal with Piggy over the tiara) that things go wrong for her. But in the end her deceit isn't that serious, and the wrongs can be righted.

But perhaps what is most interesting and surprising about a comparison between these two films is that the more 'formulaic' film, or the one with a clearer Aristotelian shape, *Gentlemen Prefer Blondes*, is the less predictable. As we will see in the next chapter, Aristotle argues in favour of 'astonishment', and against predictability. This idea that a well-known structure can still be unpredictable is somewhat paradoxical, and this paradox makes it one of the most interesting elements of storytelling. An audience can often only see the shape of a narrative once it is complete. You shouldn't be able to predict exactly what is going to happen next in a well-made narrative, even once you know all the 'rules'.

TNBLSB follows no 'rules' but is nevertheless entirely predictable. We know that Tim and Vicky must end up together, because the only other eligible male in the film is a priest, and the only other eligible woman is Tim's sister. We also know that if a family is going to have a problem with a son, the most predictable thing will be alcoholism. And we 'know' that when anything goes wrong for them, all drunks immediately go off and crash cars. We know that Tim will come back at the end of the film, because it's a musical comedy and we therefore expect a happy ending. We also know that Molly will forgive Vicky. The success of *Gentlemen Prefer Blondes* is that we are so caught up in the drama of it that we forget that this is a romantic comedy that must resolve with a wedding. Indeed, at various moments it seems impossible that anyone will get married at all. It seems impossible that Lorelei will get the tiara, then impossible that she will lose it, then impossible that it will be recovered. *TNBLSB* was a flop, both critically and commercially, while *Gentlemen Prefer Blondes* was a critical and commercial success.

Films wear their plots more obviously than novels do, which is why they are so good for introducing these principles, but the same things can go wrong in novels as in films. Most good literary novels, however subtle and unconventional, will have characters we can invest in, a sense of unity and focus, and clear narrative and thematic questions – as well as most of the other basic features Aristotle identifies in the *Poetics*. In fact, the great classic novels all work in this way, despite all being so different.

TRAGEDY AND THE COMPLEX PLOT

Tregedie is to sayn, a certyn storie
As olde bookes maken us memorie,
Of him that stood in great prosperitee
And is y fallen out of high degree
Into miserie, and endeith wretchedly . . .

Chaucer, *The Monk's Tale*

In the 1990s there was a pop group called Steps, who covered a 1979 Bee Gees song called 'Tragedy'. A key refrain in the song is the following: 'Tragedy! When the feeling's gone and you can't go on it's tragedy.' So twice in my life so far I've heard kids going around singing this line as if it were true. But is it a good definition of tragedy? Is tragedy about loss or lack of feeling, or is it in fact all about *excess* of feeling? Is tragedy, as Nietzsche suggested in 1872, actually the deepest form of storytelling there is and far removed from anything that could possibly be covered in a pop song? And how would you begin to plot it?

We're going to use three narratives as reference points: *Oedipus the King, Hamlet* and the film *Cruel Intentions*.[47] I'm going to assume you already know *Oedipus* and *Hamlet*.

Cruel Intentions is a film about two step-siblings, Sebastian and Kathryn. Kathryn makes a bet that Sebastian can't bed the daughter of the new headmaster, a virgin called Annette who is saving herself for marriage. If he can 'ruin' Annette, then Sebastian will get his prize – to sleep with Kathryn. Sebastian realises too late that he really loves Annette, and although it doesn't seem to be too late to save their relationship, other acts he's committed (seducing Cecile, the new girlfriend of Kathryn's ex-boyfriend, Court, as part of a revenge plot of Kathryn's, for example) catch up with him and he is killed by Ronald, the music teacher with whom he has encouraged Cecile to get involved.

Tragedy is a form of story in which the hero, or heroine, dies – usually literally, but sometimes metaphorically – at the end of the story. Chaucer's Monk knew this. Chaucer's Monk reminds us of what Aristotle has already told us, that tragedy features people who *fall from high places* into misery. In other words, these are very 'admirable' people, like kings, queens, celebrities and so on. Even in *Cruel Intentions* this holds true: Sebastian and Kathryn are wealthy Manhattan teenagers who are very popular at their school.

Aristotle argues that tragedy must have the following:

1. An admirable hero(ine)
2. Astonishment
3. A complex plot
4. Reversal (*Peripeteia*)
5. Recognition (*Anagnôrisis*)
6. Error (*Hamartia*)
7. A chorus

ASTONISHMENT

As we have already covered the idea of the admirable hero(ine), let's now look at astonishment. We surely already know instinctively what Aristotle tells us here, which is that every good plot contains something that is almost paradoxical: we have to be surprised by events which are, when you consider what has gone before, not at all surprising. We have to feel pity and fear 'when things come about contrary to expectation *but because of one another.*'[48] We may feel shocked and surprised, for example, when Hamlet tells Ophelia 'Get thee to a nunnery.'[49] After all, isn't he supposed to be in love with her? But he seems to have two reasons for saying this: 1) because women breed sinners like him, destined to suffer, and 2) because women make men do awful things: 'Or if thou wilt needs marry, marry a fool. For wise men know well enough what monsters you make of them.'[50] Now it becomes clear. Hamlet is angry with his mother (and is perhaps suggesting that she was either behind the plot to kill his father, or at least the motivation for it) and is taking it out on Ophelia. It's a shocking scene that certainly makes us feel astonishment, but on consideration it is found to be the consequence of the chain of cause and effect that has led Hamlet to this horrible situation. We are also astonished at the end of *Hamlet*, when Hamlet is finally killed. But it's really not that surprising, especially as Hamlet knows it is going to happen.

When Sebastian is killed in *Cruel Intentions*, it is astonishing. However, everything in the plot has led to this moment in which his pure love (for Annette) will be destroyed by the legacy of his impure love (for Cecile and for Kathryn). It might be possible to argue that the astonishment in this plot is more intense because up until the moment of Sebastian's (or, in the original, Valmont's) death the plot seems to be preparing to resolve itself as comedy. There is much confusion, and when we realise that Sebastian really is in love with Annette, surely all that remains is for him to explain the whole situation to her. But how do you explain that you have slept with someone for a bet, and your prize is to sleep with another woman? Still, we may ask whether it wouldn't be more pleasurable and satisfying if everyone did find some way of living happily ever after, with Sebastian and Annette together, Ronald and Cecile in love and perhaps Kathryn reunited with Court? The simple answer, I think, is no. Like the state of Denmark, Kathryn and Sebastian's world is rotten from the start and no happy ending can come about within it, at least not until their corrupt reign is overthrown. As we'll see later, once the central error has been committed in tragedy, there really is no turning back and making it into a comedy will only make an audience disgusted.

A COMPLEX PLOT

Aristotle makes an important distinction between what he calls 'simple' and 'complex' plots.

Some plots are simple, others complex, since the actions of which the plots are imitations are themselves also of these two kinds. By a *simple* action I mean one which is, in the sense defined, continuous and unified, and in which the change of fortune comes about without reversal and recognition. By *complex* I mean one in which the change of fortune involves reversal or recognition or both.[51]

For Aristotle, a good tragedy should have a complex plot, rather than a simple one. An example of a simple plot would be the episode of *Supernanny* we discussed before, in which the Bixleys make their journey from bad to good fortune without anything else happening that's particularly significant, or that casts the characters or the story in a new light. Makeover shows are usually simple, with a protagonist going from bad fortune to good fortune fairly unproblematically, except for the usual crisis at the end of Act 2 where they go back to their terrible clothes (or whatever) and have to be 'rescued' by the presenters. But soap operas and drama series will usually have 'twists and turns'. A simple plot is usually a chronological story told via a linear narrative, whereas a complex plot will usually turn on the revelation of previously concealed information from the past. *Great Expectations* is made complex by Pip's discovery about his real benefactor, and all the further discoveries that lead from that. By the end of the novel all our expectations, along with Pip's, have been turned upside down. *Pride and Prejudice* is also made complex by the revealing of Wickham's secret past.

REVERSAL

Reversal is a 'change to the opposite',[52] and in a complex plot there will be several reversals, or twists, along the way.

These, incidentally, are very hard to plot, but very satisfying for an audience. A good reversal will provoke astonishment, pity and fear, and will often underline major themes within the story. This is probably best understood with some examples. In *Cruel Intentions*, Sebastian intends to betray Annette in order to sleep with Kathryn. The reversal comes about when, in sleeping with Annette, he actually betrays Kathryn (because he finds he is in love with Annette). In *Hamlet*, Rosencrantz and Guildenstern take Hamlet to England to be executed, but instead it is they who are executed while Hamlet returns to Denmark. Sometimes reversals can be subtle (and they don't occur only in tragedy). In *Toy Story*, Buzz Lightyear has to accept that he is a toy – a simulation of a fictional character – in order to have an authentic life. In *The Bell Jar*, Esther Greenwood becomes mad and tries to kill herself because she is not 'normal' like Joan; later Joan ends up killing herself while Esther gets better. (Although we know now that this isn't how the 'real' story ended, it's how the book does.) In *Great Expectations*, Pip believes he is inferior in status to Estella. But he later discovers that she was inferior all along.

Here's one of Aristotle's examples of a good reversal:

> For example, in the *Oedipus*, someone came to give Oedipus good news and free him from his fear with regard to his mother, but by disclosing Oedipus's identity he brought about the opposite result.[53]

Here we see reversal happening at the same time as the big recognition: Oedipus realises that he is really the son of

Laius and Jocasta and has therefore killed his father and married his mother. And there is another big reversal within this recognition: knowledgeable Oedipus, determined to know everything, finally discovers that he did not even have the most basic knowledge about who he is, and where he came from. Reversal is a key part of any drama, and when it is well-plotted it certainly causes astonishment, understanding and pleasure. The example I used last time of the perfect girl who falls into a hole she had dug to conceal evidence that she had murdered her rival also uses reversal. Try to identify reversals in narratives you are familiar with, and look particularly for the subtle reversals in realist fiction.

RECOGNITION

Recognition is, as Aristotle describes it: 'A change from ignorance to knowledge',[54] and it is one of the most crucial parts of a tragedy. Aristotle suggests that it is best when it happens at the same time as a reversal, as in the example from *Oedipus* above. Recognition can come about when a piece of information is revealed that crucially alters the relationships or perceived facts in the hero's world. For example, two lovers may discover that they are actually brother and sister (*Home and Away*, 1988–89 season). Or consider this storyline from *The Archers* a few years ago: a woman is jealous of her husband's flirtation with another woman and so begins spending time confiding in a male friend. Her husband rejects the other woman but the wife accepts the advances of the friend. She realises, too late, that she is the adulterer, not him. This involves both a reversal and a recognition. However, true tragic recognition can often be much more complex than both these examples, and can involve a hero or heroine making a profound realisation that they've made a terrible mistake, and are probably going to die because of it.

Usually a recognition scene involves the hero or heroine stating clearly what has happened to them, often in a powerful first-person narration. You will almost always be able to find a clear recognition scene in any tragedy, usually just before the hero dies. These scenes can range from the very subtle to the overwrought. In *Oedipus*, we have this:

Oedipus:
>   Ah God! Ah God! This is the truth at last!
>   O Sun, let me behold thee this once more,
>   I who am proved accursed in my conception,
>   And in my marriage, and in him I slew.

Anna Karenina's tragic recognition takes place over several pages, and is complicated by not necessarily being an objective account of what has happened to her (which makes it in some ways more tragic). Chapter 30 of Part 6 begins, 'Here it is again! Again I understand everything.' Soon after this:

'What was he looking for in me? Not love so much as the satisfaction of his vanity.' She remembered his words, the expression on his face, like an obedient pointer, in the early days of their liaison. And now everything confirmed it. 'Yes, there was the triumph of successful vanity in him. Of course, there was love, too, but for the most part it was the pride of his success. He boasted of me. Now it's past. Nothing to be proud of. Not proud but ashamed. He took all he could from me, and I'm of no use to him any more. I'm a burden to him, and he tries not to be dishonourable towards me . . . He loves me, but how? *The zest is gone*,' she said to herself in English . . .

This was not a supposition. She saw it clearly in that piercing light which now revealed to her the meaning of life and of people's relations.[55]

A proper analysis of this passage would take many hours. But note particularly the way in which Tolstoy combines Anna's first-person subjective thoughts with free indirect style, and the way in which this makes the recognition slightly ironic. The 'piercing light' is Anna's alone, and the 'meaning of life' that has been revealed to her is almost certainly false. Indeed, it is the false nature of life that has been so 'clearly' revealed to her, and in this there is even more bitter irony. Here, the tragic recognition is just as we would expect, structurally. It is Anna's, and it comes almost at the end of the book, just before she dies. But look at all the depth it contains in its opposition of what is 'true' and what is 'false', and in setting Anna against herself. Anna does not see clearly at all, but merely tells us that she does. And Tolstoy is telling us something different. This is a recognition scene, but the 'truth' Anna has learnt is that everything is false. And that in itself is paradoxical, and cannot be true.

In *Cruel Intentions*, it is Kathryn who provides the recognition for Sebastian. She has already by now manipulated him into pretending he doesn't love Annette, but when he goes to take his prize (that he doesn't even want any more) she tells him that the game was not what he thought it was: 'You were very much in love with her. And you're still in love with her. But it amused me to make you ashamed of it. You gave up on the first person you ever loved because I threatened your reputation. Don't you get it? You're just a toy, Sebastian. A little toy I like to play with. And now you've completely blown it with her. I think it's the saddest thing I've ever heard.'

Recognition is therefore where a truth – factual or emotional – that has previously been concealed is revealed, and Aristotle says there are several ways in which this can be plotted:[56]

1. **Based on a 'token'.** Aristotle calls this the 'least artistic' kind of recognition (although he admits these can be 'better or worse'). The 'token' will be something like a scar or a necklace that confirms something, usually about someone's identity.[57] For example: Jane's father, a stockbroker, is betrayed by someone who wears a distinctive bracelet. He goes bankrupt and kills himself. Years later, Jane falls in love with Peter and they decide to get married. As they walk down the aisle, she notices – gasp – the bracelet. She is about to marry her father's betrayer . . . The main problem with this kind of plot is that is relies too heavily on chance (unless it was not completely random that her father's betrayer pursued her, and that she never saw the bracelet before then). Note that this kind of

recognition has astonishment (briefly) but no real depth. There is nothing to go away and think about afterwards. There is also no reversal.

2. **Based on a direct revelation.** Another weak type, according to Aristotle. This is recognition that is given directly to a protagonist by another character – for example, when someone suddenly declares his or her true identity (rather than having it discovered through events in the action). So perhaps just before the wedding, Peter's sister turns up and tells Jane that her brother killed Jane's father. The main problem here is that Jane hasn't done anything to 'earn' the information. It becomes episodic. Hints that add up to something, and make sense of the whole plot, are much better.

3. **Based on a suppressed memory.** Usually something triggers a forgotten memory, or enables the character to work out the significance of something remembered or misremembered. Here, Jane might dream of the night her father died. From her bedroom window, she saw a colleague of his leave the house earlier that night and this image has always haunted her. He was wearing a bracelet that is somehow horribly familiar. It couldn't be . . . ? No! It was Peter. Again, this can often appear episodic and random. Unless something in the plot itself causes the memory to surface, this kind of recognition is best avoided.

4. **Based on inference.** This is where a character works out the significance of something using logic. So perhaps one night Jane asks to look at Peter's CV and he won't show it to her. He says he hasn't got one, or makes some excuse. She realises he's got something to hide and works it back from there. This kind of recognition can sometimes work, but only if it is supported by detail in the whole plot. A clear problem here is that if Peter knows he has something to hide then his motivation for being with Jane becomes rather suspect and implausible.

5. **Based on the COMPLEX action in the narrative itself.** This is the one Aristotle favours. Let's look at our examples.

   a. No one tells Oedipus the whole story of who he really is, at least not in time to save him. There are no tokens to prove he is the son of Laius. He doesn't suddenly remember everything, although his memory of killing his father comes into it. It is the complex plotting of all these things together that make the tragedy work – and the fact that Oedipus puts his horrible story together himself. His motivation is very significant here, and involves the deep reversal we have already discussed: it is because he is so desperate for the truth that he pursues it even though it means finding out his own life is a lie.

   b. No one tells Sebastian in *Cruel Intentions* that he has ruined both his relationship with Annette (that was doomed anyway) and his love for Kathryn (also doomed). There are no tokens. The plot carefully positions him in a place where he is completely trapped, and by the time he realises this, it is too late.

c. In our made-up example, Jane and Peter would both be unaware that he betrayed her father all those years ago. Jane won't talk about her father much, or any details of her old life, but has vowed to kill his betrayer. Jane will have gone into a completely different line of work from her father, but maybe using one of his close friends as a contact. This friend will also have helped Peter in some way and so the plot is set up for Peter and Jane to meet. They genuinely are in love, but it gradually becomes clear to Peter (via complex plotting) that Jane's father killed himself because of him. What should he do about Jane? Perhaps in the act of trying to obliterate everything from his past he makes her suspicious. She finds burned pieces of paper and believes he's having an affair. Where was he on Friday night? Well, talking to his friend and trying to make everything right – but he can't tell her that. Suddenly he is in a position where he has to confess to an affair or tell Jane about her father. He pretends he was having an affair but Jane discovers that he is lying. The plot then ends with Peter's death, or at least the death of the relationship.

d. In *Hamlet*, though, there is no clear recognition. The closest thing to a traditional recognition scene is this response to Horatio's suggestion that Hamlet call off the fencing match with Laertes:

> Not a whit, we defy augury. There is special prov-
> idence in the fall of a sparrow. If it be now, 'tis not
> to come; if it be not to come, it will be now; if it
> be not now, yet it will come – the readiness is all.
> Since no man, of aught he leaves, knows what is't
> to leave betimes, let be.[58]

Hamlet hasn't made a clear mistake in the play, except perhaps his scheme of pretending to be mad. But he can't bring his father back, and he can't make Denmark less rotten. Indeed, he has perhaps inherited the tragedy of his life, and the only thing it can end with is his death. In this way, Hamlet stands for all of us. None of us fully understands the meaning of our lives, but we are surrounded by meaning nonetheless.

Celebrity stories are frequently told in the media using a tragic structure. It's interesting to begin to notice this, and to realise that these are plotted narratives, not necessarily true stories. Usually, much is made of the recognition 'scene' or interview, if there is one (and if not, often pictures of weeping and distress will do). *Celebrity Big Brother* is supposedly a non-fictional, non-scripted narrative.[59] But in 2007 there was a surprisingly coherent recognition scene when Jade Goody realised (partly because Big Brother had told her off for being racist, and partly through inference) that her career would probably be over when she left the house because of her bullying of Shilpa Shetty. There was some dramatic irony here – we realised, although Jade did not, that she had already lost most of her sponsorship at this point, and that her perfume had been pulled from the shelves. In the 'scene', she sits in the Diary Room for over half an hour sobbing. Among other things, she says 'I'm so scared . . . It's so different this time around because before I didn't have anything to lose. Nothing. Now I've got so much. I don't want to go through all that crap again.' She is falling from a high place. You might want to also look at the way the media covered the stories of Lindsay Lohan, Tiger Woods and Britney Spears. The 'death' in these tragedies is usually of the person's career, and may even be temporary. But when the celebrity actually dies, as in the case of Jade Goody or the South African cricketer Hansie Cronje, their stories stop being tragic and become simply sad (especially as neither of them died as a result of their tragic mistake – the structure broke down at that point).

However, the story of the death of Princess Diana does work as a complete tragedy, with her recognition 'scene' taking place during her interview with Martin Bashir in 1995. In this interview she says: 'The most daunting aspect was the media attention, because my husband and I, we were told when we got engaged that the media would go quietly, and it didn't; and then when we were married they said it would go quietly and it didn't; and then it started to focus very much on me, and I seemed to be on the front of a newspaper every single day, which is an isolating experience, and the higher the media put you, place you, the bigger the drop.' Diana is an almost perfect example of a tragic heroine, because she was so loved, but so flawed. She knew that going to such a high place would inevitably lead to a big 'drop'. Her fatal mistake was marrying into the Royal Family in the first place, which attracted the media attention that she could never cope with. But who among us would not have made the same mistake, if we were put into the same situation?

ERROR

That the brutal outcome of tragedy is always, in plot terms, the fault of the hero is the next thing we are going to talk about. Aristotle's term for this error is *hamartia*, which translates as a simple mistake, error or miscalculation. Although many people translate 'hamartia' as a 'tragic flaw' or 'fatal flaw', Aristotle doesn't imply that this is what he means by the term. Indeed, he is at pains to point out that tragic heroes must have *no* deep moral flaw:

> This is the sort of person who is not outstanding in moral excellence or justice; on the other hand, the change to bad fortune which he undergoes is not due to any moral defect or depravity, but to an error [*hamartia*] of some kind.[60]

Oedipus, for example, is not perfect. He has after all murdered the man he met at the place 'where three ways meet'. But we don't think he's evil because of this (and neither does the chorus, significantly), since the other man started the quarrel and Oedipus was simply defending himself. Perhaps Oedipus's big error was to leave Corinth on the basis of a prophecy, just as his father's big error was to send his son away to be killed, also on the basis of a prophecy. Many commentators will argue that it was Oedipus's 'hubris' – as a flaw in his character – that caused his downfall, and perhaps it is true that if he hadn't been so determined to know everything, he wouldn't have found out the awful truth. But then again, like many tragic heroes, Oedipus finds himself checkmated by the forces around him: the barren lands, the unhappy citizens. He has to try to find the murderer – it seems that he has no other choice. Is there a point in the narrative where he could stop asking questions? Maybe; maybe not.

It's hard to find the big fatal error in *Hamlet*, as we have observed, unless one wants to argue, with many commentators, that it is a tragedy of inaction, and that Hamlet is mistaken in not killing Claudius when he finds him praying alone after the play. Another approach might be to consider what has made the state of Denmark 'rotten'. For this we have to go back a generation and look at the behaviour of Old Hamlet, who has seized Denmark from Old Fortinbras. Is that the big moment that sets everything going in this tragedy? Was it Old Hamlet's greed for power that sowed the seeds not only for his own death but for the death of his wife and child as well?

Some tragedies seem easier to read than this, though. It's clear that Othello shouldn't have trusted Iago, for example, and it's also clear that Jade shouldn't have gone back into the Big Brother house. Or is it? These mistakes never seem fatal at the time they are made. Perhaps Othello should not have believed so much in his own power, or should have trusted Desdemona above all else. But you can see how he is the way he is. Of course Jade shouldn't have been racist, but it's clear that in some ways she was just very insecure. It's important to remember that tragedy is never simply a 'morality tale' that tells us how to act. Who knows what we'd do in any of these characters' situations, or what forces prompt us, and them, to act in one way rather than another? All tragic characters become trapped by a situation they thought they could control, and that perhaps we would think we could control, if we were them. Princess Diana could never get rid of the media, once they had noticed her; Anna Karenina can never undo the damage to her reputation that comes from being with Count Vronsky. Hamlet, once he has declared himself 'mad', no longer has any control over his life, although being 'mad' seemed like a good plan at the time. Tragedy can have a similar structure to addiction, where you smoke one cigarette, or have one drink, or gamble on one horse, and it's not so bad, and there are no clear consequences, so you do it again. Your life appears improved – you look cool, or find it easier to relax, or make some money. So you repeat the action again, and again. And it is never quite clear which repetition takes you into a realm you can never leave, and in which you are no longer in control. The important thing to remember is that tragedy is universal. An obvious point is that we all die in some sense tragically, as Hamlet makes us realise. But most of us will experience tragic structures in our lives: not in the tabloid sense of a sad, nonsensical event, but through our addictions, our weight gain, our bad love affairs, our cheating and our lying. Addicts, the obese and the lovelorn are not 'bad people' who deserve what they get. They are just people trying to make their lives better, as we all do. Tragedy is not about judging people because they are bad, it is about feeling intense compassion for people who destroy something important to them.

A CHORUS

In classic Greek tragedy, the text is always being read or interpreted as it goes along by the chorus. When we read Aristotle it's easy to dismiss elements like the *dithyramb* (tragic song) and the chorus as things we just don't have any more and can safely ignore. Then again, if we're looking for a tragic song, what about the Placebo track 'Every You, Every Me' that begins *Cruel Intentions*? And while the chorus might not explicitly exist in our dramas any more, it is certainly there implicitly. Indeed, the live audience forms much of the 'chorus' of *Big Brother* (home viewers providing the rest – 'You decide . . .'), and featured in the events of 2007 so much that it had to be taken away. Audiences that are filmed as part of 'the drama' of reality TV or talent shows are the closest thing we have now to a chorus, because they affect (by their voting, and their influence on others' voting) the outcomes of the 'characters'. Twitter can be seen as a very contemporary sort of chorus, and in the non-fictional fictions of celebrity lives it can function exactly like a traditional chorus, by commenting on, and influencing, the action as it happens. However, when people live-blog or live-tweet episodes of *The Archers*, or the latest TV drama, the chorus effect becomes para-textual: located outside of the story.

You'll probably have noticed in *Oedipus* that the chorus, which is placed right within the drama, is there to express the feelings of the general population. It forces Oedipus to act, and then stands in judgement over his actions and the outcome of these actions. You could argue that if it wasn't for the chorus (real or implied), there wouldn't be any meaning to the hero's actions in a tragedy. Or to put it another way: if no one is watching, who cares if Oedipus killed his father and married his mother? If no one was watching, and judging, do you think he'd still tear out his eyes with the golden brooches? If no one was watching, Princess Diana's story would never have become a tragedy. In this example, the chorus of the media did not just comment on her action, it eventually killed her.

In his passionate and sometimes mysterious book *The Birth of Tragedy,* Friedrich Nietzsche suggests that Greek tragedy actually *originated* from the idea of the chorus, because tragedy is so universal and connects us all. He argues that tragedy deeply expresses something of the 'primal Oneness' of being, and the ideal, or original, chorus is a manifestation of this primal Oneness. Nietzsche, like his predecessor Schopenhauer, had what is termed a 'pessimistic' view of the world. For Nietzsche, all beings are caught up in endless cycles of suffering and pain, and the more cheerful, logical and optimistic our art is, the more we are attempting to hide from the reality of existence: the dark, horrible primal Oneness where what we have in common is that we are all born to suffer and then die. It may not be cheerful, but then Nietzsche argues that the most moving and profound experiences are never cheerful. But that doesn't mean they are unpleasant. Far from it.

Nietzsche identifies two different types of artistic expression: the Apolline (after the god Apollo) and the Dionysiac (after the god Dionysus). The Apolline is a safe, logical kind of art that seeks to imitate *things* almost perfectly. This is the painting of the bowl of fruit that actually looks just like a bowl of fruit – the kind of thing Plato also wasn't that keen on since it is an imitation of an imitation. It is the perfectly structured comedy in which everything happens for a reason, and everyone ends up married and happy. It's the kind of narrative that makes you put down the book or leave the cinema feeling merely satisfied (and sometimes with that sickly feeling you get when you have watched something too formulaic), but not at all moved. The Apolline emphasises the individual as a separate part of the world of things (or phenomena) and tends to show the individual in triumph. It's the advert with the sparkling kitchen; the completed jigsaw puzzle; the wax-work museum world in which, if we screw up our eyes for long enough and believe in all the fast cars and shopping malls, we might truly believe that we will live for ever and that nobody is suffering.

The Dionysiac, on the other hand, has for its mascot Dionysus: the god of wine, women and song. Dionysiac art, according to Nietzsche, is more closely connected with music than with language, because it is expressive rather than representative. Here are a few other ways in which the Dionysiac differs from the Apolline:

Apolline	Dionysiac
Cheerfulness	Woe
Illusion	Truth
Triumph	Destruction
Words	Music
Phenomena	Beyond phenomena
Restraint	Excess
Self	No-self or oblivion
Being	Nothingness
Euripides	Aeschylus

For Nietzsche, all proper tragic heroes – Oedipus and Hamlet among them – are actually manifestations of Dionysus, and the point of tragedy, with its complex themes and ultimate destruction of the hero, is to dramatise something that is beyond ordinary existence and the world of phenomena. By glorifying death and destruction, the properly Dionysiac tragedy celebrates *eternal life*. By glorifying life and order, the purely Apolline narrative celebrates 'the eternity of the phenomenon'.[61]

Basically: there is a world of things that we know, and then *everything else beyond it* that we don't know but can sense. One is a world of language and phenomena; the other is beyond language and phenomena. You have to go beyond language and phenomena to get to truth, but of course, outside language truths are not easily expressed.

Language, the Apolline form of expression, is imitative. I can use it to imitate, for example, a table, by writing down the word *table*. I could produce an imitation of a table in other ways: I could draw a picture of it, or sculpt it or take a photograph. But how would I represent a table in music? I can't, because music is not imitative. I could write a little tune that for me means 'table', but you would never know it means that. There is no language you could learn that would tell you, either. However, music, according to Nietzsche, symbolises something beyond language – something much more profound: 'a sphere beyond and prior to all phenomena'.[62] Therefore, tragedy best expresses the primal suffering and the primal Oneness when it includes music (as in the operas of Wagner) or when it retains the 'spirit of music' somehow.

One of the ways in which writing can be 'musical' is when it doesn't just add up nicely with join-the-dots stories, themes and imagery. *Hamlet* and *Oedipus* succeed for Nietzsche *because* they are so puzzling and difficult to read. People have been wondering why Hamlet didn't kill Claudius earlier for the past 400 years: it's not a play that has an easy 'message' or 'moral' that you can read as easily as the words themselves. You can't just unpick the logic of the tragedy and say 'Well, here is the hero, and he made this error, and unfortunately everybody then died' in the way you may be able to with *Othello* or *King Lear* (although there is much more complexity in these plays than that, it is at least possible to pinpoint the precise things that the heroes could have done differently, even if you then conclude, as we did before, that they wouldn't have made any difference).

Hamlet really is a puzzle, however. Where's the bit you can fix that will make everything better in Elsinore? It's hard to find. You can suggest that maybe the *hamartia* in Hamlet lies a generation back, with Old Hamlet's conquest over Old Fortinbras. But this doesn't completely solve the puzzle, because the play is after all about Young Hamlet. Nietzsche suggests that what we see in Hamlet is someone in a Dionysiac state. The Dionysiac state may appear troubling, dark and confusing, but suggests a knowledge *beyond* an awareness of the everyday world, as well as a heightening of the experience of the everyday world. Nietzsche says that 'Dionysiac man' shares something with Hamlet:

> Both have truly seen the essence of things, they have *understood*, and action repels them; for their action can change nothing in the eternal essence of things, they consider it ludicrous or shameful that they should be expected to restore order to the chaotic world. Understanding kills action, action depends on a veil of illusion – this is what Hamlet teaches us, not the stock interpretation of Hamlet as a John-a-dreams who, from too much reflection, from an excess of possibilities, so to speak, fails to act.[63]

A sense of 'incomprehension' in the audience, of stories being difficult to understand but ultimately leaving you with a sense of the primal Oneness of existence and suffering, is very important for Nietzsche. A true tragedy should not leave you feeling pleasantly purged, as Aristotle suggested, nor leave you 'happy lingering in will-less contemplation'. Instead the effect of the pity and fear provoked by the drama should be more complicated. Nietzsche says that someone who has properly experienced a true tragic story will react in the following way:

> He sees the tragic hero before him, in epic clarity and beauty, and yet rejoices in his destruction. He understands the dramatic events to their very depths, yet he is happy to escape into incomprehension. He feels that the hero's acts are justified, and yet is all the more uplifted when those acts destroy their originator. He trembles at the sufferings that befall the hero, and yet they give him a higher, more powerful pleasure. He looks more keenly, more deeply than ever, and yet wishes for blindness.[64]

For Nietzsche, it is only through the destruction of the hero that we can really feel for him, really become one with him. We will see later that certain kinds of realist writing are compassionate in a different way, and subtle recognitions and epiphanies can be just as powerful as complete destruction. But it is worth remembering that proper tragedy should be really tragic, and that there is something particularly elevating about fictional suffering that touches something we all have in common. Not many writers nowadays like killing their protagonists. After all, when you've spent years writing them you become very attached. Killing your character feels a bit like killing yourself. Most writers don't even consider it. But it is really worth trying to plot a tragedy and seeing what happens. When I have asked students to do this, they are usually surprised by what happens. Often a much deeper and more complex narrative emerges than they would have thought.

Knowing you are going to destroy your character(s) at the end means you have more scope to do interesting things with them at the beginning.[65] Remember that tragic heroes are always ambitious. They want to do everything, know everything, go everywhere or fall in passionate love. Make them as admirable as you can; then let them make one big mistake. But whatever you do, don't slip into formula. Remember that the best plots are a little mysterious or puzzling.

Nietzsche argues that an extreme over-rationalisation of all parts of storytelling led to the death of true Greek tragedy, and that this happened with the arrival of Socratic methods of arguing in which it seems you can work everything out if you just talk it through logically. Plato, who apparently gave up writing fiction because he wanted to study with Socrates, actually ended up writing a sort-of fiction, as we have seen. But what we are left with in his work are dramatisations of people trying to make the world make sense. For Nietzsche, all of this is simply too optimistic: like the scientific method, it claims that everything is knowable if you can just sit down for long enough and work it out. This desire to make everything make sense can be seen, according to Nietzsche, in the work of Euripides, who was the major writer of New Attic Comedy, the style of drama that predominated in Greece after the death of Aeschylus. Nietzsche makes reference to a play written after the death of Euripides, called *The Frogs*, by Aristophanes, a short summary of which may provide a useful closure to this chapter.

In *The Frogs*, Dionysus goes to the underworld to stage

a competition between the dead poets Aeschylus and Euripides to see who is the better tragedian (and who should go back to Earth to save Athens). They take it in turns to criticise one another's work. Euripides says that Aeschylus was too dark, brooding and overwrought, but then Aeschylus proves that any of Euripides's clever but formulaic stories could be about someone losing a bottle of oil. The point seems to be that every formulaic story starts with a conflict that's later resolved – like losing a bottle of oil and then finding it again. While it's very useful for writers to know how to create drama, and how to successfully plot three-act stories, we must make sure that we are not just writing about bottles of oil. What we can take from Nietzsche, and from Aristotle, is that we need to go beyond formula if we are to truly move people. This doesn't mean abandoning structure, shape and traditional plots, and we will examine some of these in the next chapter. But we must think about how we can do new things with these plots, and how we can use what we put inside them to really connect with each other.

HOW TO TURN A FAIRY TALE INTO AN EQUATION

> Do you believe that every story must have a beginning and an end? In ancient times a story could only end in two ways: having passed all the tests, the hero and heroine married, or else they died. The ultimate meaning to which all stories refer has two faces: the continuity of life, the inevitability of death.
>
> Italo Calvino, *If On A Winter's Night A Traveller*[66]

If you spend long enough thinking about narrative, eventually the following idea is likely to occur to you: *What if there are only a limited number of plots that we use time and time again?* As readers, we are often able to anticipate what might happen next in a narrative, although if it is a well-made narrative we won't have any idea *how* the action must come about. We know that in every Fred Astaire and Ginger Rogers film the two romantic leads must be married (literally or symbolically) at the end. The pleasure in these narratives comes partly from the writers making this union seem impossible by placing various obstacles in the path of the lead characters. We know what *must* happen, but not how it *can*. We know what must happen because, consciously or unconsciously, we know all about basic plot structures.

By page 700 of *Middlemarch*, we know that Will Ladislaw and Dorothea must come together, but this seems impossible. There is much drama in a situation that seems as if it won't 'work out' (in all senses of the expression). Ladislaw is too proud to be seen to be chasing Dorothea's fortune, and there is the further problem of Casaubon's will, which forbids Dorothea from marrying Ladislaw. Ladislaw leaves for Europe, with no plans to return. We recognise, perhaps, the features of romantic comedy in this plot[67] (even if we don't even know the name for it), and our expectations work accordingly. We want, and expect, that the obstacles facing these two lovers will be overcome. Similarly, we don't have to be narrative theorists to know that a story about a difficult childhood is likely to have a 'coming of age' or 'rags to riches' plot, and that what 'must' happen is growth and development (and what must *not* happen is tragedy, where the child, who is already suffering, dies because of his or her own error). We know instinctively that a story about a teacher facing a difficult class of students will either end in the teacher's failure, or triumph. We know that most plots begin with some difficulty or problem, which is either overcome or not.

Much of this we know from Aristotle. We know the difference between comedy and tragedy, and we know that good people in troubled circumstances will find a solution and live happily ever after, and that admirable people with big ambitions will eventually meet their downfall. Aristotle also mentions the 'epic', which does not have such a precise structure as the tragedy and the comedy because it is longer (and recited, rather than acted out on stage), but relates roughly to what we would now call a 'quest'. But surely those three forms don't cover all possible plot structures? Where would *The Bell Jar* fit in? Or *Murder on the Orient Express*? Or a Chekhov story? Or *Cinderella*? Although there is a wedding at the end of *Cinderella*, it doesn't seem to fit what Aristotle says about comedy, that 'In comedy even people who are the bitterest enemies in the story [. . .] go off reconciled in the end, and no one gets killed by anybody.' Instead, Cinderella's step-sisters have their eyes pecked out by pigeons.

In his book *Story*,[68] Robert McKee lists what he suggests are all the possible film 'genres', ranging from 'Love story' to 'Sports Genre' to 'Mockumentary' and far beyond. Within these he specifies types of plot: the 'disillusionment plot', the 'punitive plot', the 'education plot', the 'maturation plot', the 'domestic drama', the 'revenge tale' and so on. We are probably all used to seeing films and novels classified and discussed in these sorts of ways, but we may sense that there's something not quite right about this kind of classification. We go into Blockbuster, or onto Amazon, and the films are neatly arranged for us into comedy, drama, action, horror and so on. In most bookshops, science fiction, fantasy and horror each have their own little section. Nowadays there's even a section for 'dark romance'. But these distinctions often only really relate to aesthetic differences. An action film might have a love-struck hero fighting against bad guys, rescuing his love-interest and living happily ever after. Doesn't a romantic comedy have more or less the same structure, even though its 'baddies' are more likely to be the heroine's parents than international terrorists? Many science-fiction narratives also have a happy ending, with a hero and heroine united and some sort of corruption or external threat overthrown.[69] A long, difficult journey may form the structure of a science-fiction film (*Star Wars*), a fantasy novel (*Lord of the Rings*), a quirky independent film (*The Straight Story*), a book about going to India to learn yoga (*Yoga School Dropout*) or a videogame (the *Final Fantasy* series). Perhaps aesthetic and commercial classifications don't actually tell us much about plot. It is the *underlying* structure that we need to look at if we are to come up with any theory of basic plots.

Taxonomy – the classification of things into tables, lists, 'basic types', hierarchies and so on – may not immediately seem to be the most exciting way to approach storytelling. But if you can understand the basic shapes of other narratives, you will be in a better position to construct your own. Remember that no architect designs a house by simply drawing an idea of 'home'. An architect will know the different possible shapes of houses and will work on this basis. The finished and lived-in home, complete with furniture, people, food, pets, belongings and mess, is, of course, not something that can any longer be represented by a line drawing. But without this drawing (or some sense of a basic structure), it could not exist.[70] Knowing about basic plots enables us not just to lay strong foundations for our narratives and give them a shape that works, but also to understand how to become inventive by subverting expectation, using irony and reversals on the level of plot (rather than just within the story) and working with metafiction.

PROPP'S BASIC FUNCTIONS

In 1928 the Russian folklorist Vladimir Propp published what would become a very influential book, *The Morphology of the Folktale*.[71] His project was to reduce one hundred nineteenth-century Russian folk tales[72] to their irreducible 'functions'. He found 31 of these functions (also known as 'narratemes') and argued that every folk tale was made up of some combination of them. Essentially, he found an underlying plot that was so well-used and so recognisable that it seemed really very obvious when he pointed it out: a young hero goes on a journey to recover something that is missing, facing trials along the way. This adventure can happen many, many different ways – but since there are only 31 distinct things that can happen, Propp was able to produce complex equations to show exactly how fairy tales are put together. While reducing a fairytale to an equation might seem like an odd thing to do, Propp contributed something very important to the study of narrative structure: he argued that there are elements in narratives that function like *variables*. It doesn't matter (on the level of plot) whether someone is given a magic horse, or buys some magic beans or steals a magic sword. The key thing is that they have received (by whatever means) a magical object (of any sort).[73] This is probably the most important thing we need to know about basic plot structures: in any plot, some things will be variable, and others will be static. Comedies, as we know, always end with a wedding (static), although this wedding can take any form and may even be metaphorical (details are variable).

Inspired by the eighteenth-century botanist Carl Linnaeus, Propp created a classification system for his fairy tales based on distinguishing between static elements and variables. Linnaeus had realised that all plants have reproductive systems, and so based his classification around these universal elements of reproduction (in angiosperms, this means the structure of the flower). All flowers have petals (static), but roses typically have five regular petals and sweet pea flowers have five irregular petals (variables). This, along with other differences, means they can be placed in different botanical families.[74] Before Linnaeus, plants had different names in different places and classification systems were fairly vague: based on colour, perhaps, or habitat. Before Propp, folklorists classified fairy tales according to the repetition of 'motifs' – 'a dragon kidnaps the tsar's daughter', for example – or according to whether they were 'animal stories', 'fantastical stories' or 'tales of everyday life'. But this did not lead to any useful system, and was certainly no way of comparing the structural elements of different stories. Propp argued instead that fairy tales have a 'quite particular structure'[75] and set about breaking this down and analysing it. He suggested that there are 'indivisible units' of fairy tales (and by implication other types of plot), which he called 'functions'. Functions are *actions* performed by *characters* under *certain circumstances*. Fairy tales are simply made from different combinations of these functions.

How did Propp come to this conclusion? Well, he started by ruling things out and rejecting things that were wrong or unhelpful. For example, the motif 'a dragon kidnaps the tsar's daughter' is not an indivisible unit and would not work as a function. Propp says:

> This motif decomposes into four elements, each of which, in its own right, can vary. The dragon may be replaced by Koščéj, a whirlwind, a devil, a falcon or a sorcerer. Abduction can be replaced by vampirism or various other acts by which disappearance is effected in tales. The daughter may be replaced by a sister, a bride, a wife or a mother. The tsar can be replaced by a tsar's son, a peasant or a priest.[76]

In other words, 'a dragon kidnaps the tsar's daughter' may well have the same structural effect in a narrative as 'a whirlwind takes away a peasant's sister'.[77] If we were classifying fairy tales and looked for all stories in which a dragon kidnaps a tsar's daughter, we'd be looking for the wrong thing. If we decide that dragon stories are of one type, and stories with whirlwinds are of a quite different type, we will miss many important structural similarities shared by stories 'about' dragons and stories 'about' whirlwinds. What is more interesting in this case, Propp argues, is to look for stories that include some sort of agent that brings about some sort of disappearance. In plot terms, the disappearance is far more important than its cause. His functions (and we'll come to a list of them soon) are all actions based on variables. For example, function XXV states that 'a difficult task is proposed to the hero'. The difficult task can be *anything* (although those of us familiar with fairy tales know that it is fairly likely to be something like 'kiss the princess in a window'[78] or 'deliver the hair to the king of the sea'[79]).

It's likely that we're already familiar with these kinds of variables in fiction, even if we have never before stopped to think about it. Alfred Hitchcock used the term 'McGuffin' in a 1939 lecture to describe the thing that every character in a certain kind of narrative is trying to get hold of. It is 'the mechanical element that usually crops up in any story. In crook stories it is always the necklace and in spy stories it is always the papers'.[80] The point with a McGuffin is that it does not really matter what it is, just as long as the characters are all in competition for it. In a romantic comedy, it often does not matter exactly what the obstacles are to the happy union of the two lead characters, as long as there are obstacles.[81] As we will see later, if your fiction is to have any depth then you will choose your specific details with great care. But for now it is useful to realise that there are always different possibilities for these details, once you realise how they work as part of the structural foundation of a narrative.

The ITV drama series *At Home with the Braithwaites* tells the story of Alison Braithwaite, her husband David and their three daughters, Virginia, Sarah and Charlotte. Alison has won £38 million on the Euro-Lottery. She decides to use the money to set up a charity and to keep the whole thing a secret from her family, particularly her overbearing and materialistic husband David. This provides the central dramatic question and storyline of the narrative: when, and how, will her family find out that she is a millionaire? However, other members of the family have secrets too. Virginia is a lesbian, secretly in love with the glamorous woman next door. Sarah, humiliated after her drama teacher passes a love letter she has written to him to the headmaster, gets involved with Phil, a working-class lad from next door (on the other side). David's secret is that he is having an affair with his secretary, Elaine. By the end of the narrative, all the secrets will have been revealed and the family will have had a good old shake-up. Phil's mother will find out David's secret and, enraged by Alison arranging an abortion (of her son's baby) for her daughter, will therefore tell her everything. Alison, now feeling that David can no longer dictate any terms to her about anything, will finally have the motivation to tell him her secret. A good exercise is to go through this paragraph and underline all the variable elements. How are they operating in this narrative and how could they be changed while leaving the basic structure intact?[82]

Some elements in a fairy tale (or any other kind of narrative) will therefore be variable; a dragon may as well be a whirlwind if it has the same effect, and a secret can usually be anything at all, as long as it is discovered at the right time. We clearly need to look at generals rather than specifics to find the essential action that forms the function.

It's also true that very different actions can often bring about very similar effects, and Propp warns us that outcomes that appear similar are not necessarily part of the same function. His example explains this very well:

> For example, if Iván marries a tsar's daughter, this is something entirely different than the marriage of a father to a widow with two daughters. A second example: if, in one instance, a hero receives money from his father in the form of 100 roubles and subsequently buys a wise cat with the money, whereas in a second case, the hero is rewarded with a sum of money for an accomplished act of bravery (at

which point the tale ends) we have before us two morpho-
logically different elements – in spite of the identical action
(the transference of money) in both cases.[83]

So we can see that 'marriage' on its own is not a function,
and neither is 'the giving of money to the hero'. Each has
to be understood *in context* for its function to be revealed.
For example, the money that buys the wise cat is part of
the function 'the hero acquires the use of a magical agent',
whereas the other sum of money is either the 'liquidation
of lack' or may even take the role of the 'throne' in the
function 'The hero is married and ascends the throne'. In
order to understand all this, the best thing is to look at the
list of Propp's functions. Remember that these relate to
nineteenth-century Russian fairy tales.

After 'an initial situation', the action proceeds as follows:

I	One of the members of a family absents himself from home.
II	An interdiction is addressed to the hero.
III	The interdiction is violated.
IV	The villain makes an attempt at reconnaissance.
V	The villain receives information about his victim.
VI	The villain attempts to deceive his victim in order to take possession of him or his belongings.
VII	The victim submits to deception and thereby unwittingly helps his enemy.
VIII	The villain causes harm or injury to a member of a family.
	a One member of a family either lacks something

or desires to have something.

IX   Misfortune or lack is made known; the hero is approached with a request or command; he is allowed to go or he is dispatched (the 'connective incident').

X   The seeker agrees to or decides upon counteraction.

XI   The hero leaves home.

XII   The hero is tested, interrogated, attacked etc. which prepares the way for his receiving either a magical agent or helper.

XIII   The hero reacts to the actions of the future donor.

XIV   The hero acquires the use of a magical agent.

XV   The hero is transferred, delivered or led to the whereabouts of an object of search.

XVI   The hero and the villain join in direct combat.

XVII   The hero is branded.

XVIII   The villain is defeated.

XIX   The initial misfortune or lack is liquidated.

XX   The hero returns.

XXI   The hero is pursued.

XXII   Rescue of the hero from pursuit.

XXIII   The hero, unrecognised, arrives home or in another country.

XXIV   A false hero presents unfounded claims.

XXV   A difficult task is proposed to the hero.

XXVI   The task is resolved.

XXVII   The hero is recognised.

XXVIII   The false hero or villain is exposed.

XXIX   The hero is given a new appearance.

XXX   The villain is punished.

XXXI   The hero is married and ascends the throne.[84]

The sequence of events leading up to function VIII are really preparatory incidents. They may not even be there in a story at all – they may function as un-narrated 'back-story' or be entirely absent. Function VIII is usually where the main action begins. The hero at this point has a reason to leave on an adventure: a lack that may have been caused by a villain (the kidnap of a bride), or that may just have been realised (the need for a bride). Each function has many variants. For example, in XII, where the hero is tested, there are ten distinct possibilities for this test, including 'A dying or deceased person requests the rendering of a service' and 'The hero is approached with a request for mercy'.[85]

Note that each function is connected with a specific character. There are seven key characters, according to Propp, each of whom has his or her own 'sphere of action': the villain, the donor (who gives something important to the hero), the helper, the princess and her father (counted together as one character in terms of sphere of action, and representing 'a sought-for person'[86]), the dispatcher (who sends the hero away for some reason), the hero and the false hero. Propp is clear that in one story you may not have all these characters (and it is very unlikely that you will have all 31 functions). Characters are not fixed: if a villain inadvertently gives something important to the hero, then he or she is also at that moment acting as a donor. Therefore one character may perform different roles at different times in the narrative. But the functions will never be in a sequence other than the one presented here, and each function will be connected with the designated character. So it is always the hero who ascends the throne at the end of the story, never the villain. It is always the villain who is exposed, not the princess.

Propp is talking about the chronological story here, rather than plot (although fairy tales usually follow a chronological sequence anyway). Clearly an interdiction cannot be violated until it has been expressed, and there's no point in a hero setting off on a quest unless he or she has realised that something is lacking (treasure, a fortune, a bride etc.). So in some ways, perhaps, Propp is stating the obvious. But so often the obvious is exactly what we need pointed out to us when we begin working with plot. Propp reminds us that significant moments in stories are often familiar because they are repeated time and time again. He also makes us aware of how much variation is possible around a specific function. If we think back to the example of variations of The Cave in the first chapter, we may remember that the cave can be any place of entrapment and ignorance, and escape from it can take any form.

Vladimir Propp's study examines one form of narrative, and there clearly are other forms. He's not saying that everything is a fairy tale. But it's interesting to note that his structure is not restricted only to the fairy tale. For example, Homer's *Odyssey* fits Propp's scheme very well indeed. And we can see Propp's functions cropping up elsewhere. In *Pride and Prejudice*, Elizabeth Bennett lacks a husband. She is tested (indirectly) by Darcy, and passes all of his tests. There are complications created by Wickham, who is later exposed as a villain/false hero. In

Middlemarch we also see the function 'the false hero or villain is exposed' in the resolution of Bulstrode's narrative. *Great Expectations* could be read in a very interesting way through Propp's scheme. Indeed, many of its elements are there. Pip violates an interdiction and unwittingly helps a 'villain' (Magwitch). Miss Havisham and Estella make Pip aware of his lack of refinement and he decides he must become a gentleman. There are various tests along the way, and Pip has a helper, Herbert Pocket, who shows him the 'rules' of this strange new world in which he finds himself. There is a final fight with a villain (Orlick).

Reading *Great Expectations* through Propp's scheme can open up some interesting questions. The end of the novel subverts almost everything that a conventional fairy tale is supposed to deliver. There is no marriage or ascension to a throne. Instead, Joe has the wedding that perhaps Pip should have had, and Estella remains enigmatic, even to the extent of appearing in several possible endings. Is Magwitch in the end a villain, a false hero or a helper? He occupies the role of villain at the beginning, but Orlick takes the role later on. Or perhaps Miss Havisham is the real villain of the piece. Is Pip's journey valid, given that it is undertaken for the sake of Estella, who is a strange combination of villain, false hero and princess? These are interesting questions. And perhaps we can consider the reversal with Estella in more depth when we see that she occupies the structural position of 'princess' but is revealed to be no such thing.

In contemporary fiction we will never try to construct a conventional 'princess', but we might decide to put a different sort of character in that position and see what happens. We may indeed want to *explore* the concept of 'princess' rather than merely represent it. What we often want is a kind of artistic disharmony: a dissonance, as in jazz. Propp explains the concept of disharmony in the fairy tale:

> Villainy and its liquidation (A–K) are separated from each other by a long story. In the course of the tales the narrator loses the thread of the story, and one may observe that element K sometimes does not correspond to the initial A or a. The tale is as though out of tune. Iván sets out after a steed but returns with a princess [. . .] We have a phenomenon similar to disharmony when the first half does not evoke the usual response, or else replaces it with a response that is completely different and unusual for the tale norm. In tale No. 260 the enchantment of a boy is not followed by any breaking of the spell, and he remains a little goat for life.[87]

It's quite clear that writing Estella as simultaneously princess and not-princess creates a dissonance that enables us to think deeply about the construction of social character. Leaving a boy as a little goat in a fairy tale, however, is just a mistake.[88]

Morphology of the Folktale demonstrates how it is possible to take what we might call a 'basic plot' and define its characteristics in an enormous amount of detail. We now know exactly what a Russian fairy tale is, and how it works. We know it has 31 possible components (functions) that can be put together in any combination, although not in any order. We also can see that the basic fairy tale includes some functions that are shared by many other narratives in some form or other. We also now know how other basic plots are likely to be described: each will have static elements and variable elements. If we decide, for example, that the quest is a basic plot then we can say that a static element is that it will always involve a journey. A variable would be the destination.

THE MONOMYTH

In 1949 Joseph Campbell introduced his theory of the 'monomyth' in his book *The Hero with a Thousand Faces*. The monomyth is the fundamental, archetypal adventure story that Campbell believes we all hold in our heads.[89] Campbell argues that we are all heroes taking part in our own adventures, which are all structured the same way.

> The standard path of the mythological adventure of the hero is a magnification of the formula represented in the rites of passage: *separation-initiation-return:* which might be named the nuclear unit of the monomyth.
>   *A Hero ventures forth from the world of common day into a reign of supernatural wonder: fabulous forces are there*

encountered and a decisive victory is won: the hero comes back
from this mysterious adventure with the power to bestow boons
on his fellow man.[90]

For Campbell there is only one story, one great myth, that
we tell (and live) time and time again. He asserts that every
myth, story or even personal experience is structured like
a journey, or quest. Every story begins with a 'call to
adventure' that the hero will initially refuse. The hero,
having received some supernatural aid and acquired a
mentor, will answer the call eventually, however, and will
then proceed to the 'first threshold', on the other side of
which lies an 'otherworld' of danger and adventure. The
hero proceeds down a 'road of trials' towards an 'innermost
cave' (which can be a real cave, but could equally be a
spaceship containing a 'monster', or even the headmaster's
office). The hero will return to his or her normal world
with new knowledge to share with his or her society as
well as some sort of treasure and love-interest. George
Lucas apparently used Campbell's book to plot the original
Star Wars film.

Although he takes a very different approach to laying
out his material (he fuses, rather than attempts to separate,
different stories, so that the book is made up of lots of
beginnings, middles and endings all swirling into one
another), Campbell ends up describing a structure very
similar to the one that Propp has already explored. The
focus is on a long and difficult journey, full of tests, personal
growth and self-knowledge that includes light and dark

forces, great danger and usually ends with specific rewards: sex (marriage) and money (treasure, a kingdom, an 'ultimate boon').[91] Campbell does not accept that tragedy and comedy are distinct plot structures but sees them as part of a cycle within the monomyth.[92] The idea of one single, underlying structure common to all myths was also explored by the French anthropologist Claude Lévi-Strauss in 1958, in his book *Structural Anthropology*. Like Propp, Lévi-Strauss was particularly keen on turning things into equations: myths, in his case, rather than fairy tales.[93]

FIVE BASIC PLOTS

In 1957, in his book *Anatomy of Criticism*, the critic Northrop Frye proposed a system of five basic plots (which he calls *mythoi*, plural of *mythos*).[94] Frye connects each of his five mythoi with a season, as follows:

Spring	Comedy
Summer	Romance
Autumn	Tragedy
Winter	Irony and satire

In comedy, argues Frye, a young couple are in love, but cannot get together because of some authority figure – an interfering father, for example, or the old-fashioned or restrictive conventions of society. In the end, the young lovers get together and the ways of the authority figure are finally exposed as ridiculous. As we already know, this type of story usually ends with the wedding of the young lovers, and, Frye adds, often a party which celebrates the coming-together of the whole society, in which everyone seems to be matched with the right partner. Shakespearian comedies work in this way, as do lots of American high-school films (several of which have, in recent years, been based on Shakespearian comedies, including *10 Things I Hate About You*, *She's the Man* and *Get Over It*). We'll look more closely at contemporary romantic comedy in the next chapter.

Romance, the mythos of summer, is what we'd recognise as the quest or adventure story that we have just explored. In a romance, the hero will travel to a site of conflict where a dragon (this may be read metaphorically) threatens a kingdom or society, and specifically a king and his daughter who may well be the next sacrifice for the dragon. Frye points out that these adventure stories often include quite simplistic characterisation, where the characters are either good (for the hero) or bad (against the hero). It is in these stories that we meet magical animals, giants, wood nymphs and other fairy-tale characters. These are adventures that take place in a natural setting. There will be an emphasis on the number three (three wishes, three attempts at solving a puzzle, three brothers etc.). At the end of this story the hero will be 'killed' and reborn, and will overcome the dragon and be rewarded with a bride (the daughter of the king) and treasure. Frye, in some ways like Campbell, describes this structure as a 'central unifying myth' inside which all the others occur. Examples of this type of plot would include J.R.R. Tolkien's *The Lord of the Rings*, Homer's *Odyssey* and *Monkey* by Wu Ch'êng-ên.

Tragedy is the mythos of autumn, the season of death. We already know what Aristotle says about tragedy, and Frye agrees with all of it. These are stories of the downfall of an admirable person, involving reversal and recognition and, usually, some kind of hubris, which Frye defines as: 'A proud, passionate, obsessed or soaring mind which brings about a morally intelligible downfall'.[95] Frye reminds us that tragedy focuses on the individual, not the group. Furthermore, this hero is isolated in some way. There are no magical creatures or helpful figures. Frye points out that tragedy is the only kind of story that is not based around wish-fulfilment, and in this sense it is more 'realistic' than the others. Proper tragedy cannot be thought of as simply a moral or cautionary tale, of course. It is arguably the most complex mode of storytelling, leading us to ask the most profound questions about the human condition. Frye notes Hegel's concept of the '*Augenblick*' (the blink of an eye): the crucial moment where both possible 'roads' available to the hero or heroine (one to destruction and one to salvation) are seen by the audience. The tragic hero always, of course, chooses the former – not usually, however, because he or she is simply a 'bad' or 'stupid' person but for very complicated reasons, as we have seen.

Satire and irony are the mythoi of winter, the season where natural processes close down and drama is reduced. These tend to be plots in which the hero does not have any kind of transforming experience, good or bad, and usually does not try to change the world. Frye argues that each of his mythoi bleed into one another, just as seasons do. So a particularly difficult comedy with lots of obstacles may be very close to a romance; and a romance in which the goal is too ambitious, and from which the protagonist may not return, starts to become tragic. Here he connects light satire with comedy and dark irony with tragedy. Irony emphasises the human over the heroic, according to Frye. This is a kind of 'tragedy from below', featuring explicit, sincere realism, fatalism and metaphysical doom. The novels and stories of George Orwell and Franz Kafka would be a part of this mythos.

Satire, Frye argues, like comedy, is about challenging convention in society. However, while comedy is usually optimistic, and shows a society resolving its problems, satire focuses on the challenge to society, and rarely includes a happy resolution. The 'Going for an English' sketch from *Goodness Gracious Me* highlights how ridiculous British people can be when they 'go for an Indian' by dramatising a group of professional young Indians 'going for an English' and asking how bland the food is likely to be and ordering 24 portions of chips. Nothing is resolved at the end of the sketch; no one lives happily ever after. But we see something about society that we didn't see before. 'Going for an Indian' can no longer be seen as culturally neutral. Indeed, we are invited to consider how patronising and, indeed, embarrassing, it can be when viewed from another perspective. Satire often uses defamiliarising reversals and exaggerations (no one really 'goes for an English'; ordering 24 portions of chips is comically excessive) in order to challenge society's conventions, assumptions and habits.

Satire can also use an 'ingénue' figure as narrator: someone who is unaware that the way they describe their society may make it seem problematic. Ricky Gervais's character in *The Office*, David Brent, is such a figure. He has no idea that the world is not the way he says it is. He believes himself to be an 'entertainer', as well as a good, popular boss. In fact, he is predictable, embarrassing, tedious and disliked by his staff. Here he is discussing John Betjeman's poem 'Slough' (which is where *The Office* is set):

This is the poem 'Slough', by Sir John Betjeman. Probably never been here in his life. 'Come friendly bombs and fall on Slough, it isn't fit for humans now.' Right, I don't think you solve town-planning problems by dropping bombs all over the place; he's embarrassed himself there. Next: 'In labour saving homes with care, their wives frizz out peroxide hair, and dry it in synthetic air, and paint their nails . . .' They wanna look nice – what's the matter, doesn't he like girls? 'And talks of sports and makes of cars, and various bogus Tudor bars, and daren't look up and see the stars, but belch instead.' What's he on about? What, has he never burped? 'Come friendly bombs and fall on Slough, to get it ready for the plough. The cabbages are coming now, the earth exhales . . .' He's the only cabbage round here. And they made him a knight of the realm. Overrated.

David Brent is clearly wrong about the poem on many levels, and of course it has far more depth than he realises.

But there is great humour in his strange analysis, and the way in which he positions himself as more of an 'expert' on Slough than Betjeman. Humour, like irony, relies on reversals. Here, David Brent thinks he's being funnier than the poem, but the poem is both funnier and more profound than he will ever be. And when he is funny, it's unintentional. There is further humour in the juxtaposition of Betjeman's language and David Brent's. Although 'Slough' is written in a fairly conversational register, it seems almost formal in comparison with David Brent's colloquialisms ('He's the only cabbage round here'; '. . . he's embarrassed himself there'). We don't expect this kind of language in a serious discussion of poetry. More humour, and in fact sadness, comes from David Brent's unawareness that the poem may be addressed to *him*, and may therefore be asking *him* to dare to 'look up and see the stars'.

Whose 'side' are we on here? David Brent's or Betjeman's? As the final object of satire is always ourselves (because it is ultimately *our* societies, habits and conventions that we are criticising), it must be both. Clearly, in the world of *The Office* Betjeman is more 'right' about Slough than David Brent is: the programme sets out to show us as much. But who hasn't at some point felt the need to defend their home town, or made fun of a poem, painting or piece of music that threatens them? Satire, at its best, should be, I think, both compassionate and affectionate, even though its aim is to hold failure up to ridicule. We are all failures, and we are all ridiculous at some moments in our lives. Frye argues that in particular satire has to be funny; it cannot just be an unmediated attack.

Irony and satire certainly exist, and there is something pleasingly earthy about Frye's use of the seasons to show how each mythos blends into the next. But I'd prefer to classify irony and satire as *styles*, or even modifying structural factors, rather than deep structures in their own right. After all, neither can provide a complete shape for a story. How does 'classic' satire begin and end? How does irony begin and end? Do satires and irony have weddings, deaths, journeys? In what order? There are no fixed, recognisable moments in either. But we know that both will challenge our views of something, often including the very structure of the narrative in which we find them. We'll be exploring this further in the next chapter.

SEVEN BASIC PLOTS

So far, almost everyone is in agreement that there are at least three basic plots: tragedy, comedy and the quest/romance/epic. This is also true of Christopher Booker, whose book *The Seven Basic Plots* was published in 2004. Booker's argument is quite different from the others we have met so far, although he shares with Joseph Campbell the idea that the point of narrative is our own psychological growth. For Booker, there are good plots and bad plots. The good ones follow a universal pattern focused on the growth of the self and the overcoming of the ego. The bad ones (there are lots of these, including Mary Shelley's *Frankenstein*, Herman Melville's *Moby Dick* and the works of Franz Kafka) do not show a hero (or society, in tragedy) moving from darkness into light, but may show the reverse, or an incomplete process. Each of Booker's seven plots is presented as archetypal, as are the characters and other elements within them. So we have 'dark' and 'light' forces; we have Mother and Father figures, the Wise Old Man, the Child, the Innocent Young Girl and so on; we (again) have the 'rule of three'; we have the hero united with his anima (or a heroine with her animus) at the end of the narrative.

Booker's seven plots are as follows:

- Overcoming the Monster
- Rags to Riches
- The Quest
- Voyage and Return
- Comedy
- Tragedy
- Rebirth

I have often hesitated to recommend *The Seven Basic Plots* to students. Why? After all, this is the one book that they actually go and borrow from the library, often on the strength of the title and a brief summary. I bought the book on the day it was published, on the strength of not much more. As a readable and easy introduction to the idea of basic plots, it is great. Friends who read Part One of this book can have an enjoyable weekend arguing over whether the film they just watched is an 'Overcoming the Monster' or a 'Voyage and Return' plot. I worked out that my novel *PopCo* could be classified in this system as a Rebirth plot, and it gave me a little thrill of recognition when I did. People who are plotting novels for the first time do find it useful to declare that they are writing 'a Quest' or 'a Tragedy', and Booker's breakdown of these plots is certainly more accessible than Northrop Frye's, partly because he uses so many examples from popular culture.

But there are a number of problems with *The Seven Basic Plots* that may be overlooked by someone encountering these kinds of ideas for the first time. The first major problem is that Booker is not really describing seven *different* basic plots. When it comes down to it, this is another monomyth theory. Each plot (apart from comedy) has five distinct stages, beginning with a call to adventure (except for the Voyage and Return plot, which begins with a 'fall' into adventure), followed by a 'dream stage', a 'frustration stage', a 'nightmare stage' and then a resolution (either a 'thrilling escape' followed by happily-ever-after, or death). Comedy has only three stages: initial confusion, greater confusion and a happy resolution. Of course, Booker provides enough differences so that it is possible to argue about whether a particular narrative follows one plot structure or another and, as I have already said, this can be great fun. But essentially this is a highly conservative argument that requires fiction to be of only one sort and to 'improve' us somehow. Booker himself acknowledges that each of his plots

> . . . begins by showing us a hero or heroine in some way incomplete, who then encounters the dark power. Through most of the story the dark power remains dominant, casting

a shadow in which all remains unresolved [. . .] [T]he ending shows how the dark power can be overthrown, with the light ending triumphant. The only question is whether the central figure is identified with the light, in which case he or she ends up liberated and whole; or whether they have fallen irrevocably into the grip of darkness, in which case they are destroyed.[96]

In other words, the 'archetypal pattern around which our human urge to tell stories is ultimately centred',[97] is all about darkness being overcome by light. While all ideas about basic plots are reductive, this one seems unnecessarily so. The book is 700 pages long, but the ideas in it reduce further and further like a sauce on the boil until, in the end, they don't amount to much more than the idea that stories should always show goodies triumphing over baddies. The Jungian theory Booker uses is much richer than it appears in this book, and he really does not do credit to Jung's many interesting ideas.[98]

It is quite bizarre that Booker rejects so many well-known narratives because they don't fit his scheme.[99] Surely a theory of basic plots should give us a scheme into which we can fit (with some interesting wriggling) any coherent, popular or classic narrative, and which we can also use to help us work out where our own narratives are not working, or perhaps even sticking too rigidly to formula? Booker's argument is problematic in many other ways. If this is all there is to narrative (and if telling well-structured stories is such a fundamental part of being human), then why is it so hard to write a successful novel? Why are we not all born with the ability to write Harry Potter books or Agatha Christie's mysteries? And why are there so many classic narratives that refuse to moralise about 'light' and 'dark' but are still loved by readers?[100] And if one story is all we ever really needed, why do we keep making up new ones?

THE EIGHT BASIC PLOTS

'. . . all that ruddy fiction! Hero goes on a journey, stranger comes to town, somebody wants something, they get it or they don't, will is pitted against will . . .'

David Mitchell, *Cloud Atlas*[101]

Merry and tragical! tedious and brief! That is, hot ice and wonderous strange snow.

Shakespeare, *A Midsummer Night's Dream*[102]

In 2010 my third-years and I read *The Restraint of Beasts* by Magnus Mills. The story is quite a simple one. Tam, Richie and their unnamed foreman are high-tensile fencers. They are to travel from Scotland to England to work on a difficult fencing project. While there, they are approached by the sinister Hall brothers, who build seven-foot-high fences and make a lot of sausages. They end up working for the Hall brothers, and the novel ends uncertainly, with a sinister sense that our heroes (such as they are) are the beasts who will be restrained, either literally or thematically, by the fences they build. We sense that they may even get turned into sausages, although this is left very ambiguous.

The novel is written in a minimalist, matter-of-fact style and includes much repetition. There are a few accidental deaths, which are treated with deadpan humour. Otherwise, Tam, Richie and their foreman work, smoke, go down the pub and spend all their money and so then must work again. They have no ambition and few romantic prospects. Here's a short extract:

> And so another day passed and the long fence slowly grew around the foot of that hill. The next light at the end of the tunnel was Wednesday night at Carmens [sic]. I didn't mention it at all to Tam and Richie but I could tell during Wednesday afternoon that expectations were beginning to rise again. Now the post hammer was back in action, guarded closely by Tam, we were able to work in a tight three-man squad, section by section, along the fence. About four o'clock, as an incentive, I told Tam and Richie that we would finish the bit we were on and pack up for the night. I never saw them work so fast.[103]

In our seminar, my students and I focused on themes around work in late-capitalist society and the concept of fencing: restriction, entrapment and the lack of possibilities for escape or transcendence. I'd been encouraging the students to draw plot diagrams for their novels, and we soon began wondering 'what kind of plot' is at the centre of *The Restraint of Beasts*. At first glance, there would seem to be none; no light forces fight dark forces, so it's likely that the narrative would not be at all acceptable for Christopher Booker; Northrop Frye would presumably have it lurking somewhere in the winter of his scheme. No one gains anything. No one is reconciled with anything. There is no love story. But this is nonetheless a very gripping novel that does feel satisfying. It does have some sort of 'shape', and (albeit understated) moments of drama. It almost won the Booker Prize.

So the students and I went through the plots we were working with at the time (tragedy, comedy and the quest), to see if any of them seemed to fit. We realised that the novel could be read as either a tragedy or a quest, and, importantly, that these kinds of readings added great depth to our experience of the novel. *The Restraint of Beasts* is in many ways a tragedy, but a tragedy of low people. We know that one of the 'rules' of tragedy is that it dramatises the downfall of admirable people. Tam, Richie and their foreman are not admirable in any classic sense. They are not famous, rich, assured, successful or happy. They have nowhere significant from which to fall. They are, however, pretty good at putting up fences. And they are funny, in a deadpan way. We care what happens to them, even if we are never going to feel about them the way Nietzsche feels about tragic characters from great operas. They may have very little ambition, but they still aspire to work with the Hall brothers in order to make a bit more money. This is their – or at least their foreman's – big mistake: their *hamartia*.

Like tragic heroes, these characters get mixed up in a scheme that is too ambitious and dangerous for them, and they will die (even if this ends up being a metaphorical death) because of it. If we do consider Tam, Richie and their foreman as tragic heroes, what we end up with is a profound comment on a late-capitalist society in which, if you are working-class, the smallest amount of ambition can lead to your downfall, and possibly kill you. And at no point do you even get to enjoy being a hero. We see here that characters can be killed by a small, almost imperceptible level of ambition within exactly the same structure in which it is usually an abundance of ambition that is dangerous. This is a reversal (a change to the opposite) on the level of plot. It is what I would like to call an *ironic* plot.[104]

Irony relies on reversal, on things being turned upside down. Irony is where the stated meaning is the reverse of the implied meaning. When I am planning to go for a run and someone tells me it's going to rain and I say 'Oh, *great*', I am being ironic because I mean the opposite of what I'm saying. When this happens on the level of plot, the result is that some standard part of the plot is replaced with its opposite. A tragedy is of low people, for example, or a quest is for something trivial. If this is done well, instead of a plot that has 'gone wrong' or doesn't work, what we get are all the pleasures of reversal, but on the level of structure. We know what is 'supposed' to happen; then we see what actually does. A pattern forms in our minds that includes the plot-that-isn't as well as the plot-that-is. The pattern forms in our minds (if it does) because this process involves a clear reversal, rather than just a random divergence from the standard plot. So in *The Restraint of Beasts* we have a tragedy with low people rather than high people. And in the disruption caused by the reversal there is great thematic depth. Most good contemporary plots have some level of irony. Many will also be metafictional (and we'll be looking at some examples at the end of this chapter).

In order to read – or write – plots in a playful way we need to know something about narrative shapes in general. If a narrative is working against convention, it helps if we know what the convention is. So often it is crucial to look at what is *not* dramatised, and what does *not* happen when we expect something will. In order to do this we have to know what a more typical structure would include. This is why I still think that some theory of basic plots is helpful, even though we may never agree on how many of them there are, or what each one should contain. Knowing about basic plots enables us to read more deeply; in particular, we are better equipped for encounters with irony, satire and metafiction. It also enables us to control our own plots when we write, and to see what the possibilities are for experimentation.

Here are what I believe to be the eight basic plots:

- Tragedy
- Comedy
- The quest
- Rags to riches
- Coming of age
- Stranger comes to town
- Mystery
- Modern realism

The first three of these we by now know very well. I'd agree with everything that Aristotle says about tragedy and comedy, everything Nietzsche says about tragedy and most of what Northrop Frye says about tragedy, comedy and romance, except that I think in this case 'quest' is a clearer term than 'romance'. In fact, the quest narrative is still, I think, best described by Vladimir Propp. Rags-to-riches and coming-of-age narratives can actually both also be covered by Propp's functions, but I think they are different enough from the usual quest narrative to need categories of their own. So that's where we will begin.

RAGS TO RICHES

In a rags-to-riches plot we meet a young, innocent individual who is oppressed in some way, often in a domestic setting. This character then receives a special invitation. Cinderella is invited to the ball. Neo in *The Matrix* is invited to follow the white rabbit.[105] Pip in *Great Expectations* is invited to go to Miss Havisham's house. Harry Potter is invited to go to Hogwarts School.[106] There is often some kind of miracle or 'fairy godmother' element in a rags to riches story, where the hero[107] is chosen for transformation and help by seemingly supernatural forces, or 'luck', or by believing, rightly or wrongly, that he or she is a wizard, princess, gentleman or some other type of special person. Although this initial call to adventure is similar to that in the quest, what follows is different. Heroes in rags-to-riches plots do not tend to refuse the invitation they receive, in the way a hero on a quest will usually refuse his or her call to adventure. This will be the invitation they have been waiting for all their lives.

The drama that follows may well be focused on the hero coming to terms with his or her new riches or powers. The story will usually also remain more or less domestic, as in *Cinderella* or *Great Expectations*. Pip does face tests and trials, but these are mainly cultural, rather than natural or supernatural. He only goes into battle once, with Orlick, and this is in self-defence. The focus in this kind of plot is on the transformation of the individual from someone who has nothing to someone who has something. There is often a significant reversal involved, whereby characters who have had riches at the beginning of the narrative – and who have been unwilling to share these with the protagonist – will lose them. As the protagonist experiences good fortune, the antagonist(s) will experience bad fortune. Sometimes the protagonist will help the antagonist(s) out of their bad fortune. There will often be a connected love story, but this will often be abandoned, forsaken or resolved unexpectedly. The emphasis in this plot is on an individual's relationship with new wealth, of whatever sort. This relationship is primary, and any other relationships will be secondary.

The film *Lourdes* tells of Christine, a young sufferer of multiple sclerosis, who is almost completely paralysed. She travels to Lourdes as part of a coach trip, among a group of other variously disabled people. She seems to enjoy these coach trips, not much caring about the destination. In fact, as she confides to the attractive helper Kuno, she prefers the cultural trips to the religious ones. She is depressed about being paralysed, often asking 'Why me?'. She is not brave or particularly saintly. When the priest asks her 'Do you believe that someone who can use their legs is automatically happier?', it is clear that Christine does believe this. She has no faith in anything beyond the happiness of the 'normal'. Given that Christine does not believe in miracles, it is ironic that after being bathed in healing waters she is able to start moving her arms and her legs. A miracle has happened, but to a non-believer. What follows is darkly funny and intensely thought-provoking. Now that Christine can move independently and take part in 'normal' life, she is bound to be happier, surely? Normal life, as we all know, however, is often disappointing. But after being graced with a miracle, is it right to be dissatisfied with 'normal'? And, what's more, should Christine have been chosen for this miracle at all? Why not someone with faith instead?

It's clear in the film that the other 'pilgrims' have found a way to believe in miracles without ever actually seeing or experiencing any. So when one does take place – and indeed happens to the wrong person – many other features of 'normal' life emerge: conflict, jealousy, envy and suspicion. Here, director Jessica Hausner has used a subtly ironic rags-to-riches plot to explore profound themes about faith, and the extent to which the recipients of miracles are expected to be happy with less than everyone else: with the 'normal' mundane life that many of us are trying to transcend in some way. Is simply 'being able to walk' all that we should require from life? And are we asking for too much if we desire more? If normality is offered to us as a miracle, should we be content with it?

Rags-to-riches plots can also often be seen in non-fictional contexts. Popular culture always seems to favour true-life stories that are structurally similar to basic plots.

So we will read more in newspapers about the bus driver who was shortlisted for the Booker Prize (Magnus Mills) than the more usual bourgeois author on the same short-list;[108] we will hear more about the overworked nurse who wins the Lottery than we will about the company director who does. Makeover shows will often focus heavily on how 'impoverished' (in terms of their house, their garden, their wardrobe or whatever) their subjects are before the make-over. Sports commentators often talk about the possibility of a 'Cinderella story' if a team is losing very badly but there is still hope that they might win. A football team winning 4–3 after being 3–0 down makes a 'better story' than one that simply wins 4–0. In rags-to-riches plots, it seems that the bigger the gulf between the 'rags' and the 'riches', the greater the drama.

In an episode of *DIY SOS* we see three beautiful but very poor teenage girls who are crying because they have to live with their grandparents. Their family home is in a terrible mess. Dad was about to do some serious DIY – and had in fact ripped out the whole kitchen – when he was taken ill. We see Mum and Dad crying, and the grandparents, too. We see the girls performing in a dance production at school. These are clearly good people, who have been very unlucky. The *DIY SOS* team have promised that they will do up the kitchen. Instead, with such limited time that it seems like a miracle, they redecorate the entire house and replant the garden. The three girls finally have lovely bedrooms, and a little stage area downstairs where they can perform.

It seems to be a feature of rags-to-riches plots that deserving people get far more than they ever could have hoped for, although of course these riches can also be misused, as in *Great Expectations*, or oddly disappointing, as in *Lourdes*. Rags to riches also provides the structure for the surprise party, where someone's friends initially pretend to have forgotten them or not be interested in them in order to make the resulting party all the more pleasurable. One Christmas I was tempted inside an old shop by the large crowd of people already there. Inside was a man with a microphone 'selling' expensive items for £5 to the first people who put their hands up. In my rational mind, I must have known this was some sort of con. But the rags-to-riches plot took over and as far as I, and everyone else, was concerned, this was a fairy-godmother figure, and we were very lucky to be in the right place at the right time. When the man asked everyone to give him £10 for a 'mystery gift', I'm sure we all expected to receive vast riches for a relatively small outlay. Most people handed it over. What everyone got was a very cheap-looking 'collectible' coin that was clearly worth nothing.[109] While this structure can clearly produce highly sentimental or even deceitful narratives, it can also lead to profound explorations of what wealth – of whatever sort – means for people who receive it.

Not all narratives that include a protagonist receiving a sum of money are rags-to-riches plots. We should remember Vladimir Propp's distinction between the sum of money that buys the wise cat, and the sum of money given as a reward. In the film *It Could Happen to You*, Charlie, a cop, does not have enough money to tip a waitress, Yvonne, and so promises to return the next day with either double the tip or, if he wins the lottery, a share of his prize money.

When he unexpectedly does win the Lottery, his wife wants all the money. However, Charlie honours his promise and he and Yvonne immediately begin doing good deeds – and falling in love. Crucially, the money is not important to them. They only care about making other people happy, and about each other. By the end of the film, the balance sheets are clear. Everyone's (very complicated) debts have been paid off, somehow,[110] but Charlie's wife has taken the Lottery winnings and then lost them. Charlie and Yvonne are therefore as poor as they were when they began but have gained love, which in the world-view of the film is more important than money. This is in fact a romantic comedy, and finishes with a society coming together to honour the young couple, and leaves everything in its right place.[111]

COMING OF AGE

A coming-of-age plot differs from rags to riches in some important ways. In a rags-to-riches plot, as is also so common in the quest, the hero is chosen because they are special. They may be poor in some way (financially, culturally, physically) but they are already rich in some significant (but hidden) way that makes them a target for more good luck. They are secretly a princess, or have magical powers. Or they are 'The One' as in *The Matrix*. Alternatively, they are worthy of good fortune simply because they have been so poor. The hero of a coming-of-age narrative is usually not special at all. He or she may not even be particularly oppressed, but will be lacking crucial knowledge, skills or trust in the world. This may even be someone who has riches but must cast them off, as in the story of the Buddha, which is perhaps the most classic coming-of-age narrative in existence.

The man who will become the Buddha begins as Siddhartha Gautama, an Indian prince born into great comfort, prosperity and fortune in around 500 BCE. Siddhartha is compassionate from the beginning, caring for sick animals and not comprehending the pain and suffering he sees (for example, a bird eating a snake). His father tries to protect him from the world, having been told that if the young Siddhartha sees an old person, a sick person, a dead person and a monk, he will wish to become a monk himself. He builds him his own palace, and arranges for dancing girls to entertain him. But like all fictional prophecies this one comes true, and, after abandoning his young wife and son, Siddhartha sets off into the wilderness to find himself, and to seek the answers to the biggest questions in life: why do we suffer, and why do we die? Siddhartha makes several mistakes along the way. At one point he tries being an ascetic, but finds this is not the correct route to enlightenment. Eventually, he meditates under the bodhi tree and the secrets of life are finally revealed to him. Where a rags-to-riches hero relies on external assistance – the benefactor or fairy-godmother figure who provides the riches – the hero of a coming-of-age plot must find strength to change within him or herself. This is a narrative of transformation by experience.[112] It is a narrative of enlightenment. It must be undertaken alone.

If in *The Bell Jar* Esther Greenwood had succeeded in

killing herself, the result would be a highly ironic quest. As it is, the plot sees Esther come of age. Almost everything she tries fails – even her attempted suicides – and she must find greater and greater reserves of strength within herself. Her problem does not relate to suffering in general. Instead, Esther's suffering is presented as a synecdoche for the suffering of young women in 1950s North America. How can she exist in world in which she is expected to marry Buddy Willard and turn into something like his mother, who spends hours constructing a beautiful rug that is then just used as a kitchen mat that soon becomes 'soiled and dull and indistinguishable from any mat you could buy for under a dollar in the Five and Ten'?[113] There is a sense here, as with the Buddha's story, that Esther's is a crisis of both too much and too little: she appears to have a lot of options, but is unable to choose any of them. Her encounter with a tree is far less rewarding than the Buddha's:

> I saw my life branching out before me like the green fig-tree in the story. From the tip of every branch, like a fat purple fig, a wonderful future beckoned and winked. One fig was a husband and a happy home and children, and another fig was a famous poet and another fig was a brilliant professor, and another fig was Ee Gee, the amazing editor, and another fig was Europe and Africa and South America, and another fig was Constantin and Socrates and Attila and a pack of other lovers with queer names and offbeat professions, and another fig was an Olympic lady crew champion, and beyond and above these figs were many more figs I couldn't quite make out.

I saw myself sitting in the crotch of this fig-tree, starving to death, just because I couldn't make up my mind which of the figs I would choose. I wanted each and every one of them, but choosing one meant losing all the rest, and, as I sat there, unable to decide, the figs began to wrinkle and go black, and, one by one, they plopped to the ground at my feet . . .[114]

The fig-tree at first seems almost like a device we'd encounter in a quest or a rags-to-riches plot; there's something magical about the idea of choosing something important by simply plucking it from a tree. But *The Bell Jar* does not dramatise what happens when Esther chooses one of these figs. Instead it explores what happens because she realises she can't choose. It isn't just Esther's depression that makes choice impossible for her but also the culture in which she finds herself. In 1950s North America it was very difficult for a woman to be able to have a family, an exciting career and opportunities for travel. We've already seen something of this problem dramatised in *Gentlemen Prefer Blondes*. But this is a more authentic world than the one depicted in *Gentlemen Prefer Blondes*, and there aren't many diamond tiaras going spare. Esther can't find a way to do everything, and so she finds herself with nothing.

Most memoir that deals with the difficulties of childhood adolescence or early adulthood (note that there aren't really any that deal with happy or easy times) will use a coming-of-age structure. *Oranges Are Not the Only Fruit* sees the young protagonist, Jeanette, come of age as a result of struggling with a conflict between family and identity. She is gay, and her family are Pentecostals who believe she is possessed by Satan. *Anna Karenina* is created by interweaving two distinct plots. Anna's story is the tragedy, of course. But Levin's story has a coming-of-age plot. We see him struggle with love, religion and work as he tries to learn how to live a good life that benefits himself and others. His is a life to be lived through reason and therefore stands in opposition to Anna's reckless, passionate, tragic life. Coming-of-age narratives are about people learning hard lessons over a fairly long period of time. Most people do not come of age in a couple of days.[115]

Jane Austen's *Emma* tells of a young heroine, Emma Woodhouse, who believes herself to be an expert in good taste and deeply knowledgeable about the workings of the society around her in Highbury, Surrey. She is something of an amateur psychologist, confident in her assumptions about who loves whom and why. When her governess, Anne Taylor, leaves to marry a neighbour, Mr Weston, Emma finds herself alone with her father, a hypochondriac who has never quite got over the death of his wife. Like the Buddha, Emma has a comfortable life, but lacks worldliness. She finds a new companion to replace Miss Taylor, an unsophisticated lower-class girl from the nearby school called Harriet Smith, for whom she has great plans. Mr Knightley, a worldly and sophisticated man and great friend of the Woodhouses, warns Emma about her schemes, and becomes angry when she prevents Harriet from accepting a marriage proposal from Robert Martin, a farmer. Emma's ambition for Miss Smith backfires when the eligible Mr Elton, whom Emma believes to be in love with Harriet, declares his love for Emma instead. Over the course of the novel Emma must learn that she is not as sophisticated as she imagines, and that the world is much more complex than she thinks.

Coming-of-age narratives usually include some kind of epiphany[116] or enlightenment scene that is comparable, in structural terms, to tragic recognition. Emma's includes this:

> With insufferable vanity had she believed herself in the secret of everybody's feelings; with unpardonable arrogance proposed to arrange everybody's destiny. She was proved to have been universally mistaken; and she had not quite done nothing – for she had done mischief.[117]

While the enlightenment scene in a coming-of-age narrative usually occupies the same *position* as the recognition scene in a tragedy, it has quite a different result. Any 'mischief' or mistakes that have occurred can be put right and will therefore lead to new knowledge rather than downfall. Coming-of-age heroes generally mean well, and often are not acting in their own interests, but in what they believe to be the interests of others. Emma may be arrogant and vain, but she is also quite charming. She is also a very caring person, who shows great devotion to her father. We know she is not a bad character, or someone destined for tragedy. After her enlightenment scene, she is rewarded for her new self-knowledge with the love of Mr Knightley.

In *Middlemarch*, Fred Vincy's reward for coming of age is his childhood love, Mary Garth. He has been promised great riches but has not received them. His ambition for wealth and status has got him into all sorts of trouble. This is someone who is reduced to nothing, and has to build his own character without wealth. Coming-of-age narratives don't always end with a wedding, though. The reward for enlightenment is often a new sense of freedom, rather than a new commitment. They may even dramatise the end of a relationship and show a young hero arriving at a place of self-knowledge from which they can (after the end of the narrative) perhaps seek a more meaningful kind of love.

Ironic coming-of-age plots may leave the protagonist none the wiser, or realising how much more they have to learn. Chekhov's story 'The Lady with the Little Dog' tells of an adulterous love affair between Dmitry Dmitrich Gurov and Anna Sergeyevna von Diederitz, which begins when the pair meet while holidaying in Yalta. We expect that Gurov may come of age in this story (or alternatively have a tragic downfall); after all, he begins as someone who has already learnt some lessons about illicit love.

> Repeated – and in fact bitter – experience had long taught him that every affair, which at first adds spice and variety to life and seems such a charming and light-hearted adventure, inevitably develops into an enormous, extraordinarily complex problem . . .[118]

The two lovers have their affair in Yalta and agree that they will never see one another again after they part. Anna Sergeyevna will return to St Petersburg, and Gurov will return to Moscow. But once home, he can't get her out of his mind. He seeks her out in St Petersburg and they find themselves continuing their affair. Gurov realises that he is getting old, and also that he is in love for the first time. The story ends with these lines: 'And it seemed – given a little more time – a solution would be found and then a new and beautiful life would begin. And both of them clearly realised that the end was far, far away and that the most complicated and difficult part was only just beginning.' Gurov has learned how to love, and in this sense he has come of age. But he has not learned how to love freely, and the end of the story is therefore not a happy one. The final word in the story is 'beginning', which is as far from a resolution as it's possible to get. But although it would have been straightforward to turn this into a tragic love story in the style of *Anna Karenina*, Chekhov does not do this. He leaves us, like his characters, without the satisfaction of either complete tragedy or complete enlightenment. But, like Gurov, we have been changed by our experience.

STRANGER COMES TO TOWN

Just as there are a limited number of plots, there are a limited number of ways in which a narrative can begin. All beginnings involve some sort of change: some spark that gets the plot moving. Often, as Vladimir Propp has demonstrated, narrative begins with an acknowledgement of some sort of lack. Someone wants something and they set out to get it. Emma lacks a companion, and so seeks out Harriet Smith. The Buddha lacks true understanding of the world and so sets out to find enlightenment. But there is a distinct category of narrative that begins with someone new coming into a town, family or community, and it is this arrival that makes the community aware of some great lack, or desire, or question that was unknown before.

Many narratives have newcomers or visitors at their centre: Darcy in *Pride and Prejudice*; Ladislaw in *Middlemarch*; Buzz Lightyear in *Toy Story*; Magwitch in *Great Expectations*. But the basic plot 'stranger comes to town' is not merely a narrative that begins with someone unknown turning up out of the blue. This plot dramatises both a profound rejection of an outsider and an examination of the ways in which outsiders shake up communities and change them for the better. In this plot, a family or community is disrupted by the arrival of a person or animal. The new arrival is usually (but not always) initially rejected. He or she will certainly be misunderstood, though, and there will be a mystery about him or her. Who is this? Why are they here? Where have they come from? Why are they so weird? But gradually it becomes clear that the presence of the stranger is changing everyone's lives for the better. Perhaps truths are told or deception is uncovered. Perhaps people are provoked into inhabiting their true identities. Perhaps they are able to love, or live, in a new way. However, the community often realises how helpful the stranger has been only after they have sacrificed him or her in some way. This plot always ends with the death or departure of the stranger, and the renewed life of the community.

One of the most familiar and ancient versions of this story is, of course, the New Testament.[119] Here we follow the story of Jesus Christ, the son of God, sent to Earth to suffer for our sins. We learn that 'He [had] no stately form or majesty That we should look upon Him, Nor appearance that we should be attracted to Him. He was despised and forsaken of men, A man of sorrows and acquainted with grief; And like one from whom men hide their face He was despised, and we did not esteem Him'.[120] But, of course, he changed the world, and many of us now live in societies where the main belief system is based on remembering just how Christ was forsaken, how he suffered and what he taught us.

Often, a stranger-comes-to-town plot has at its centre an ingénue figure who befriends the stranger and attempts to protect him/her/it from the rest of the community. The film *E.T.* tells of Elliot, a young boy whose family has broken down, and who finds a lost extra-terrestrial in the garden shed. Before he returns to his own planet, E.T. will teach Elliot's family the meaning of hope and love. He will also die and be resurrected before his spaceship arrives. This kind of plot is always highly emotional, dealing as it does with some kind of profound innocence that is broken (here we see that E.T. is too pure and fragile to survive on our harsh planet), or a great love that is refused, squandered, forsaken, or accepted for a time but ultimately betrayed or lost. E.T. somehow stands not just for all the 'strangers' we have tried to help, but for the stranger in ourselves: ugly, awkward, desperately fragile – and bound to be rejected by mainstream society.

Ali Smith's novel *The Accidental* tells of the Smart family, who are renting a holiday cottage in Norfolk for the summer. When an enigmatic young woman called Amber turns up,

Eve and Michael Smart each assume that she is the other's visitor. Eve believes that Amber is just another student with whom Michael is having an affair. Michael thinks Amber might be part of his wife's latest writing project. Amber affects the whole family very deeply. She befriends 12-year-old Astrid Smart and begins a sexual relationship with Astrid's traumatised older brother Magnus. It soon becomes clear that each member of the Smart family is in love with Amber, despite the fact that she is often quite rude to them, at one point saying to Eve, 'God, you're boring.' Amber has a curious kind of honesty; her lies are often more truthful than the Smarts' sincerity. And she does such unbelievable things (rescuing Magnus from hanging himself; throwing Astrid's camcorder off a motorway bridge) that when she is honest about them no one believes her. Even though she breaks their hearts and eventually goes to their London home and steals all their possessions, it is clear that Amber has changed this family for the better. Magnus stops being suicidal. Astrid grows up and discovers herself. Eve learns to be reckless. Michael starts appreciating his family more. Everyone lives happily ever after, even to the point of enjoying the way the empty house echoes. It's just as Eve thinks to herself on the night that Amber appears: 'Couldn't it sometimes take an outsider to reveal to a family that it was a family?'[121]

Amber, like many strangers who come to town, is a morally ambiguous character, more a dose of harsh medicine than any sort of fairy godmother. In this basic plot the stranger may certainly be unpleasant, but is more likely to be misunderstood. He or she may be animalistic in some way, or childlike, or unusually innocent. The stranger will certainly not conform to the usual codes and conventions of the society that he or she is visiting, whether this is deliberate (as in Amber's case) or simply not possible (E.T.). In the story 'Sea Oak' by George Saunders, the stranger who comes to town is the narrator's Aunt Bernie, who, after being murdered in a robbery, returns as a zombie to force him, his sister and their cousin to make more of their lives. A gentle, optimistic person who had no expectations of life, never swore and found living on minimum wage in a slum rather pleasant, Bernie comes back from the dead with a different set of objectives entirely.

> Well I am going to have lovers now, you fucks! Like in the movies, big shoulders and all, and a summer house, and nice trips, and in the morning in my room a nice vase of flowers, and I'm going to get my nipples hard standing in the breeze from the ocean, eating shrimp from a cup, you sons of bitches, while my lover watches me from the veranda, his big shoulders shining, all hard for me . . .[122]

Here Bernie is fulfilling the classic disruptive function of the stranger. It's not just that she's a zombie: she's a virgin zombie who wants to get laid. She is disturbing, in every sense of the word.

As we have seen, basic plots always have a mainstream or pop cultural form as well as their more 'literary', highbrow, subtle or ironic versions. Here we find the stranger-comes-to-town plot at the centre of the ghost story, the horror film and most narratives of infection or illness. The stranger that comes to town can be a plague, a serial killer, a shark or a killer ape. But even in conventional versions of this plot type there is always something horrific, weird or unusual about the stranger. Strangers who come to town are never ordinary. They never fit in. They always travel alone (often in summer). They go places that they were never invited, and even if they are invited they are unwanted (as in the story 'Cathedral' by Raymond Carver, where the stranger is a blind man who teaches the narrator how to see). The stranger will not necessarily be alien or supernatural, but from the way people treat them they may as well be. *Housekeeping* by Marilynne Robinson tells the story of Sylvie, a drifter who turns up to look after orphans Ruth and Lucille in the small, desolate town of Fingerbone in north-west America. The narrator is Ruth, the less conventional of the two sisters. Here we have a subtle, ironic version of the stranger-comes-to-town story where the only person transformed by Sylvie is Ruth, who ends up becoming a transient like Sylvie when they leave Fingerbone together.

The enduring fear of the stranger is perhaps what makes these narratives so powerful. Wherever there is fear there is also desire, and there is often a love story at the centre of these narratives (such as Elliot's love for E.T., or Magnus's love for Amber). But the stranger, while having 'odd' or seemingly supernatural powers, will usually be poor and materially powerless. This, therefore, is the plot type that most vividly attempts to dramatise encounters with the 'other' (while hardly ever putting the audience quite in the other's shoes). These dramatised encounters with the other are, structurally, the reverse of the colonial encounters in which it is the powerful community, or its representatives, that turn up on the doorstep of the 'stranger'. Indeed, an ironic version of this plot can be seen in Sylvia Townsend Warner's novel *Mr Fortune's Maggot*, where the stranger is a missionary who ends up 'going native'. But the true version of this plot type is manifested when the 'other' turns up in a metropolitan setting. In this plot type, therefore, it is often 'exotic' wisdom that is passed on; everyone learns to loosen up a little, and there may even be some dancing. There are very few 'classics' that use this structure, although many folk tales and fables from around the world do. But it is central to our understanding of fiction partly because the writer often occupies the structural position of stranger.

MYSTERY

Mystery is probably the most fundamental basic plot, and perhaps the most well-recognised. After all, every narrative contains mystery. Mystery is the engine that powers every story. We open a book and we are confronted with mysteries. Who are these people? Why are they doing these things? And that's even before we find out that a crime or murder has been committed (if indeed it has). Whodunnit? Whydunnit? Howdunnit? These are the fundamental questions of life, not just the murder investigation. Even so, I hesitated to include mystery in my list of basic plots. Why? Well, most mystery stories are structured in such a way that once the mystery is cracked, another story emerges that is not a mystery but usually some other kind of plot. *Oedipus the King* is often cited as one of the earliest examples of detective fiction. And indeed it is. Oedipus investigates a murder and uncovers the truth. That is the part of the plot that works according to the rules of mystery. But once the truth is uncovered the plot re-shapes itself as a tragedy (and absorbs the mystery into this larger plot).

Does this mean that *Oedipus the King* was only ever a tragedy and we should disregard the mystery plot altogether? I think not. *Oedipus the King* uses *both* a mystery plot and a tragedy plot. In a similar way, Plato's Simile of the Cave, another fundamental mystery story, opens out to reveal a coming-of-age plot. Here is a mystery that when solved has a profound effect on the 'detective' figure, who is fundamentally changed – enlightened – by his discovery of the truth. Like Oedipus, he finds that the subject of the mystery is his own identity, and his own perception of reality. We may note that there are basically two different ways to solve mysteries: to use logic and reasoning, as Oedipus does, or to use experience and empirical knowledge, as the prisoner in the Cave does. These form the basis for two different forms of mystery narrative: one based on inductive reasoning (where a hypothesis is created from evidence), and one based on deductive reasoning (where a hypothesis is tested by experience). These happen to be the two major post-enlightenment epistemological strategies (or ways of knowing things), and this is certainly the plot type that is closest to philosophy. This is a plot about knowledge: about moving from a state of ignorance to a state of understanding. It is about finding – or at least seeking – the truth.

While other narratives may or may not 'layer' their plots – a coming-of-age narrative for one character and tragedy for another, say – the mystery *always* has at least two central plots, one of which concerns the detection process and the other of which is the plot revealed by this process. The first Sherlock Holmes mystery, *A Study in Scarlet*, by Arthur Conan Doyle, separates these two plots entirely, to the extent of having the first as Part I of the novel and the second as Part II, where at first it appears to belong to a different narrative entirely. In Part I we are introduced by Dr Watson to Sherlock Holmes, an intense, clever man whose 'ignorance was as remarkable as his knowledge'[123] and who, when Watson tells him that the Earth orbits the sun, says he never knew this and pledges to forget it again.

> 'But the Solar System!' I protested.
>   'What the deuce is it to me?' he interrupted impatiently; 'you say that we go round the sun. If we went round the moon it would not make a pennyworth of difference to me or my work.'[124]

For Sherlock Holmes what is important isn't knowledge based on hearsay, but knowledge based in experience and experiment. He is someone who totally inhabits the real world. As he writes in an article that Watson reads:

> By a man's finger nails, by his coat sleeve, by his boot, by his trouser knees, by the callosities of his forefinger and thumb, by his expression, by his shirt cuffs – by each of these things a man's calling is plainly revealed. That all united should fail to enlighten the competent enquirer in any case is almost inconceivable.[125]

Although Watson is initially unconvinced by this, he soon changes his mind when Holmes uses his methodology to solve a real murder mystery. Holmes's summary of his method shows exactly how this kind of mystery plot works. The detection process is a hermeneutic method: a way of finding deep meaning. The murder scene, like the body of the man above, is seen as a text that can only be read by someone (the great detective) who has learnt its particular language. In other words, there are clues, or traces, which, when interpreted correctly, reveal a larger truth. This method (which Holmes describes as deduction, but is really induction – as we have seen, the prisoner in the cave practises something closer to deduction[126]) is pleasingly, perhaps comfortingly, deterministic. With the right clues, anything may be known, understood or even predicted. For Holmes, this means that 'all life is a great chain, the nature of which is known whenever we are shown a single link of it'.[127]

In *A Study in Scarlet* a man has been found dead in a house on Brixton Road, London. Sherlock Holmes is invited by Gregson, an incompetent Scotland Yard detective, to view the body and help with the case. Another detective, Lestrade, is also struggling to work out the meaning of the clues left on the scene. However, from clues unseen by Watson (and indeed by the reader) Holmes works out the age, height and complexion of the murderer. There are, though, several areas where the reader can join in. The murderer has written the word 'Rache' in blood on the wall. The Scotland Yard detectives believe that the murderer intended to write the word 'Rachel'; Holmes knows that Rache is German for 'hate'. If the reader knows this too, then he or she can share the thrill of detection. There is also a wedding ring, which the astute reader can assume means that there is or was a woman involved in the story. Indeed this proves to be the case, and once Holmes has apprehended the murderer we are off to Salt Lake City for Part II of the novel in which we meet some murderous, polygamous Mormons, the beautiful Lucy Ferrier, and the man who will avenge her death. This plot, revealed by the mystery, is another tragedy.

An important feature of the mystery plot is that it is always, to a greater or lesser extent, interactive. This has developed a great deal since the first Sherlock Holmes mystery was published, and mysteries are deemed to be more or less 'satisfying' on the basis of whether the clues given really can be intelligible to a reader. It's true that other plot types also often ask for the reader's involvement: the reader may be required to fall in love with a hero or a stranger, for example, in order that the plot may work. But this is the only plot type that works specifically as a puzzle that the reader can solve. In order to work like this it needs much specific detail. As Holmes says to Gregson:

> It is a mistake to confound strangeness with mystery. The most commonplace crime is often the most mysterious because it presents no new or special features from which deductions may be drawn. This murder would have been infinitely more difficult to unravel had the body of the victim been simply found lying in the roadway without any of these *outré* and sensational accompaniments which have rendered it remarkable.[128]

Like any good plot, a mystery is built from specific, memorable detail. And murder mysteries do tend towards the remarkable, rather than the realistic. Here we find, for example, the locked-room mystery, which is virtually unknown in real life. Like the romantic comedy, the mystery relies on obstacles. The mystery must provide a taxing enough puzzle for the reader/detective, who, as we are beginning to see, function as one. At the beginning of the mystery plot we have no idea what has happened: neither the reader nor the detective knows the solution to the puzzle. The reader and detective are one, but the detective represents the reader's more active and inquiring self who, if given the right information, could solve anything. The detective is who the reader would be if only he or she were paying a bit more attention.

But there is another type of mystery altogether: one that places the reader ahead of the detective, positioned somewhere closer to the person who has set the puzzle (an antagonist usually, but not always) than the person who must solve it. This is the situation in The Cave: we, the readers, are introduced to the set-up (which is the solution to the mystery) before we see the drama of the prisoner coming to his own understanding of his situation. We know what he is going to discover before he does. The TV series *Columbo* also works in this way. Every episode begins with a murder being committed, and we see who has done it. Then the eccentric detective Columbo turns up and begins his investigation. We know, if we are familiar with the 'formula' of these mysteries, that Columbo will solve the mystery; and of course we also know the solution. What we do not know is the process by which Columbo will move from the mystery to the solution, from ignorance to knowledge, and so this becomes the question that drives the narrative, rather than the usual question of whodunnit.

The mystery plot is all about uncovering truth, as we have seen. But what if the purpose of the 'detective' or narrator figure is to cover up the truth: to conceal it not just from us but also from him or herself? What if the narrator positions him or herself in the place of the detective figure but actually turns out to be the perpetrator of the mystery we're reading about? In these cases we have an unreliable narrator, and therefore an ironic version of the mystery. *The Horned Man* by James Lasdun has precisely the structure I have just described, as, more or less, does Zoe Heller's novel *Notes on a Scandal*. But not all ironic mystery plots have such a straightforward reversal, or such an unreliable narrator.

Julian Barnes's novel *The Sense of an Ending* begins by positioning the reader some way behind the narrator, Tony Webster, as he examines his memory of a set of events leading up to his friend Adrian Finn's suicide: once without the benefit of any sort of proof, and then again after his memory has been jogged by a letter and a diary. Tony admits from the start that he is only a semi-reliable narrator. And Adrian tells us early in the novel, "'History is that certainty produced at the point where the imperfections of memory meet the inadequacies of documentation.'"[129] This is what the novel dramatises. We are given a set of memories as clues on the very first page, but we are never sure that these are quite the right memories, or quite the right clues. We also have no idea why we need clues, because we don't know what has happened. This seems to be a mystery with no mystery. In the event, the astute reader will probably catch on to what has happened a little faster than the narrator, but 'what happened' is hardly the point of the novel. The point is the exploration of the central themes: history and memory.

We see the mystery plot playing out in every classroom, every seminar room and in every PhD project ever undertaken. Education turns us all into detectives. We formulate research questions and set off deductively to test our hypotheses (like the character in the Simile of the Cave, who, when freed from his chains, immediately wonders what is outside). Otherwise we may engage in what's known as 'blue skies' thinking, which is what Holmes does, and actually also what great writers do. We may decide to look at the detail of life and see what conclusions (or even better, further questions) we may draw from it.

MODERN REALISM

Sometimes a narrative can become hugely successful while breaking all the structural rules we have come across so far, and we realise we are faced with a completely different kind of plot. An example of this is the novel *One Day* by David Nicholls, which at the time of writing has sold more than a million copies worldwide. The novel opens in 1988. It is Emma Morley and Dexter Mayhew's graduation night and they are in bed together. Although she is in love with him, he is not particularly attracted to her. The two become friends, and we follow their lives over the next 20 years. The way we do this is to 'visit' them on 15 July – St Swithun's Day – each year. This is the 'One Day' of the title.

Emma is an instantly likeable, admirable character, with a sense of social justice and a good deal of humour. Dexter is self-obsessed and dishonest and remains so for the rest of the novel. Throughout the novel Emma is in love with Dexter. But he gets work as a TV presenter and dates famous and beautiful women, while she makes do with an unfunny stand-up comedian she meets while working in a Tex Mex restaurant. Dexter becomes an alcoholic; Emma has an affair with the headmaster at the school where she ends up teaching for a while. There are some deft structural moves in the novel. Over the course of the novel Emma follows something like a rags-to-riches trajectory while Dexter's story is more of a tragedy. She becomes a best-selling writer, while he gets unhappily married and drinks even more. His TV work dries up. The two of them do get together eventually, although Dexter has not really changed and does not really seem, in narrative terms, to 'deserve' her. Still, they are happy. They are trying for a baby. They are looking for a house to buy together. This is where we sense their story should end. But it doesn't.

On 15 July 2004, while Emma is cycling to meet Dexter to look at a house, she is involved in an accident. This is how the chapter finishes: 'Then Emma Mayhew dies, and everything that she thought or felt vanishes and is gone forever.' Much of what is written about this book in the press focuses on its ability to make grown men (or, actually, anyone) cry. The book does indeed tend to reduce people to tears. But why? It is not a great tragedy. Emma does not deserve to die. She is not dying because of some great ambition: it was just an accident. The structure of the novel becomes rather more interesting and poignant at this moment. *Aha*, we realise. *That's why we have visited 15 July every year. This is the day she dies.* It's a very neat structural moment. But it still doesn't work according to any conventional notion of plot. Emma is too admirable to be killed; Dexter is not admirable enough to learn anything interesting as a result. If Emma's death is part of 'Dexter's tragedy', then we are left wondering why she has been placed at the centre of the book, both morally and in terms of her actions.

So where does the popularity of this novel come from? We know from Aristotle, and from 99 per cent of other narratives we experience, that good characters like Emma don't, shouldn't, just randomly die. In fact we can rely on it, usually. Random death is not what fiction is supposed to provide. Fiction is supposed to be a secure structure in which we can explore ideas and experience emotion without, well, without *really* experiencing it. But Emma's death is somehow 'like real life'. That is how death really happens: you don't plan for it, and it's never all right. The 'grown men' who are moved to tears by the novel are probably experiencing something closer to real grief than fictional pleasure. Perhaps the book is in the end recommended as an 'intense experience' rather than a 'good story'.

While *One Day* is highly problematic in many ways, and probably owes much of its success to dubious factors,[130] it is an example of a novel that ultimately eschews conventional plot. It is not metafictional, ironic or satirical, however. Rather, it rejects plot in such a way that any criticism of it on this basis could well be met with the response, 'Well, that's what real life is like. That's what *happens*.' Any narrative that prioritises 'what real life is like' at the expense of recognisable plot structure fits into a category that I want to call modern realism. And as with all the other basic plots, it has better and worse types. Of course, it isn't exactly a basic plot in as much as it *has* no definite plot; it differs from all the others in that it doesn't have a recognisable Aristotelian structure based on change from one state to another. But it does have some notable features. It can be a 'glimpse', as in the modern short story, or a novel-length impressionistic account of 'not much happening'. It is what the character Charlie Kaufman describes in his conversation with (the fictional) Robert McKee in *Adaptation*:

> Sir, what if a writer is attempting to create a story where nothing much happens? Where people don't change, they don't have any epiphanies. They struggle and are frustrated, and nothing is resolved. More a reflection of the real world.[131]

Modern realism is different from what is termed 'classic realism', or 'nineteenth-century realism'. In fact, for me these terms refer to style rather than structure. Classic realist novels are, when you break them down, usually an intricately constructed combination of the basic plots we have already looked at. They are long and highly ambitious in their attempts to depict what is real, but they do this *with* narrative, not at its expense. They usually attempt to represent, in some way, a whole society, and show its workings in detail. Just as *Middlemarch* has many plots, not just one, big (in bulk and theme) contemporary novels tend to be rather similar. We follow one or more characters through one or more plots and explore contemporary life as we go. Novels like *White Teeth* by Zadie Smith, or *number9dream* by David Mitchell don't have a single 'plot' but a complex narrative, made up of several plots, made up of many stories.

Modern realism is quite different. Modern realism is where art imitates life; where the writer or director seems to be saying, 'Life doesn't work out like art, so why not reflect *life*, in all its disappointment and disconnectedness? Why make everything so damn *perfect* all the time?' As I have argued in previous chapters, there can be huge problems with letting go of structure. *There's No Business like Showbusiness* rambles along, a bit like 'real life', but does not enrich us in any way. In the end it's just boring. In order for modern realism to have any depth, and to be recognisably different from real life, it must do something that real life does not do. Usually, therefore, modern realism focuses on some sort of close-up examination of the real. In each narrative not much may seem to happen, but under the surface rather a lot is going on. We are left, undistracted by plot, to closely read images, moments, emotions, ideas and textures, among other things.

In 'Bliss' by Katherine Mansfield, Bertha and her husband Harry are to hold a dinner party. In the run-up to the dinner party Bertha feels an inexplicable sense of bliss 'as though [she'd] suddenly swallowed a bright piece of the late afternoon sun'.[132] She feels a particular affinity with a pear tree in the garden, which is 'in fullest, richest bloom; it stood perfect, as though becalmed against the jade-green sky'.[133] Indeed, Bertha realises after she has dressed for dinner that she has more or less come as the pear tree. 'A white dress, a string of jade beads, green shoes and stockings. It wasn't "intentional".'[134] One of the dinner party guests is Pearl Fulton, a beautiful, 'strange', blonde, single woman described as a 'find' of Bertha's. In the story Bertha never quite shakes her feeling of bliss, and after dinner finds that she truly desires Harry for the first time. But then she sees Pearl Fulton in the corridor in a clinch with him. He is telling her he adores her, and the two seem to be planning to meet the following day. This scene is enclosed in a strange parenthesis. Another of the dinner party guests, Eddie, is trying to tell Bertha about a poem called 'Table d'Hôte'[135] that begins with the line 'Why Must it Always be Tomato Soup?'. Before Bertha sees her husband and Pearl Fulton in the hall Eddie has been searching for the poem. After the scene he has found it.

'Here it is,' said Eddie. '"Why Must it Always be Tomato Soup?" It's so *deeply* true, don't you feel? Tomato soup is so *dreadfully* eternal.'[136]

What is this story? What does it ask of us, and what does it offer in return? It certainly resists immediate interpretation. The tree here is not as easy to read as Sylvia Plath's fig tree, or the Buddha's tree, each of which has a definite figurative or literal place in its respective narrative. What is the significance of the pear tree here? At first it does seem to function in the same way as Plath's tree, when Bertha 'seemed to see on her eyelids the lovely pear tree with its wide open blossoms as a symbol of her own life'. There then follows a list of all the ways in which Bertha has 'everything' – a life in full bloom like the tree – finishing rather unexcitingly with 'and their new cook made the most superb omelettes . . .' Does Bertha have everything or not? The story never tells us. We suspect not, especially at the end, but we can't really be sure. Is the story a satire? Are we supposed to sneer at these silly 'modern' people who are frightfully keen on things, or are we supposed to feel compassion for them? When Pearl Fulton arrives at the dinner party resembling the pear tree in the evening (she wears silver), does this mean she eclipses Bertha in some way? Does Bertha actually desire her in the way generations of students have fantasised?[137] And what are we to make of the other key piece of imagery in the story, the two cats stalking one another?

The story doesn't tell us.

Much fiction tells us how to read it. For example, Sherlock Holmes stories break down the detective process for us so that we may join in. They, and other satisfying mysteries, remind us of significant clues (although if they do this too much we may find them patronising). In *The Accidental* we are reminded that this is a stranger-comes-to-town plot in the line 'Couldn't it sometimes take an outsider to reveal to a family that it was a family?'[138] In the novel *Clear* by Nicola Barker the characters read Kafka's short story 'The Hunger Artist' to try to make sense of David Blaine's 2003

stunt 'Above the Below', in which he was suspended in a
clear box over the Thames with no food for 44 days. Readers
get more out of the novel if they read Kafka as well. The
novel also opens with a quotation from the opening of the
novel *Shane*, in which a stranger comes to town just as
Blaine does. *Northanger Abbey*, as we will see, provides a
guide to Gothic romance so that we can better appreciate
its metafictional treatment.

Most mainstream narratives come with paratextual
devices (book blurbs, plot summaries and so on) that tell
us how to read and enjoy them. There will be various other
non-diegetic factors too. A TV thriller will have creepy
music so that we know when to be scared; a comedy may
have a laughter-track to show us when to laugh. Mainstream
entertainment always tells us how we should be feeling and
what we should be expecting. We can usually pick up what
kind of story we are experiencing within seconds of
switching on the radio or TV. Modern realism does not do
any of this. But it does give us hints. In 'Bliss' we hear of
a play that someone wants to write:

> One act. One man. Decides to commit suicide. Gives all
> the reasons why he should and why he shouldn't. And just
> as he has made up his mind either to do it or not do it –
> curtain. Not half a bad idea.[139]

And just after this we hear that the dinner guests remind
Bertha of a play by Chekhov. Perhaps, then, *this* is a story
we are to read in the same way we might read Chekhov's
fiction? Perhaps this story is going to be as inconclusive as

the suicide play, and perhaps that's 'not half a bad idea'? While these references don't tell us *exactly* how to read the story, we are now aware of its mode. This is something to be read slowly, to be thought about deeply. This is like real life, only more so.

Compared with many other examples of modern realism, however, 'Bliss' is full of action and drama. Indeed, we might want to argue that this is a subverted version of some other plot. Could it, for example, be an ironic mystery, where we get the solution (Harry and Pearl Fulton are having an affair) without the question? I think not. After all, ironic versions of plots involve significant structural reversal and I'm not sure that happens here. But we must be careful not simply to file anything 'weird', inconclusive or seemingly plotless as 'modern realism'. Raymond Carver's stories, while held up as great examples of plotless minimalism, almost always have recognisable plots. 'Cathedral', as we have seen, is based on a stranger coming to town. 'Feathers' seems to be an ironic rags-to-riches narrative. Most of Carver's stories involve change from one state to another, even if this is quite subtle. And Carver's stories are honest with us. They tell us what they mean to do to us, often from the first line. They have clear narrative questions: a fridge has broken down; a car needs to be sold; people are going to attempt to talk about love. While the stories are often inconclusive, we get the sense that by the end something has changed; something has happened.

Many plots will answer narrative questions while leaving thematic questions unresolved. Modern-realist fiction answers no questions of any sort. We are left with the feeling that things may simply carry on as they are, or that what has changed is so subtle as to have very little effect on the characters. Modern-realist characters have small epiphanies rather than a great enlightenment. At the end of Mansfield's story 'The Doll's House', in which two low-class girls are allowed to view a doll's house belonging to a wealthy family, one of the low-class girls says to the other, "'I seen the little lamp.'" This is exactly our experience as readers when we encounter this plot type: we hope for no more than to see the little lamp. Modern realism implicitly suggests that life-changing enlightenment is not easily achievable for most of us. Indeed, its structure will rarely promise to change our lives. We will have a small epiphany when we encounter it: we will see the little lamp and then, like the girls in 'The Doll's House', we will fall silent. After watching a modern-realist film we will not cry, pledge to take up ballet, wish we were more glamorous or muscle-bound or decide to go on a diet. We will not dribble sun-tan lotion on the latest modern-realist novel as we frantically turn its pages. Indeed, many modern-realist novels position themselves against the classic realist novel by having deliberately frustrating plots. The novel *C* by Tom McCarthy kills off its most engaging character in the first fifty pages and leaves us caught in the wake of her brother's complicated bereavement for its remainder.

The modern-realist plot may function as a 'glimpse' of life, and these glimpses may often seem like fragments from a story. We usually don't need to see a story ending to know how it will end. But much of modern realism completely disrupts what we expect from narrative. David Lynch is an example of a modern realist who uses the screen to represent something beyond 'consensus reality' or 'narrative reality'. This is a different kind of real: what is real for him. Of course, when artists do this, the audience needs to be able to share the same exact vision. I can perhaps now finally admit that I have never been so bored as when I was 16 and watching *Eraserhead* because it was a 'cool' thing to do. I had no idea what was going on. I felt alienated and freaked out, as well as bored. If someone had told me I was *supposed* to be feeling these things, would it have made any difference? Probably not.[140]

When I went to see the film *Le Quattro Volte* more recently I didn't need to pretend to be cool, and I read a detailed review first so that I knew what to expect. From the review I learned that the film, which has a lot of goats but no dialogue and no narrative, is a dramatisation of Pythagoras's idea of the four stages of life: human, animal, vegetable, mineral.[141] Once I knew this, I could 'read' the film (which, I'll admit, for me means constructing a narrative from it). The film moves very slowly indeed, but it offers a profoundly moving experience. But if I hadn't known how to connect the images I was seeing I'm sure I would have had a far less moving experience. It's undoubtedly important to be given a space in which to think about how a man may become a goat, who may become a tree, which may then become charcoal in a great cycle of life. I'm not sure quite what the point is of hiding the fact that this is what a film is about (especially if you then have to explain it in the press conference).

Should modern-realist texts therefore come with internal

'reading guides', as 'Bliss' does? I'm not sure. The best examples of modern realism are inscribed with many possible readings, and however good authors are at creating texts, the best ones don't tell us exactly what to do with them. But Mansfield's nudges are still very important. They at least direct us to a tradition; they offer us the play of intertextuality, and help create what Barthes might call a 'tissue, a woven fabric' from not just one, but many texts.[142] However, we must take care to remember that in fiction it is *theme* that needs to be deeply read, not narrative. Most of the best plots are very clear about what is happening on the level of narrative, but very complex on the level of theme. *Oedipus the King* would gain nothing from being difficult to read on the level of story. We know absolutely what has happened to Oedipus, but we may spend the rest of our lives thinking about what this means. The same is true of *Waiting for Godot*. We know without doubt what happens, just not what it means. Modern realism may be unconventional, but it must still attempt to enlighten rather than obfuscate. Art should try to let us see things that are difficult to see in ordinary life, not make things that are simply difficult to see.

SUBVERSION

Many people who successfully write fiction do it without any conscious idea of basic plots. But whenever I have talked about basic plots with my students they have been quite liberated by being able to understand these shapes and do something with them. It is, as we've seen, often much more interesting to use a plot ironically, or in some way 'against' the themes of the narrative, than it is to use it straight. But usually it is useful to know (even if it is only semi-consciously) what plot you are subverting and why. *Lourdes* and *Great Expectations* both use a rags-to-riches structure in order to ask questions about the importance of wealth. But a typical blockbuster like Jackie Collins's *Lucky* will enable characters to gain riches without leaving them (or us) with any difficult questions. So many romantic comedies end in almost self-parodic fashion, with a wedding, followed by weddings of all the other characters, sometimes even followed by one or more pregnancies. There is often a lot of bunting. But despite my students' reluctance to use romantic comedy (for them, it is the 'cheesiest' of plot structures), interesting things can be achieved with it.

The 2004 film *Eternal Sunshine of the Spotless Mind* tells of two ex-lovers, Joel and Clementine, who have had their two-year relationship surgically wiped from their memories. All is confusion – as it must be in romantic comedy – but they somehow manage to come together again. The question that the film asks – is it worth continuing with a relationship that you know can only ever be flawed? – is a huge one, and is handled with ambiguity and depth. And, of course, no one knows the answer. Nicola Barker's novel *Five Miles From Outer Hope* is another edgy romantic comedy. Medve and her eccentric family live on an island in Devon, in a run-down hotel. Medve's mother is absent and her father is distracted. It is summer 1981 and the awkward, teenage Medve spends her days painting Margaret Thatcher mugs and waiting for something exciting to happen. When La Roux turns up from South Africa, Medve is wearing a 'cheap, synthetic nightdress (a garment so flammable that if I fart the buttons tinkle) and a long crocheted knee-length waistcoat', through which he can see her nipples. Later, when she finds him reading *Black Beauty*, she becomes

> momentarily distracted by the sight of his genitalia in his preposterously high-yanked boiler suit, where they hang on his left thigh, all limp and lopsided, like a small bag of crushed intestines newly liberated from the back end of a turkey.[143]

Here are two people fascinated with their own (and each other's) repulsiveness. They fall in love but find themselves part of a game of one-upmanship that goes wrong. La Roux is sent back to South Africa, and he and Medve will be apart for years before they find each other once again. But they *do* find each other again.

Knowing about basic plots means you can create interesting clashes and subvert expectation without writing something disappointing. It also means you can explore metafiction, as Jane Austen did when she wrote her first novel, *Northanger Abbey*, in 1798–99. *Northanger Abbey* relies on the reader's knowledge of two different types of plot: the romantic comedy and the Gothic romance.[144] It continually asks us to reflect on the process of fictionalisation: how we fictionalise ourselves and others; when this may be useful and when it may not. The first chapter prepares us for some self-reflexivity, a central feature of most metafiction. The novel opens with this: 'No one who had seen Catherine Morland in her infancy, would have supposed her to be an heroine.'[145] What an odd way to begin a novel. After all, we are supposed to be suspending our disbelief at this point, not thinking about characters as 'heroes' or 'heroines'. This sentence reminds us that Catherine is someone who is going to take part in a fictional narrative, as 'an heroine'. The novel does not pretend that this is a 'real person', but, by admitting that this is a story, instead immediately breaks the frame, and with it our suspension of disbelief. This works on two levels. Catherine, the fictional heroine of a romantic comedy, will imagine herself the heroine of a Gothic romance. Austen plays on this throughout the novel, as we will see. It's as if Austen is dramatising her writing process on the page in order to tell us that it's OK not to believe; it's OK to acknowledge that this is just a story or a fantasy (and perhaps one that we hope might happen to us).

The teenage Catherine then goes into 'training' to become a heroine, reading Pope, Gray, Thompson and Shakespeare. Here Austen works a neat double-bluff: this 'real person' attempting to become a fictional character (in order that 'fictional', dramatic things will happen to her) is in any case already a fictional character, as we well know (and have been reminded in the first line). The arch, knowing narrator then tells us that 'when a young lady is to be a heroine, the perverseness of forty surrounding families cannot prevent her. Something must well happen to throw a hero in her way'.[146] Of course it will! This is fiction after all. And something does indeed. Catherine is taken to Bath, where she

meets Henry Tilney, a rich and eligible young man who
lives in Northanger Abbey. The novel continues to follow
the structure of a romantic comedy, and Catherine and
Henry are, after some difficulties, brought together in
marriage. One obstacle to their happy ending is, interestingly, *fiction itself*. Catherine's love of Gothic romances
means that when she goes to stay with Henry's family, she
begins to suspect that Henry's father, Colonel Tilney, killed
his own wife. When the family hear of her suspicions they
are, of course, not amused.

We learn the conventions of the Gothic romance during
a three-page conversation between Henry and Catherine
when they are on their way to Northanger Abbey, which
Catherine fancies will be a tremendously spooky Gothic
mansion. After asking Catherine whether she is '. . .
prepared to encounter all the horrors that a building such
as "what one reads about" may produce?', Henry introduces
us to some of the conventions of the genre.

> But you must be aware that when a young lady is (by
> whatever means) introduced into a dwelling of this kind,
> she is always lodged apart from the rest of the family. While
> they snugly repair to their own end of the house, she is
> formally conducted by Dorothy the ancient housekeeper
> up a different staircase, and along many gloomy passages,
> into an apartment never used since some cousin or kin died
> in it about twenty years before.[147]

This kind of parody is so often metafictional: it is fiction
about fiction, after all.[148] But it is also satirical, and the more

familiar we find Henry's summary of Gothic romance the funnier we will find it. We need to know something about fictional form and basic plots to read this novel, but it helps us along with scenes like the one quoted from above, which more or less functions as a primer for learning about Gothic romance. As well as offering a critique of some of the predictable elements of contemporary fiction, *Northanger Abbey* contains many other metafictional strategies often wrongly termed 'postmodern', including addressing the reader[149] and frame-breaking.[150] Metafiction isn't postmodern at all; it has almost certainly been around as long as fiction has.

The film *Adaptation* tells the story of Charlie Kaufman, a screenwriter who is struggling to adapt *The Orchid Thief* by Susan Orlean. Being 'great, sprawling *New Yorker* stuff',[151] Orlean's book is hard to turn into a conventional screenplay. She has tried to see a rare ghost orchid and has failed. She has attempted to overcome her journalistic objectivity and find passion and has failed. She has become close to her main subject, the orchid thief John Laroche, but the two have never fallen in love. As Charlie Kaufman tells screenwriting guru Robert McKee in a scene later in the film, 'I wanted to present it simply, without big character arcs or sensationalising the story. I wanted to show flowers as God's miracles. I wanted to show that Orlean never saw the blooming ghost orchid. It was about disappointment.' McKee responds to this: 'I see. That's not a movie. You gotta go back, put in the drama.'[152]

Intriguingly, Charlie Kaufman is a real screenwriter, and *Adaptation* is his real adaptation of Susan Orlean's book.

Using a classic metafictional strategy, Kaufman has dram-atised the script's creation within the script itself. The film opens with the character Charlie Kaufman (played by Nicholas Cage) worrying about having no good ideas, being fat, bald and a failure. He has taken the commission to adapt *The Orchid Thief*, but has no inspiration beyond not wanting to 'ruin it by making it a Hollywood thing. You know? Like an orchid heist movie or something, or, y'know, changing the orchids into poppies and turning it into a movie about drug-running, you know?'[153] To make things worse, he has his twin brother Donald staying with him. Donald is working on his own script, called *The 3*. He has been to a seminar given by Robert McKee and believes wholeheartedly in McKee's principles of storytelling. Donald believes his brother to be a genius and asks him for help and advice. But Charlie only ever disapproves of Donald's project, ignoring him completely when he enthuses about Robert McKee ('My genre's thriller. What's yours?'[154]). But this doesn't stop Donald excitedly telling Charlie about his 'Image System', or helpfully posting a copy of McKee's 'Ten Commandments' above both his own and his brother's desk.

We are frequently invited to laugh at Donald. At one point we hear about some good ideas he's been having:

> I'm putting in a chase sequence. So the killer flees on horseback with the girl. Cop's after them on a motorcycle. And it's like a battle between motors and horses. Like tech-nology versus horse.[155]

Part of the humour in this comes from subversion of expectation. We expect Donald to say 'technology versus nature', but instead he finishes with 'horse'. We recognise from this that his understanding of theme and character is not at all sophisticated. But somehow, while Charlie loses Amelia (his love-interest), sweats, worries, masturbates and doesn't finish his script, Donald becomes more popular, gains a girlfriend, does not get stressed and finishes his script. The last straw for Charlie is when his agent takes on Donald's script and sells it for a vast sum of money. Charlie now attends Robert McKee's seminar, but ends up none the wiser. All of his experiences so far have gone into his script, so it has become a self-referential, angst-ridden, intellectual film without very much obvious story. At a particularly low point, Charlie asks his brother to read his script. 'So what would you do?' he asks him. 'Just for fun, how would the great Donald end this script?'[156]

At this point the tone dramatically shifts, and we soon understand we are now in Donald's version of his brother's film. We find that Susan Orlean and John Laroche are embroiled in a drug-fuelled love affair. The drug? It's a luminous green powder processed from the ghost orchid. When Laroche and Orlean find out that Kaufman is onto them, they attempt to kill him. Donald saves him, but is then killed himself. In a ludicrous final scene in the swamps, Laroche is killed by an alligator.

Ultimately, the delicate realist screenplay Charlie dreams of is never realised. It remains as remote as the ghost orchid. As well as being thematically consistent with the book (Orlean never does find passion, never does see the orchid), the whole film works thematically on several other different levels. The 'adaptation' of the title does not just refer to adaptation for screen, but to biological adaptation. Charlie's script mutates, in the hands of his brother, and becomes something more obvious, successful and recognisable; in other words, it becomes something more likely to survive. Those 'in the know' will read it satirically, but this is not always the effect it has. I have shown this film in class a couple of times. Responses vary from 'I liked the second half more than the first half – it had more action' to 'It went a bit stupid and clichéd in the second half'. The film certainly does have complexities that are hard to completely grasp on a first view, but it is worth watching twice to see exactly how it works.

It's not just that this is a script about a script about a script (etc.). The film sets us up to believe that Charlie is superior to Donald, and we therefore expect that his ideas will triumph in the end. Do they, or not? On one level they do not, as Donald takes control of the final section of the film (and, as McKee has told us earlier, 'The last act makes the film. Wow them in the end and you've got a hit.') But then again, this material is clearly highly unsophisticated, and we are invited to laugh at it, as we have laughed at Donald throughout. So Charlie wins after all? Has he shown that his film would have been superior? Well, not exactly. This, after all, *is* his film. Donald's material makes the final cut. In practical terms, a film that contains all the things that Charlie doesn't want to write about – 'sex or guns or car chases . . . Or characters learning profound life lessons. Or growing, or coming to like each other, or overcoming obstacles to succeed in the end'[157] – is, of course, more likely to be commercially successful than one that does not, even if these things are handled ironically. Like *Northanger Abbey*, *Adaptation* allows us all the pleasures of trashy fiction – including the significant metafictional pleasure involved in ripping it to shreds.

Susan Orlean's response to the film is interesting. She says that the screenplay

> . . . has ended up not being a literal adaptation of my book but a spiritual one, something that has captured (and expanded on) the essential character of what the book, I hope, was about: the process of trying to figure out one's self, and life, and love, and the wonders of the world; and the ongoing, exasperating battle between doing what's easy and doing what's good; and the ongoing, exasperating battle between looking at the world ironically and looking at it sentimentally. Oh, and orchids. It is about orchids, about how they adapt to their environment, sometimes resulting in the strangest and most marvellous forms.[158]

What a wonderful idea that a film about orchids can be a film that *behaves* as an orchid does! Just like the orchids featured in the film, *Adaptation* itself is adaptive. It becomes more and more likely to succeed in a cruel and competitive environment. We can see by now I hope that the ironic, satirical, metafictional or playful version of a plot is not a plot that has gone wrong, or might corrupt us, as Christopher Booker seems to imply, but instead is one that can have profound thematic resonance. But in order to be playful writers or readers we must be aware of the shape of traditional plots.

We must also respect the fact that fiction is mysterious. Fiction is paradoxical. Like Catherine Morland, we may think we know everything there is to know about familiar plots, but great fiction uses these plots and still remains unpredictable. Any good theory of basic plots must celebrate the mysteries and paradoxes of storytelling, rather than seek to finally explain it. It should do away with moralistic notions of good versus evil and right versus wrong, and instead adopt a compassionate approach. As we will see in the chapter on character, no one in real life looks into a mirror and sees an antagonist, a 'monster', a 'baddie' or evil. So why should fictional characters be cast in these two-dimensional roles? Why should structures be based on one type of person overcoming another? *Anna Karenina*, undoubtedly one of the greatest novels of all time, has no evil in it at all. There is also no evil in Chekhov's work or in any Jane Austen novel.[159] In these texts, the darkness, if that is even what we want to call it, is often personal and self-inflicted. Everyone is trying to live a good life, even though for Anna Karenina and so many other characters this goes spectacularly wrong. In *A Midsummer Night's Dream*, Oberon is trying to make everything go *right* with his various applications of love-in-idleness. He isn't evil, just careless.

In Katherine Mansfield's story 'Marriage à la Mode' we see a couple, William and Isabel, living more or less apart. She and the children are based in a house by the sea with a bunch of feckless modern artists; William works to pay for it all and visits at weekends. At the end of the story,

William has written Isabel a love letter, which she reads out, laughing, to her friends. Afterwards, she feels terrible.

> Oh, what a loathsome thing to have done. How could she have done it! *God forbid, my darling, that I should be a drag on your happiness.* William! Isabel pressed her face into the pillow. But she felt that even the grave bedroom knew her for what she was, shallow, tinkling, vain.[160]

Isabel has the chance to come of age in this story by deciding to write back to William. But at the last minute she goes swimming with the others instead, resolving to write to William 'Some other time. Later.' Is Isabel evil? Of course not. She is simply making a mistake, as we all do. The mistake is profound. The (subverted) structure in which it is made is well-known.

MORE THAN ONE PLOT

Most novels contain more than one basic plot, if we look hard enough. With 'big' novels, we often don't have to look that hard at all. *Anna Karenina*, as we have observed, very clearly contains a tragedy and a coming-of-age story. If we look closely at it, however, we'll see that it contains other structures as well, or hints of structures. How should we classify the minor narrative concerning Varenka and Sergei, when he decides not to propose to her because of what she says about mushrooms? This scene seems to me to be an example of beautifully wrought modern realism. No one lives happily ever after; everyone is a bit relieved.

If On A Winter's Night A Traveller by Italo Calvino uses many basic plots in partial form. Part of the frustrating pleasure of that novel comes in realising that we don't really need these stories completed, as we know what is likely to happen.

How do we know plot so well? Is it simply because we encounter plots from an early age, perhaps in comforting settings, and grow to love their familiarity? Or are they, as many theorists of basic plots, including Jung, Lévi-Strauss, Joseph Campbell and Northrop Frye, believe, archetypal? Do they really form part of the blueprint of the universe? Is it written into the DNA of the universe that there is a distinction between individuals and groups, that the concepts of the 'gift' and the 'mistake' (among others) are part of physics rather than language? Narrative seems to imply that heterosexual, monogamous relationships are in some way fundamental, but I'm not sure this is true. Evolutionary psychologists and the literary theorists who use their ideas may claim that telling stories is an adaptive behaviour: that we are primed to respond to plot because when we were cave-people we learned all sorts of useful things about woolly mammoths around the campfire and were able to remember this information better because it came in a familiar structure. But it could also be argued that storytelling is maladaptive. Go out and look around a contemporary city and try to decide how useful storytelling is to us now. Does it make us happy or sad? Fat or thin? It certainly makes us get things wrong.[161] And what kinds of stories do we mean anyway?

My sense is that narrative is cultural and historical.

Modern realism is by no means a 'basic plot' in the sense that people have been using its structures for all time. Instead, it is a structure that developed during the early part of the twentieth century, fuelled by, among other things, global warfare, extraordinary technological acceleration and the arrival of hermeneutic reading methods such as 'new criticism' and psychoanalysis. It is essentially modernist. Rags-to-riches plots are also culturally and historically specific; you need economics for rags-to-riches plots just as you need alienation for modern realism. Indeed, far from being fundamental, both these plots can only make sense in established, complex societies with market economies.

Does that mean that there are far fewer than the eight basic plots than I have outlined here? The Brazilian novelist Paulo Coelho has argued that there are only two narratives: 'the voyage of discovery — and a stranger comes to town',[162] and it is certainly possible to see story in this way: either *I go somewhere and things change*, or *someone comes to me and changes things*. Googling 'stranger comes to town' leads to lots of articles based on this idea of there being only two basic plots. But for me this would be a bit like reducing the whole of storytelling to Freud's 'fort da' game. It would mean that we could consider *Anna Karenina* – in which perhaps Vronsky is the stranger who comes to town and Levin is the hero who goes on a journey – without ever having to think about tragedy. But life isn't all merely comings and goings, and we need to know tragedy to understand *Anna Karenina*. And, in fact, if I happened to be looking for the one basic plot that underpins all the others I would not choose either the quest or stranger comes to town. I would choose tragedy. Not everyone goes on a journey, but everyone dies.

My eight basic plots are based on the main fundamental forces for change that we are likely to encounter in our lives. You might go on a journey, or someone might give you a life-changing gift, or you might fall in love, or you might learn something, or you might make a terrible mistake, or someone new might knock at your door one day, or something mysterious might happen, or *nothing* of consequence might happen for a while. I'm not sure there is much else. Notice how all the basic plots (except modern realism) deal with exciting things. Work, reproduction and survival do not, oddly, give structure to most of our stories (although they will, of course, give it content). Clocking in is not enough to begin a story. Hammering away at something all day is not a story. Giving birth begins a life, but it does not begin a story. Cooking a meal is a nice thing to do, but it is not a story. No one is gripped when you begin chopping broccoli. The beginning of a day is also not enough to begin a story. We always want to know: what is so different today that a story may begin? What has changed? Our story structures come from the things that happen to *disrupt* normal life. Things that can go dramatically right or wrong. Things that are in flux. Of course modern realism is the exception here. But what it gives us is *art*. It takes ordinary life and turns it into something beautiful and thought-provoking and often funny. At no time does storytelling ever just give us ordinary life.

My eight basic plots are not definitive. I have provided a table below that summarises the essence of each of them, but this is just one way of organising and understanding narrative. Why not try making up your own scheme?

Structure	Summary	Classic example	Contemporary example
Tragedy	An individual is destroyed by his or her ambition.	*Oedipus the King; Genesis*	*The God of Small Things*
Comedy	Two people overcome obstacles and live happily ever after.	*A Midsummer Night's Dream*	*Eternal Sunshine of the Spotless Mind*
Quest	A group of people led by a hero set off on a journey to accomplish something important.	*The Odyssey; Monkey*	*Final Fantasy VII*
Rags to riches	An individual is transformed by a gift.	*Cinderella; Great Expectations*	*Lourdes*
Coming of age	An individual must become enlightened.	The story of the Buddha	*The Bell Jar*
Stranger comes to town	A community is changed for ever by a visit from a stranger who is then sacrificed.	The New Testament	*The Accidental*
Mystery	An individual must discover the truth.	*The Cave; Oedipus the King*	*The Sense of an Ending*
Modern realism	Art imitates life	*Waiting for Godot*	*The Straight Story*

PART II

PRACTICE

HOW TO HAVE IDEAS

It is bad for the artist to undertake something he doesn't
understand. We have specialists for specialised questions; it
is their function to discuss the peasant commune, the fate
of capitalism, the evil of drink, shoes, women's diseases.
The artist, however, must treat only what he understands;
his sphere is as limited as that of any other specialist's.

Anton Chekhov[163]

What's normal to you is exotic to somebody else.

Jarvis Cocker[164]

When I wrote my first five novels, I had very little idea
what I was doing. I didn't know most of the things that are
in this book. I got through the first three by the skin of my
teeth, hoping that what I lacked in depth I (almost) made
up for in plot, but really knowing that I wasn't writing the
sort of authentic, deep fiction I really loved.[165] I knew that
when I had a good idea there was usually something quirky
or subversive about it, and my next two novels were a bit
better. In *Bright Young Things* I took the well-known narrative of 'clashing stereotypes are stranded on an island and

try to escape' and tried to do something new with it (my 20-something characters, all of whom are very similar, only try half-heartedly to escape, preferring to sit around talking about sex, drugs and the meaning of life). With *Going Out* I took the well-known narrative of *The Wizard of Oz* and used it as the basis for a quest through Britain's flooded B-roads as Luke, who has been allergic to the sun for his whole life, goes in search of a cure. I have always been lucky enough to instinctively understand structure (or at least to realise I do) and I managed to have some success by using a combination of this, my love of the quirky, and much well-fictionalised autobiographical material.[166]

Then the autobiographical material ran out.

Well, OK, it never really runs out. And, of course, you're always gaining more. But I'd written quite a lot about being young and anxious, and the obvious stuff was gone. I needed something else to write about, or at least a new way of writing about being young and anxious.[167] I had a strong sense that for my next novel I wanted to write something big and sprawling and complicated. I wanted to try something really ambitious, something more important, deep and fascinating than I'd written before. And, from somewhere, I had a hunch about how I might do this: I got a big notebook and a pen and sat down and wrote a list of everything I was interested in at that moment, big and small. Then I set myself a challenge: I was to make a meaningful novel out of all those things – *all* of them, mind – and in so doing, work out how they were connected. This is what I wrote:

- Code-breaking
- Marketing
- Crosswords
- A toy company
- Mathematics
- Pirates
- Cellular automata
- Having ideas
- Boats and sailing
- Animal rights
- Veganism
- The Voynich Manuscript
- Cool grandparents
- Anti-capitalism
- Interactive elements (maybe a crossword in the book?)
- World War Two
- Being a teenage girl
- Cricket

This list represents my main interests in 2002, when I began writing the novel. The reason I put 'a toy company' on my list was because I had read somewhere that corporations like Mattel and Hasbro were having real trouble cracking the teenage-girl market. At the time, teenage girls apparently did not buy toys. Boys bought videogames, balls, skateboards and so on, but girls just bought make-up and clothes. I was intrigued by this. And I love a challenge, so I thought, *What would I sell to teenage girls?* What I came up with was an identity necklace that tells people who you are: sort of Facebook on a string (before Facebook). One of the great

things about being a novelist is that you can use your idle
fantasies *for* something. I was never going to really make this
thing; but I could write about someone who did. It was an
idea I could have a character come up with in my novel. So
there'd be a toy company, and they'd arrange a 'thought camp'
(another weird thing I'd read about) in which their brightest
young talents would be given the challenge of coming up
with an idea for a toy for teenage girls. Someone would come
up with the necklace idea. I knew this person would end up
abandoning the idea, because she would realise that she didn't
really believe in exploitative marketing to teenagers.

But that on its own would make a very thin novel. So I
began trying to work in my other elements. I had a feeling
that it was really worth pushing hard with this, and that
the elements that didn't seem to fall naturally into the story
would be the most fruitful ones, both in narrative terms
and thematically. All the stuff I'd written down had been
floating around in my mind after all; it wasn't random. I
had the feeling that it *did* connect. At that stage I still didn't
quite know what my book was really about, but I hoped I
would find meaning in the connections. In the end, plotting
the novel felt like completing a cryptic crossword. But in
working like this I found I *was* able to make connections I
hadn't anticipated, and fictionalise a lot of my own interests
and experiences. Writing itself felt like an adventure, full of
interesting things to be discovered. At no point did I have
the feeling that I already knew the answer to some question
and here I was writing it up. The writing was the formulation of the question.

The resulting novel, *PopCo*, has as its protagonist Alice

Butler, who has been brought up by her mathematician grandparents (one of whom was a code-breaker at Bletchley Park in the Second World War). In the backstory, there is mathematics, cryptanalysis and pirate treasure. As a child, Alice was given a necklace with a code on it that would lead her to the treasure, if she knew its solution. But she's never found the solution, and now works for PopCo, a toy company. Alice has been selected for the 'thought camp' on Dartmoor, where, unknown to her, vegan anti-capitalists are plotting to take over the world (in a good way!). Alice eventually comes of age and has a political awakening. The novel is full of interactive elements: readers can learn a lot about secret codes, mathematics and ideation. There is indeed a crossword at the end of the book. And, in later editions, a solution to the puzzle of the code on Alice's necklace.

It didn't come together easily or quickly, but it did come together. I was able to make thematic links between, for example, capitalism, mathematics and piracy, which fascinated me; I also explored contemporary marketing practices by focusing on teenage girls' experiences of them (which I have shared). I also found that I wanted to write something about compassion. In 2003 I had become a vegan and this led me to reconsider many philosophical questions that exist around animal rights. Creating a resistance movement based on compassion allowed me to dramatise some of these questions. I also wanted to explore in some detail the ridiculous things that creative industries do in the name of making money. I'd even heard of fast-food companies commissioning extensive studies on the psychology of queuing, and the most effective ways to organise queues so that people bought more stuff.

My strange list had proved fruitful, and while *PopCo* might not be a perfect novel, I learned an awful lot from writing it.

While I was researching the concept of ideation (idea-generation), I came across the concept of the creative matrix. In *PopCo* I show how such a matrix could be used to create a new concept for a toy:

There is a five-columned matrix on the desk in front of me. This is what it says:

Product Category	Special Powers	Theme	Kid Word	Random Word
Ball	*Lights up*	Pirates	*Cool*	Round
Board game	*Explodes*	Witches/ghosts	*Clever*	Lawn
Wheels (bike, skateboard etc.)	*Floats*	Wilderness	*Scary*	Mountain
Doll	*Big*	Saving the world	*Silly*	Elves
Videogame	*Small*	Animals/fish/environment	*Mysterious*	Complex
Building kit	*Invisible*	Outer space/UFOs	*Gross*	Serpent
Activity set	*Fast*	Martial arts	*Special*	Extinct
Plush/soft	*'Real'*	Acquiring/collecting	*Cute*	Bubble
Robot	*Shows emotion*	Mastery	*Grown up*	Armour

Everyone else has roughly the same thing in front of them, as this matrix is what we have been making all afternoon, with a facilitator called Ned. Most of the columns have been created by us all just shouting ideas out as they have come to us but now we have been left on our own to finish compiling the random word columns individually [. . .] With Ned, we are 'recapping' the process of compiling matrices, most of us having done it before, and adding this new thing: the random words column, which is pretty new to most of us.

The notion of randomness is a big part of any kind of lateral/creative thinking. It's all connected to that idea that you can't really trust your brain, that any ideas you have on your own may well turn out to be simply bad ideas or just ones that aren't at all original. Just as routine kills creative thought, so too apparently does, well, thought itself. Our brains are just not wired up to be original on their own. But with this thing called 'Random Juxtaposition' (an idea of Edward de Bono's, of course), well, you can have many good ideas.[168]

As may be clear from this, my intention when I began investigating ideation was to satirise its techniques. I wanted the process to seem silly and pointless and perhaps also faintly sinister. And I think in *PopCo* it does, to some extent. However, when I drew up this fictional matrix I found it surprisingly easy to use to create Alice's ideas for new toys. Or, at least, it was a great deal easier that just trying to get my brain to come up with 'several ideas for new toys' on its own. Perhaps routine does kill creative thought; perhaps PopCo wasn't wrong about everything. Here's Alice's description of what she does with her matrix:

What you do with a matrix is as follows: you write the columns out, as I have done, and then you take one thing from each column until you have made an entirely new thing. For example, you could have a small ball that is connected with mastery and is perceived as special. So this could be a brand where each ball is unique, perhaps with its own signature pattern or design (like Cabbage Patch Dolls, which each came with a unique 'Adoption Certificate'). Using mastery, you would be able to learn tricks with the ball, and perhaps take part in regional or 'street' competitions. If we add a word from the random column we could take, for example, 'complex' and make this product complicated and challenging to learn. This would fit in with children's desire to be special, to learn special (secret?) skills and 'be the best'. This product would also have collecting/trading appeal because of the uniqueness of each ball. Perhaps kids could be encouraged to buy the whole set of a particular theme (sea, space, monsters etc.). You wouldn't know which type of ball you were getting when you bought it and then you may want to swap. To further encourage kids to buy more than one ball, there would also be multi-ball tricks that could be learnt.

Or what about a 'Snake Board': a skateboard that is 'real', connected with animals and the words 'silly' and 'serpent'? This would be a product for 9–12 year old boys and would be sold in the form of a 'create-your-own' kit. The 'real' factor is the wood and wheels and so on, which the kid can put together in various ways. Each Snake Board kit can take on the shape and character of different types of snake.

There'd be the Python, the Adder and so on. The 'silly' factor could be achieved by having things like 'wobbly wheels', 'crazy eyes' and 'killer tongues' as features that could be added to the board. Perhaps the boards could also shoot 'venom' when you stamp on a foot pedal?

What about a building set that shows emotion, is connected to the environment and the word 'cute'? This would be something like Meccano (a product that makes all toy creatives, engineers and architects go a bit misty-eyed due to the fact that everyone learned to build things with it and it isn't made any more). However, when you build things with it, it becomes 'happy' or 'sad' depending on certain factors. A wall without windows would be 'sad', perhaps? Or the building material would become sad about things that are bad for the environment? I'm not sure this is feasible – it's a bit too AI – and sounds altogether too educational. Still, a building set with 'cute' features would work – definitely for girls. I add the random word 'elves' and spend the next fifteen minutes working out a product with which girls could build miniature elf dwellings, shops, and, in theory, whole towns, which they would then put in their gardens. Like bird tables – but for magical creatures! At the point when I catch myself thinking, *How would you know if the magical creatures had visited or not?* I give this up and start doodling instead.[169]

It turns out that our imaginations are very good at doing new things with specific material we give them. But they are not so good at coming up with new material on their own. When you ask your imagination to come up with 'a story' it either won't do it, or it will come up with something too familiar and predictable: something full of stereotypical characters and soap-opera scenarios; or pure autobiography. To predict is, after all, to imagine. Is it any wonder that unguided imagination leads to predictability? My teaching job means that I encounter students' ideas all the time: some good, others not so good. The best ones always involve the student using his or her own experience, ideas and feelings in an innovative way. They don't just write down what has happened to them, but they spread their experiences, ideas and feelings around various characters, work in any philosophical ideas they have, along with their hobbies and interests and unique world-view. They work a bit like I did when planning *PopCo*, with all that crazy and unique *stuff* from their heads, but rearranged a bit. There are some, but not many, people who can do this without sitting down with a pencil and a piece of paper and making the actual list. It's a bit like anagrams: yes, there are some crazy geniuses who can do them in their heads; but I (and perhaps you) need to write the letters down and look at them to solve the puzzle.

It wasn't long before I realised that the way I'd come up with the idea for *PopCo* in the first place – challenging myself to include all items from a list I'd written down – wasn't that different from the way I had Alice work with her matrix. Using a matrix essentially mimics the process of good fictionalisation. You take the things you know, the experiences you've had and the ideas that interest you and make a narrative by combining them in new ways. This is, after all, how great fiction must always have been written.

This method forces us out of predictability (what we simply 'imagine' might happen), but keeps us grounded in what really matters to us (and what has emotional truth for us). It has integrity. Unless we are foolish, we are not doing this primarily to make money (as poor Alice is). We are doing it to find an innovative, truthful and entertaining way of examining the world.

Over the years I have experimented with using various sorts of matrices in my teaching. All of them ask students to ransack their own minds for things like 'problems you have faced' and 'your current obsessions'. My latest ones also include a question-and-answer section that asks people to reflect on their views on relationships, religion, culture and philosophy. Most literary novels do present some sort of 'world-view', and it is important that people work out a rough idea of their own before they begin, even if all it amounts to is the reason they don't have one.[170] The matrix that I've included in this book (see Appendix One) is the one I use with MA students. I use it because I need to get people up-and-running with an idea quickly so that we can get on with thinking about plotting, characterisation, sentence-level writing and all the other complexities that we need to cover in only ten weeks. Often, I get the students to bring their completed matrix to class and then give them as few as fifteen minutes to come up with a plot. I am amazed that in this situation people almost always come up with something really good. Something you could imagine seeing in a bookshop and wanting to read. Something an agent wouldn't immediately delete from his or her inbox because it's so boring, familiar and could be written by anybody.[171]

Something a bit real and a bit wacky all at once. It's a shame that a few students abandon such ideas for the teen horror novel they were writing before they came on the course. But most people find they can do great things with their matrixes.

At the University of Kent, our technology has improved to the extent that I can now get students to upload their completed matrixes to the course website before the first class so I can see who they are and what kinds of interests they have. No one else can see the matrixes, just me. As a result, the students are very honest. Shockingly so. And I feel like something of an anthropologist, looking at all this data. I've discovered that *everyone* worries about death, not just me. Ninety per cent of women worry about their weight and/or appearance, not just me. Most people worry about their family, not just me. There are plenty of universals out there. On relationships, however, people split. There are people (like me) who think relationships are of crucial importance in life, and couldn't imagine not having, or wanting, a partner. But a surprising amount of people believe that relationships in fact 'hold you back'. This is great! If someone genuinely believes this, I want to read about it. For me, this idea is exotic. When I read a novel, I like it to deal with universals, but I also want it to be a bit exotic. I want to experience a different worldview from my own. If you think about it, you probably feel this way too. When you're using your own matrix for working out an idea, the key is to focus on the more strange, distinctive or quirky things on there, at least to begin with. The problem with this is that to you everything will seem normal and not strange at all. But imagine that someone else was looking at it. What three things would they pick out? What three things do you have on your matrix that they are unlikely to have on theirs?

At the beginning of term I ask the students to swap matrixes (for this I get them to do smaller, less potentially embarrassing versions) and plot each other's stories. I thought this was quite a bad idea until I tried it, but it's actually quite useful. For one thing, people realise how interesting their material is when someone else looks at it, and they get some sense of the particular things that are exciting to another person. They get an objective view of it. But they also usually realise what a bad job we tend to make of working with someone else's material, because we don't know it well enough. When we plot someone else's material we have to make all sorts of assumptions about it. It can often turn quickly into soap opera, or just feel 'wrong'. When I was researching *PopCo* I read a book about resistance fighters in the Second World War who were to be dropped behind enemy lines and pretend to be French. In order to do this convincingly, they had to have intensive training. They even had to have their dental work changed, because English dentistry would give them away. They also had to remember to look right rather than left when crossing the road, and many other things. If you work with material you know, you won't have to spend a lot of time on your characters' dentistry – or equivalents – to make them believable; they just will be. And you can therefore spend more time on the important parts of writing: making it beautiful, and making it meaningful.

In order to show you how to use a matrix to have an

idea for a novel (or a story) I have completed two of my
own (to be found in Appendix Two). I know from experience that trying to create a fictional 'dummy' matrix with
a made-up character does not work. The matrix has to be
completed honestly by one individual. What you find is that
matrixes come out differently at different times. Most
people have much more material than will fit on one; and
of course we forget things, too. Anyway, I have filled in one
as I imagine my 18-year-old self may have done it, and one
as I am today. As soon as I did it, I realised that today's
one would probably have come out a bit differently had I
done it yesterday, or three weeks ago, or in a different mood.
I also find I am more comfortable being honest about my
18-year-old self (because she's long gone) and less so about
myself today. If you find yours doesn't work very well, do
try doing it again. Remember that you are not publishing
the raw version in a book like I am so you can be as honest
as you like. You might like to do a new one each time you
want to write something creative. You may find that eventually you don't need to use this technique any more,
because your brain has become more used to putting things
together creatively. But for now remember that while doing
things in your head seems impressive if someone is watching,
no one is watching.

So let's begin by looking at my matrix from 1991. The
first thing to do with a matrix is to look at the whole as
objectively as possible. Are there any interesting things to
note immediately? What are the themes of the novel likely
to be? Here I immediately notice that we have a young
white girl who is immersed in elements of black culture.

Not totally – but it's something this person definitely knows about. But this doesn't mean that the novel she should write will be about black culture because she 'knows it'. She doesn't really know it; she knows what it's like to hang around the edges of it, wishing she had an identity as fixed as 'being black'. After a lot of soul-searching, this person would need to write about *this* experience. Going back to the matrix we can see that this 18-year-old wants to impress people, but she also wants to be authentic. There's some good potential tension there, and I wonder whether this will be a novel that explores authenticity in some way. This also goes with the theme of white girl who (sort of) wants to be black. Another thing that I immediately notice is that this is someone who has had a complicated life, with all kinds of family disruption. Could this be a novel about family?

Next: what are the individual items on the matrix that are the most quirky and unusual? (On your own matrix they may seem completely normal or even dull. If you can't get beyond this you may need to get a friend to help you look at it.) I'd immediately pull out of this one the dreadlocks, the cricket club and the market stall. These are items I'd definitely like to have in the novel. I also like the idea of someone having a memory for numbers, and the concept of a perfect circle. Being an architectural assistant is also fascinating but I happen to know I've already written a short story about this.

There are several options with a matrix like this. But the simplest thing is to pick one (semi-random) item from each column and create a simple storyline as you go along.

To do this, take a character name and start to build a storyline for the person by working across the matrix. Remember that you are creating fiction, and so try not to select things that simply add up to 'real life' for you or a friend. For example, from my matrix we might come up with Abby, who is working at Chelmsford County Cricket Club when the West Indies are on tour in the UK (although I don't have this exact detail on my matrix, they did tour when I was working at the cricket club in 1991). She falls in love with a black politics student, Eliot, who is obsessed with cricket, and supports the West Indies. She knows nothing about cricket but tries to learn from Bob, the man in charge of the score-board at the cricket club. He gives her knowledge in return for cups of tea and pieces of cake, perhaps. None of this is set in stone; it's just brain-storming. And you will come up with lots of elements that work as variables that will need to be refined further. But from a basic idea you can start to build something. Don't assume that you necessarily need lots more characters; and don't become too restricted by your matrix. In a big, complicated novel you might use every element on it; but you won't usually. You'll also use an awful lot of material that you didn't think to write down (like the detail about the West Indies tour). That's fine. You'll also reject most ideas you have at this stage; that's fine too. In fact, ideally you will have rejected around 20 ideas, or details, for every one you eventually use.

At this stage you can also consider what type of plot you might use, but without completely committing to anything. For example, the cricket idea above could easily be written as a romantic comedy (perhaps the obstacles are to do with the mixed-race relationship between Abby and Eliot). It could take the form of stranger comes to town (perhaps with the West Indies cricket team functioning as the strangers who somehow manage to change everything in the small community of the cricket club). It could certainly be a coming-of-age novel, where Abby learns about cricket, and, at the same time, about herself. Perhaps her love for Eliot is unrequited. Keep these kinds of thoughts in the back of your mind while you try out different ideas. You don't want to be too controlled by structure at this stage, but knowing about various basic plots (as outlined in the previous chapter) can help you to see where your idea might go and what you think about that.

If you want to build up more storylines (and usually you will need more than one, unless you are writing short fiction), you repeat this process of picking a character name and then 'giving' this person things from your matrix as their own. In the idea above, I'd certainly have to distribute some more things from my matrix between Eliot and Bob. Eliot already has 'student' and 'political knowledge'. Perhaps he is also French. He could work on a market stall. He may have grown up in Barking. He may be really good at cooking. Bob might be an ex-architect whose wife has just died. There are two things to remember here. First of all, you should try to connect things on your matrix in a way that is *different* from the way things were connected in real life. For example, in real life the person I knew who wanted to smuggle drugs to Jamaica wasn't a close friend at all. But in the story she could be a sister, a best friend, a man or anything. She might want to smuggle drugs to anywhere. Or she may actually be smuggling exotic pets or plants (although I'd then have to know something about exotic pets or plants). The second thing is to make sure you build up links with the first character you thought of. How do your characters meet one another? And how do their lives become connected? Where is the drama?

So in an entirely different plot we may have Clare, who lives in Chelmsford. She is a student who works in her spare time as a waitress. She's obsessed with creating dreadlocks and spending as much time as possible at the local reggae club, trying to impress the DJs with her knowledge of dancehall music. Her sister Abby is depressed after her botched abortion, but Clare finds she is too busy learning about dancehall to be of much help to her. Clare's friends are Kaia and Charlie. Kaia wants to become a chef, but her washed-up Rasta father desperately wants her to do law or politics and 'better herself'. Kaia's white stepfather is an architect who is obsessed with cricket, and particularly the 1991 West Indies tour (see how this has become a useful detail?). Charlie runs a market stall selling alternative/political badges, t-shirts and so on. His mother has cancer, and he is her main carer. He wants to be a rapper, but he has too many responsibilities to be able to really do it properly. While he and Clare help each other rub beeswax into their hair, Kaia begins trying to straighten hers. Kaia then becomes involved with a seemingly glamorous drug dealer, Josh, who persuades her first to take cocaine to his brother who is in prison, and then to smuggle cocaine to Jamaica. At the last minute she realises she can't do it, but she's already swallowed several of the packages. Clare has to decide whether to take her to hospital or not. And so on. (What happens to Charlie's mother? What does Josh do when he finds out? With a plot like this there will be lots of questions, and lots of decisions to make.)

This is the kind of thing you should end up with if you use a matrix properly. It's a bit of a mess, and will probably change entirely as you begin writing, and ideally even before you begin. Indeed, I have resisted the urge to tidy it up too much at this point, so you can see how the raw material might look before it is shaped. The way it looks at the moment, it could be written as a coming-of-age story, modern realism or tragedy. Kaia doesn't have to be rescued; she could die during her drug-smuggling attempt. But you'd need to think how realistic that would be for this character. Clearly people do die smuggling drugs. But has this ever happened to anyone you know? Is it likely to happen to you? The answers to these questions will give you some sense of your emotional truth here. I know that if I were in Kaia's situation I would never be able to swallow the cocaine. Or if I did, I'd maybe manage one or two packages and then wonder what the hell I was doing.

I'll never forget actually seeing my friend preparing to do this and feeling very shocked, even though I didn't say anything and instead pretended I saw things like that all the time. I think at that point I longed to be at home eating toast and Marmite, laughing with my mum and stroking one of our cats. This was my emotional truth inside that scene. Remember to consider what the emotional truth of any situation is likely to be for you. What would your characters (who are all going to be a bit like you) *really* feel, and what would they *really* do? In this exact situation, if you were this exact character, what would you do? The main thing at this stage is that you have characters you recognise, in settings you know well, doing things you understand, and things that you would also do in their situation. There will be more on this in the chapter on characterisation.

If you don't like the first idea you come up with, try it an entirely different way. Again, don't let the most obviously dramatic elements on the matrix guide you (teen pregnancies; drugs etc.). You can also do more subtle things with your material and create great tension and depth from less extravagant situations and moments. So a different plot from the same matrix might be this: Clare has been expelled from boarding school for sneaking out in the middle of the night. The head teacher was convinced she was meeting a boy, but she was actually going to feed a hedgehog. (Is this too sentimental? Unbelievable? Remember that you are just brainstorming but do evaluate your material as you go along and work out which bits might need to be changed. Basically, however, we can see here that Clare needs to be expelled for something 'light'.) She can't restart her A-levels for another year. So back in Chelmsford she has to get a job, but she doesn't know anyone. She develops a crush on Pepper, the ethereal girl with dreadlocks who sells clothes on a market stall every Saturday, but can never get up the courage to talk to her. Clare wants to *be* Pepper. She thinks everything would be great if she were exactly like her, so she starts creating her own dreadlocks.

She gets a job working in an old-fashioned video shop and amuses the owner, Bob, by only ever watching cookery programmes because she hates war and violence. Bob is obsessed with the videogame *Streetfighter II*, and holds tournaments in the back room every Friday night. One night Pepper comes along and wins. She and Clare get talking and become friends. Clare finds out Pepper's life history. She was a brilliant politics student who dropped out after her best friend died while trying to smuggle cocaine to Jamaica. Meanwhile, Bob's world is shattered when Eliot turns up. Eliot is his long-lost son from Cambridge. Eliot is a very geeky but good-looking mathematics student. He has always been a completely authentic person: he is what he is. But his mother has just died and he's very confused by finding out that his father back home isn't his real father. He starts to go off the rails. This seems as if it's going to be a coming-of-age story, but it doesn't have to be. It could be a quirky mystery. Perhaps someone is stealing horror films from the video shop and Clare, Pepper and Eliot have to come together to find out who it is. Or Eliot could be re-cast as the stranger who comes to town. Or perhaps this is a romantic comedy in which Clare thinks she loves Pepper, Pepper really loves Bob and Eliot really loves Clare.

When I work with people on their matrixes, I often pick

out one or two things to ask questions about. It's interesting to see how people talk about the elements from their matrixes, and it's also very useful to crack open the general to get the specifics out. Recently I asked a student what it was like working as a lawyer on the trading floor of an investment bank (her current job). What she told me was the basis for a novel in itself. Here, if my 1991 matrix belonged to someone else, I'd ask about the racism column. Why does this person worry about racism if she is white? I'd discover that her stepfather is black and her brother is mixed-race and I'd tell her that I wanted to read about *that* experience – of being a white person in a mixed-race family. She might tell me that it's not just that – she is an outsider in many respects. She feels that she doesn't fit in anywhere. I'd reassure her that all writers feel this in some way (just as all writers seem to go through periods of struggling with depression, anxiety and self-doubt). How could her novel include something of this feeling (without becoming directly autobiographical)?

I'd also ask about her terrible taste in books. OK, *The Temple of My Familiar* is a good novel. But Jackie Collins and Lucy Irvine? And Choose Your Own Adventures? Then again, even this is revealing. This is a person who likes fairly easy books. She has been so caught up in the drama of life that she hasn't yet begun to read challenging or classic fiction, and she's actually scared of it. She has, however, tried to read plays by Samuel Beckett and Edward Albee, and likes the strange conversational rhythms of absurd drama. She also likes gritty realism, and lots of explicit detail. This could work well in her novel and I'd certainly encourage her to be as graphic as possible. I'd definitely put her on a reading diet (I'd suggest beginning with *The Bell Jar*). But I might just suggest that she think about structuring her novel as a Choose Your Own Adventure . . .

The truth is that I did try to write a novel when I was eighteen. It didn't have any of the elements from my matrix in it (except that it was in fact a Choose Your Own Adventure). It was called *A Mercy Killing* and was a graphically violent Marxist feminist novel all about over-throwing the patriarchy and getting men to do the washing-up. Even though I'd experienced real sexism in all my part-time jobs, and I could have written interestingly about, say, running the players' restaurant at the cricket ground, where the boss kept telling me, cryptically, that tables 'are for rissoles not arseholes' and the players often asked me to sit on their laps, I let the material control me. So I automatically began writing about a housewife much older than I was (as if sexism never happened to anyone apart from 'housewives'), and her very stereotypically male husband. I was just replicating the cultural myth that the theme 'sexism' has to be encountered in a domestic setting, between a husband and wife, where she is a doormat and he is brutish and violent. I wasn't doing anything new with this idea at all. My characters were predictable and one-dimensional.

Why on earth did I do that when I had all this rich material of my own? I didn't actually know any brutish and violent men; at the time, most of my parents' male friends were trying hard (and often failing) to be feminists.

That would have been much more interesting to write about because it would have been true. It would not have been literally true, because I would have fictionalised it. But it would have had emotional truth. It would have been authentic (and probably funny, too). In my novel I had the woman murder the man in various graphically violent ways (it was a Choose Your Own Adventure, remember, so in theory he could die in different ways) because he wouldn't do the washing-up. But, in real life, do people *actually* murder their husbands because they are pissed off about the washing-up? I imagine more men get killed by wild animals each year than by women pissed off about the washing-up. Outside TV drama, this stuff just doesn't really happen. There is so much more drama in a really bitter, authentic row than there is in a completely unbelievable murder. So be very careful not to let your material control you. Keep asking yourself what would *really* happen in this situation, not what would happen if this were a scenario on *Columbo* or *Coronation Street*. And be true to yourself, and what you have learned and not yet learned from experience.

When I was about sixteen I had this idea that I could get a flat of my own and live independently. My parents told me not to be so silly; that I didn't realise all the hidden costs of living, because I'd never actually had to pay a gas bill or shop for loo roll. They were right, of course, but I had no way of knowing this until I'd lived it myself. It took me years to be able to live it myself, because I never quite had the money to set myself up. And in fact my first experiences of living away from home were with other people's parents. So imagine me, only two years later (and still living with my own parents), trying to write my domestic drama about a husband and a wife who presumably did between them work out how to buy loo roll and put the rubbish out. I really didn't have a clue. Having good ideas means being able to make decisions about what you can and can't write about. Often you can find a more authentic angle on something that means you don't have to abandon an inauthentic idea entirely. Say you want to explore aging, but you're only 21. You'd ideally like to have an elderly protagonist, but know you'd never be able to pull this off. But aging must matter to a 21-year-old, or you wouldn't be interested in it. Perhaps this is a novel about a 21-year-old who is particularly concerned about aging, despite being young; or perhaps this 21-year-old has some grandparents, or even an aging pet, and you decide to write about his or her relationship with them.

I have included a matrix I completed in 2011 so that you can see just how different an older person's matrix is from a younger person's – even when, as in my case, they are the same person. I originally planned to show you some examples of plots from the 2011 matrix, but, however I tried it, it kept turning into the novel I'm writing now – despite me trying to keep many of its obvious elements off the matrix. I guess that just goes to show: when you have an idea burning in you, *nothing* is going to distract you from it. Anyway, for now note how different the 2011 matrix is. My reading has improved at last, and I've experienced some of the big things in life: death, addiction, relationship breakdown and so on. Potentially, I have a lot more to write about than the 18-year-old; but this also means I'll need to make some choices. I probably won't fit everything in. But wouldn't it be great if I could . . . ?

Older people may well find their matrix potentially contains a huge novel like *Middlemarch, Great Expectations* or *Anna Karenina*. If that happens to you, it's great; but it can be daunting for a first-time novelist to try to write on this scale. Don't be afraid to use one main strong storyline and either ignore some of the details on your matrix, or incorporate them quite subtly. Know the strengths given to you by your age and experience. The younger novelist can show the teenager at the centre of the family row: exactly what she is thinking and feeling and doing and just how angry and misunderstood she is and why. The older novelist may well be able to show authentically what almost everyone is thinking and feeling in this row. Thoughtful older people who have spent many hours in this kind of combat (as parents, lovers, children and so on) can really get deeply into these scenes. But the 18-year-old may simply toss her hair, leave the room and move on to a different scene. Both approaches are of course fine. But know yourself, and know what you can write. Completing a matrix for some past version of yourself is also a very fruitful way of coming up with ideas, especially for the backstories of characters, although I'm not quite sure if I'd be able to do my 18-year-old self justice now. But completing a matrix that represents who you were two or three years ago may be a great help.

If using a matrix doesn't appeal to you, then just make a list, as I did with *PopCo*. Or perhaps you already have an idea that you plan to work on, like many of my students do. However you get to your initial idea, be honest with yourself about it. Is it a good idea or a bad idea? Bad ideas include those that you feel you 'have' to write for some reason, perhaps because you promised someone else you'd tell their life story, or because you feel obligated to an idea in some other way. Good writing is not what you do under duress, feeling guilty, because you have made a promise (to yourself or someone else). If your old ideas were any good you'd have written them by now. Abandon them, or incorporate them into a matrix, and see what happens now, today.

How do you know when your idea is a good one? Well, when you can't stop thinking about it. When you go over and over the characters in your mind. When you are desperate to begin writing. When you find yourself getting up at 5 a.m. (or staying up until 3 a.m.) to work more on your idea, or even to begin writing it, even though you've never done this before. When you love your characters and want to spend as much time with them as possible. If writing feels to you like a job or a chore, then your idea isn't good enough. It's as simple as that. If you are not in love with your idea now, then you never will be. So dump it and find a new one. I know that many of you will be panicking at this point because you don't think you have anything 'exotic' or special or interesting in your life and you find it hard to imagine any idea *really* exciting you. All I can say is that everyone thinks that. Just do your matrix and see what comes out. See if you can find a way to connect the material that excites you, even if you don't believe the material to be exciting on its own. That's the key to a good idea.

STYLES OF NARRATION

In watching effects, if only of an electric battery, it is often necessary to change our place and examine a particular mixture or group at some distance from the point where the movement we are interested in was set up. The group I am moving towards is at Caleb Garth's breakfast table . . .

George Eliot, *Middlemarch*[172]

So now you have an idea for a story, how are you going to tell it? Who is going to be the narrator? What style of narration are you going to use? Are you going to use a third-person, past-tense narration (Lucy walked down the hill)? A first-person, present-tense narration (I walk down the hill)? Or some other combination? *The Bell Jar* is written in first person, past tense, as are *Great Expectations* and *The Great Gatsby*. *Middlemarch* is written in the third person, past tense, as is *Emma* and *The God of Small Things*. *The Accidental* is written in third person, present tense, as are my novels *Bright Young Things* and *Going Out*. David Mitchell's *number9dream* is entirely narrated in first person, present tense – even the long flashbacks. I also used first person, present tense in my novels *PopCo* and *The End of Mr. Y*. Some novels and stories use more than one form of narration. *Bleak House* has two main sections running parallel to one another: one is told in first person, past tense, and the other in third person, present tense. *Cloud Atlas* by David Mitchell has six distinct narrators. Every single writer who begins a novel or story eventually finds some workable combination(s) of tense and perspective. Ideally, they do not do this without giving it some thought. Or to impress their teacher.

I have an embarrassing confession to make: I used to make all my students write in the first person. I was generous enough to let them decide whether this would be in the present or past tense but many of them chose the present tense anyway, perhaps thinking this was the correct thing to do. What did I happen to write in at the time? That's right: first person, present tense. I even got into an interesting debate with Philip Pullman about use of the present tense.[173] Why was I so sure students should use first person? Well, I wanted them to get good marks, and we marked high for authenticity. It is surely easier to be authentic if you write in first person than it is in third person, right? Well, yes, often it is. Unfortunately, it's also easy in first person, and especially if you use present tense, to over-narrate, to over-explain, to tell rather than show and to lose sight of your structure. And you don't necessarily get marks for authenticity if you decide to make your first-person narrator a serial killer. Or a unicorn. Nowadays I'm not at all strict about how my students choose to narrate their fiction. And I've drifted out of first person, present tense (the style of the young?) and towards a more mature free, indirect style, which has perhaps made me more mellow.

The only thing I demand now is that people think hard about the choices they make with narration. First person, present tense is fine. Third person, past tense is fine. But why have you chosen this combination? Have you tried it other ways, to be sure? And have you taken into account all the other aspects of narrative style and worked out how you will treat time, for example? As with so many things, there is a kind of dreary consensus about narrative style that says it doesn't really matter, and that all we are doing is *telling* a story, not creating it. You might not begin with *Once upon a time* exactly, but you might begin with something like 'Amanda woke up sweating' without even realising that in writing this you have already made at least two major choices regarding narrative style. You have chosen third person and past tense (unless of course this is being narrated by Amanda's partner, in which case you've chosen first person, past tense).[174]

When I started writing, at the beginning of a project all I would do was choose a grammatical person[175] and a tense from a chart in my head and then begin. This is what the chart in my head looked like:

First person	Past tense
Second person	Present tense
Third person	Future tense

So I'd pick one thing from the first column and one thing from the second column and get on with it. Most people (apart from Italo Calvino in *If On A Winter's Night A Traveller*) don't use the second person successfully, at least not in a genuine way, but I wanted to have it in my chart because it existed and was possible.[176] And I did end up using it, sort of, in *The End of Mr. Y*. Similarly with the future tense: I wanted to have eliminated it consciously, not just unconsciously ruled it out because it's weird. I like this chart, because in some way it seems to contain the whole universe: there's me, you and everyone else; there's the past, the present and the future. Until we discover other dimensions of time and being, all narrative – and all of life – must happen within these coordinates.

When I first started writing, I felt that for every new project there were only three narrative possibilities: first person, present tense; first person, past tense; and third person, present tense. At that time I had some strange moral objection to third person, past tense, because I thought it was 'traditional' and conservative: the language of the 'dead white male'. I was wrong, as we will see. For a long time I didn't really consider first person, past tense either because I'd used it for my crime novels and therefore thought it was cursed somehow. After writing *Bright Young Things* (which was in third person, present tense) I'd also come to the conclusion that present tense was my 'special' tense: it was what I wrote best in. So basically, for me, for a long time, the choice came down simply to first person or third person, as I knew I'd be writing in present tense. I changed from this (to first person, past tense) only for *Our Tragic Universe*.

If you know you are better at one narrative style than

another, and if your writing 'just flows' in past tense, for example, but 'looks wrong' or 'feels weird' or is hard to sustain in present tense, then stick to what you're good at, at least for now. I've had students who write wonderfully in, say, first person, past tense, then get to their all-important third year and suddenly declare that they are going to 'try' multiple narrators and present tense. When I ask them why, they say they think they should be challenging themselves. They say they think it shouldn't be this easy. If you are lucky enough to have 'found your voice', stick to it for at least a couple of novels (or at least until the end of your degree programme). Refine it; push it to its limits; see what it's capable of. Abandoning your voice because you think you relish a challenge is like throwing out your best outfit because you think it'll be interesting to try to look just as good in something else. Being a writer doesn't mean being able to competently (re)produce every kind of style there is. It means being brilliant at your own style. But you also need to recognise when you are sticking to a style that does not suit you, and that is not helping produce your natural voice.

In many ways it seems as if all you have to do is choose a grammatical person and a tense to go with it and start writing. It's certainly what I used to do (and still do, to some extent). You might like the sound of first person, past tense because you enjoyed *Great Expectations* and *The Bell Jar*. You might always work in third person, past tense and so that's what you're going to continue with now. But there is one more question to answer before you can really begin: *Who is actually going to tell the story?* Again, we need to watch out for the unspoken consensus that says that in a first-person narration the protagonist must tell the story and that in a third-person narration the person telling the story is definitely the author – or even God. It's not that simple. In fact, it's so complicated that by the time you've finished answering the question of who tells your story, you will have decided on an entire narrative style.

It might seem 'obvious' that you should choose your protagonist as your first-person narrator if he or she is a detective solving a crime (unless of course he is Sherlock Holmes, who is far too wrapped up in himself and his latest research to bother writing down what he does but luckily has someone to write everything down for him), or someone coming of age (unless they are just too unreliable to see what is happening to them). But what if you're writing a stranger-comes-to-town plot? Convention suggests that while the stranger is a central figure in this type of plot, he or she rarely narrates it. Or what if the main character dies? Can they still narrate? It's unlikely, but still faintly possible. The question of narration is complex enough with just one main character, but what if there are several? Should you use multiple first-person narrators? Should you go omniscient? Or will your writing gain focus from being restricted to the consciousnesses of just one or two of these characters? In fact, now we're thinking about it, what on earth does it mean to 'restrict' the telling of a story to one consciousness or other? When it comes down to choosing a narrator, suddenly narrative style becomes much more complicated and also much more interesting.

Often, these initial decisions about narration are clustered together and called 'point of view', but there is much more to point of view than just knowing who narrates and roughly how they do it. 'Point of view' implies looking rather than telling: used in the conventional way, it seems to suggest that there is a story happening 'out there' and all we need to do is switch on the consciousness of one character or another – like flicking on a light switch in a particular room – and we will see the story play out from their 'point of view'. If we want we can switch the light off in one room and another on somewhere else and we will see the same story from someone else's point of view. But this is not how fiction is written. Two characters will never tell the same story from two different perspectives; they will tell two different stories. Stories are *told*, as we have seen, and the way they are told, or plotted, creates the final narrative. Thinking that you can just switch point of view and keep the same story is a mistake.

George Eliot famously switches 'point of view' from Dorothea to Casaubon at the beginning of Chapter 29 in *Middlemarch*. Indeed, Dorothea's perspective is abandoned mid-sentence:

> One morning, some weeks after her arrival at Lowick, Dorothea – but why always Dorothea? Was her point of view the only possible one with regard to this marriage?[177]

While George Eliot (in the form of the persona that narrates *Middlemarch*) appears to have dropped Dorothea's perspective temporarily for Casaubon's, we might argue that this section of the novel, and, furthermore, the whole novel, still

adopts Dorothea's point of view in the sense that it takes
her *side*. The question of whether Dorothea's point of view
is 'the only possible one with regard to this marriage' can
be answered in different ways. It is not the only possible
one, the novel tells us: but it is the best one. After all,
Dorothea can love passionately and Casaubon can't; she is
quick and intelligent while he is slow and set in his ways;
she is kind while he is spiteful; she does not bear a grudge
but he punishes her in his will. The book repeatedly
compares these two characters and finds Dorothea to be
the better one. So although it claims briefly to adopt
Casaubon's point of view, does it really ever do so?[178] Point
of view implies more than just the position and direction
of the narrative 'lens': it also implies something like a world-
view.

Point of view implies which character is being favoured
by the narration, not which character is doing the narrating.
In Katherine Mansfield's story 'Marriage à la Mode', the
third-person narration is filtered mostly through William,
although we enter his wife Isabel's consciousness for the
last scene. However, the point of view is always William's;
Isabel, we discover, in the last scene, has betrayed him. In
The Great Gatsby, Nick Carraway hardly narrates from his
own point of view: he doesn't really have one. Nick is not
telling his own story; he tells and un-tells Gatsby's story.
The novel is to a large extent narrated from Gatsby's point
of view even though he is never its narrator. We might
decide that a character like Gatsby could not exist without
a narrator like Nick, and that Gatsby and his 'point of view'
are only ever fictions anyway, invented to prop up some

bland idea of 'Nick': the clean-living American who does no wrong. But then every Nick needs his Gatsby. In the end perhaps the *novel itself* has a point of view that exists separately from that of all its characters. Each novel takes a position, which is really what a point of view is.[179] This doesn't necessarily imply a moral judgement, but does accept that most novels and stories have something like a main character and in some strange way this character is simply the one that is *loved* the most.

Even if we work out who tells the story and how this is accomplished using grammatical person, tense and perspective, and even if we work out the point of view of each of the characters and that of the whole narrative, we still need to consider what restrictions we will place on our narration. In a novel with ten characters, why can we hear the thoughts of only four of them? And why do we shift perspective every chapter but never mid-chapter? How does narrative time work? How much of it is there in the story and how is it dealt with? All of these questions may be answered naturally when you are writing. When I wrote my first crime novel I assumed I must write in first person and I'm sure I didn't really think much before using the past tense. Throughout the novel there are (terrible) flashbacks that tell the story from the murderer's perspective, and these are written also in past tense but in third person (and printed in italics). In later novels I spent more time considering logically just how the murderer's perspective came to exist as a text within a text, but in the first novel it just hangs there, unexplained. I also assumed that a crime novel should take a few weeks of narrative time. In the early days

I never felt comfortable leaving my characters on their own for hours at a time, let alone days or weeks. The main action of *Bright Young Things* takes place in less than a week. But *Great Expectations* begins when Pip is seven and ends when he is thirty-seven.[180] How should we make decisions about all these things?

Now that everything has become so complicated, let's abandon all terminology just for a moment so that we can be clear about what we need to decide in order to write a piece of fiction. I think the main decisions are as follows:

- Who tells the story?
- How much do they know?
- What is stopping them knowing more?
- When are they telling it?
- How has someone come to be reading it?

What you eventually write will be as much a result of these decisions as it is a result of those you make about plot, character and theme. Would *Great Expectations* be the same narrative if it were narrated by Joe or Estella? Would *Middlemarch* remain the same if it were told in the first-person present tense from Dorothea's perspective? How would *The Bell Jar* change if equal weight were given to Esther's mother's version of the story? One of the most interesting questions to ask about fiction is therefore, *Who tells the story?* Before we even consider any of the other questions, we should ask, *Who is telling this to me?* And, maybe, *Why?* And, perhaps also, *What's in it for them?* We have already started considering these questions. But what does it really mean to make these decisions? What does it really mean to create a 'point of view' (in all senses)?

Let's assume you've got a rough idea of your plot and characters. As an example we'll use one of the ideas I proposed in the earlier chapter 'How to Have Ideas', in which Clare gets expelled from school and then gets a job in a video shop, where she works with Bob. Clare is secretly in love with Pepper, who works on a market stall. Eliot, Bob's long-lost son, and maths genius, turns up at some point during the narrative. You might know your plot in more detail than this, but actually it's a good idea to think about narrative style at a point when your idea is rather sketchy, because it might change things in an interesting way. The first question to ask is whether or not there is a main character. There is: Clare. So one obvious option is that she could be the narrator and she could tell her story to us in first person. That's simple enough. But what if Clare isn't that articulate? What if she is prone to long periods of emotional outpouring and teenage angst? What if, conversely, she's too shy to tell us much? Is she the best person to tell her own story? Does being narrator suit her character?

We could certainly make any seeming deficiency work for us artistically. For example, the emotional outpouring and teenage angst could be quite funny. Or Clare's apparent inarticulacy could allow us to explore themes of language – perhaps she is highly articulate in her own way, like the character Victor in Niall Griffiths's *Kelly and Victor*, a first-person, present-tense novel with two narrators who take it in turns to tell the same events from their own perspective.

Bright lights an activity behind me up on the promenade and in front of me the sea's endless blackness, always rolling in. Easy to understand suicide here, at night-time on a beach, the way the dark water pulls you, draws yer in. Sucking you towards something which seems to offer a promise deep inside you of a destination strangely like light. As if the cold an slime under the waves with the crawling an flopping goggle-eyed creatures you'd find a place warm and well lit. Where you'd wanner stay forever and where yer'd never rot.[181]

Similarly, the narrator of Anne Donovan's *Buddha Da* has a first-person narrator telling in the past tense – in very much her own way – of her father becoming a Buddhist in Glasgow.

At first bein a Buddhist didnae seem tae make that much difference tae ma da. He used tae go doon the pub on a Tuesday and noo he went tae the Buddhist Centre tae meditate. Same difference. He never talked aboot it, wis still the same auld da, gaun tae his work, cairryin on in the hoose. He stuck a photie of the Buddha up on the unit in their bedroom and noo and again he'd go in there and shut the door insteid of watchin the telly – meditatin, he said.[182]

Restriction of any kind always works well in fiction, especially if there is a plausible reason for it. If your narrator sees the world in a particular way, or is likely to have an unconventional voice, then this can be emphasised in the narration. A good example is *The Curious Incident of the*

Dog in the Night Time by Mark Haddon, where the narrator is a child with Asperger's syndrome. Clearly this means he creates a different story from the same initial events than Nick Carraway would, or Pip or Esther Greenwood – but think about the subtle limitations that each of these characters has, too. Think too about your own limitations. A Glaswegian can attempt to write in the way Anne Donovan does. If you are from Surrey, you cannot.

So if I am considering letting Clare tell her own story, I'll need to work out what kind of voice she is likely to have, and whether this is the kind of thing I want to write. Most of the time Clare will be a bit like me and her voice will be a bit like mine and a first-person narration will work out fine. A first-person narration, like everything in fiction, will never be one hundred per cent real. Clare will have a narrator's voice in the same way people have a 'telephone voice' and it will be plausible that, for example, she blurts out her life story to Pepper in a different voice from the one she uses to narrate the rest of the book. Indeed, if Clare narrates the story in the past tense from some distance – say ten years on – her voice can be rather more grown up than if she does it in present tense, in the now.

Great Expectations is narrated at some distance from the main action and Pip's grown-up voice is quite different from the voice he has as a child, and even as a young man. Look at the different registers at work in this one extract:

> I walked away at a good pace, thinking it was easier to go than I had supposed it would be, and reflecting that it would never have done to have had an old shoe thrown after the

coach, in sight of all the High-street. I whistled and made nothing of going. But the village was very peaceful and quiet and the light mists were solemnly rising, as if to show me the world, and I had been so innocent and little there, and all beyond was so unknown and so great, that in a moment with a strong heave and sob I broke into tears. It was by the finger-post at the end of the village, and I laid my hand upon it, and said, 'Good-by O my dear, dear friend!'

Heaven knows we need never be ashamed of our tears, for they are rain upon the blinding dust of earth, overlaying our hard hearts.[183]

The opening statements appear fairly factual, and although the narrator is describing the feeling of leaving home, at first neither the far-away narrator nor the character (they are the same person, of course, but not the same persona) is very emotional about it. In the phrase 'it would never have done to have had an old shoe thrown after the coach' we see something of Pip as a young man leaving home, as he is in the scene. But when we get to the phrase 'and I had been so innocent and little there' suddenly he is the boy again. Abruptly, wonderfully, we are there with Pip, and we are feeling what he is feeling about his past. After the paragraph break, however, the more solemn narrator's voice is back to tell us not to be ashamed of our tears. In the space of a few lines we have therefore visited the consciousness of Pip first as an adult narrator, then as young man leaving home, then as a boy (using the boy's word 'little') and then as adult narrator again. Note that the remark at the end of this extract exists outside the main narrative time of the novel in the shadowy, uncertain place from which the novel is being narrated. We know this because the tears '*are* rain'. This thought is happening now, in the present tense, at the point of narration, not in the past with the rest of the narrative.

Before we leave first person behind altogether, let's consider what would happen if we wanted Clare to remain the protagonist, but have someone else tell her story. Is this 'someone else' inside the narrative or outside it? In other words, is it another character, or is it me, the author, using some persona? If Clare is to remain the central character but someone else in the novel is going to narrate, then this person has to have the motivation to do so. Could this be Clare's little sister, for example, perhaps telling an admiring story about her big sister? Could it be Eliot, who is secretly in love with Clare and therefore notices all the things she does that summer? Could it be Pepper, telling us a very different story and experiencing Clare as anything from a stalker to a first love? All of these would be first-person narratives, but with Clare as a focus, except for the last one, where it actually becomes a story that is more about Pepper (and might, in the end, turn out to be the story I really want to write – so let's not rule anything out at this stage). In a sense, this is how *Buddha Da* works: the story is ostensibly about the narrator's father and what happens to him as he 'comes of age' and becomes a Buddhist. But, like *The Great Gatsby*, it can't help being about the narrator too.

So the next option is that as the author I can decide that

I am going to tell the story myself using a third-person narration. But let's not get carried away here. Let's remember that, as I'm the author, I am *always* going to be the person telling the story. Just because I pretend Clare is doing it doesn't mean it's not really me in the end. Although another way of looking at this is that as author I can in fact *never* tell the story, and for one simple reason: it is fiction and I am real. When George Eliot tells of Dorothea and Lydgate and Mary Garth she is describing characters from her imagination, not real people. There are two different dimensions here: the real and the fictional, and a first-person narrator – of any sort – within the fictional world is unlikely to refer to the real world and therefore break the frame ('Here we are at Chapter 29 of *Middlemarch* and I've really had enough of narrating this through Dorothea's consciousness, so I'm going to try Casaubon's. After that I might have some tea. Gosh, my hand hurts from all this writing.[184]). The conventions of realist fiction after all require us to treat the fictional world in every way *as if it were real*, but without ever believing that it is literally real. We require most fictional worlds to be logical, but closed. I can believe everything in *Middlemarch*, but I can't believe that George Eliot ever went there and met these characters. Therefore she herself can never be the narrator of the novel. Her third-person, intrusive narrator is in fact a persona, not a person: it's another character created by the author.

So what would it mean to narrate our story in the third person – where Clare and everyone in it are referred to by name, or as 'he' or 'she' and there is no longer any acknowledged 'I'? Well, for one thing we'd need to write third-person sentences: 'Clare wanted a cup of tea', for example, rather than 'I wanted a cup of tea', or even 'I was dying for a cup of tea'. In fact, if that's how Clare would say it, that she didn't just want a cup of tea, she was *dying* for one, then we could even have it in our third-person version: 'Clare was dying for a cup of tea.' Now things get interesting – and more complicated – again. Just how much of a third-person narration 'belongs' to the third-person narrator, and how much to the characters themselves? Whose voice is it really?

Often, a third-person narration will be quite subtle, and it will appear as if the story is being told by nobody-in-particular. George Eliot (or at least her persona) might address the reader in *Middlemarch*, but in many third-person narrations the narrator just hangs out in the background quietly, pretending not to be there. They won't sit the reader on their lap and begin with *Once upon a time*, and they won't say things in a film-trailer voice like, 'Little did Clare know what a surprise was in store for her that afternoon . . .' They just tell the story in such a way that it seems as if no one is telling it at all: as if it has no explicit narrator. But even if the author/narrator sets him or herself at some distance from the action, the characters are always there right at the forefront of what's going on. If I am writing a third-person narration with Clare as the main character, then some of the language I use will inevitably be Clare's. I may have chosen to tell her story for her, but I will need to let the reader know what she is thinking and feeling. I can show much of what Clare thinks by her actions, of course, but what about the narration itself?

Let's say we have a scene with Clare in the video shop. She's shelving some horror films and thinks that the covers are pretty nasty, or what I, in a certain kind of 'writing voice', might call lurid. I could write 'Clare started shelving the horror films. She thought, "These covers are really lurid."' I probably wouldn't write it like this because it's awkward and clumsy, but if I did I would be using what is called *direct discourse* to express Clare's feeling about the lurid covers. I might be more likely to write it like this: 'Clare started shelving the horror films, thinking that the covers were really lurid.' This is called *indirect discourse*, because we express the feeling Clare has about the lurid covers indirectly. We say she's thinking it, but we don't mess around putting the thought in quotation marks. Notice that in both examples so far we remain at a distance from Clare, and never depart from the narrator's voice, which is perhaps what we'd expect from a third-person narration. The covers are lurid because I think they are, even though I give the thought to Clare.

But let's look at a final example: 'Clare started shelving the horror films. The covers were so lurid. They were like puke.' This is called *free indirect discourse* or *free indirect style*. What's happening here is that the narrator's voice and Clare's voice have become fused. 'Clare started shelving the horror films' is an objective fact that is simply reported. 'The covers were so lurid' belongs half to the narrator and half to Clare. Clare is thinking/saying it, but still using the narrator's word 'lurid'. But 'They were like puke' is definitely Clare's expression. Note how the sentence sits there on its own without attribution. It's not 'Clare thought they looked a bit like puke.' (indirect discourse) or even 'Clare thought, "They look like puke."' (direct discourse). Isn't the free indirect style far more elegant? I mean, obviously we're still talking about vomit, but you must agree that it's the more dignified way of doing it.

In James Wood's excellent discussion of free indirect style in his book, *How Fiction Works*, he discusses the difference between words that seem to 'belong' to the author and those that belong more to the character.

> Free indirect style solves much, but accentuates a problem inherent in fictional narration: do the words these characters use seem the words they might use or do they sound more like the author's?
>
> When I wrote, 'Ted watched the orchestra through stupid tears', the reader would be likely to assign 'stupid' to the character himself. But if I had written, 'Ted watched the orchestra through viscous, swollen tears', the adjectives would suddenly look annoyingly authorial, as if I were trying to find the fanciest way of describing those tears.[185]

We will see later when we discuss sentence-level writing that the character can usually be forgiven for saying things we would not forgive the author, and that overuse of adjectives and adverbs is a problem for the author in a way it isn't if they are plausibly attributed to the character. But we should be able to see that free indirect style is one in which the author is able to choose when to use the words and expressions of a character in the narration, and when to use his or her own. Here it differs from first-person narration, where all we have are the words of one character (plus the spoken words of others) to tell the story. Although sometimes it doesn't differ that much, as in this extract from Katherine Mansfield's story 'Marriage à la Mode':

> But the imbecile thing, the absolutely extraordinary thing was that he hadn't the slightest idea that Isabel wasn't as happy as he. God, what blindness! He hadn't the remotest notion in those days that she really hated that inconvenient little house, that she thought the fat Nanny was ruining the babies, that she was desperately lonely, pining for new people and new music and pictures and so on. If they hadn't gone to that studio party at Moira Morrison's – If Moira Morrison hadn't said as they were leaving, 'I'm going to rescue your wife, selfish man. She's like an exquisite little Titania' – if Isabel hadn't gone with Moira to Paris – if – if . . .[186]

We may wonder what the point is of free indirect style when we could just render everything in the voice of the character. Why not narrate this story entirely in the first person from William's perspective? Why go halfway, into this strange place where William is thinking these things, but not quite admitting them directly to himself or anyone else? There are several reasons not to use a first-person narration for a whole narrative, as we have just seen: the narrator's voice may be unbelievable, overwhelming or too unreliable. And perhaps there are interesting contrasts to be explored between the narrator's voice and the character's. But it is quite rare for an author to choose free indirect style and then limit it to exploring just one character's consciousness (although it does happen). Most of the time an author chooses this kind of narration because he or she wants to visit the consciousnesses of more than one character, and this is the most effective way to do it, especially within scenes. In 'Marriage à la Mode', William sends a letter to Isabel and we need to see her reading it without him being there, and we need to know how she feels about receiving it.

The God of Small Things by Arundhati Roy has a particularly fluid kind of free indirect style that can inhabit any character's consciousness at any time. In fact, sometimes it inhabits more than one character at once: when a roof rack 'rattled and made fallingoff noises' we understand that this lovely word 'fallingoff' belongs not just to the young twins Rahel and Estha but in some sense to everyone in the novel. But it is definitely not the narrator's word; it is not neutral. In the novel adult expressions are frequently processed through the consciousness of the twins (and perhaps 'children in general'). After the twins fail to appreciate a gift of a Susie Squirrel book, 'Miss Mitten, who belonged to a sect of born again Christians, said she was a Little Disappointed in them when they read it aloud to her, backwards.'[187] The capitalisation of 'a Little Disappointed' is a subtle form of free indirect style. It's the child's experience of being told off: of the weight that adults can give to things like being a little disappointed (and note the ironic use of the word 'little' here too, which is what makes it funny. If someone is going to bother to be 'a Little Disappointed' with capital letters, you'd think they could manage to admit that they are actually very disappointed). The use of capitalisation continues through the novel, rendering adult phrases or ideas childlike and defamiliarised. There's Chacko's 'Reading Aloud voice', the 'Orangedrink Lemondrink Man', the 'History House' and wisdom like 'Anything can Happen to Anyone' and 'It's Best to be Prepared'.

But this isn't the only voice in *The God of Small Things*. When characters are alone – particularly Estha and Rahel – the narrator gets us closer to them by using a more conventional free indirect style.

> From the way Ammu held her head, Rahel could tell that she was still angry. Rahel looked at her watch. Ten to two. Still no train. She put her chin on the window sill. She could feel the grey gristle of the felt that cushioned the window glass pressing into her chinskin. She took off her sunglasses to get a better look at the dead frog squashed on the road. It was so dead and squashed and so flat that it looked more like a frog-shaped stain on the road than a frog.[188]

We can see here the classic blending of narrator and character that characterises free indirect style. Some of the thoughts are attributed to Rahel by the narrator, and we are told, for example that 'She could feel the grey gristle of the felt . . .' But when we get to the description of the frog we find that this thought or observation is attributed to no one. Nevertheless, we know that we are inside Rahel's consciousness, and that these are Rahel's words. And being able to use Rahel's words means the narrator can be more playful and childlike.

But let's look at a slightly different mode of narration from the same novel:

> Once a month (except during the monsoons), a parcel would arrive for Chacko by VPP. It always contained a balsa aero-modelling kit. It usually took Chacko between eight and ten days to assemble the aircraft with its tiny fuel tank and motorized propeller. When it was ready, he would take Estha and Rahel to the rice-fields in Nattakom to help him fly it. It never flew for more than a minute. Month after month, Chacko's carefully constructed planes crashed in the slushgreen paddy fields into which Estha and Rahel would spurt, like trained retrievers, to salvage the remains.[189]

This is a more adult voice. At first it seems fairly objective. This is the narrator simply telling us what has been happening with Chacko's model aircraft. But when we get to the description of Estha and Rahel and find that they 'would spurt, like trained retrievers' we are alerted to the fact that we have drifted into Chacko's consciousness, because these are his words, and this is how he sees the twins. They certainly wouldn't see themselves like this. Although we spend a lot of the novel looking out at the world through the twins' eyes, the novel twists its perspective like a kaleidoscope, enabling us to look at them, or, through them, to look at ourselves. In this novel, we don't know exactly what everyone is thinking all the time, but we have the potential to know. The narrator can choose to tell us anything about anyone.

This is what is usually called an 'omniscient' perspective.

The primary OED definition of 'omniscient' is as follows: 'Esp. of God: all-knowing, having infinite knowledge'. I am suspicious of the way this term is used in literary criticism, because it implies that in other perspectives – a 'limited' third-person narration,[190] for example, or in first person – authors don't occupy this god-like position. What nonsense. Of course we do. We are the creators of our own little worlds and therefore their gods. We do potentially know what everyone is thinking and doing at any one time. Except here we end up falling headlong into the rabbit hole of theology. Is it really possible, even for a god, to have *infinite* knowledge of everything? Probably; but for us this state is unimaginable. What would it be like to never be surprised by anything in our creation, or delighted by it, or moved by it?

I abandoned the concept of omniscience around the same time I first abandoned the concept of God, thinking that the problem with it was its impossibility and its arrogance and its implausibility. One of the reasons I used first person and then a strictly limited third person (which we'll come to in a moment) was because I didn't believe in this entity that could zoom around reading everyone's mind. I didn't want to believe it. I was so wrapped up in myself that I imagined that no one could ever understand me. I did manage to extend this courtesy to others, thinking that if no one could understand me then I could understand no one and all I could offer literature therefore was my own little limited first-person world.

It's true that there is a terrible kind of omniscient perspective in fiction that trivialises, rather than celebrates, subjectivity (*Richard thought he had got the better of Jack, but Jack knew something Richard didn't. He knew that behind Richard stood a huge monster, hungry for flesh. As Richard was devoured his last thought was that he hated Jack. Jack was not at all sorry to see Richard die.*) But done properly, what I would like to call simply 'free indirect style' instead of 'omniscience' can be the most compassionate, inclusive kind of narration possible. It's not that the free indirect narrator does not take sides: indeed, in *Middlemarch* it takes Dorothea's side, and in *The God of Small Things* it takes the side of those characters who love authentically and freely: Rahel, Estha, Ammu and Velutha. But we see the possibility of other perspectives, and we potentially understand more about why people act because we see them from the inside. Baby Kochamma in *The God of Small Things* betrays Ammu and Velutha, the characters that stand for love and truth. But we understand why she does this. She has lost all hope of love, and become afraid of the future. The narrative does not ask us simply to condemn her, but to see where she is coming from, even though we may still decide she is wrong.

Objectivity is one of the items on a list that Chekhov sent to his brother Alexander in 1886 to help him be a better writer. The whole list of the conditions Chekhov sets out that a work must meet in order to be 'artistic' reads as follows:

- Absence of lengthy torrents of a politico-socio-economic nature
- Total objectivity

- Honesty in the descriptions of characters and objects
- Extreme brevity
- Daring and originality; shun clichés
- Compassion[191]

When Chekhov talks about total objectivity he means that the writer should say what happens without judging it. He does not mean that we should strive to create works that readers will be able to approach objectively, or that our work will not inspire great feeling in them, but that we should not attempt to tell readers what to think. The centre of this whole list, I would suggest, is compassion, through which we might try not just to love all our characters, but perhaps to love them all the same amount. Even if this is too hard for us, it's certainly a liberating experience – and a very worthwhile exercise – to try writing without formulating opinions of everything, when you attempt to just show things as they are. Of course, we don't require our characters to be objective, just the narration. Rahel can hate Baby Kochamma; we can, if we like, hate Baby Kochamma; it is only the narrator who cannot. The narrator takes the position of a god, but not the judgemental, Old Testament kind of god who sets out to torment and punish his creations. This is, rather, as the title tells us, a god of small things.

Perhaps the master of a non-judgemental free indirect style is Tolstoy, who even manages to make Karenin, Anna's unreasonable husband, seem like a sympathetic character. In *Anna Karenina* it is virtually impossible to judge anyone. Even though Tolstoy apparently set out to write a condemnation of Anna, he found he couldn't do it. He was just too good a writer and his compassion shines through everything he writes. Whom do we love more, Kitty or Anna? It's hard to say. Do we love Levin more than Karenin? Yes, but probably only because we see more of him and perhaps also because in the novel Levin takes the 'everyman' role with which it is easiest to identify. But importantly, we do not despise anyone in the whole novel, even though no one in the novel is without flaws.

In *Anna Karenina* there seem to be some rules about the way that the free indirect style is executed: more than in *The God of Small Things*. The novel is broken up into short chapters, each usually containing only one scene, and in each of these we usually visit only one consciousness. In Chapter 23 of Part One we find Kitty waiting for Vronsky to ask her to dance the mazurka. The only thoughts we know are Kitty's; when she watches Vronsky and Anna dancing together we only know what she thinks and not what they are feeling. Of course, we can surmise some of what they are feeling by the objective facts, and also from Kitty's description. Although I am describing Tolstoy's narration (and really all third-person narration) as 'free indirect style', it is a feature of this style that indirect discourse is also used ('She thought that during the mazurka everything would be decided'). Tolstoy also uses direct discourse, where a character's thoughts are enclosed within quotation marks, as in the beginning of this extract:

'But what about him?' Kitty looked at him and was horrified. What portrayed itself so clearly to Kitty in the mirror of Anna's face, she also saw in him. Where was his quiet, firm manner and carefree, calm expression? No, now each time he addressed Anna, he bowed his head slightly, as if wishing to fall down before her, and in his glance there were only obedience and fear.[192]

Kitty can see that Vronsky is in awe of Anna; that he probably loves her. Who else could tell us this? Anna certainly couldn't tell us the truth about this scene herself: it would be too arrogant and vain. It probably needs to be seen with the clarity only an outsider can provide. If this were a first-person narration from Anna's perspective, it would be awkward to describe this moment at all.

In this scene we only inhabit Kitty's consciousness and no one else's. However, Tolstoy also moves between consciousnesses within scenes from time to time, as does George Eliot in *Middlemarch*. Both writers seem to take the approach that while each scene 'belongs' to one character more than another, and their consciousness will be dominant, other consciousnesses may also be included. This is a stricter system than that in *The God of Small Things* but not as strict as Ali Smith's system of narration in *The Accidental*.

Here we have five main characters: the Smart family, comprising the mother, Eve; the stepfather, Michael; the son, Magnus; and the daughter, Astrid. Amber is the fifth character: the stranger who comes to town. There are some ambiguous sections of first-person narration that concern Amber, but the main part of the novel is narrated in third person, present tense, using free indirect style. Each member of the Smart family takes their turn to 'own' a chapter. Although there is a narrator telling their story, this is nothing like the 'I' of *Middlemarch* that has thoughts and feelings and opinions of its own. This third person is as close as it is possible to get to first person.

> Astrid isn't totally broken yet. But if a window could throw a brick at itself to test itself that's what she'll do, she'll break herself, Magnus thinks, then she'll test how sharp she is by using her own broken pieces on herself. Everybody at this table is in broken pieces which won't go together, pieces which are nothing to do with each other, like they all come from different jigsaws, all muddled together into one box by some assistant who couldn't care less in a charity shop or wherever the place is that old jigsaws go to die. Except jigsaws don't die.[193]

Here Magnus provides not just many of the words but also the punctuation and rhythm of the narration. Why not just use first person here? Indeed, why not use multiple narrators, and have each member of the family tell their own part of the story? Well, what's so lovely about this extract is that while the metaphor about the jigsaws is rendered in perfect free indirect discourse and absolutely comes from Magnus's head using Magnus's words, I don't believe he'd bother to think of it himself in a first-person narration. Someone like Magnus needs a third-person narrator to bring him out of himself. The narrator has gone in there, right into his brain, and found the metaphor that he would use if he could be bothered to think of a metaphor. But Magnus has not provided us with it directly. In fact I'm not sure any member of this family would be as honest in a first-person narration as the narrator forces them to be in free indirect style. What would Eve do in a multiple first-person narration? She'd probably keep a journal that would be far less interesting than her thoughts, which we can get at in free indirect style in a way that we can't get at in any form of first person.

Why is this? And why would she need to keep a journal in a multiple first-person narration? Well, convention seems to dictate that first-person narration is dramatised in a way that third-person narration doesn't have to be. It has to be plausible. No one asks who is this character in *Anna Karenina* who seems to be able to visit everyone's thoughts, and knows exactly what is happening with everyone. I suppose we just assume it is Tolstoy, and since it's his story we wouldn't want to argue with him. No one is too concerned about the 'I' in *Middlemarch*, and how it has access to the whole story in the way it does.

But the moment you write in first person, people start to wonder how the story is being told. One clear first-person narrator – as in *The Bell Jar*, or *Great Expectations* – seems to be fine, and it does seem fairly plausible that someone might sit us down and tell us a story about themselves, as if we were both down the pub. Or as if they'd phoned us up. Therefore it's OK for a single-narrator first-person narrative to sort of 'hang in the air'. The narrator may explain when and where he or she is narrating from, but we don't necessarily expect this. We don't require that the writing-down of the story be dramatised, although some first-person narrations are written in that way, and are therefore presented as diaries or letters or as some other fictional artefact. But the moment *another* first-person narrator is added, the plausibility falls away and we begin wondering what kind of mortal consciousness could contain another – or at least what coincidence has led to these two narrators coming along to tell two parts of the same story at exactly the same time (or, even more coincidentally, *one right after the other*)?

It just seems weird. It jars. Suddenly we're not in a normal pub any more, or having a normal telephone conversation. Imagine if *Les Liaisons Dangereuses* were narrated by the Marquise de Merteuil and the Vicomte de Valmont simply taking it in turns to tell us the story of how they came to make their bet and the tragic result of it. For one thing, a past-tense narration would be impossible, as they both die at the end of the story. But even a present-tense narration always has a sense of the past about it.[194] It just wouldn't be plausible. But even if we could believe in it, I imagine it would feel rather flat. At least with the epistolary structure we sense that these two did not just self-consciously begin telling us A Story (perhaps using something like Chacko's 'Reading Aloud voice'). After all, they were completely wrapped up with living their lives and experiencing all that drama and it's only because we can read their letters that we have any sense at all of what is happening between them. The narration once again becomes part of the story, and is plausible for these characters. We believe that someone found the letters and brought them together to create a narrative for

us: we do not believe that its characters would sit down
and tell it to us.

For these kinds of reasons, most multiple first-person
narrations take the form of fictional artefacts – letters,
journals, stories-within-stories and so on – that are put
together in a way that makes sense within the fictional
world. In *Hey Nostradamus!* by Douglas Coupland the story
of the events and aftermath of a 1988 high school shooting
is told by four narrators in turn: Cheryl, one of the victims,
tells her story in the first person, past tense, from a kind
of afterlife. The next section is told by Jason, whom she
secretly married shortly before the shootings. He is writing
his part of the story in 1999 as a letter to his nephews.
Most of this is in first person, past tense, although sections
that dramatise the actual writing of the letter are narrated
in present tense.

> Just so you know, I've been writing all of this in the cab of
> my truck, parked on Bellevue, down by Ambleside Beach,
> near the pier with all its bratty kids on rollerblades and the
> Vietnamese guys with their crab traps pursuing *E. Coli*. I'm
> using a pen embossed with 'Travelodge' and I'm writing
> on the back of Les's pink invoice forms. The wind is heating
> up – God it feels nice on my face – and I feel, in the most
> SUV-commercial sense of the word, *free*.[195]

The next section is dated 2002, and is narrated by Heather,
also in first person, and a mixture of past and present tense.
Heather is a court stenographer, and often (although not
always) writes her journal entries in place of her court

transcription. 'I wonder how many other stenographers across the decades have sat here pumping out their inner self while appearing prim and methodical?'[196] The last section is narrated by Jason's father, Reg, in 2003. It takes the form of a letter, but has a more direct style than the one Jason wrote to his nephews. In this one, Reg addresses Jason almost constantly as 'you'.

In *Cloud Atlas* by David Mitchell, each narration contains the one that came before it, which creates something of a Russian-doll structure similar to, and indeed inspired by, Italo Calvino's *If On A Winter's Night A Traveller*.[197] Not all are in first person, but of those that are, one is a journal, one takes the form of letters, and one is something like a video recording. But there is a sense that these documents and artefacts have been put together in precisely this order for us by one single consciousness. In the world of the fiction, we assume that these documents have been found, ordered, perhaps even edited. This is also the logic by which Bram Stoker's *Dracula* is put together. Sometimes this putting-together is itself dramatised; sometimes it isn't.

In the end, every form of narration that works seems to lead back to the idea of a *single* storyteller, whether that is an author-narrator, a first-person character or an 'editor' or 'curator' of found documents and artefacts. It seems that we want our narratives told, or at least put together, by one consciousness, however many consciousnesses are then raided within the text. Perhaps one of the reasons for this is that we expect this single consciousness to restrict the narration somehow and therefore frame the narrative in a way that is coherent, both in terms of the plot, and thematically. Why should the Smart family have to take it in turns to have their consciousnesses visited? Why can't we just hear whoever has the most interesting thought at any given moment? One reason is that the story has more drama this way. When Amber declares to Eve that she and Magnus (Eve's teenage son) are going into the village to have sex, we are in Magnus's consciousness at that moment and we feel what he feels: complete stupefaction, until he realises, and we realise, that Eve is bound to think this is just a joke. And she does, or she seems to. As we are in Magnus's section, we have no idea what Eve thinks.

In *Bright Young Things*, I decided I would restrict my third-person, present-tense narration so that each chapter 'belonged' to one of the characters. I decided that the focus would go round in a set order – Anne, Jamie, Thea, Bryn, Emily and Paul – and would never deviate from this order. The characters spend most of their time together, so we can usually hear what everyone is saying, but we can only know what one character at a time is thinking, or secretly doing. When dramatic things were due to happen in the novel that concerned just one or two characters I had to decide whether the event should happen inside or outside 'their' chapters and how this would affect the telling of the story. Why would I set restrictions like these for myself? Well, because it is only through restriction – or obstacle – that drama can happen. At the very least it forces the author to think, and solve problems, and *plot*. Narrative when left to its own devices can become formless and uninteresting. It is virtually impossible to find a story or novel that doesn't have some kind of consistent internal structure based on rules created by the author. Every narration is somehow consistently organised.[198] Here is David Mitchell talking about how he decided to organise his novel *The Thousand Autumns of Jacob de Zoet*.

> I tried writing it in the first person, and it just wasn't right. The book gave me a lot of trouble, which is why it took four years. I restarted it twice, and it only came to life when I tried it in the third person. Then I had to decide which characters' thoughts we'd be able to hear. In the end I devised a rule: each chapter has a single principal observer who wears an imaginary recording digicam, like a coal miner's hat with a spike tapping his brain, so his thoughts, but only his, can become known to the reader.[199]

The rules you set for your narrative style won't just concern whose consciousness can be visited at what time, or who narrates in what order. When you decide on a particular tense, for example, you must stick to it and be consistent. One of the commonest problems I see in students' early work is tenses that shift about quite randomly. The only way to really check whether you are consistent in this way is to read your work aloud to yourself. Think about the logic of your tense structure as well. In *Hey Nostradamus!* there are often shifts in tense between present and past depending on what is being described. Three of the four sections have a clear 'now' and a 'then' and the tenses are used quite logically: present for now and past for then.

And these shifts are often dramatised as part of the narration, when the characters tell us where they are and what they are doing now, before continuing to reflect on the near or distant past. In *number9dream* every scene concerning Eiji is narrated in the first person, present tense, regardless of when it is taking place. As long as you are consistent – as long as you set rules for yourself and stick to them – you can do almost anything you like. But it would seem odd if David Mitchell suddenly wrote Eiji in the past tense for no apparent reason, or if the characters in *Hey Nostradamus!* suddenly began narrating wholly in the present tense.

Every narrative choice you make will affect all the others. Some time ago now we began thinking about who would narrate this story of Clare in the video shop, and in thinking just of this question 'Who narrates?' we have had to answer virtually all the others. As soon as we begin thinking of the narrator, we must begin wondering how much they know and what restrictions they have and when they are telling the story. You will have realised by now that grammatical person is more than anything a matter of knowledge: a first-person narrator knows far less than a third-person narrator because the first-person narrator cannot know beyond his or her own thoughts. But we have seen that this is complicated in the sense that everybody who writes any kind of story automatically inhabits a first-person position ('author') that paradoxically knows everything (although perhaps not an 'infinite' amount). In any case what then matters are the restrictions placed on the narration. In a first-person narration we may wonder how the story has made its way to us. Was it written down as a journal, say? And how many people narrate, directly or indirectly? How many consciousnesses are going to be available for us to inspect? Can we visit them in any order at any time? What are the codes and conventions of this fictional world that we are visiting?

Consistency – in all senses of the word – is, in the end, what this is all about. How will you get all your material to hang together? To retain its form? To be harmonious? Although making decisions about narrative style can seem very complicated, once you've decided whose story or stories you want to tell you can work out the rest quite logically. Some people just begin writing and see what happens, but this can go wrong because you may naturally fall into your most conservative style, when perhaps it would be far better to try something you wouldn't auto-matically think of. A good exercise is to try your idea several different ways to see which one works best for you. At the very least this is bound to give you a new perspective.

I have included a technical matrix (in Appendix Three) for a hypothetical story about a boy and a rabbit, which is good for practice, especially as the subject is a 'silly' one and there's no need to feel anxious about it. Try choosing one thing from each column as randomly as possible and apply the resulting narrative style to the idea. Let your imagination be as free as you like in this exercise. There's nothing stopping you from deciding that Olive is a hundred years old, for example. You might create a technical matrix yourself containing all the narrative options you want to consider or are interested in and pick several paths through it. Then see how your prose would look if it were written according to the parameters you have chosen. Choose three different ways of doing it – one conventional, one risky, one ridiculous, say – and try writing a paragraph.

CHARACTERISATION

One should also, as far as possible, work plots out using gestures. Given the same natural talent, those who are actually experiencing the emotions are the most convincing; someone who is distressed or angry acts out distress and irritation most authentically. (This is why the art of poetry belongs to people who are naturally gifted or mad.)

Aristotle[200]

Keep away from depicting land captains. Nothing is easier than to describe unsympathetic officialdom, and although there are readers who will lap it up, they are the most unpleasant and limited kind of reader.

Anton Chekhov[201]

You must make up your mind once and for all, did you come here to serve art, and to make sacrifices for its sake, or to exploit your own personal ends?

Constantin Stanislavski[202]

Imagine you are at a big party. It is very full, and, if you are to break through the crowds, you need to work out where you are headed. Directly ahead of you is the food: a table laden with whatever is delicious in your culture. Perhaps some bread and cheese; perhaps several different curries. Off to the right is a table with a limited amount of vintage champagne, or whatever is your favourite party drink. Through some French doors is the moonlit garden, a place you can be alone. In one corner of the room you're in now there is a good friend who has just gone through a horrible break-up. In another corner is someone you can rely on to complain about things – in quite an entertaining way – for half an hour. Standing in the middle of it all is the host, whom you find a bit intimidating. You can hear music coming from somewhere, and you expect that there is a dancefloor in another room.

You probably already know where you'd head first at this party. I know that I'd go for the champagne, then quickly see if my friend was OK, then head for the garden and eventually the dancing. For me, a good party should be just like an evening in a Fred Astaire and Ginger Rogers film where everything is beautiful and there is no real conflict. Therefore I would avoid the complaining person. I'd mean to thank the host, but might forget. Anyway, we're all different, so what would you do? Champagne or host? Or something else entirely? How about a close friend or relative you know well? What would they do? A friend of mine who always tries to do the right thing would, I imagine, first thank the host and then go and talk to her heartbroken friend. She'd get a drink later. Someone else I know would head straight for the food. Now imagine the same scene with the addition of the person you secretly love (if that person is now your partner, imagine a time before you were together). You hadn't expected that this person would be at the party. He or she hasn't yet seen you. *Now* what do you do? It is different from your first choice? How? Why?

Characterisation is based on the choices that people make in different situations. As Aristotle has told us already, we see characters through their actions, and in action there is always choice: Do I do this thing or another? Having chosen this thing, *how* do I do it? Some choices are conscious; some are unconscious. Some choices are based on obstacles, some on incentives. Others are (or seem) completely free. Most of the choices we make are quite small and amount to little more than whether we get a drink or food first at a party. But in these choices we see character – personality – emerge. Character isn't what someone thinks they should be, or hopes they are, or tries to be. We see character in what people *actually* do when given a certain amount of choice. Whatever I believe about myself, if I stand on the table and shout to a whole room of people that I am *REALLY SHY* it is clear that I am not. My action, based on my choice, shows that.

Character, or personality, is the glue that holds people together. It means that people are fairly predictable, if we know them well enough. This isn't a bad thing; it's just part of life. Most of us can predict whether a particular friend is more likely to choose to watch a soap opera or a football match tonight. Most of us know which things a particular friend takes seriously, and what is likely to please or offend him or her. Even if we find someone we know well doing something surprising, we will usually cease to be surprised once we know the reason for it. If fictional characters' actions astonish us, then this should be *because* of what we already know, not in spite of it. Great characterisation leads to wonderful reversals and just because a character is predictable on some level, that doesn't mean we should be able to predict exactly what he or she will do. Pip's response to Magwitch's return, Hamlet's anger with Ophelia and Ladislaw's reaction to Casaubon's death all have depth and drama because they are both astonishing *and* predictable. They are not random; they are the actions of people we feel we have come to know. But they are not what we necessarily expected either. They are dramatic but still 'in character'. Each is the choice of one thing rather than another, and while this choice may not make sense for everyone it makes sense for this character, in this situation.

Some guides to characterisation ask you to consider what your character would do if someone murdered their parents, or if they ran over a child, or if they had to choose between a life-saving operation for a friend and a million pounds for themselves. But these problems are not common ones that you are likely to face, and so it is unlikely that your characters will either. Watch out, too, because as soon as you think of something as abstract as 'a character' it becomes possible to think of murder and revenge and all sorts of unrealistic actions. Always ask, *What would I do? What are the choices I would be likely to have in this situation?* And it is much more likely that you'll be faced with the choice of black or blue socks for the day; toast or porridge for break-fast. Ordinary choice is based around things like where to go, who to see, what to eat, what to drink and what to say, just as in our party scenario. And it is difficult enough to fictionalise ordinary choice, let alone the big stuff. Many choices are of course not 'free'; they are based on obstacles, problems, compromises and incentives. And they can require some close reading to appreciate their complexity. If I find my rugby-obsessed friend watching a soap opera with his wife, it doesn't mean he suddenly loves soap opera. It means he loves his wife.[203] Most of the time we have to look beyond the surface to see real character. And when we look we find a special kind of coherence.

A mistake that beginning writers make (and it's one I have definitely made too) is to have a character arrive at a party and go through vague 'party actions' without being faced with real choices appropriate to his or her character. So, for example, I may have a character who particularly enjoys being comfortable. She never gets drunk (because this is uncomfortable for her), hardly talks to people she doesn't like but very much enjoys eating cake and other comfort foods. This character will not arrive at the party, calmly survey the room, greet the host, get a drink, eat something from the food table, talk to the other people in the room one by one and then go and stand in the garden. This set of actions makes no sense for this character. These are the actions of a generic party guest, and there isn't any such thing.[204] Our character will head for the food, probably telling herself that she 'deserves' it after her long drive. And she will probably feel a bit guilty that she doesn't greet the host first, or only does it in the most cursory way. We must remember that these are the actions of someone normal, not a villain. If we start to moralise about how she should have done this or that instead and then punish her for not being perfect – for example, if we decide to make her fall over because she didn't greet the host properly or because she ate too much cake – then, like cruel gods, we have cheapened our creation. We will think about this in more depth later.

When I first started writing, I didn't know how to do anything. I remember trying to work out how to write a fight scene (which was in itself completely implausible) and not being able to visualise which fist a character might use to punch someone, and in what direction the other person might fall. As a teenager I'd been obsessed with acting. I did my LAMDA medals and dreamed of becoming a professional actor. So I soon found myself out in the corridor trying to 'block out the scene'. After trying and failing to do this on my own I roped in a friend, staged my fight and wrote down what I learnt about the positioning of limbs and so on. Afterwards I thought to myself, 'Writing is a bit like acting.' Then I thought: 'OH MY GOD WRITING IS EXACTLY LIKE ACTING.'

After that, my first-person narration became a lot easier. All I was doing, I worked out, was a kind of role-play in my mind. And as long as my characters did things I was likely to do, they'd be authentic and plausible. So my character would get up, get dressed in clothes similar to mine, maybe a pair of jeans and a t-shirt, put on her left trainer before her right trainer and so on. She'd have a cigarette, because I would have done in those days. She'd drink a mug of tea. Then maybe she'd go to the shop, with her money in her jeans pocket rather than a handbag. When she got to the shop she'd look around at all the things on sale and maybe make a comment on consumer society and the price of baked beans, whether or not this fitted with the themes of the novel. She'd exchange some witty banter with the shopkeeper, which might establish things about how the local neighbourhood is going downhill or something like that. She . . .

Is it time for lunch yet? Wow, what a dreary scene. But if you're anything like me, you'll have got yourself lost in scenes like this before. You take your character somewhere for no real reason and then you are surprised when they don't seem to want to do anything. While other writers talk thrillingly about their characters 'taking over' their novels, all your characters do is just stand there. Why did my character have to go to the shop? I don't know. I probably thought it would be something for her to do while I tried to work out the rest of the plot. Perhaps it would 'establish character' if we saw her interacting with the shopkeeper? But, of course, it doesn't, not if there's no drama to keep the reader engaged. People do not go to shops simply to show off their witty exchanges with the shopkeeper or to establish their characters. These things can happen inci- dentally, but real people (on whom we want to base our characters) go to shops because they *want* something. They go because they *need* something. They make a choice to go because they desire change in their life, even if that change is simply to have a loaf of bread. And usually, if this is to form a scene in fiction, the bread won't be there, or it will be too high to reach, or a naked woman will be standing in front of it, or just as the character reaches for it his or her mother will phone with some important news. But if your character didn't need to go to the shop in the first place, then none of this will have any truth.

I was beginning to realise that there was a lot more to characterisation than just acting things out in my head, or in the corridor outside my study. After all, there is good acting and bad acting. Was it possible that some of my writing was based on *bad* acting? Was it possible that just having characters do things in a plausible, 'realistic' manner wasn't enough? I again thought back to my teenage acting days and remembered how fascinated I'd been with the great Russian theatre director Constantin Stanislavski. Of course I'd never actually read any of his books, but like most other people at the time I'd heard something about the principles of method acting, where you prepare for your role by actually living it as authentically as possible – like Robert de Niro apparently did to construct his character in *Taxi Driver*. Indeed, at the time I often fantasised about being in New York (or some other glamorous location) having to method-act the part of a beautifully wasted dropout, ballet dancer or star-crossed lover . . .

But ten years on I'd realised from writing myself into many corners (and corner shops) that there was more to characterisation than just looking the part, or even being able to 'do the things this kind of person would do'. There was more, I realised, to acting than just actions. Feeling a character's pain means *really* feeling it, not just going through the motions of acting it out. Total plausibility must mean that a character goes to a shop for a reason, and only then can she act authentically when she gets there.[205] Acting authentically means understanding the motivation for every little choice a character makes. It means there always is motivation and there always is choice. It means realising that truth inside an illusion is not truth at all. With all this in mind, I went to the library and read Stanislavski properly and discovered just how crucial his work is for writers creating characters.

Constantin Stanislavski (1863–1938) revolutionised Russian theatre by encouraging actors to locate the truth of a role inside themselves in order that they could present authentic, psychologically accurate characters on stage. Stanislavski realised that while it was possible for actors to adopt flat, familiar forms of characterisation, and that in some forms of theatre this would work as a kind of bland entertainment, there was a deeper truth in a kind of acting that a) shows a true understanding of the character (and therefore all of humanity) and b) draws this understanding, and therefore the character him- or herself, out of the *actor*. The actor does not copy other people 'acting joyful'; he or she acts as he or she does when feeling joy.

Stanislavski shows us that the major problem with stereo-typical, flat characters is that they cannot lead anything forward, let alone a plot, because they do not desire. They have no *objectives*. Stanislavski says that:

> It is possible to portray on the stage a character in general terms – a merchant, a soldier, an aristocrat, a peasant etc. [. . .] For example, a professional soldier as a general rule holds himself stiffly erect, marches around instead of walking like a normal person, wiggles his shoulders to show off his

epaulettes, clicks his heels together to make his spurs ring, speaks in a loud, barking tone out of habit. A peasant spits, blows his nose without a handkerchief, walks awkwardly, speaks in a disjointed manner, wipes his mouth on the tail of his sheepskin coat. An aristocrat always carries a top hat, wears gloves and a monocle, his speech is affected, he likes to play with his watch chain or the ribbon of his monocle. These are all generalised clichés supposed to portray characters. They are taken from life, they actually exist. But they do not contain the essence of the character and they are not individualised.[206]

These are examples from Stanislavski's own time, but we could equally say that the chav wears a hoody and trainers and carries a can of lager or a bag of McDonald's; the geek has pale skin and acne and glasses; the yummy mummy has blonde highlights, big sunglasses and expensive holidays; the member of the Women's Institute wears frumpy tweed skirts, makes her own marmalade, listens to *The Archers* and hates all young people. The student, in this way of looking at things, stays in bed until after lunch, gets drunk all the time, never washes, is terrible with money and spends all his or her time having sex and talking about philosophy. These examples are from post-millennial Britain (except the portrait of the student, which I realise owes a lot to the 1980s TV programme *The Young Ones*), but each culture has its own versions. As Stanislavski points out, there is some truth in these rather brutal characterisations, but they are not individualised, and they are static rather than dynamic. These characters can't make change happen because they don't need anything to change. Like plastic action figures they are already set, moulded and complete. They will never change their clothes, let alone surprise us in any meaningful ways.

Stanislavski's work represents a profound rejection of cliché, stereotype and commonplace assumptions. It is compassionate, and suggests that we all have the potential to understand and experience pain, love, hatred, frustration, ambition, failure and so on – all the things that make us human. By acting, or writing, we can share this compassion and understanding with each other and we can connect with people by representing, as authentically as we possibly can, the deep complication of human emotion. If I can do a good job of representing anger (and writing it down isn't that different from acting it out because both involve the choice of specific details), then there is a chance that you will recognise this as your own anger and you will be able to examine it in more detail. But I only know anger because I have felt it. And I have only felt it because – to be scientific about it – I have been in a dramatic situation where an obstacle means I cannot meet some objective. And it is only because of this that I have the first clue about writing fiction. I have suffered, I have experienced drama and I am prepared to share this with you.

Stanislavski's system urges the actor to find the particular in the general, to find his or her own unique way of presenting a deep character rather than a flat stereotype. Like his first lead-dramatist Chekhov,[207] Stanislavski wanted audiences to be able to experience a narrative without constantly being told what to think about it or how to judge the characters. Long before 'new criticism' and 'The Death of the Author', Stanislavski argued that a play often needs to be performed before the 'main theme' can be grasped. 'Sometimes the public helps us understand its true definition', he says.[208] This understanding is the point of art, and in theatre it must be the actors as much as the writers who produce characters of sufficient depth to help us understand things better and explore things deeply. A pantomime full of stereotypes does nothing to challenge what we think of as life, and our place in it. It is not art.

In order to present his theory of acting, Stanislavski fictionalised the lessons of a group of novice actors as they study under the great director Tortsov.[209] His books include *An Actor Prepares*, *Building a Character* and *Creating a Role*. In *Building a Character* we see our narrator and the other students grappling with the problem of acting 'old age'.

A minute later Vanya was hobbling around the room all doubled up as though he had had a stroke.

'No,' said Tortsov, stopping him, 'that's not a human being, that is a cuttlefish, or some kind of monster. Don't exaggerate.'

In another minute Vanya was hobbling around with youthful speed.

'Now that is too boisterous!' said Tortsov, again checking him. 'Your mistake lies in the fact that you follow the line of least resistance: you indulge in purely external imitation. But copies are not created works. That is a bad line to follow. It would be better for you to begin by studying the nature of old age. That would make clear to you what you should search for in your own nature.'[210]

Although it is difficult to write old age when you are young (and poverty when you are rich and so on), we do nevertheless frequently have to write outside our own experience. I may want to describe my protagonist's grandmother walking across the room, for example, and so I need to understand something of old age. Will I have my old woman shuffle slowly across the floor, exaggerated to the point of one dimension? Or will I focus on the little objective details that comprise this action? As I am not an actor, I perhaps have the luxury of being able to say 'The old woman walked across the room' without having to show how she does it.[211] An actor has no choice but to create every moment of the action. But if I *do* decide to portray the old woman, I can learn from Stanislavski not to exaggerate, belittle, condemn or patronise. Instead, I will know that I should consider deeply what it means to be 'old'. And I will know not to do this just by imagining, or even observing, elderly people but by considering how *I* would do something if I were very old. I have to find the role inside myself.[212]

Stanislavski also teaches us to look for the motivation behind the action. I may be able to convey how an elderly person sits in a chair in great detail if I think about it hard enough. But I also need to know *why* he or she is sitting at this moment, and in this chair. Because people act for a reason it is always plot that drives character forward, not the reverse, just as Aristotle said. We don't see characters just 'being', we see them 'doing'; we see them *acting*. Again, I can verify this by looking at myself. Do I do things for no reason at all? Or does everything I do have a motivation? In fiction characters move from a happy beginning to a sad end (good fortune to bad fortune), or the reverse, and in many ways that's all there is to it, as we have already seen. But writing this kind of trajectory is not easy.

One of the reasons it can be so hard to plot convincingly is because we are working with the complexities of cause and effect. We know that every part of the action in a narrative should be linked, so that if you take one piece away the rest comes with it. For example, it is because Oedipus's father Laius, ruler of Thebes, thinks Oedipus is cursed (to kill his own father and marry his mother) that he sends the baby away to be killed. But the baby is rescued, and adopted by a couple in Corinth. Oedipus makes his way back to Thebes, killing his father (a stranger) on the way. He marries his mother and, when it is revealed to him that Thebes is suffering under a great curse because of the murder of Laius, he, being a heroic kind of person, sets out to discover whodunnit. Of course, it was him.

What you'll notice about cause and effect is that it is always driven by character. But more than that – by characters who *desire*. Laius doesn't send his baby off randomly, or to help Sophocles along with his plot. Having been given the problem of the curse, and *desiring* to live, and, of course, believing in the curse, because he's that kind of person: only then does Laius choose to send off his baby. Oedipus doesn't just set out randomly to find out who killed Laius because he has nothing better to do. The citizens of Thebes say the murderer must be found, and because Oedipus *desires* truth and justice, he acts. The very fact that each of these events leads directly to the next, indeed *causing* it to happen – and doing so in a completely seamless way – is the reason that this is an excellent plot. At every moment, every character has an objective and these objectives make things happen. Change takes place.

In *An Actor Prepares*, Stanislavski introduces the concept of the unit and the objective. As we will see later, working on the level of the scene can help a writer to organise and focus his or her material. Actors already have scenes written for them, but they often need to be able to break these into distinct units, especially if their character is performing one 'unit' while another character is engaged with their own. Say I am going to post a letter. I leave the house and walk down the street, taking in trees, people, a plane flying in the sky and so on. There are a few spots of rain. A dog sniffs me and I exchange a few words with his owner. Then I stop to look in a shop because I am hoping to buy a new bag. I continue down the street to the post-box and post the letter. How many distinct units are there here? Do we count them as follows: street, trees, people, plane, rain, dog, dog-walker, shop, post-box? Do we take all of these as the units, or episodes, that comprise me walking to the post-box? Stanislavski suggests not. The effect of seeing all these things separately would make the event 'going to post a letter' tedious, episodic and unfocused.

Instead, he suggests breaking an action like this into more distinct units, each with its own objective. Here we see that there is one main objective: *go to the post-box*. There is also a minor objective: *look for a new bag*. These are not part of the same unit but are distinct units in themselves. In the main unit I am *going to the post-box* and looking at the trees and greeting the dog-owner and so on are all part of that. In an entirely different unit (contained within the first) I am *looking for a new bag*. Do these objectives go together or not? If my objective in the main unit changed slightly to *I must reach the post-box before 4 p.m. so that my love letter gets to its recipient tomorrow*, then suddenly looking for the bag seems incongruous. If I was an actor, I would not dawdle on my way to post this letter. I would give up looking for a new bag and would probably not greet the dog-walker either. As a writer, I would also not want to create all these different, distracting actions. I'd be guided by the main objective for this character in this scene, and reduce it from two units to one.[213]

We can see clearly that each unit is created by an objective that is itself created by desire. Stanislavski stresses how important it is for actors to choose *verbs* to express their objectives. As he says, 'Every objective must carry in itself the germ of an action.'[214] Action is formed from doing, not being: from concrete verbs rather than abstract nouns. Kenneth L. Stilson, Charles McGaw and Larry Clark, in their book *Acting is Believing*, explore the distinction between 'being' and 'doing' here:

> A state of being is not actable because it provides nothing specific to do. It leaves the actor stuck with a general emotion, leading him into stereotyped movements and gestures – clenching his fists to show he is angry, putting

his hand to his head to show he is thoughtful, or contorting the muscles of his face to show he is in pain.

Burning your hand may *be* painful. But you *want* to relieve the pain by applying salve, butter, cold water or some other remedy. When a celebrity is pointed out in a crowd, you may *be* curious. But you *want* to secure a position where you can see to advantage . . .[215]

Just as an actor cheapens a performance with a predictable expression of vague 'anger', so we cheapen the concept by simply writing the word, or using a cliché to describe it. Thinking instead about what our character desires at this moment, and how he or she might try to achieve this – in other words what he or she would *do* – is a fundamental principle of characterisation. So we must always remember the desire, and then the action that comes from desire. The character goes to the shop because she wants a loaf of bread; she goes to the post-box because she wants to post a letter. A very useful thing to do with desire is to keep asking *why?* of it. Why does the character – or why would *I* in her position – want a loaf of bread? Is it because she wants to relieve her hunger? Not necessarily. Sometimes I buy bread because I think I might want toast tomorrow morning, or because my mother has come to stay, or for my partner. I might be buying bread because I want to be organised, or because I want more time to do something else tomorrow, or because I want to impress someone. Of course it's also possible that I might want to make a sandwich for lunch. Think about how the actions around buying the bread would differ in these scenarios. How likely am I to chat to the shopkeeper if my objective is to make a sandwich as soon as possible?

It is important to identify the correct objective in each scene and not get tempted into shallow characterisation by making 'obvious' or simplistic assumptions. As we saw above, I don't buy bread only when I am hungry. Always put yourself into the character's place and ask what *your* objective would be in this precise situation. Robert McKee is helpful here:

> If your character's up to no good and you place yourself within his being, asking, 'If I were he in this situation, what would I do?', you'd do everything possible to get away with it. Therefore you would not act like a villain; you would not twist your moustache.[216]

Think about cartoons for children. The villains simply have to *be* villains, which means twiddling their moustaches, cackling loudly and so on. This is a generalised portrait that is not intended to explore anything in any great depth: it's just shallow entertainment. But a real villain is, of course, busy trying not to get caught. When I used to let my dog off the lead in a place where this had just been banned, I didn't run around laughing and declaring that I had foiled the council's plans. But I did glance over my shoulder a bit more often, and carried the lead in my hand rather than in my pocket. I acted in these ways because I desired not to be caught. This was my objective. I was not offering myself up as a 'character'. One problem with the stereotypes we have already looked at – the soldier, the chav, the geek

and so on – is that they are static images rather than active
characters. OK, a soldier might go to war, and a chav might
get into a fight, and a geek might stay indoors all the time,
but we have no idea why they are doing these things, apart
from, 'Well, he's a soldier and that's what they do', or 'He's
a chav, and that's what they do.' We are not seeing these
characters making any choices. Indeed, stereotypes have no
choices because everything has already been decided for
them in advance.

It is horribly easy to write stereotypes. But remember
that if you do write them, then not only are you in danger
of misrepresenting humanity (just as you are not a stereotype, neither are other people), you are also in danger of
bad plotting. *A geek walks past a chav and the chav attacks
him for no reason.* That's a terrible plot, because there's no
problem to be resolved, and no motivation for the action,
and, because of that, no cause and effect. But it's what we
expect these clichéd characters to do. The only way we can
make this 'chav' character act convincingly and meaningfully is to first strip away the label 'chav' and, second, to
think seriously about what he desires and what obstacles
he faces. What are his units and his obstacles? What's his
story? The danger here is that we can end up adding senti-
mentality to stereotype. We might say that the chav is a
chav because of the government, or because of his parents,
or because he went to a bad school. Poor old chav, so
mistreated and bullied and downtrodden . . . We could also
construct a whole story for the geek that 'explains' who he
is. Perhaps his parents worked too hard, leaving him to be
cared for by a cold au pair. Perhaps he found he could

only be happy playing videogames. Perhaps because his parents didn't love him he has never learned to love himself. He escapes further and further into fantasy but never learned the basics of personal hygiene . . .

That's not characterisation: that's just a lot more clichés.

I remember the first time I tried teaching characterisation with an MA class. We do it differently now, but in that class I asked the students to think of a stereotype, write a description of it, and then work out what could be changed to make the character rounded and likeable. Again and again the students removed flaws that needed to remain, or made excuses for the character. So a barmaid with tattoos had only got the tattoos to cover up a painful skin condition she'd had as a child. A 'white van man' only drove fast because he was anxious about his newborn baby and so on. Note the judgement in these edits. Tattoos are *bad*. Driving fast is *bad*. Anything to do with children and babies is *good*. The students were pointlessly trying to neutralise 'bad' actions with sentimental or passive reasons. It wasn't the students' fault – it was, after all, a terrible exercise. But I learned a lot from getting it wrong. The main thing I learned is that we always have to begin with the character's desire and build up from there, otherwise characterisation will be patronising. I slap my friend in the face not because I am 'cold and cruel', and not because I was horribly abused as a child and can only react violently, but perhaps because in this situation I *want* to be the centre of attention, or I *want* her to shut up and stop speaking about my sister that way. I may never have slapped someone before; I may do it all the time. But in this scene, at this moment, I *want* something – however unconsciously – and that is why I act.

Stanislavski argues that all a character's objectives should come together as part of one great *superobjective*.[217] This, for me, is the most profound part of his teaching, and the one that has most use for us as writers. When I used to give my lecture on characterisation, I would ask the students to think about why they had turned up to hear it. What was their objective in this 'unit' in their lives? Given that they were not simply robots programmed with a timetable, why were they there? Lots of students don't come to lectures, after all, and as we record our lectures in some form and put them online, it would seem to be much more efficient for students to just read the lecture while lying in bed. So why do students go to lectures? I'm sure many of the students didn't immediately know why they were there. Some of them were presumably simply following the 'rules'. Some of them may have wanted to impress me. Some of them may have feared failure. Some may have promised their parents that they would attend all their lectures. Some of them may have saved to pay their tuition fees and wanted to get everything they could out of their degree. One of them may have been in love with one of the others. Another may have just turned up because she was cold.

Behind every surface objective lies a deeper desire – to be a better student, or a better person, or to not get into trouble, or to be a better writer, or to fall in love, or what-ever. Behind this desire lies something even more profound. A need for control, or perfection, or love, or success, or approval, or knowledge, or to be truthful. The surface reason for going to a lecture, visiting a shop or getting a drink at a party is your 'motivation', or your 'objective'. The reason for *this* (once you go back through enough 'Why?'s), ultimately, is your personality or, if you like, your character – and the essence of your character is something like a superobjective: a big wish, an ultimate wish, the thing you desire *more than anything else.*

Whether or not you want to fish around in your own psyche for your own final superobjective (which can be very difficult, if not impossible[218]), and whether or not you believe you have one, it can certainly help you if you give each of your characters one big thing they want – a superobjective and then one little (connected) thing in each scene. Like many principles in this book, this may sound reductive. In practice, it isn't: it's extremely difficult to get right. The first thing we need to do to get it right is to look at ourselves enough so that we see our true motivations for things. What things do *I* want? Why am *I* really doing this? Am I actually bitching about this person to make myself look better? Perhaps that's why my character is 'bitchy', too. She's not 'a bitch'; she's insecure, just like me. She *wants* to be liked. Why does she want to be liked? Who does she want to like her? Perhaps being liked makes her feel safe, loved or in control. Writing means looking deeply into ourselves and being very, very honest about why we do things, in order that we can create honest and authentic characters.

The second thing we need to do is state each character's superobjective carefully. In practice this can take a very long time for each character. Stanislavski discusses the problem of naming the superobjective in this significant passage:

Suppose we are producing Griboyedov's *Woe From Too
Much Wit* and we decide that the main purpose of the play
can be described by the words 'I wish to strive for Sophy'.
There is a great deal in the plot that would confirm that
definition. The drawback would be that in handling the play
from that angle the theme of social denunciation would
appear to have only an episodic, accidental value. But you
can describe the super-objective in the terms of 'I wish to
struggle, not for Sophy but for my country!' Then Chatski's
ardent love of his country will move into the foreground.
At the same time, the indictment of society theme will
become more prominent, giving the whole play a deeper
inner significance. You can deepen its meaning still further
if you use 'I wish to struggle for freedom' as the main theme
[. . .] [T]he whole play loses the personal, individual tone
it had when the theme was connected with Sophy; it is no
longer even national in scope, but broadly human, and
universal in its implications.[219]

Note how the naming of the superobjective can change its
level of significance from the personal to the national to
the human and finally to the universal. It should go without
saying that we are always aiming for universal significance
in our work. That doesn't mean that nothing will happen
on a personal or individual level, but that these personal,
individual events will have some resonance for all of us, as
part of a larger thematic whole. Another thing to note from
this passage is that Stanislavski often blurs the boundaries
between the main theme, or superobjective, of the play, and
that of the main character. This is because in any fictional

whole, the superobjective of the main character and the superobjective of the whole narrative are usually very closely connected. We will look at examples of this later.

A character's superobjective is their *prime motivating desire*. It is what he or she wants more than anything else. In a sense, almost everyone's prime objective is to be happy. But different things makes us happy. Examples of super-objectives are 'I wish to be comfortable', 'I wish to be perfect', 'I wish to be in control', 'I wish to be loved', 'I wish to be a success', 'I wish to have knowledge', 'I wish to be entertained', 'I wish to be important', 'I wish to have power' and 'I wish to be superior'. There are lots of others.[220] I like the way Stanislavski frames the superobjective in terms of a wish. And it is helpful to begin 'I wish . . .' as if you, or your character, had come across a magical object that granted you just one wish. With *one wish*, what would your character want? No, not the thing you'd tell your whole family about. What's the one big secret thing you want, the thing you'd probably be embarrassed to admit in public? It's likely you don't know. But your unconscious does.

Imagine you've just won a million pounds. What will you spend it on? Perhaps a nice big house. Will you spend more time working out the furnishings or the alarm system? Will you install a gym or a videogames room? This is a fairly crude example, but I'm sure you can see that someone who spends more time thinking about an alarm system than a sofa probably values control more than comfort even if they don't realise this. Our hang-ups and problems, and of course those of our characters, will also relate back to a superobjective. I would imagine that someone whose main desire is to be perfect would be more likely to develop an eating disorder than someone who desires to be comfortable. Of course, one set of actions doesn't immediately lead us to a superobjective. Someone with an eating disorder may finally want to be safe, or loved, or powerful or successful or any number of things – we'd need to have other actions to make a full picture. But we can say for sure that he or she wants this *more* than he or she wants to be comfortable, because an eating disorder is absolutely not about comfort.

Much of the time the superobjective does not tell you exactly what someone will do, and there are lots of situations where most people do exactly the same thing, like have a slice of cake at a children's birthday party, or sunbathe on the beach. Most of the time the superobjective tells us more about how an action will be undertaken. Think of three different superobjectives and imagine how different sunbathing would be for each of them; then do the same for eating a slice of cake at a children's birthday party. Think about how this person would react to a telesales call or a thunderstorm. Many of the things that happen to us – like telesales calls and thunderstorms – can't be controlled by us anyway. All we can do is react.

One important thing to consider is that your character will be unaware of his or her superobjective. Most people will tell themselves, and others, stories about who they really are that are nice, but not necessarily true. I may believe that all I want is to do good things for other people. But if I have ever walked past one single unhappy person without trying to help them, then this can't be my superobjective.

Helping people might be something I desire; it certainly isn't what I desire *above all else*. In my novel *The End of Mr. Y*, the protagonist Ariel wants a lot of things (to have more money, to have sexual relationships, to finish her PhD etc.) but the thing she wants *more than anything else* is knowledge: her superobjective is therefore 'I wish to know everything'. So, in Chapter One, when she goes into a bookshop and finds a rare, cursed book on sale for £50 (almost all her money in the world), she buys it and decides to worry about food later. A character whose superobjective was 'I wish to be comfortable' or 'I wish to be safe' would not buy the book.

Another important feature of the superobjective is that the character has not achieved it and cannot possibly hope to ever achieve it. Giving characters a superobjective that is achievable might seem kind and modest but it will severely limit your theme. If we consider Pip's superobjective in *Great Expectations* as 'I wish to become a gentleman to win the affections of Estella', we are being far less ambitious than if we consider it to be 'I wish to get the best of everything'. Look at these two options carefully. One is possible, limited and finite; the other is impossible, unlimited and infinite. Stated objectives – the things that characters admit to wanting – are usually of the first type; superobjectives, the second. Just because Pip states that 'I had loved Estella dearly and long, and that, although I had lost her and must live a bereaved life, whatever concerned her was still nearer and dearer to me than anything else in the world',[221] that does not mean it is absolutely true.

Part of Pip's appeal is that he believes that he has thrown

over good, innocent Joe for the cold temptress Estella. Pip probably thinks that to be a moral and good person he should have settled down with Biddy and not become so obsessed with being a gentleman at any cost. We love Pip for thinking like this, of course. We love his regret because it is personal and human. But the book is bigger than that. The book allows its characters to view morality on a personal level, but as a whole it frames these questions in a universal way. It asks us to consider whether Pip would *really* do things differently if he was given another chance. And would we want him to? Would we have him settle down with Biddy and never have any further ambition in life? Do we want him to become Joe?

Furthermore, do we really believe that Pip would never have had it in him to want to become a gentleman if he had not seen Estella, and that nothing else could have had the effect of her harsh words about his hands and his boots? *Great Expectations* is not about the damage that Estella can do, or about the damage women can do, or even about the damage that sexual attraction can do. It is about the damage that *pride* can do, and the mistakes we all make in trying to get the best of things. And, in the end, Pip is actually transformed by his desire for betterment and carries out his duty to Magwitch properly: he does his best for him. Like seed words, which we will come to later, superobjectives work well when they have a multiplicity of meanings. 'I wish to get the best of everything' does not just imply material and moral improvement. Getting the best (better) of things also means gaining knowledge, getting on top of things, winning. It's all ego, as Pip is, and as we probably are too.

More than one character means more than one superobjective, and drama is created from having two (or more)
superobjectives in competition or conflict with each other.
Characters will already face significant obstacles, of course.
As we have seen, superobjectives are impossible to achieve.
But the character who wishes to be comfortable might just
achieve it for ten minutes with a big tub of ice cream – if
it wasn't for his wife telling him that he should go to the
gym instead. If he wants to be comfortable, and she wants
to be, say, a success, these two are going to clash over all
sorts of things.

Stanislavski uses the example of Henrik Ibsen's play
Brand to demonstrate how competing objectives and superobjectives work. In a central scene in *Brand*, Agnes is
mourning the death of her young son. Her husband, the
Pastor Brand, had refused to try to save the health of his
son by moving his family. Now his son is dead, he insists
on Agnes giving the baby clothes to a neighbour. We have
a 'clash of principles'[222] in which

> Brand's *duty* wrestles with mother *love*; an *idea* struggles
> with a *feeling*; the fanatic *preacher* with the sorrowing *mother*;
> the *male* principle with the *female*.[223]

Of course, these principles still need to be translated into
objectives. At one point Tortsov's students decide to brainstorm this and we learn that Brand's duty makes him desire
'to obtain power over Agnes in order to persuade her to
make a sacrifice, to save her, to direct her in the right path',
and Agnes's love makes her want to 'remember my dead

child', and 'to be so close to him that we can never be separated'. Brand meanwhile wishes 'her to understand man's larger destiny'.[224] Here we begin to understand even more about the conflict between these two. Brand imagines himself fighting for universal principles against those that are merely personal.

It would be possible to argue that in *Adaptation* the character Charlie Kaufman's superobjective is to 'be loved'. He agonises about his appearance, and wants to please people. This looks neat set against the superobjective of Susan Orlean, which is 'to love something else', or 'to be passionate'. Love is set against objectivity; fiction against journalism . . . But wait. Let's test this out. Is Kaufman really *all about love*? His first minor objective in the plot of the film is to write a successful screenplay: this has nothing to do with love; indeed, he does it so intensively that he loses Amelia. He is also not writing the screenplay because he wants to be a big deal in Hollywood, or he would immediately make the 'orchid heist film'. His superobjective therefore isn't about love, power or wealth. It seems to be something more to do with truth. He wants to write about real life. In fact, it turns out that he doesn't want to be loved so much that he will bullshit to get love as his brother seems to do. His superobjective becomes something like: 'I wish to tell the truth about life'. Not 'I wish to be thought truthful', which is different. *I wish to be truthful.* But he is a writer of fiction, which gives a very special kind of internal conflict. Susan Orlean's superobjective is still, I think, that she wishes to be passionate, and her obstacle is that she is required to be objective, because she is a journalist.

Another character who desires truth above all else is Ammu from *The God of Small Things*. We see this in all her actions: her desire for true love is clearly of high importance, as is her desire to tell the police the truth about Velutha. But we also see it in her everyday actions, such as her cynical responses to Chacko, her Oxford-educated brother. After Chacko thanks a Marxist protestor for closing the bonnet of their car, this is what follows:

> 'Don't be so ingratiating, comrade,' Ammu said. 'It was an accident. He didn't really mean to help. How could he *possibly* know that in this old car there beats a truly Marxist heart?'
>
> 'Ammu,' Chacko said, his voice steady and deliberately casual, 'is it at all possible for you to prevent your washed-up cynicism from colouring everything?'
>
> Silence filled the car like a saturated sponge.[225]

Here we see Ammu's desire for truth set against Chacko's optimism. While he continues to send his doomed model airplanes into the sky, she keeps metaphorically shooting them down. If Ammu was only cynical around Chacko and no one else, her action would be limited to the personal sphere. As it is, her cynicism comes from a deep desire to tell the truth. In her desire for truth above all else, she embodies a universal concept.

In David Mitchell's *number9dream* we could read Eiji's superobjective as 'I wish to find my father', but then much of the novel seems irrelevant. Why the fantasy love affair? Why the gangster plot? Why the exploration of reality and fantasy? 'I wish to find my father' is in fact just an objective in a larger whole. If we re-cast Eiji's superobjective as 'I wish to be a hero', then the whole plot makes sense. And heroism, being a hero and the place of the real-life hero in relation to fictional heroes are all universal themes, whereas the search for Eiji's father relates only to Eiji. Good super-objectives don't just help us to understand our characters and make them act – they connect our fictional characters with the bigger themes of our plots and, if we do it right, with wider concerns outside the plot.

It's a good idea to build your characters using super-objectives. In practice it's almost impossible to do this before you begin writing and get to know the characters a little bit first. I want to see what the characters will do on their own before I begin crafting them, and so I usually begin working intensively on character only once I am a few chapters into a novel. I first read Stanislavski between *PopCo* and *The End of Mr. Y*, and so Ariel Manto is the first char-acter I have written with a superobjective. I didn't start thinking about it until I was halfway into the novel. Characters usually do take on some coherence on their own. I didn't need to know Ariel's superobjective to know that she would buy the cursed book. But I needed it later, when I wanted to keep her actions consistent. She gets stuck in the Troposphere because she desires knowledge more than safety, freedom, love or control.

Working with superobjectives also helped me with *Our Tragic Universe*. Sometimes a superobjective becomes a real puzzle, and working it out can be very productive. In *Our Tragic Universe* I spent a very long time working on Meg's superobjective. Here's part of the table I created when I was writing the novel:

Meg	I wish to make sense (. . . to write (define, create, make, limit) reality, to tell a true story, to distinguish between reality and fiction, to know what is real, to define reality, to rationalise, to 'make sense' out of the world, to make fiction real, or realist, to embrace the material world, rather than faith, stories and language, to make a scarf, to make sense myself, or be the author of reality rather than the passive reader of fiction, to be able to make predictions – to actively create meaning and sense, but also to have meaning in myself, to 'make sense' to other people and in the universe).	But . . . I write fiction, I make nonsense, or bad sense; I am in a relationship that is not real, but appears that it should 'make sense' but only as fiction. The limits of reality don't stay where I set them. I sense things I don't like.
Libby	I wish to follow a pattern (. . . to be a heroine; for life to work like fiction. If I do something good I wish to be rewarded, if I do something bad I wish to be punished). Libby wants instructions, models, fictional versions. Not advice, exactly, but patterns. She likes the pattern of the beginning of a relationship. She would have read *The Rules* when it came out and laughed at them but secretly followed them. Is this why she likes SF, too, and therefore read Meg's books?	But . . . Real people feel pain, and tragedy is not much fun when it's happening to you.
Vi	I wish to eliminate drama (. . . stories, heroes, overcoming).	But . . . In wishing this I wish therefore to be a hero and overcome something, therefore I am a living paradox . . .

This is exactly how I found it, buried in a folder called 'Characterisation' in a folder called 'Our Tragic Universe'. I tend to do a lot of 'working out' when I am writing my novels, both on paper and increasingly on computer files as well. This table does not accurately represent the way the characters actually turned out, but it does show some of what I was thinking when I was writing them. Much of the thinking process happens naturally while writing a novel, and if this level of working-out is not for you then don't panic. I'm not sure I could have managed quite this much detail for the characters in *Going Out* or *Bright Young Things* at the time I was writing them. Looking at the table now, I can see that while I worked on the internal conflict of each character, I did not work on the conflict between characters as much as perhaps I would now.

At this stage it is important to make sure that you are not consciously or unconsciously creating a character that is basically a portrait of someone you already know. Well-crafted characters will represent some aspect of yourself or 'people in general' (which you can only really know from yourself), not someone else. It feels very uncomfortable taking about characters and even giving them objectives and superobjectives if you know they are in fact your own mother, or your flatmate, or your cousin. Of course you will be inspired by things that people do and say in the world, but you should always look inside yourself for what you can make from these observations. Again and again I see students struggling to write the actions of someone whom they know in real life. It's limiting, embarrassing and also, of course, morally dubious. So let your characters develop as a part of you. Ask yourself what *you* would do in this situation if you were this person. And at some point it will probably become clear that you need a superobjective to help you, if you are not to let your character become a cliché. It is very, very easy for this to happen. In *Our Tragic Universe* it was almost impossible to keep Libby from being a stereotype ('the mistress'; 'the adulterous woman') until I pinned her down with this idea that she wants to follow a pattern. Then she became much more interesting.

I recently did an exercise in a tutorial with a PhD student that was quite illuminating. She was trying to work out a minor but important character, so I asked her what the character would buy from a supermarket for dinner on an evening that her husband was away. My student had no idea. In fact, imagine now a middle-aged woman in the supermarket. What do you think she's buying? Without some sense of her personality – and therefore her super-objective – we have no idea. Therefore we fall back on stereotypes. A middle-aged woman must like cakes and chocolate, we might think. Or she might be on a diet. She'd buy a magazine. A salad, perhaps. Why? We don't know. Maybe because these are things that middle-aged women buy in TV commercials. But I bet we don't automatically imagine her buying a crate of beer and a large steak. We have created a stereotype – and chosen to accept consensus reality rather than deep reality.

Now let's give her a superobjective. Let's choose the same one my student chose: *I wish for balance*. Now we see that the woman in the supermarket does not want to get too much or too little of anything. She's not going to binge on biscuits, or wine. She's going to have a little of every-thing. And she probably won't even know that this is what she's doing; she will just do it. If her superobjective is to achieve balance, ideally she'd have a job where she can prioritise this (or, if she hasn't, this will be a source of great tension). Perhaps she's a yoga teacher, a ballet dancer, an accountant, or an interior designer. Obstacles are likely to involve unbalancing in some way: this is where this character will find tension. Perhaps this comes in the form of a partner or colleague with a competing superobjective. Or perhaps she is actually very poor and trying to balance her books as well as her life.

Much of what she does in the supermarket will be the same as other people. Most people, after all, try to save money, go quickly and ignore everyone else. But what if this woman's desire for balance means she wants fairness and equality in the world? What if she's a slow shopper, and her basket is actually full of organic, local and fair-trade groceries, because these seem the most 'balanced' and there-fore the most fair? Remember that my idea of balance and yours are likely to be different. Just knowing the super-objective of the character does not predict exactly what they will do, or how the superobjective will become evident. Let's now think about what would happen if she notices a special offer. She can get three jars of supermarket own-brand coffee for the price of one jar of her fair-trade brand. What does she do now? Try to work it out. (But remember that she doesn't know she is constantly looking for balance.)

There are other sources of tension and drama apart from just the obstacle. The incentive also creates drama, because it also forces us to choose one thing rather than another, or modify our behaviour in a way we think will be beneficial to us. Most people will do something if there's a financial reward for it, or they will avoid doing something if there is a fine. At least that's what the theory says: people actually react in all sorts of interesting ways to incentives. In the popular economics book *Freakonomics* we hear about the nursery that started fining parents who were late to pick up their children. Suddenly the rate of late pick-ups increased rather than decreased. Why? Because people now felt they were paying for their lateness and so didn't have to feel guilty about it.[226] Similarly, a library fine of 20p examined from another angle is quite a good price to pay for not having to go out in the rain today. A parking fine may for some just be a reasonable price to pay for parking in the best spot in town. Perhaps that is why councils now use wheel clamps, and in Vilnius, Lithuania, the mayor apparently runs over illegally parked Porsches and Rolls-Royces in a tank.

Contemporary behavioural economics shows us all this and more. It shows that given the chance to steal without being observed, most people don't do it. Surely in a completely rational, self-interested world, we would steal at every available opportunity? In a way, of course, we do. Every 'special offer' in the West rips someone off somewhere. But most of us won't cheat the staff kitchen contribution scheme at work.[227] In some way we clearly want to think of ourselves as good people, or people in control, or people who are well-off, or better than 'all those thieves out there' or whatever. After all, quite a large proportion of people on this planet believe they will be judged at the end of their lives, or even before then.

Behavioural economics shows again and again that although we are sometimes oddly rational despite ourselves,[228] probably more often we are the reverse. Elinor Ostrom's Nobel Prize-winning work debunking the so-called 'tragedy of the commons' shows us that we are actually not often 'rational', if rationality means getting as much as we can for ourselves regardless of others in our community. As we saw earlier, the psychologist Daniel Kahneman (also a Nobel laureate) has shown how 'fast thinking' is often wrong even though it *feels* completely right. There is evidence all over the place that although people act for a complex brew of reasons, much of the time we are irrational, emotional, moral, yet somehow oddly predictable. Yes, we may be self-interested animals, but something stops most of us running around with a machete stealing everyone else's stuff. We don't, after all, just want 'stuff'. Much of what we want involves good relationships with other people, and this, as we have already seen, is almost impossible to understand. This is what fiction is for. After all, if people were programmed like computers then we'd know exactly what everyone would do in any set of given circumstances and there'd be no pleasure (or gain) in reading Tolstoy. What we actually find is that one single action can be investigated for hours, weeks, months if we really want to go that deeply into it. We probably don't want to go that deeply into it, but we do want to go further than just making quick assumptions.

Think about the last time you bought a pair of shoes.

Did you buy new shoes only because your old ones were worn out? Did you buy them as a treat? Did you buy them because you were bored, or feeling insecure? Think about the shoes you bought. (Yes, even if you don't think shoes matter to you, and only 'silly' people think deeply about shoes.) Are they beautiful? Comfortable? Sensible? Cheap? Expensive? And I bet if you think about it you will find a similarity between the shoes you last bought and what you have for breakfast. For example, if you wear sensible shoes, I bet you'll have a sensible breakfast, too. I bet you have bran. If your shoes are very comfortable – like Ugg boots, or favourite old trainers – I bet you have something sweet or fatty in your breakfast (even if these occur in a healthy form as raisins, honey or coconut), because these are comforting foods.

Things do not always follow from one another in such a simple way, of course. We can't tell just by knowing that someone buys expensive shoes what kind of breakfast he or she has. We'd need to know more before we could predict anything. We'd need to know *why* this person bought expensive shoes. But if we kept asking 'Why?' of all her decisions, we'd probably get a similar answer each time, just as we'd discover that the person who likes comfortable shoes also likes a bit of comfort food as well (and would probably head for the food table first at a party . . .) Just because people aren't always textbook-definition rational (for example, only buying new shoes when an old pair has worn out), that does not mean they are not in some way consistent.

Last time I bought shoes, they were sensible and slightly ugly. If a friend had seen me, she might have asked what had happened to my personality that I was suddenly buying these ugly things rather than shoes I really like. But in fact I was buying ugly shoes for the same reason I buy my other shoes: because I am quite vain. How does that work? Well, earlier this year I had to give up running because of shin-splints and since then I have put on weight. I don't like putting on weight. The only way I can get back to running is if I fix my shin-splints. So I saw a physiotherapist, who told me to also see a podiatrist. He tells me I have to wear sensible, ugly, sturdy shoes (with orthotic insoles) for 97 per cent of the time from now on. But I can wear high heels *sometimes*. The choice I was faced with, to put it in very blunt terms, was this: to wear nice shoes all the time but forget about running (but as I said to the podiatrist, 'What's the point of wearing nice shoes if I'm fat?'), or to run, be thin and wear nice shoes for only 3 per cent of the time. If we look at this situation closely, we can see that in buying ugly shoes I am committing an act of vanity far greater than if I was buying beautiful shoes.

What a lot of explanation about one pair of shoes! But I bet you've got similarly detailed explanations about your own shoes, if you really think about it. In fact, you'll have similarly detailed explanations about many of the things you do. My explanation above only scratches the surface of me-as-character. Why do I want to be attractive? Why do I feel I must make jokes with healthcare professionals? Why do I run? Is it to win or to take part? Why? And even though I seem to be baring my soul to you, am I *really*? Were the shoes I was buying really that ugly, or was I in fact trying to buy the most beautiful ugly shoes I could?

Why did I just edit the paragraph above so that instead of admitting to being 'very vain' I am now admitting to being only 'quite vain'?

Really thinking about these things is part of being a writer. If you don't already do it, begin now. Think about the last thing you bought or did and ask yourself why. *Really why*. Keep asking why until you get to something big like 'I wanted to be comfortable' or 'I wanted to be in control'. This takes a lot of practice, and you might not get anywhere near the final big thing for a while. But here's a hint: all shoes are designed to be as comfortable as possible, as sturdy as possible and so on. You might choose shoes that are comfortable *and* sensible *and* attractive. You need to ask yourself which is the *most important* of these factors for you, and why it is important. You may have been clever and bought shoes that are both beautiful and comfortable. But if you were in a shop that was about to close and you had to choose between a pair of shoes that were beautiful but uncomfortable and a pair that were comfortable but ugly, which would you choose? Character is seen most clearly in choice under pressure. But, as we should have noticed by now, it is also seen when there is no pressure at all. People are still consistent when there is no one watching. On their own, what do people do and why? What stories do they tell themselves about what they are doing and how close is this to the truth?

When you create characters you have committed a god-like act. It doesn't matter whether you are religious or not, you have still behaved as a god would. Characterisation is after all not mere representation, since in fiction you are not (I hope) representing anyone real on the page. It is an act of creation. Even if you have avoided taking a god-like role in your narration, you can't avoid it when you create characters. So act as you hope a god would. In my experience, many people who are not religious feel that all versions of God they have come across are not good enough. They let people starve, for example, or don't answer every prayer. Well, when you create characters you must be the perfect god, whatever you think that should be. At the very least this means you must love your characters – yes, even the antagonists. You must not judge them. You must show them compassion. Give them free will, a superobjective, some obstacles and incentives and see what happens. They will make mistakes because we all do; they will be lonely sometimes because we all are; they will hope for things to get better, as we all do. If you do it well, we will see ourselves in them.

WRITING A GOOD SENTENCE

Specificity, precision, and brevity, applied in language, drive us towards compassion. Conversely, all attempts at world domination begin with weak, evasive, impersonal language.

George Saunders[229]

Cross out as many adjectives and adverbs as you can. . . . It is comprehensible when I write: 'The man sat on the grass,' because it is clear and does not detain one's attention. On the other hand, it is difficult to figure out and hard on the brain if I write: 'The tall, narrow-chested man of medium height and with a red beard sat down on the green grass that had already been trampled down by the pedestrians, sat down silently, looking around timidly and fearfully.' The brain can't grasp all that at once, and art must be grasped at once, instantaneously.

Anton Chekhov[230]

Good writers are those who keep the language efficient. That is to say, keep it accurate, keep it clear.

Ezra Pound[231]

You can always count on a murderer for a fancy prose style.

Vladimir Nabokov[232]

I used to love Enid Blyton. When I was about eight, I would often make myself some toast and a cup of strong tea with three sugars and lie on the brown carpet of our council flat to read *The Magic Faraway Tree* or *The Enchanted Wood*. I can't quite express how much I loved escaping to this world where children were nice to each other, had lots of food and went on adventures. I remember reading very, very fast, sucking up the stories as if they were milkshakes. Adults commented on how quickly I could get through books. It's a good job there were decent libraries then, because sometimes I read three or four books in a day. I got through books fast because, like most fast-reading children, I read just enough words to get a sense of what was going on. I don't think I ever read whole sentences. At that age I would definitely skip any particularly long descriptions and head straight for the dialogue. Years later, one of my PhD students told me that she'd learned exactly these skills on a speed-reading course. But perhaps all eight-year-olds are natural speed-readers. At eight, no one wants to linger over a simile. At eight, you just want to know What Happened. But even when I read a book a second time and a third time, I read it exactly the same way.

It wasn't just that I'd fallen into bad reading habits. These books seemed to encourage me to read this way. None of the sentences demanded my attention. None of them said, *Stop and read me because I will tell you the truth about life.*

When I was eight, the truth about my life was that it was boring and confusing and I wanted to escape it, and it was as if these books knew that. They were comforting. They were soothing. They had good characters and bad characters, and good things happened to the good characters and the bad characters learned the error of their ways. The sentences were easy to read, or at least easy to skip. Many of them had what I quickly recognised as 'filler': adjectives and adverbs that didn't make any difference to what was happening and that often told you what you knew already. I wouldn't swap that early reading experience for anything, but it's not how I would want to read as an adult. Now, most of the time, I seek out the best writing I can and savour it. When I choose a book to read, I expect a good plot, good characters, deep themes and some humour. I also want it to contain good writing.

When people talk about 'good writing' in this way, they are usually talking about what happens on the level of the sentence. They mean the way a writer chooses to put words together. 'Good writing' is usually understood to be different from 'bad writing' in the same way that gourmet food differs from junk food; world-class cricket differs from the family game on the beach or ground-breaking architecture differs from a dusty old portakabin. As we must know, there are always problems with all these classifications. While they are not entirely subjective, and most people can identify gourmet food, high-level sport and exciting new buildings, sometimes people can be shocked by what is deemed gourmet food (snail ice cream, for example), high-level sport (the original West Indies fast-bowling attack) or great architecture (modernist concrete). But we should probably acknowledge that what disagreement there is goes on around what is newest and what takes most risks. Apart from that, most of us will enjoy a Michelin-starred meal in the same way that most of us appreciate a six that has been swept out of a cricket ground. Most of us look up at the London Eye, the Sagrada Familia or the Chrysler Building and feel some kind of tingle.

Good writing is an art. When we look at it, sentence by sentence, we should feel joy. We should feel the thrill of being the person who by reading it makes it mean something. We might even learn sentences by heart to comfort us in the middle of the night. We should feel excited to turn every new page to see what this writer has done next. And we shouldn't feel this because someone tells us we have to, or because the work has made us feel intimidated and threatened (because of all its big, formal words, for example). We should be able to discover the kinds of sentences we love on our own. It took me a long time to understand how to do this. My childhood reading habits made me lazy, and, as I've already said, I was one of those teenagers who read Jackie Collins rather than Tolstoy. The only 'classics' I read were for school, and even then I often didn't finish them. When I was about 19 I fought my way through Umberto Eco's *Foucault's Pendulum* only with the help of a dictionary. Eventually I discovered Douglas Coupland and finally felt that someone was speaking to me. I was getting somewhere with my reading. Then a friend loaned me a battered paperback copy of *London Fields* by Martin Amis.

At the time I was about 22 and working as a live-in care assistant to a blind woman. I got in the habit of going to bed early with painkillers (I had toothache), whisky (which made the painkillers work better) and *London Fields*. It was like nothing I'd ever read before. I became particularly obsessed with the 'dead clouds' that recur throughout.

> Dead cloud. Just then – awful sight. Just then he saw that a dead cloud was lurking above the near rooftops. Awful sight. What did he think it was doing there, so out of kilter? They were always lost, dead clouds, lost in the lower sky, trembling drunkenly down through the thermals, always looking in the wrong place for their brothers and their sisters.[233]

At some point during those long, lonely evenings, Martin Amis convinced me that I wanted to be a writer. It was probably Enid Blyton who made me want to write stories in the first place. And Douglas Coupland had reassured me that I had something to say. But Martin Amis made me want to be a *writer*. He made me want to write good sentences. At first I simply wanted to do what he did with sentences, which is very hard.[234] Of course, I didn't succeed. I wrote things like, 'I felt a sudden wave of sickness engulf me, moving in a matter of seconds from my feet to my throat in a rush of adrenaline.'[235] Oh dear. And I still don't write like Amis – who does? It turns out I am naturally a more minimalist writer who admires, but just can't do, all that expansive stuff. But I still love his sentences. In fact, I love all kinds of sentences: long ones, short ones, complex ones and simple ones. And I agree with George Saunders that the sentence is 'where the battle [is] fought':[236] where we find truth.

So what makes a good sentence, and how can we write

them? How can we make our writing as beautiful and meaningful as possible? And is there only one way to do this, with a lot of prescriptive rules, or can we make the rules up ourselves as we go along? This is a complex subject to teach, because it's very difficult to tell another person exactly how to write. No one can say they know precisely what good writing is, and exactly how to do it. If they could then it wouldn't be art. But what we can say is that we want to write beautifully and meaningfully, and we want to know enough to be able to define that ourselves. We can also say that we want to know something about what great writers think is good writing. We can look at writing we think is bad and learn from it, as well as from our own mistakes. We can try, in our own way, to tell the truth, whatever that is for us.

When Ernest Hemingway was a young writer in Paris in the 1920s and his writing was going badly, this is what he would do:

I would stand and look out over the roofs of Paris and think, 'Do not worry. You have always written before and you will write now. All you have to do is write one true sentence. Write the truest sentence you know.' So finally I would write one true sentence, and then go on from there. It was easy then because there was always one true sentence that I knew or had seen or had heard someone say. If I started to write elaborately, or like someone introducing or presenting something, I found that I could cut the scrollwork or ornament out and throw it away and start with the first true simple declarative sentence I had written.[237]

I think this is one of the best pieces of advice that any writer has ever given. It's absolutely right: if you can write one sentence that you think is true, in all senses of the word, then you can be a writer. All you have to do is write one of these sentences, and then another. You keep writing them until you have a paragraph, then a scene, then a story or a novel. So what is a true sentence? Hemingway defines it as a 'simple declarative sentence', but that is just the kind of true sentence Hemingway would write. A true sentence for Hemingway would be something like this one, which begins his story 'Hills Like White Elephants':

> The hills across the valley of the Ebro were long and white.[238]

And in the same kind of spirit, this is from *The Bell Jar* by Sylvia Plath:

> The lawn was white with doctors.[239]

Both of these sentences are what I will call 'minimalist'. Almost every very good minimalist sentence is the result of much more intensive drafting and re-drafting than is apparent in the end result. Minimalist sentences are usually produced by cutting every unnecessary word so what remains communicates the idea as efficiently as possible. There are different levels of minimalism, because 'unnecessary' can be defined very differently. While Arundhati Roy, along with all the best writers, also produces minimalist sentences ('A leper with soiled bandages begged at the car window'[240]), a true sentence for her might be much more expansive. It might be something like this:

> Chacko, in his *What happened to Our Man of the Masses?*
> suit and well-fed tie, led Margaret Kochamma and Sophie
> Mol triumphantly up the nine red steps like a pair of tennis
> trophies that he had recently won.[241]

For Nicola Barker, a true sentence may be more expansive still. In her novel *Five Miles from Outer Hope*, this kind of sentence is fairly typical:

> Immediately after – as if nothing at all significant has
> happened – he starts telling a fascinated Patch, at length,
> about his troubled South African school-days (about the
> unflattering shorts he wore and the horrible haircuts, about
> the corporal punishment and the compulsory rugby. Oh,
> the eternal smarts of a *thousand* indignities!) while I slide
> around silently on the sloppy tiles, do a spot of mopping,
> grab a fresh cloth, the bean-bag, a Pomfret cake, and then
> skid grimly off to try to tackle the too-tender, one-wheeled,
> wet-bellied plane wreck of little Feely.[242]

These sentences are both beautiful in their own way, I hope you'll agree, even if they lack the clean, brisk clarity of the minimalist sentences. They include what Hemingway would leave out – the 'scrollwork and ornament' – but they make it very much their *own* kind of scrollwork and ornament. Embellishment in expansive writing cannot just be there for its own sake. It must add something to the beauty or meaning of the sentence.

True sentences can even seem quite wrong. Geoffrey Willans's *Molesworth* books are modern classics praised by critics everywhere, but just look at the writing:

> There is only one thing in criket and that is the STRATE BAT. Keep yore bat strate boy and all will be all right in life as in criket. So headmasters sa, but when my bat is strate i still get bowled is that an omen chiz. Aktually i usually prefer to hav a slosh: i get bowled just the same but it is more satisfactory.[243]

What should we conclude from this? Is the concept of the true sentence simply subjective? Can anyone write anything and declare it a true sentence? Well, yes, of course they *can*. But it won't be recognised as such unless it seems true to a reader. In order for something to be true it must be one or more of the following: realistic, authentic, correct, sincere, loyal, faithful, honest, unfeigned, consistent with fact, accurate or natural. This isn't completely objective truth we are talking about, of course. The truth can be presented metaphorically, as in Arundhati Roy's simile about tennis trophies; partly figuratively, like Sylvia Plath's 'the lawn was white with doctors'; or (almost) entirely factually, like Hemingway's description of the hills. The truth can be complicated. The truth can be deceptively simple. The truth can be the way someone sees, or says, something, as with Nicola Barker's narrator Medve, in whose 'grown-up' voice we actually see her youth, or Nigel Molesworth, who with his inaccurate language presents an entirely accurate picture of a particular kind of childhood.

When someone tells the truth they can say something direct like, 'I was standing outside the Odeon at midnight.' That is a true sentence. It doesn't need to be factually true to appear true on the page. It's true in the same way a grain in a piece of wood is true. An untrue sentence will usually be characterised by one or more of the following attributes: vagueness, long-windedness, wordiness, uncertainty, formality, repetitiveness, passivity, humourlessness, use of old-fashioned words (to impress the authorities?), clichés and abstraction. So an untrue sentence may sound something like this: 'At approximately midnight, that is to say some time between eleven o'clock and one o'clock in the morning, it would be fair to say that I could have been witnessed in the general vicinity of the cinema known locally to most people as the Odeon.' This is also the kind of language we get in spam emails, like this one that I received today: 'Firstly, I must solicit your confidence in this transaction; this is by Virtue of its nature as being utterly confidential and top secret. Though I know that a Transaction of this magnitude will make anyone apprehensive and worried, but I am Assuring you that all will be well.' Indeed, we can usually identify a spam email immediately because it is written like this.

This doesn't necessarily mean that all short sentences are true and all long sentences are false, but it does remind us that scrollwork and ornament need to be used thoughtfully, if they are to be used at all. A short, declarative sentence is, as Hemingway says, a good start. Once you have your central, true idea, there's nothing to stop you expanding on it: but all parts of the expansion must also be true. They must not sound like lies. They must not be vague, waffly and obfuscating. They must not sound like something you are saying to a policeman, or writing to your great-aunt. They must not sound like you are puffing yourself up to impress someone, or desperately trying to make someone believe you.

True – or good – writing is usually inventive, original and daring, which means it's far easier to describe – and compose – bad writing than it is to describe and compose good, true writing. If you are producing a business report, a reference, a mission statement, a slushy romance novel or a certain kind of humour project, then you may well need to use some 'bad writing'. And, of course, in the right hands even the worst types of bad writing can become good. Michel Faber's satire of Dan Brown-style novels, *The Fire Gospel*, is hilarious. But most of the time you should be aiming to write the best possible prose you can. This doesn't mean prose that strains and looks effortful. It means *your* version of 'The lawn was white with doctors', or Baby Kochamma's 'armfat', or Amis's dead clouds. It means finding a way to put your world on paper without making it sound like something a crooked politician would say. The good news is that there are thousands of ways of being a good writer, but only very few ways of being a bad writer. As Tolstoy (almost) said: all bad writing is the same, each piece of good writing is good in its own way.

When I first started teaching sentence-level writing I felt uncomfortable because so much of it seemed to involve pointing out what was wrong with bad sentences, rather than celebrating the really amazing ones. But the point is that it is possible to define bad writing in a way that it is just not possible to define good writing. We can admire 'The lawn was white with doctors' all day long, but I'll never be able to tell you how to write it. I can suggest that you might cut all unnecessary words from your sentence about doctors standing on the lawn, but you might just end up with something like, 'There were doctors on the lawn.' That would be fine. It's a good sentence. It's a true sentence. But it's not a *brilliant* sentence. Of course, before we can aim for brilliance we must aim for simple truth (and if we get it right, our exact simple truth may well be brilliant). But again, this is hard to define unless we say what it isn't. It is only by studying false sentences that we can see what sorts of sentences are likely to be true.

False sentences are likely to be:	True sentences are likely to be:
Abstract	Specific
Vague	Precise
Long-winded	Concise
Formal	Informal
Repetitive (unintentionally)	Clear
Inauthentic (tone, vocabulary etc.)	Authentic (tone, vocabulary etc.)
Passive	Active
Old-fashioned	Contemporary
Shallow	Deep
Familiar	Defamiliarising
Clichéd	Inventive

The first step in learning to write a true sentence is to work out what a false one would be. Therefore, we need to identify bad writing. We need to study it and see what it looks like. So I'm going to do an experiment, now, right here on this page. With the above table in mind, I am going to write as badly and untruthfully as I can and see what happens. I think I'll write the scene from one of my ideas in the chapter 'How to Have Ideas', where Clare finds Kaia preparing to smuggle cocaine to Jamaica. The most dramatic scenes usually lead to the worst writing, after all. Here goes.

When she slowly turned around to face me I could see that her whole being was contorted in pain. Her usually glossy hair was frizzy and unkempt and her once-stylish clothes looked as if they desperately required a wash. I couldn't believe my eyes. I couldn't believe that my friend, who usually possessed such a sunny and happy disposition, was now reduced to this. Of course I knew exactly what she was doing. Charlie had told me to expect the worst. But I still wasn't prepared for the shock of seeing what was lying right there in full view on her bedside table. There, right in front of me, were twenty bulging condoms full to bursting with bright white powder. As I saw her calmly and coldly prepare to swallow another one my whole body filled with revulsion and adrenaline suddenly coursed bitterly through my veins, making me a nervous wreck. I wanted to scream but it caught in my throat. I wanted to tell her not to do it, not to ruin her life like this, but I knew it was too late. I ran hurriedly from the room, bile welling up inside me, getting out of there as fast as my legs would

carry me. Downstairs, eggs were being cooked inexpertly
by Josh.

It pains me to have just written that. It took two and a half
minutes, and the only effort required was in not deleting
what I had written as soon as I had done it. I have to be
honest and say this is not 'my' bad writing: it's not the kind
of bad writing I do in the first draft of a scene, for example.
It is a deliberate parody of the 'bad writing' I find elsewhere.
Why am I doing this? Am I showing off because as a
professional writer I find it easy to churn out something I
think is terrible in a couple of minutes? (And surely that's
not really something to show off about . . .) No. In fact,
why don't you try it? Take a couple of minutes to think
about what 'bad writing' is for you. Think of an untrue
sentence. Now write an exaggerated version of it. Take
about five minutes and see what you come up with. If you
can't easily think of scenarios, then write a love scene, or
the scene where a hero and a villain meet for the first time
(*Finally I have you in my grasp, my darling / you puny weak-
ling . . .*). You'll realise, I hope, that it isn't very hard. And
that's the point I want to make: anyone can write badly
because it's actually very easy. That's why bad writing
doesn't (usually) win big literary prizes, and also why it
doesn't get very high marks on writing courses.

Good writing can be easy, sometimes, as well. If you
know a true sentence, you can simply write it down
(although to get it to be exactly right, and perfectly true,
might take quite a lot of time in cutting and revising). Once
you've warmed up, and you know your characters and what

they are doing, and you have found your 'writing voice', you can occasionally write a good short paragraph (or at least the basis for one) in two and a half minutes. It's rare, but it can happen. But bad writing is *always* easy. Bad sentences have a tendency to just 'write themselves'. Clichés tumble over one another trying to get into your sentence as if it were the first day of a sale. Your brain can just go to sleep. Why not? After all, every animal on the planet conserves energy when it can. Anyone who has written badly (and that certainly includes me) will know, however, that while bad writing can start off by being easy – almost addictively so – it can end up treating you rather cruelly. As untruth follows so easily from untruth and the word count rises, the whole gets wobblier and wobblier until nothing – the plot, the characters, the descriptions – makes any sense any more.

Bad writing is usually formless, so although it's easy to keep going with one particular idea for quite a long time (*I was shocked and disgusted because I had never, not in all my years, seen anything quite like it, not once, not ever as long as I had lived . . .*), when that sentence is over it's not clear what the next one should be about. And bad writing leads to plot problems too, partly because it happens too fast for you to keep up, and partly because it leads to melodrama and overreaction. If characters are always jumping into and out of things (I jumped out of bed; He jumped in the shower), they will get quite tired. If they are always fearing for their lives, with their hearts hammering in their chests and fear pounding in their skulls, they will soon burn out. The reader will have a hard job believing they want anything other than a good long nap. Because it generally tells rather than shows, bad writing can distort the pace of your narrative as well. But the main problem with bad writing is that anyone could have done it. It is not distinctive in any way. I don't think we should be timid about admitting this. It's not 'all subjective'. There is not a critic in the world who would think my paragraph (above) is any good. The good thing about admitting that there is such a thing as bad writing – and having some in front of us – is that we can start to examine it closely to see exactly what is wrong with it.

We'll begin by looking at the paragraph as a whole and considering what's wrong with it before looking at it sentence by sentence. At the moment the paragraph describes someone entering a room, being shocked to see her friend swallowing condoms full of cocaine and then running out without saying anything. First of all, this is a scene reduced to a paragraph. There's nothing necessarily wrong with that, but should this be a full scene with dialogue? When we look at what is happening in the scene, how believable is it? Why is Kaia swallowing condoms full of cocaine in an unlocked bedroom into which anyone can walk? Why hasn't she waited until she gets to the airport? Is it realistic that she would have 'twenty bulging condoms full to bursting with bright white powder' on her bedside table, given that the street value of this much cocaine would be at least £100,000? Could someone *really* swallow twenty condoms full of anything if they'd never done it before? Does Kaia want to be caught? Is she expecting Clare? Do people even smuggle cocaine out of Britain? Now I come to think of it, I'm pretty sure my friend was practising a technique she was planning to use on the way *back* from Jamaica. These are all questions about the plausibility of the scene. You can't write a good sentence in a bad scene. And if you do, you'll end up deleting it anyway.

Now let's look at the sentences. In the first one I don't much like the adverb 'slowly' but it's not doing too much harm. The main problem with this sentence is that it is vague, and, when we consider it, faintly ridiculous. What is her 'whole being'? This is very abstract and not necessary. We gain nothing from this phrase and may as well use 'she' or 'her body'. What does it mean to be 'contorted in pain'? Since 'contortion' means 'The action of twisting or writhing; the fact of being twisted; distortion by twisting' (*OED*), what we have in this first sentence, if we break it down, is someone who is simultaneously turning around slowly while her body twists and writhes. This is a very peculiar action that seems more like something we'd encounter in a contemporary dance performance than a teenager's bedroom – and I don't believe it for a moment. And what is this 'pain'? Where would it be on a scale of one to ten? Is it more of a stubbed-toe pain? A bruise? A toothache? Using a word like 'pain' is lazy here. It tells the reader that we don't really care about them understanding anything about Kaia's experience at all. It's a real 'Yeah, whatever . . .' word. It means too much and is therefore too big for a sentence.

The sentence is not a place for backstory. If we want the reader to know that Kaia's hair was usually glossy, then we should have shown it before now. In fact, if we had depicted this glossy hair in an earlier scene, then a detailed

description of Kaia's frizzy hair now would do a good job
of showing (rather than telling) something of how she's
been feeling. We can still do this, of course, we'd just need
to go back and put in the earlier scene. But a good description in our current scene is not 'frizzy and unkempt'. These
words are vague and abstract and they repeat the same
idea. Frizzy hair, on someone whose hair is usually glossy,
is unkempt (which actually means 'uncombed'). And there
is a further problem with the word 'unkempt'. It is not a
word I would have used at 18, and it's not even a word I
would use now. It's a bit old-fashioned and fusty. Where
has it come from? My theory is that these over-formal,
write-to-your-great-aunt words come from the reading you
were forced to do as a child. All those 'improving' classics
of yesteryear do not improve our writing today. Write in
your own voice. Do not do what I just did and use words
like 'yesteryear' unless you are sure you'd use them in an
email, or a conversation with a friend.

In the same sentence we discover 'once-stylish clothes'.
What exactly are these? Presumably Kaia's crisis hasn't
been going on so long that her clothes have had time to go
out of fashion? This is vague, abstract and wordy. Instead
of saying 'her once-stylish clothes looked as if they desperately required a wash' could we not just say instead, 'Her
501s were covered in fag ash'? Whatever you decide about
using brand names in your work, they do have the benefit
of being highly specific (as long as people know what you're
talking about), and you want to lose the waffle wherever
you can. But actually, now that we are examining this
sentence, the once-stylish, dirty clothes make even less

sense. This is the early 1990s: the height of grunge. Why would Clare point out that Kaia looked a bit scruffy? It has to be worse than she has described, or there'd be no point mentioning it. The only way to rescue this is with details. A soup stain on a Bob Marley t-shirt? But again we'd want to consider why Kaia has been spilling – or even eating – soup. And 'desperately *required* a wash'? What's wrong with just saying 'needed'? Remember not to write as if you're filling in a form for the council, or making a statement to the police.

'I couldn't believe my eyes' is a cliché. Then immediately we have 'I couldn't believe that my friend . . .' This clearly repeats 'I couldn't believe', and so normally we would decide that it is bad writing and cut the repetition. It is, in this case, bad writing by association, but this kind of repetition can be used effectively: just look at the opening of *The Bell Jar*.[244] We don't need 'my friend' as we already know that Clare and Kaia are friends. Good writing never states the obvious. This is a long-winded sentence that tells us nothing new. It starts with a repetition, continues by telling us something we know already, then tries to do backstory/characterisation in a third of a sentence. Then it repeats something else we know already, that Kaia is in some way reduced. '[W]ho usually possessed such a sunny and happy disposition' is another hangover from children's books. What teenager has a *sunny and happy disposition*? What teenager has a *disposition*? Again, 'disposition' is a great-aunt word. It's a police-statement word. It is far too formal. These over-formal words usually have a Latin origin. As Shakespeare and Chaucer both knew, for those of us writing in English Anglo-Saxon words are far more gritty and down-to-earth.

More backstory follows. Do we already know that Clare and Charlie have spoken about this problem? If so, we don't need reminding here. If not, then again we are faced with this problem of a scene being reduced to a sentence and then thrown in as quick backstory. Sometimes scenes will be reduced to sentences, and we don't want to plod through every little action with a character. But including this detail here needlessly breaks the scene. If we are to explore what's going on in Kaia's bedroom, we need to be able to fully concentrate on it. 'But I still wasn't prepared for the shock . . .' You don't say. Something like this should almost always be shown with action rather than told with narration, otherwise it also risks stating the obvious, or undervaluing an emotion. Then: '. . . of seeing what was lying right there in full view'. This is an incredible *three* ways of saying the same thing: that Clare is seeing something. The only precise thing amidst all this waffle is the bedside table. Then we're back to the *fourth* repetition of the idea of seeing something ('There, right in front of me') before we get to the main point of the paragraph: the condoms full of cocaine.

The reader doesn't really have the chance to appreciate this because he or she is still being bombarded with repetition. 'Bulging' and 'full to bursting' describe the same thing. Neither is quite right for the mood required in this piece. 'Bright white' states the obvious, and verges on repetition. Next we have 'calmly and coldly', which are inconsistent with the painful contortions with which we began the paragraph. But quite apart from this, we must remember that whenever we use an abstract word without exploring it we are in some way ripping off our readers. We are telling him or her, 'Here is this concept, "calmly", and I can't be bothered to make it come alive for you so you'll have to do it yourself.' I often think that readers should get a small refund every time an author uses an adverb or abstract noun in this way. It is the writer's job to bring 'calmly' and 'coldly' to life, not just type them onto a page.

The next problem with our paragraph is the cod-biology: '. . . my whole body filled with revulsion and adrenaline suddenly coursed bitterly through my veins'. Biological descriptions almost never work in fiction. Many of them (like 'adrenaline coursed through my veins') are clichés. Most of them are inaccurate. For example, adrenaline does not course through one's veins exactly. Among other things it turns glycogen into glucose so that one's muscles work more effectively. Most clichés about the body are pseudo-scientific, which is one reason to avoid them. But there is also something boring about them. Adrenaline is released in my body in exactly the same way as it is in yours. But art must be more than just biology. If you are going to describe a sensation that I have experienced, I'd like you to do it so that I can see my experience in a new way. Just as we don't talk about love in terms of blood rushing to the genital organs, we should not talk about fear in terms of adrenaline. Watch out too for vague biological descriptions like 'fear pounded through my skull' or 'my heart felt like it was going to explode'. These descriptions leave no room for the reader to feel anything. They are also lazy, consensus versions of emotion: the sorts of emotions people write when they haven't really felt them. By the time I'd finished my first crime novel I realised I'd run out of ways to describe someone's heart beating fast. That should have been a clue to something.

The next two sentences are just out-and-out lies. If Clare really wanted to scream, she would. If Clare really wanted to tell Kaia not to do it, she could. Clare obviously wants to do *different* things. So what does she want and what does she do? This scene, such as it is, is crying out for some dialogue and for us to get out of Clare's head. So it would be good if she could say something here, rather than just running away. The final sentence in the paragraph also repeats the same idea – running – three different ways, one a well-worn cliché ('as fast as my legs would carry me'). Every word you use that you don't need will clutter your sentences and detract from what you want to say. Don't use unnecessary words. Running is hurried, so no one in any of your sentences should ever have to run hurriedly.

The last sentence is passive rather than active. Writing 'Eggs were being cooked by Josh' (we can lose the 'inexpertly' or try to dramatise it by showing they have shell in them or something) makes the eggs the focus of the sentence rather than Josh. We should usually try to turn something like this around so that it reads 'Josh was cooking eggs'. Too many passive sentences will make your work seem formal and, like a police statement, full of victims who never admit to doing anything but only ever have things done to them. The passive voice is at best a bit whiny. At worst it says things like 'The bombs were launched in the dead of night' without ever telling us who is being bombed by whom and why. It is cowardly and weak and never takes the blame for anything.

So that's approximately 2,000 words explaining why 200 words don't work. I should have thought myself lucky when all I got from my first editor was a seventeen-page letter listing all the mistakes I'd made in my text. Some of the editorial suggestions were quite funny, especially the proposition that my heroine should be tied to a chair and then rescued by her love-interest at the end. But I actually learned a lot from that letter. I learned about split infinitives (which no one much bothers about any more) because I kept writing that my heroine 'put the kettle on', rather than 'put on the kettle' (although I must admit I fought to keep the more natural, and therefore more true, 'put the kettle on'). But I also learned not to write passive sentences, and not to let my protagonist be too negative. I learned not to repeat myself or state the obvious. But the main thing is that I learned to look closely at my sentences to see what they contained. I realised I'd just never really looked at sentences before. I'd never looked at individual words before. I'd never really thought on the level of the sentence before.

Gradually after that I became obsessed with words and sentences. I became particularly interested in what other people did with their sentences and why. I didn't find out about Hemingway's concept of the one true sentence until much later but, mainly through reading Raymond Carver, I became more and more interested in short, minimalist sentences. When I was free of the contract for my crime novels I immediately began trying to find my own voice. I started experimenting with short, declarative present-tense sentences like 'The room contains a desk, a woman and two large stacks of paper', which is how *Bright Young Things* begins; or, simply, 'Mice', which is the first paragraph of Chapter Six of *Going Out*. I started trying to reduce my sentences as much as possible, while keeping them true to the voices of the characters. My prose wasn't always beautiful, but it was a start.

This is George Saunders's rather lovely description of what happened when he first became obsessed with sentences after reading Esther Forbes's novel *Johnny Tremain*:

> Standing around the schoolyard in those post-Forbes days, I tried out sentences meant to describe, with Forbes-like precision, whatever I happened to be seeing: 'Sister Lynette hovered in the doorway like a nun hovering in a doorway holding a peanut-butter sandwich, which was what he, George, also was probably having later today, in terms of lunch.' This, revised, became: 'Sister Lynette, with sandwich, stood in the door.' And then: 'Sister, sandwich, in door.' Well, maybe that was taking it too far.[245]

Every writer who develops their own style does so first as a celebration of a style they deem to be excellent, or against another style they believe to be 'bad', 'dead' or offensive in some way. Because of this, some fashions in writing change. Authenticity is currently more important than exact correctness, which is why people do not correct every split infinitive. Indeed, you even find them in newspapers, along with people saying things like 'OMG'. But some things never change, and I feel quite confident that the paragraph above, about Kaia and the cocaine, will never, ever be considered good writing. Time is not going to make a single one of those sentences true. Shakespeare and Chaucer both wrote true sentences, using their own blend of informal, authentic vernacular and traditional prose. Those sentences remain true today, and will remain true for all time. There is something universal about good writing. It even transcends language: after all, Chekhov's advice on sentence-level writing, translated from Russian, works perfectly well on English sentences. When he urges us to delete all our adjectives and adverbs it is because these are vague, abstract types of word in any language.

All good writing is specific rather than abstract, and precise rather than vague. When I first started teaching this idea, I would put a picture up on the screen in the lecture theatre of a man walking on a beach alone. The picture was full of little details. For example, there was only one bird in the sky, in the distance. There were no boats. There were not even any footprints. The beach was large enough that the man looked very small. And he was all hunched up, as if the world was too much for him. I would show students this picture and then switch it off and replace it with the word 'Loneliness'. Which is the more evocative, I would ask them, the word or the image? Which is more specific? Which one attempts to give us a picture of loneliness that we can think about, and which just prompts us to provide our own specific details to go with the word?

Every time we use an abstract word rather than a specific

word or image, we will either be saying nothing at all, or, at best, saying something millions of people have said before. 'She was jealous and angry and hurt' could have been written by anyone. There's nothing specific there; nothing concrete. No image that we can see in our minds. We may remember Aristotle talking about showing with action rather than telling with narration. As writers, we are expected to explore abstraction and complex emotion by creating scenes and drama. We are surely cheating a bit if we just write down what someone is feeling! Why should we expect someone to pay us for our work, or spend hours reading it, if all we've said is 'She was jealous and angry and hurt'? However, if we find a new, or particularly powerful way of expressing, exploring or dramatising jealousy or anger or pain, then we have actually done something artistic, rather than formulaic and boring.

Let's look at an excerpt from the story 'Sea Oak' by George Saunders:

At Sea Oak there's no sea and no oak, just a hundred subsidized apartments and a rear view of FedEx. Min and Jade are feeding their babies while watching *How My Child Died Violently*. Min's my sister. Jade's our cousin. *How My Child Died Violently* is hosted by Matt Merton, a six-foot-five blond who's always giving the parents shoulder rubs and telling them they've been sainted by pain. Today's show features a ten-year-old who killed a five-year-old for refusing to join his gang. The ten-year-old strangled the five-year-old with a jump rope, filled his mouth with baseball cards, then locked himself in the bathroom and wouldn't come out until his parents agreed to take him to FunTimeZone, where he confessed, then dove screaming into a mesh cage full of plastic balls.[246]

There is nothing abstract here at all: it's all specific detail. Saunders gives us the space to examine this kind of world for a few moments – but in the special, clear way that he sees it. Imagine this written differently, with abstract words instead of specific ones:

> I live at Sea Oak, which is a very disappointing place. My sister and my cousin like watching stupid confessional TV shows while feeding their babies. Today the show is about a ten-year-old who killed a five-year-old in a horribly violent way and how his parents extracted a confession from him.

Although this yields fewer words, and we should always aim for conciseness and brevity, we should be able to see that this version also says a lot less, and is far less beautiful. We don't get a picture to look at. Note also how much work the abstract version asks the reader to do. While I'm sure we all grew up learning that hard work is good, and that good writing can be demanding, having to work hard to produce images is not the job of the reader. The reader must have the images provided by the writer so that he or she can be engaged in working hard on the *meaning*.

Raymond Carver says that details, rendered in 'clear and specific language' are what 'light up the story for the reader'.[247] And Chekhov says that:

I think descriptions of nature should be very short and always be *à propos*. Commonplaces like 'The setting sun, sinking into the waves of the darkening sea, cast its purple gold rays, etc.' 'Swallows, flitting over the surface of the water, twittered gaily' – eliminate such commonplaces. You have to choose small details in describing nature, grouping them in such a way that if you close your eyes after reading it you can picture the whole thing.[248]

See how much fun even Chekhov has inventing 'bad writing'! Here the really important thing is that the details you choose must be small. In other words, they must be precise. They must be the little things you notice in the world, and that perhaps no one else sees. Small details are not just good for creating a fuller image for the reader, they also create depth. They give the fictional world more dimensions. They give us more to think about. In *The God of Small Things*, Arundhati Roy builds up a whole world based on small details. Estha is not just sexually assaulted by 'a man'; it is the Orangedrink Lemondrink Man. Rahel, on the way to Cochin, does not just simply have her hair 'tied back'. Instead:

Most of Rahel's hair sat on top of her head like a fountain. It was held together by a Love-in-Tokyo – two beads on a rubber band, nothing to do with Love or Tokyo. In Kerala Love-in-Tokyos have withstood the test of time and even today if you were to ask for one at any respectable A-1 Ladies Store that's what you'd get. Two beads on a rubber band.[249]

Here the Love-in-Tokyo isn't just identified and named, it is examined. We get to spend some time with it. It is inserted, gently, into history, and we know Rahel's world, and Kerala, better because of it.

I am always trying to get students to use more specific details. It is a rare sentence indeed ('The lawn was white with doctors') that cannot take one or two more specific details. Here you do need to begin to identify your own style. Are you a minimalist writer, like Hemingway, Carver and Plath? Or are you more expansive, like Arundhati Roy, Martin Amis and Nicola Barker? Although these aren't real categories, exactly, and the line between them is sometimes more blurred than I am making out, it's still worth making some decision about what you are aiming for at the moment. Every time I begin a new novel I think I'm going to be much more expansive than I was in the last one, but it doesn't always turn out that way. You need to have confidence to write expansively. You must have it in you to be lyrical. The more expansive you are, the more likely you are to riff on your specific details, or repeat them, or turn them into refrains or make them rhyme. You'll be just as specific as a minimalist writer, but you are more likely to invent neologisms, write long lists, or use poetic devices like assonance and alliteration. You can write, as Arundhati Roy does, 'The silence gathered up its skirts and slid, like Spiderwoman, up the slippery bathroom wall.'[250] Say it out loud. See what texture it has.

The more minimalist you are the fewer details you will include – but you are likely to spend a good deal of time choosing the right details and making them as specific as possible. Reading our sentences out loud won't necessarily bring them to life: in fact, the sentences will look just right on the page: clean and simple. If minimalist writing is read out loud, it will sound cool and low-key. The kind of thing you could say in a bar. Expansive writing is much more performative. I know minimalist writers who don't use words of more than two syllables, or who try never to let a line of dialogue cover more than one line of text. Others, like George Saunders and Sylvia Plath, put in as much specific detail as possible, but each single word earns its place. There is nothing in this description that doesn't need to be there, for example:

> They imported Betsy straight from Kansas with her bouncing blonde ponytail and Sweetheart-of-Sigma-Chi smile. I remember once the two of us were called over to the office of some blue-chinned TV producer in a pin-stripe suit to see if we had any angles he could build up for a programme, and Betsy started to tell about the male and female corn in Kansas. She got so excited about that damn corn even the producer had tears in his eyes, only he couldn't use any of it, unfortunately, he said.[251]

Pace, character and plot will also affect how much specific detail is needed at any one time. Not everything in a novel can be described in the same amount of detail as the Love-in-Tokyo (or at least it can, but you'll have to accept that not much else is going to happen in the novel). But if a character is reading a book on a train, most readers will want to know what the book is (or at least what kind of book it is) and where the train is going. Make sure this is as concise as possible, though, and not vague. 'Beth got the last seat on the 5.31 from Charing Cross' is usually better than 'Beth got on a busy train from London'. If a character is reading a newspaper over breakfast, then the reader will probably want to know what the newspaper is and what comprises the breakfast. If the character is on their way to the cinema, then the reader will want to know what he or she is going to see. The reader can't always be told every detail, of course. But on the principle of Hemingway's iceberg, you should always know what the details are.

A problem will arise at some point about how you treat pop culture. There are three possible approaches. The first one is that you name everything exactly as in real life, as Bret Easton Ellis does in *American Psycho*, Martin Amis does in *Money* and I do in *Bright Young Things*. This is direct and authentic but can make your writing seem cheap: as if it has become a disposable pop cultural artefact by association. The second option is to describe popular cultural artefacts without naming them, as I tried to do occasionally in *Going Out*.[252] This can have a subtle, defamiliarising effect, although it can seem disingenuous if the writer and reader both know what is actually being described. The third option is that you invent fictional TV shows, brands and fashions that plausibly represent the kind of popular culture you want to explore, as George Saunders does in many of his short stories, and as I do in *PopCo*. These can exist in isolation, or in combination with real pop cultural references. This can be great fun to do but can make your fictional world seem inauthentic. There is also a temptation to exaggerate, and satirise. Satire can be fine, of course, but it is not the only way to treat popular culture.[253]

Of course, within each option there are plenty of opportunities to develop your own style and make your own comments on the things you see in the world. Watch out here that specificity does not turn into judgement. Try to remain 'objective', in Chekhov's sense of the term. 'The woman wore red lipstick' is objective. So, just about, is the more specific, 'The owner of the shop wore a Chanel lipstick the colour of a million pillar boxes.' But 'Her cruel boss was wearing expensive red lipstick' is not objective. The sentence contains an explicit judgement of the woman and her lipstick. Similarly, we can say that 'The cat sat on the mat', which is just an objective statement of fact. 'The Persian cat sat on the cashmere mat' also states facts, but with more specific detail. But 'The pampered cat sat on the luxury mat' is judgemental. More judgement takes place on the level of the sentence than we might think, and we must be alert to it.

Here we also begin to see the main problems with adverbs and the more abstract adjectives. Not only are they often judgemental words that tell the reader what to think, they are also very vague. If I know that the cat is on a cashmere mat, I can see that in my mind. Cashmere is not just a luxury item: it is warm, comfortable, soft, hairy, safe, relaxing. But a 'luxury mat' asks the reader to do all the work. It also turns the world into a grey sludge. In 500 years' time people might wonder that kinds of fabrics were particularly luxurious in the early twenty-first century and if all that the books of the time say back to them is 'luxury fabrics' then they will never know. They will have to insert luxury fabrics from their own time and will never get the pleasure of really visiting the twenty-first century. At the beginning of *Pride and Prejudice*, we hear not just that Darcy has come to visit Netherfield, but that he has come in a chaise and four. Each time you use a specific detail, you are recording an important part of your world. And it may well be something no one else has noticed.

Most of the time a well-chosen noun will create more associations and pictures in our minds than an adjective will. A noun is a thing. A verb is an action. Your writing should be full of these because they are true. You can't argue with a cup on a table, or someone running up a hill. Adverbs and adjectives are describing or modifying words. They are what you find in the sentence's dressing-up box: old hats and suits that are familiar and worn out and often full of holes. Adverbs and adjectives can make sentences appear more serious or meaningful from a distance, but when we look close up we see that they can actually be very distracting, or even meaningless. They also lead to long-winded, 'wordy' writing, which is quite different from what we've been calling expansive writing. Wordiness implies that there are extra words that don't mean anything, or that tell the reader what to think. Most of the words could be deleted or rearranged and the sentence would be better as a result.

One of my favourite opening lines is from *Neuromancer* by William Gibson.

The sky above the port was the colour of television, tuned to a dead channel.[254]

Look at all those nouns: *sky, port, colour, television* and *channel.* Virtually the whole sentence is made of nouns. It's lean and colourful. It says exactly what it means. Imagine how different this opening could have been if Gibson had been long-winded:

Case stood alone near the port regarding the sky which loomed high above him, bearing down on him in a most unnerving fashion. It was a grey, indeterminate colour, rather similar to the colour, not white although equally not black, that you sometimes see on television screens when the reception isn't quite as good as it would ideally be.

I'm not suggesting for one moment that Gibson started off with something as terrible as this description and then 'edited it down'. But if you find you have written something like it (and I certainly have, especially in the early days), don't stand for it. Take hold of it and shake it until all the junk falls out and you are left with nouns and verbs. 'The sky above the port was the colour of television, tuned to a dead channel' has no junk. It tells us something truthful, specific – and rather beautiful – about the colour of the sky above the port. It tells us something of the tone of the narrator. It tells us that we're in a world that is so degraded that even nature appears like broken technology. But it doesn't use silly expressions like 'broken technology': it shows us what this looks like. I can use phrases like 'broken technology' now because I am writing in a semi-formal, semi-academic register. That's what all the fancy Latin words are for. It's not that these words are always 'bad' but in fiction we want to be able to look at things closely before we start analysing them: before we decide what we think.

I'd known for a long time that good sentences had few adverbs and adjectives. But once I realised that what they had instead were more nouns and verbs, I created the following exercise.

THE BANK OF WORDS

Imagine you have a budget for your writing. This means that every time you use a word, you have to pay for it. The thing is, some words are cheap and some are expensive. How can you stay within budget and still say what you want to say?

Say that for every 500 words, you have £100 to spend (although you can try adjusting this budget if you like). I'd suggest beginning this exercise using a 100-word descriptive passage (which would give you a budget of £20) and then move on to trying a whole page. But before you start working on your own writing, try costing up 100-word excerpts of published fiction. Which writers are more economical with their prose?

The point of this exercise is to teach you economy. This isn't just about cutting words (although that may happen) but about using the best words.

Type of word or phrase		Cost
Concrete noun	A thing you can see, touch or count like *table, bowl, cat, water.*	Free
Abstract noun	A thing that you can't see, touch or count like *justice, friendship, horror, fear.*	£10
Concrete verb	Something you can see happening like *walking, talking, saying, making.*	Free
Abstract verb	Something you could never see actually taking place, like *loving, feeling, ascertaining, deciding.*	£10
Concrete adjective	A 'describing word' where you can see the thing being described, like *curtained, muddy, wet, red, faded.*	Free
Abstract adjective	A 'describing word' that relates to an abstract quality like, *big, small, heavy, pathetic, lacklustre, beautiful, amazing.*	£5
Adverb	For these purposes, anything ending in 'ly' like *abjectly, quickly, sorrowfully, stupidly.*	£20
Modifier	Usually some kind of adverb or adjective, but can be used to modify adjectives, adverbs and nouns. Includes *really, very, a little, quite.* For example: *very small* or *quite wet.*	£5
Cliché	A well-known figurative phrase like 'He felt like a rabbit caught in headlights' or 'The dead of night'.	£50 per whole cliché

- Any other words like *as, of, its, the* and so on are free.
- Dialogue, free indirect discourse, or anything clearly 'in character', should be disregarded but only if the words seem true for that character. You may need to discuss what this means.
- Note: this is a very simplified version of grammatical rules, with a few made-up bits for ease of use (verbs and adjectives aren't usually divided into abstract and concrete in the same way that nouns are).

Appendix Four contains some passages of around 100 words each for you to try this with, but you can easily find your own passages to try it on. I would recommend doing it at least once with something very commercial and with something more literary to see the staggering difference in cost that can occur between two different types of writing.

I have invented a lot of writing exercises in the last seven years, and this is the one that the students enjoy most, and that has the most impact on them. I still get emails from ex-MA students that say 'Whoops! Another £20' each time they use an adverb. For many students, this is the first time they have had reason to examine every single word in a sentence to see what it is doing there. For this reason I do not apologise for turning the whole thing into a monetary system. After all, we are talking about economies of style: how much we value particular words, and how costly the wrong ones might be to our artistic intentions. We are taking account of words and seeing what they add up to. Of course, in each class someone will suggest that perhaps the writers who 'spend' the most money on their sentences end up making the most money back. But this is actually untrue. There are far more bad writers not making any money and not getting published than there are good writers in the same position. And the few bad prose writers that do make a lot of money do so because they are exceptionally good at plot and connecting with a big audience, not *because* they are bad writers.

I ended up learning a lot from the Bank of Words, too. When I began teaching I'd made it my mission to eliminate the adverb. I forbade my students from using any clichés at all. Without thinking too much about other options, I based all my sentence-level teaching around a safe minimalist style, and used the advice given by the great minimalists in my teaching materials. It's amazing how many writers turn out to be minimalists once they begin writing about the composition of sentences. Or maybe it's only the minimalists who can really explain how they compose sentences. Even Stephen King's (wonderful) book *On Writing* comes out in favour of a style that has no adverbs, no way of attributing dialogue apart from 'he said' or 'she said' and only advocates the passive voice if a dead body needs to be carried out of the room. (He admits in the book that he hasn't always followed his own advice.) I really thought I'd found the answer to everything, which should have been a hint that I hadn't. *Cut, cut, cut!* I would tell people. Of course, if someone turned up writing like Martin Amis (and someone did), I didn't stop them. But most people didn't, and so I carried on with my minimalism. I invented another exercise that I actually still rather like, where students would take a paragraph of their prose, turn it into a haiku and then put it back on the page as three clean, lean sentences.[255] I interviewed George Saunders and virtually all we talked about was cutting. In fact, Saunders went so far as to say that 'Cutting is really writing' and I enthusiastically agreed.[256] This is all true and useful, up to a point, and it is definitely the place to start. But it led to a particular problem.

I had never worked out how to account for many great writers – past and present – who clearly work outside this severe minimalist paradigm. I tried teaching Nicola Barker novels, only for my students – who had all been trained to fear the adverb – to declare them 'overwritten' and 'annoying'. I sent one of my best research students off to read Tolstoy, but she 'couldn't get on with the language'. Another PhD student saw me reading Jane Austen. 'How can you read that?' he said. 'It's so abstract, man. It's full of adverbs.' This was all my own fault, I knew that. But how could I account for both types of writing I liked in some sort of coherent, teachable system? How could I live with this weird situation where it was OK for Nicola Barker, Martin Amis and Arundhati Roy to use adverbs, but not all right for my students? I got around the problem of Tolstoy, Jane Austen, Katherine Mansfield and George Eliot by declaring them 'authentic for their time', but if adverbs can go in and out of fashion then was I just teaching 'today's fashion' by teaching everyone to despise them?

The answer came when I was creating my Bank of Words exercise. Every time I create a new exercise I test it, like a recipe, and the first thing I noticed with this one was that it didn't work if dialogue was treated like the rest of the text. After all, real people do use adverbs and clichés when they speak. Indeed, informal speech takes place on a different level of discourse than 'art'. If I turn up at yoga and one of the women says to me, 'It's raining cats and dogs out there', I don't search around in my mind for the most artistic way to respond. I say something like, 'Yeah, it's really coming down.' So when I first trialled the exercise I instructed the students to ignore dialogue. However, when I came to choose the extracts for them to practise on, I found myself cheating slightly. I still wasn't choosing just

any good writing to make my point. I was still choosing
only minimalist writing. I certainly wasn't choosing something like this, from Katherine Mansfield:

> Harry had such a zest for life. Oh, how she appreciated
> it in him. And his passion for fighting – for seeking in
> everything that came up against him another test of his
> power and of his courage – that, too, she understood. Even
> when it made him just occasionally, to other people, who
> didn't know him well, a little ridiculous perhaps . . . For
> there were moments when he rushed into battle where no
> battle was . . .[257]

Or this, from Nicola Barker:

> Rather too soon she finds me large as life – if not *larger* –
> sitting cross-legged on the cocktail counter, painstakingly
> dissecting a troublesome verruca (I've learned over the years
> that if you soak your foot for long enough in slightly salted
> warm water and then pluck at the offending growth with
> tweezers, the whole organism can be extracted in one
> complete segment, like a perfectly-formed miniature cauli-
> flower).[258]

The Nicola Barker example in particular began to really
bother me. If a student wrote like this he or she would get
a very high mark, even though on the surface the sentence
appears to break all the 'rules'. It would certainly be very
expensive to buy its components from the Bank of Words.
But it is authentic, exuberant and full of personality. It's

so true, even though it contains so many 'false' words – and one big cliché. If we edited it according to the basic rules of minimalism, we'd end up with something like this:

> She soon finds me sitting cross-legged on the cocktail counter. I've learned that if you soak your foot for long enough in slightly salted warm water and then pluck at a verruca with tweezers, the whole thing can be taken out in one complete segment, like a miniature cauliflower.

It's cleaner and leaner, sure. But it has also become rather serious and lost all its personality. It is no longer playful. It has not become a better piece of writing.

Around the same time I was puzzling over this, I was becoming more and more interested in the possibilities of free indirect style. Indeed, I'd begun to write my new novel using it. As I worked on the early pages I realised that it wasn't just dialogue that needed to be excluded from my Bank of Words exercise: everything written (successfully) *in character* needed to be ignored. In 'Bliss', it's not an objective, 'neutral' narrator who says 'Harry had such a zest for life'. These are Bertha's words. And the neutral narrator is not the one trying to convince us that Bertha 'appreciated' this quality: this is the word Bertha uses to try to convince herself, and us. If there is something hesitant and false in Bertha's tone, that is because she isn't really that certain of Harry. The uncertainty in the sentences is their truth. And Medve's voice in *Five Miles from Outer Hope* is simply not intended to be minimal and tasteful and quiet. It is *supposed* to be over-the-top, garrulous, arrogant, playful, faux-knowing and wrongly arch. It is the authentic voice of this character. Again, the truth is in the pretence.

So abstract words do have a place in fiction. Of course they must never be lies that a neutral, 'objective' narrator tells to us. But they work when they are the lies – or at least the stories – characters tell to themselves and others. They must be authentic, though. I don't think I could ever write that one of my characters had a 'zest for life' because it's not an expression I would use, and by extension it's not an expression many of my characters would use. But it is an expression that Bertha would use, and that is why it works. None of this means that 'anything goes' and it's all subjective again. Adverbs still cost £20 each unless they are genuinely being used by a character, directly or indirectly. And I would still strongly suggest that any beginning writer develops a workable minimalist style as a foundation before trying to add to it. After all, every writer, even the most expansive, has to know how to produce a simple declarative statement.

One of the ways of doing this is, as we've seen, by saying 'literally' what happened in as few words as possible. 'The man sat on the chair', for example, or 'The flowers were on the table.' But economy – and considerable depth – can be achieved with figurative expressions as well. Metaphors enable us to take the properties of one thing and apply them to another thing, which can sometimes lead to a greater understanding of both things. Lots can go wrong with metaphors, but they are the main way that we can achieve depth on the level of the sentence. Depth implies layers of meaning, and a metaphor gives us not just one thing to visualise, but at least two, layered on top of one another. If you imagine a word as one dimension (a point) and a sentence as two dimensions (some kind of timeline), then figurative language adds another dimension. The sentence goes down, into meaning, as well as along, into time.

For example, if I say 'Peter was a lion in battle', then ideas connected with a lion are applied to Peter. The properties of one are overlaid on the other, which means that every time we reach the word 'Peter' we don't just see Peter, we see a lion too. If we have seen or thought about more than one lion in our lives (on TV, at a safari park, in pictures or in poems) then all these images and ideas will pile on top of the concept of Peter. Peter now has more depth, because we see in him everything we know about lions. This is a very basic example, of course. But from it we should see the usefulness of metaphor. Metaphor means that instead of listing lots of abstract words ('strong', 'courageous', 'fierce', 'sleek', 'animalistic' and so on) or even using specific description that would show Peter being strong and fierce, which can be difficult (he killed ten more men per hour than any other man and didn't even stop for lunch), we can find an image that somehow already holds all the ideas we want to invoke and then apply this image to the man. Saying that Peter is a lion in battle is therefore also an extremely economical way of saying all those things about his being tough and fierce and so on all at once. Instead of extending the sentence lengthways, into time, we have extended it downwards, into meaning.

Many well-known metaphors – like 'He was a lion in battle' – are clichés. Some clichés were originally good metaphors that have become overused and familiar. But a lot of them are metaphors that sounded good at first but actually don't work when you think about them. Men can't really be that much like lions in battle because lions don't have wars. The image does not quite work and becomes shallow, rather than deep. We use metaphors all the time: mostly clichés, which are fine – indeed, expected – in informal discourse. I might say, 'I was bored to death' or 'I am drowning in work', for example. A common mistake in speech and writing, though, is for people to say things like 'I am *literally* drowning in work', as if a metaphor is too 'pretend' and therefore not 'strong' enough. In a recent rugby game, the commentator said that the eyes of the nation were 'literally on the players', which would be rather gruesome.

The whole point of a metaphor is that it is *not* literally true. It alerts us to a deeper truth. Look at all the work the metaphor is doing even in these clichéd examples. When you tell someone you have been bored to death you're using the metaphor to exaggerate and for humour. Here the 'reader' or listener knows that you are not dead, because you're talking to them. But they know death comes as the result of something extreme – violence, deprivation and so on. They are invited to imagine what kind of boredom would lead to death (an experience that went on for so long that you starved, perhaps), and dead people: corpses, coffins and so on – all of which have associated images of people lying flat on their backs. Here, what you are really saying is that you were simply extremely bored. If you say 'I was bored to tears' you're doing the same kind of thing with metaphor, but instead of invoking death you are invoking crying – again, probably a response out of proportion to just 'being bored'. In both examples the metaphor characterises the speaker. Both, in slightly different ways, are telling us that they are interesting, because boredom makes them die, or start crying. The metaphor does a lot more here than an abstract word could. It gives us something to visualise.

One of the clearest descriptions of metaphor is in Aristotle's *Poetics*. He says,

> A metaphor is the application of a noun which properly applies to something else. The transfer may be from genus to species, from species to genus, from species to species or by analogy.[259]

If we don't want to get too far into taxonomic language, we can simply treat 'genus' as 'abstract' and 'species' as 'specific' here. Most metaphors involve a specific thing being used in place of an abstract quality. For example, if I say 'I have a mountain of laundry to do', a mountain is a specific example of the abstract category 'large things' and I am therefore using it in place of 'I have a large amount of laundry to do'. This can go the other way. If I say I have to read 'a whole library' before my class tomorrow, I probably mean I have to read several books. Several books are part of a library, so in this case I have replaced the specific with the abstract (or the genus). Hemingway's story 'Hills

Like White Elephants' uses a metaphor (or at least a simile, which we will come to) as its title. Here both the hills and the concept of the white elephant are used to stand for 'something big'. When the girl says that the hills look like white elephants, she is substituting one big thing for another big thing: elephants for hills, of course, but also, more subtly, white elephants for the burden of an unwanted pregnancy. Here, then, the specific is being exchanged for the specific.

Aristotle says, 'By analogy I mean cases where B stands in similar relation to A as D does to C; one can then mention D instead of B and vice versa.'[260] This is one of the easiest forms of metaphor to understand. For example, as Aristotle says, old age may be described as life's twilight because old age is to life as twilight is to the day. If I describe a tree's 'arms' as having 'bracelets of blossom', then I have taken the idea that a branch is to a tree as arms are to humans. This exact analogy does not work the other way (I do not wave my branches at my friend). But we find something similar in *Middlemarch*, when Mr Farebrother has agreed to put Fred's romantic case to Mary Garth:

> That very day Mr Farebrother went to Lowick parsonage on the nag which he had just set up. 'Decidedly I am an old stalk,' he thought, 'the young growths are pushing me aside.'[261]

This analogy is more complex. It's not just that a man, like a stalk, can become old (as both men and stalks are biological entities that must age and finally die). When this happens to a stalk, it is commonly pushed aside by new parts of the plant. Since the whole point of new growth is eventually reproduction, this metaphor becomes even fuller. This is someone being pushed aside by those who are more youthful and vigorous and more sexually potent. Indeed, this is a very economical description of such a complex idea. And we are now able to visualise Mr Farebrother as both a man and an old stalk. We can really *see* this idea.

A metaphor is distinct from other figurative forms of language because it involves one idea or image being *directly* substituted for another. However, there are other types of figurative expression. For example, a simile is where one idea is *compared* with another, not directly exchanged for it. In 'Bliss', the character Bertha tries to describe this new feeling that has come upon her.

What can you do if you are thirty and, turning the corner of your own street, you are overcome, suddenly, by a feeling of bliss – absolute bliss! – as though you'd suddenly swallowed a bright piece of that late afternoon sun and it burned in your bosom, sending out a little shower of sparks into every particle, into every finger and toe?

Oh, is there no way you can express it without being 'drunk and disorderly'? How idiotic civilization is! Why be given a body if you have to keep it shut up like a rare, rare fiddle?

'No, that about the fiddle is not quite what I mean,' she thought, running up the steps [. . .][262]

There is something light, airy and pleasingly uncertain about a well-used simile. If Katherine Mansfield had written that Bertha *had* swallowed a piece of the later afternoon sun that burned in her bosom the image would suddenly seem rather more heavy. Similarly, the point of the 'rare, rare fiddle' is that it is not quite right as a description. If Mansfield had written that 'Bertha's body had been shut up in its case like a rare fiddle for all these years' all the humour and contemplation is gone. It's not that metaphors are always humourless, of course. But here one probably would be. Mansfield instead gives us two levels of simile: the body is *like* something that is *like* a rare, rare fiddle. In a good simile meaning is often hazy and uncertain – not vague, exactly, but not final either, as in this example from *The Bell Jar*:

My hand advanced a few inches, then retreated and fell limp. I forced it toward the receiver again, but again it stopped short, as if it had collided with a pane of glass.[263]

Metonymy is a device that works by association, and often, but not always, replaces a thing with a symbol for the thing. So we might hear that he was 'on the bottle', for example, even though his drinking habit might consist entirely of that wine that comes in a box. Or we might hear news 'from' Downing Street, Brussels or the Oval Office that actually comes from the authorities we associate with these places. Metonymy is probably the hardest kind of figurative expression to use inventively on a sentence level as it relies on using already existing associations. Indeed, where metaphor involves swapping one thing for another quite different thing (but with similar properties – like a man for a lion), metonymy implies a contiguity: a *touching* of ideas or concepts. Here, the ideas that will be swapped do not necessarily share properties but may follow one another in a game of word-association. So garden fences are connected with gossip; roses with love; ink with fingers and so on.

In *The God of Small Things*, the children in *The Sound of Music* are described as 'Clean children, like a packet of peppermints'.[264] This idea is extended later:

> Captain von Trapp's seven peppermint children had had their peppermint baths, and were standing in a peppermint line with their hair slicked down, singing in obedient peppermint voices to the woman the Captain nearly married.[265]

Here, peppermints do not stand for children in a directly metaphorical way. How could they? Peppermints themselves are sticky and sugary, and the ideas being invoked here are cleanliness, freshness, innocence, purity and whiteness. This is possible metonymically partly because peppermints are white, but mainly because peppermint oil is used as the fragrance for toothpaste. Peppermint therefore implies freshness of breath, which itself implies being clean inside. Metonymic associations are usually cultural, not natural. As long as there are men and lions and sleep, we can see how a man could sleep like a lion. But the link between cleanliness and peppermints is highly contingent. It means something now that it might no longer mean in a hundred years, or a millennium.

Synecdoche is where a part is used to describe a whole,

or a whole is used to describe a part. This is similar to, but not exactly the same as, Aristotle's genus-to-species and species-to-genus metaphors. If I call a few books 'a whole library' then I am using a whole to describe a part. Synecdoche is probably the most important figurative device used in fiction, because it allows us to travel between the sentence and the world and make important connections between the two. Look at the synecdoche in William Blake's poem 'And did those feet in ancient time':

> And did the Countenance Divine
> Shine forth upon our clouded hills?
> And was Jerusalem builded here
> Among these dark Satanic mills?

Here, of course, 'our clouded hills' implies the whole of the countryside, and 'dark Satanic mills' implies the whole of industry.

Whenever you write figuratively, you will be creating depth by adding two or more different ideas together, hopefully in new and original ways. Sometimes – indeed, often – you will use a 'set' of imagery in the same piece of fiction. For example, you may decide that many of your descriptions in a particular short story will be based around water. Perhaps more often than this, however, you'll extend one metaphor over a few lines. And the key thing here is that your metaphor continues to make sense as you extend it. The first thing to realise is where you want to extend a metaphor. If I write that 'She sounded like a cat in distress. On and on she went like a broken violin', I am evoking two different images at once, and they clash. Here we'd need to decide whether to keep – and probably build on – the cat image or the violin one. Neither is particularly original. But in any case we could extend either of them if we wanted to:

> She sounded like a cat in distress. As if she'd just lost all her kittens.

> On and on she went, like a broken violin played by a drunk.

Note here that while it's easy to write or say that someone sounded like a cat in distress, and aim for humour, the moment we begin to examine the idea in more depth we see that it is in fact quite a sad image. A broken violin played by a drunk is a good, plausible image (a drunk might well play a broken violin) but if 'she' is like this broken violin, then who is the drunk who is playing her? Metaphor often involves a strange kind of plotting, because the images we create must make sense in themselves, and when applied to the more literal world we are trying to describe.

A mixed metaphor is what we get if we try to extend a metaphor but let go of the logic that connects it to the real or literal world: if we 'plot' it badly or use clichés without thinking about what they mean. For example:

> She wasn't the brightest cookie in the pot.

> He tossed the white flag into the ring.

You've got to turn round and face your Achilles heel.

Anger galloped through my mind like a streak of lightning.

While you certainly can't judge a book by its cover, you can bathe luxuriously in its sharp, glittering truth that sadly always feels just out of arm's reach.

Although at first we were looking for a needle in a haystack, at the drop of a hat the shoe was on the other foot as we probed the witnesses to see what wells of knowledge were hidden under a bushel.

In Tom Stoppard's 1968 play *The Real Inspector Hound*, one character says to the other (quite deliberately): 'The skeleton in the cupboard is coming home to roost.' When I Googled this phrase, I found someone using it, completely without irony, in a book about war and responsibility. However much we might laugh at mixed metaphors, they are easy to create by accident (not on purpose, oddly), especially when we are in a hurry. I know I unwittingly create them in speech quite a lot, especially when I'm teaching. Sports commentators produce so many mixed metaphors that the satirical magazine *Private Eye* has a column called Colemanballs that reproduces them alongside other sentence-level gaffes, like Geoffrey Boycott's observation that 'Sometimes you've got no choice where you're born', or John Inverdale's reflection that 'The best horse won, and that's all you can ask for in any sport.'

All of this should remind us to think about the words

we put on the page to make sure that at the very least they make sense. A good general rule is not to use more than one figurative expression per paragraph. But you can extend your figurative idea as much as you want to, as long as you do it logically, like George Eliot does in *Middlemarch*:

> There was a peculiar fascination for Dorothea in this division of property intended for herself, and always regarded by her as excessive. She was blind, you see, to many things obvious to others – likely to tread in the wrong places, as Celia had warned her; yet her blindness to whatever did not lie in her own pure purpose carried her safely by the side of precipices where vision would have been perilous with fear.[266]

Here the metaphor is doing exactly what great metaphors should do. It takes something that is abstract and difficult to understand and makes it possible for us to visualise it. And it makes sense. Someone blind is likely to 'tread in the wrong places' but is also likely to be fearless in some ways because of what he or she can't see. Most people reading this passage will create their own image of Dorothea walking along the side of some precipice, and can then use this image as a way to consider and explore this intriguing mixture of sophistication and credulity that she has.

In her story 'Je ne parle pas français', Katherine Mansfield has her first-person narrator Raoul say this:

> I don't believe in the human soul. I never have. I believe that people are like portmanteaux – packed with certain

things, started going, thrown about, tossed away, dumped down, lost and found, half emptied suddenly, or squeezed fatter than ever, until finally the Ultimate Porter swings them on to the Ultimate Train and away they rattle [. . .]

Not but what these portmanteaux can be very fascinating. Oh, but very! I see myself standing in front of them, don't you know, like a Customs official.[267]

Again, this is a metaphor that is extended quite logically. If a human being is a portmanteau (a suitcase, a container), then you'd expect to find it filled with things. In fact, you'd also expect it to be tossed around and perhaps chucked on a train. Suddenly we are able to see the human condition (or Raoul's idea of it) in an understandable, easy-to-visualise way. But just because we can visualise it, that does not mean it is solved. Being able to visualise something sometimes just means it is easier to contemplate. By making the human being into a suitcase, Mansfield invites us to consider the temporary nature of life, and the body as a container for something, even if this is not a soul. In the pilot episode of *Friends*, Joey says that having a relationship with a woman is like choosing a flavour of ice cream. When Ross says later that he has just 'grabbed a spoon' we understand that he means he is trying to embark on a new relationship. Sometimes metaphors help us say things obliquely that would be hard to say directly.

Metaphors are not just used to describe abstract concepts, feelings and objects. Almost anything in a piece of writing can be read metaphorically, and sometimes a whole description, scene – or even an entire narrative – will function metaphorically. For example, the setting of Hemingway's story 'Hills Like White Elephants' can be seen to stand for other things. Here we have a story about a relationship in crisis, and a big decision, and it is set at a train station. Train stations are stuck between one place and another; they are places where you wait; they are places that you do not stay. Does the train station here represent the state of the relationship in the story? Or something about Jig's indecision? Both? An object, location or set of actions in a narrative that figuratively represents the emotional state of one or more of the characters is called an 'objective correlative'.[268] This is where metaphor begins to drift out of the purely figurative and into the world of objects (albeit fictional ones) and drama: this is where we'd have Dorothea walking along a 'real' precipice rather than just imagine her walking along a pretend one. Note that in the Katherine Mansfield story we are directed to the metaphor – Raoul specifically tells us he is comparing the human body with a portmanteau. But in the Hemingway story we have to read the metaphorical content for ourselves. You don't always need to tell the reader that you are using a figurative device ('The train station reminded him of their relationship . . . '). Often it is better to let the reader make connections on his or her own.

Metaphor, whether it is used to describe a single feeling or a whole society, should, when it functions properly, give us something we can actually look at, instead of an abstract idea that is difficult to comprehend. The very best metaphors replace something we can't examine with something that we can. In a sense, all fiction is metaphorical. All fiction uses synecdoche, where a part (for example, a dysfunctional

middle-class family like the Smarts in *The Accidental*) is
used to at least imply a more important whole (the entire
English middle class). Other examples of this include
Gatsby, who stands for any nouveau riche who just can't
fit in. Then there are characters like Levin in *Anna Karenina*
or Pip in *Great Expectations*, who in some way stand for all
of us. In *The Bell Jar*, Esther Greenwood stands for a whole
generation of young women who are restricted by cultural
assumptions about what they should and should not do.
Metaphor is a wonderful way of using the specific to suggest
the general, which is what fiction does. But beware of
metaphor that does little more than make your sentences
pretty. And beware, too, of a pile-up of metaphorical content
in your work. The fact that you can describe something in
terms of something else doesn't always mean you should.
But do practise. If life is just a box of chocolates, then what
is death? Take some well-known clichés and play around
with them, and then practise extending your own metaphors.
Remember that extending metaphors relies a little bit on
plotting. They have to make sense when you have finished.

If metaphor is figurative, and involves saying what something is like, but isn't, then the technique of *defamiliarisation*
is all about telling things exactly as they are. Defamiliarisation,
or 'ostranenie', is a term that was first used by the Russian
formalist Viktor Shklovsky in his 1917 essay 'Art as
Technique'. In this essay, Shklovsky argues that the purpose
of art is to make us look at things anew. He says:

> And art exists that one may recover the sensation of life; it
> exists to make one feel things, to make the stone *stony*.[269]

Most of us probably feel the need to 'recover the sensation of life' in some ways. Shklovsky describes ways in which we can act so unconsciously that it's as if we have done nothing at all. When things are so familiar to us – for example, driving down a particular stretch of road, or making a cup of tea – we can often forget them entirely and never notice their detail. Indeed, you have probably had the experience of forgetting whether or not you have even done something habitual, like turn off your hair straighteners or the oven, or put your keys in your pocket. For Shklovsky, this is a kind of living death. He says:

> And so life is reckoned as nothing. Habitualization devours work, clothes, furniture, one's wife, and the fear of war.[270]

Similarly, we may have ideas and opinions about things that are so familiar to us they are rarely challenged. We may believe that only the most important stories make it onto the news, for example, or that going to a shopping mall or a supermarket is a normal thing to do. Defamiliarisation makes us look at such familiar things again, perhaps as an alien would, or an anthropologist from a long way away. Shklovsky uses various examples from Tolstoy to illustrate what he says:

> Tolstoy makes the familiar seem strange by not naming the familiar object. He describes an object as if he were seeing it for the first time, an event as if it were happening for the first time [. . .] For example in 'Shame' Tolstoy 'defamiliarizes' the idea of flogging in this way: 'to strip people

who have broken the law, to hurl them to the floor, and to rap on their bottoms with switches', and after a few lines, 'to lash about on the naked buttocks'. Then he remarks: 'Just why precisely this stupid, savage means of causing pain and not any other – why not prick the shoulders or any part of the body with needles, squeeze the hands or the feet in a vise, or anything like that?' I apologise for this harsh example, but it is typical of Tolstoy's way of pricking the conscience.[271]

Of course, flogging isn't familiar to us now, but we can see that it was, for Tolstoy, and why he defamiliarises it in this way. Classic defamiliarisation techniques include describing an object as if it were being viewed by a child, or some other being who has not (yet) been socialised simply to accept the way things are. Shklovsky also uses the example of Tolstoy's story 'Kholstomer', which is narrated from the perspective of a horse. The horse, Serpukhovsky, is describing how humans see the world. He says:

They agree that only one [person] may say 'mine' about this, that or the other thing. And the one who says 'mine' about the greatest number of things is, according to the game which they've agreed to among themselves, the one they consider most happy.[272]

Using a child, animal or other 'unknowing outsider' as narrator is a device that enables an object to be described as if it were being seen for the first time because, in these cases, the narrator or describer is not familiar with the object. But there are examples where a more knowing narrator will break something down for us, so that we can look at it as if for the first time.

Most people when they receive a get-well-soon card may just glance at it, think 'Oh, that's nice', and put it on a shelf. But Esther Greenwood, narrator of *The Bell Jar*, goes out of her way to describe such a card:

> I reached for the book the people from *Ladies' Day* had sent.
>
> When I opened it a card fell out. The front of the card showed a poodle in a flowered bedjacket sitting in a poodle basket with a sad face, and the inside of the card showed the poodle lying down in the basket with a little smile, sound asleep under an embroidered sampler that said, 'You'll get well best with lots and lots of rest'. At the bottom of the card somebody had written, 'Get well quick! From all of your good friends at *Ladies' Day*' in lavender ink.[273]

Here a familiar object seems strange, and we suddenly realise how absurd it is to send people pictures of poodles when they're not well. Plath doesn't need to overplay this: she just has Esther tell us what she sees in simple, declarative sentences. In this novel, it is Esther's depression that gives her a special, defamiliarising, way of looking at the world. She has seen the truth, free of scrollwork and ornament, and can tell it to us as it is.

So can we say that expansive writing has lots of metaphors and minimalist writing doesn't have any? Is expansive writing figurative and minimalist writing defamiliarising?

No. It's not just that it isn't that simple – I don't think that is anywhere near where we draw the line between these two types of writing. In fact, minimalists use metaphor all the time, on all kinds of levels. Look at Hemingway's white elephants, for a start. And Sylvia Plath's bell jar provides not just the central symbol for her novel, but also leads to a lot of glass imagery.

When you really examine them, you find that the sentences in minimalist writing and in expansive writing follow very similar 'rules'. Neither should have unnecessary words. Both should be as specific and precise as possible. Both should have considerable depth, which will usually be provided by figurative devices. We should be able to see sentences playing out in front of us as we read them. They should be full of nouns and verbs and colourful, interesting *things*. However expansive a sentence becomes, it should never become 'baggy'. In the end, the expansive sentence simply uses a greater range of poetic devices. It draws attention to itself with its neologisms, repetition, alliteration, assonance and half-rhymes. It won't say 'Lolita', when it can play with the word so that it becomes 'Lo-lee-ta: the tip of the tongue taking a trip of three steps down the palate to tap, at three, on the teeth. Lo. Lee. Ta'.[274] It calls people things like 'the foil, the fool, the poor foal'.[275] But minimalist writing shows off, too. It says, *Look how clean I am. Look how little of me there is*. Or, perhaps after editing, *See? So clean*. It is likely that although you will be able to write passably in each of these styles, you will love one more than the other, or, perhaps more importantly, one of them will love you more than the other one does. Start now trying to identify which appeals more to you and then decide what you are going to do with it that no one else has done. Look at each word in your sentences and make sure you know what it means and why it is there.

BEGINNING TO WRITE A NOVEL

It's like driving a car at night. You never see further than your headlights, but you can make the whole trip that way.

E.L. Doctorow[276]

The trouble with our young writing men is that they are still too romantic. You can't put out to sea without being seasick and wanting a basin. Well, why won't they have the courage of those basins?

Katherine Mansfield, 'Bliss'[277]

If you have the slightest interest in writing a novel then I would encourage you to attempt it. My MA students usually find that they have embarked on writing a novel less than an hour after coming to their first class. Why do I encourage people to do such an ambitious thing? Well, because I want them to stop being afraid. I want them to see that completing a novel is a highly pleasurable achievement, like running a marathon. You might not be able to write an award-winning, or even publishable, novel; that is sadly true. But then people who run marathons enjoy them even if they don't win. Most people can write a novel if they really want to, just as most people can complete a marathon if they train correctly. And many people (including me) have to complete one bad novel before then being able to write a good one (in my case I had to get through four before I wrote something I was happy with, but that is unusual),[278] so you may as well get on with it and get one out of the way.[279]

A novel is a continuous narrative usually made up of around 90,000 words. Let's say that you work all week, but you have a couple of hours free on a Saturday and a Sunday. You could write 1,000 words on each day.[280] At a rate of 2,000 words a week, you'd have 8,000 words in a month. Your novel would be finished in just under a year. If you wanted to complete a first draft more quickly than that and were able to write 2,000 words a day on three days a week then you'd have 6,000 words a week, which makes 24,000 words a month. You'd get a rough draft complete in three months. Except this doesn't take into account all the deleting you will do. We'll discuss deleting properly later. But for now assume that the faster you write the more you'll delete. So let's add a couple of months (which seems about right) and say that, at a rate of 6,000 words a week, you could have a good first draft in five months. That doesn't quite mean five months from this moment, as we will see, but five months of writing steadily once you know what you're doing.

When I began writing novels, I wanted information like this more than anything else. I thought I knew how to write a good sentence (I didn't, but never mind) but I wanted – needed – to know roughly how many of them I had to write before I could call myself a 'novelist'. Nowadays the

Internet tells beginning writers how many words different types of novels contain, but when I started there was no easy way of finding out how long a novel was, apart from doing a rough estimate based on tallying up words in a line, lines on a page, pages in a book, which I did with the shortest novel I could find in the house, which was *The Hound of the Baskervilles*. I estimated that it was roughly 60,000 words long,[281] which didn't seem too bad as a total. I mean, it wasn't completely forbidding. After all, it's only 6 × 10,000 words. Or 30 × 2,000 words – like 30 longish letters or emails – which sounded a bit better.[282] That figure really stuck with me and to this day I look forward to the moment that I hit 60,000 words in a project because it is precisely then, when I have written something as long as *The Hound of the Baskervilles*, that I feel I have written 'a novel'.

This is crazy really because most of my novels are much longer than *The Hound of the Baskervilles*.[283] But at that point, at 60,000 words, I can tell myself that the job is complete and I am once again a novelist, and so anything else I do is 'extra'. I always enjoy writing those 'extra' words so much more than I enjoy the first 60,000. Do you see the psychological trick I'm playing on myself there? You'll need to work out your version of this. Do whatever it takes: breaking it into small pieces and aiming for far fewer words than I know I'll end up writing works for me. But you might require a completely different strategy, like making a bet with a friend that you can do it. Genius, or just thinking hard, can give you the idea, the characters, the depth and the theme, but it is the cunning (and desperate) personal trainer within that gets the words on the page in a reasonable period of time.

So do you just have an idea one day and then sit at a desk every day after that until it's written down? What do 'real' writers do? Let's imagine you were going to work in the way some people think you should, and sit at your desk at 9 a.m. to write for seven hours (with a one-hour lunch break). In seven hours, if you kept writing and never went on Twitter or YouTube, you would complete roughly 7,000 words. This means you could write a novel in a couple of weeks, surely? I don't think so. Even at my very top speed, writing things like 'I felt a sudden wave of sickness engulf me, moving in a matter of seconds from my feet to my throat in a rush of adrenaline', it took me 30 days to write a novel. If I'd been writing for seven hours a day, I would have completed 210,000 words. The universe would probably fold up in horror at the idea of so much bad prose all at once. At the very least my hands would have fallen off. It's just not possible to write at that speed. No one does it. Apart from anything else, at that speed you'd need to do a lot of deleting, which is impossible if you're writing all day. So now that we have scientifically proven that the writer's day is not made up of writing, and cannot possibly be made up of writing, we must ask how it *is* comprised. What do novelists do all day? What *should* novelists do all day?

First of all, it depends where you are with your project. Let the novel dictate the speed at which it needs to be written. Do you know all your characters so intimately that you can predict every single thing that happens to them?

If so, go ahead and type so fast you bruise the tips of your fingers. Or are you, like most of us, a bit stuck? Well, maybe the book needs to be left alone for a few weeks while you work out what you want to explore. At the very end of a project, as you gradually stop washing, speaking or moving from your desk at all, you may well spend more than seven hours writing in a day. I've done that (and bruised my fingers). But at the very beginning of a project you should spend very little – if any – time actually writing (as in composing, not note-taking, which is fine, as we will see).

Once you've had your initial idea you need to let it germinate and take root properly in your mind. Ideally at this stage you will be doing something very different from writing, something where you can be physically absorbed but with your mind free enough to wander a bit. Gardening is good. Any kind of manual job works well. Anything monotonous like housework, dog-walking, driving and low-intensity caring work is good too. You'll need a big notebook, but not much else, at this stage. I like ring-bound notebooks because you can easily have them open on a desk without them trying to snap themselves shut. Anyway, get one with lots of pages and devote it to your novel.

You'll be doing three different kinds of thinking at this point. In a given day, you might do all three types, or just the first two. The first type, which you'll be doing while you work, bath the baby, knit, weed or drive down the motorway, is just gentle daydreaming. Don't try to think of your novel exactly, but let your mind know that you'll be interested in hearing what it has to say later on. If your mind does immediately zoom off and start planning scenes and characters and themes this is OK, and it does happen from time to time, but try to find some way of remembering or recording what you have thought. Depending on the circumstances I use a scrap of paper or the notebook app on my phone, but a small notebook is good if you have one handy. I heard once that Thomas Hardy used to make notes by scratching with twigs on leaves, if he was out walking and nothing else was available. Sometimes I email myself, which is actually a very effective way not just of making a note, but remembering I've made a note. Whatever method you use, keep it separate from your 'official' novel notebook, which should be too big to carry everywhere anyway. And in any case, you're not actively trying to have the kinds of thoughts you need to write down at this moment. Just relax and get on with what you're supposed to be doing. It is important for your mind to have quiet time. If you find it difficult to stop intensively thinking, you could learn to meditate and try to practise it every day.

The second type of thinking is more active but still relaxed. It's what you do when you're sitting around in the evening, perhaps watching TV or reading a newspaper. It's when you're reading bedtime stories to your children or at a dinner party with friends. It's when you're listening to the radio in the car on the way to work, rather than day-dreaming. Again, you don't have to consciously think about your novel, or choose films, books and TV programmes that count as research. Just be open to interesting conversations, ideas, thoughts and images. Notice in more detail what's going on around you. What are people wearing? What are they doing? How do they move around in the world? Look at walls, flowers, mud, pylons, stitches in blankets – whatever interests you. In the first mode of thinking you might just notice the canal bridges on the way to work. In this mode you might count them, or wonder what they're made from or even ask someone about their history. You might think deeply about the rules of football, or how the newspaper article was constructed. Become excited and childlike. Ask stupid questions. Read as much as you possibly can. If your mind is receptive, then it doesn't really matter what you do as long as it genuinely stimulates you. You could even watch a really dumb TV programme, if that's what you feel like doing, but try not to get stuck in a comfortable rut of always watching the same kind of thing. This kind of thinking is undirected, and therefore allows for happy accidents.[284]

The third kind of thinking is more directed and exciting (and tiring). It happens when you sit with your notebook and deliberately brainstorm ideas. The film *Adaptation* shows how frenzied this can be, for example in this voice-over section in which the character Kaufman is brainstorming the beginning of his screenplay:

Okay, we open with Laroche. He's funny. Okay, he says – Okay, he says 'I love to mutate plants.' He says 'Mutation is fun.' Okay, we show flowers and . . . Okay we have to have the court case. Okay, we show Laroche. Okay, he says, 'I was mutated as a baby. That's why I'm so smart.' That's funny. Okay, we open at the beginning of time. No. Okay we open with Laroche driving into the swamp.[285]

In the film Kaufman often speaks his ideas into a mini tape-recorder. I have tried this – and in fact used it in the last stages of writing my first novel – but the amount of material you generate can be overwhelming. Nowadays I just stick with my notebook, but I do talk out loud a lot when I brainstorm. My conversations with myself often begin 'OK. So what if . . .?' as I test out a strand of plot or characterisation and see where it logically goes. Often that particular strand doesn't work, and so I go back to the beginning and try again. I only write down ideas that seem to work and that I therefore want to remember. In any case I think it is very useful to be able to speak your ideas out loud during this brainstorming stage. Much more than for the actual writing, this is where you need a room of your own, or some private space in which to work. If you don't have a private space at home, you could always drive some-where remote and talk to yourself in the car. Or get up an hour before everyone else and whisper to yourself in the kitchen.

So what exactly are you brainstorming at this stage? Well, everything. Hopefully you've got an initial idea from doing a matrix or a list or something similar. Or you might even be brainstorming from a matrix with no initial idea at all. Let's go back to one of the matrix-inspired ideas I used as an example in the chapter 'How to Have Ideas'. 'Abby is working at Chelmsford County Cricket Club when the West Indies are on tour in the UK. She falls in love with a black politics student, Eliot, who is obsessed with cricket, and supports the West Indies. She knows nothing about cricket but tries to learn from Bob, the man in charge of the score-board at the cricket club. He gives her knowledge in return for cups of tea and pieces of cake, perhaps.' One of the first things I'd do with this idea (or any idea) is work out the ending. Not the actual ending that I will write – because I can't know that until I get there – but some idea of where this narrative is heading. Remember that there are only really three different types of ending. Is this one going to be happy, sad or open? And what does a happy ending actually mean for these characters? If this is a romantic comedy then Abby and Eliot must end up together. But if it's a coming-of-age novel then this doesn't have to be the case.

Let's say it is a coming-of-age novel. Who is going to come of age? Just Abby? Or all the characters? And what do they need to learn? Perhaps Abby will learn more independence. Bang! There's a potential ending. Now we can work backwards. So why does Abby need independence? It implies she has been trapped or dependent before. Perhaps she has been the lone carer of a parent with cancer? No, that's just too sad, and not something I know well enough, even though it happened to a friend. What about if she had an abortion that went wrong and now she's trying to recover from the panic attacks she had as a result? OK, so what if Eliot assumes she's a perfect white girl with no problems and then it turns out that she's actually had this abortion that went wrong?

No. This is no good because a) it pushes Eliot towards stereotype (the 'black guy with the chip on his shoulder' who spends his time worrying about 'white people') and b) it's not very romantic to find out that someone has had an abortion that went wrong. Unless . . . if the tone of the whole is very gritty, and both Abby and Eliot have lots of problems, then perhaps it will be cathartic for them to share their deepest secrets. And perhaps it's good that Abby's is so complex. Notice how far we've now come from 'Perhaps Abby will learn more independence'. Perhaps this is not the focus at all. Maybe Eliot does not begin as a cricket fan but will come of age through learning about cricket. Maybe he's written it off as a colonial game (cliché alert) and he and Abby learn about it together. Or maybe she's the one who teaches him? Do they end up competing and, if so, who wins? Keep looking for the ending and working back from that.

Writing a novel is a bit like going on a journey. It is only once you know your destination that you can start working out how to get there. People rarely set off to go 'anywhere'; most people go on journeys to specific places. If you are going from London to Edinburgh you are more likely to go through Newcastle than you are to go via Wales.[286] Get a start-point and an end-point and then you will become aware of some places that it seems logical to go through. I remember once being told the difference between aims and objectives, which I had never understood (and to be honest had never particularly wanted to). An aim is a whole task, like 'get to Edinburgh by midnight'. An objective is a part of an aim that is somehow measurable, like 'arrive at Newcastle by ten'. So if I want to get to Edinburgh by midnight, I'll need to go through Newcastle by ten. This description stuck with me because of how similar it is to plotting. Once you know the aim (Abby and Eliot will live happily ever after together) then you know at least one of the objectives (they must fall in love). In order for this to be surprising and interesting there needs to have been some conflict between them before (perhaps Eliot bullied Abby's brother at school). Before you know it you'll have a rough map with a destination and some key points you need to go through along the way.

Every time you come across a possible variable ('something bad' happened between Abby and Eliot in the past, for example) try to come up with as many different ideas as possible before you choose one. Here I've chosen 'Eliot bullied Abby's brother at school' but it could equally be that Eliot humiliated Abby by asking her out on a date as a dare, or that she did something similar to him, or that her mother was his cleaner or his mother was her cleaner and something happened . . . As a general rule, try to reject many more ideas than you accept. And be aware that the first idea that comes into your mind as the solution to a particular problem is very likely to be a cliché. After all, it is the cheapest and quickest thing your mind can offer you. It wants to save energy, but don't let it. Think harder.

Draw some kind of plot diagram in your notebook. In fact, once you've got a few details for your plot, try linking them in different ways. What would this look like as a tragedy, or a modern-realist novel? You can also use your notebook to plan and record research. Is there a book you need to read for your project? Make yourself a reading list and a 'to do' list. If you're writing about the 1991 West Indies cricket tour, are there key matches available on DVD? Are there any relevant sports biographies? If you have always been interested in existentialism, then now is the time to read Sartre. Start creating characters with super-objectives. Build up impressions of all of them. Make a family tree, if several of your characters are related to one another. Start planning scenes. Write snatches of dialogue and rough descriptions. You might also want to continue your study of narrative, but in your own way. You've seen how I've done it in this book. Why not make a pile of your five favourite novels and analyse how they work?[287] Make yourself a writer's manifesto of what you think is great writing and terrible writing. Are you going to be a minimalist writer or are you planning to do something more expansive? Try out a few sentences and see what they look like. What sorts of sentences do you love?

I've seen other writers' notebooks, and they are all strangely familiar. Early pages of your notebook will probably contain long lists of terrible potential titles, abandoned character names and so on. There'll often be questions that you are asking of yourself, in order to keep your plot on track (or even to get your plot going). In my *PopCo* notebook I have the list of different subjects I wanted to write about that I discussed in the 'How to Have Ideas' chapter. Here's a page from my *Mr. Y* notebook, from somewhere towards the end when I knew more or less what I was doing, but still trying to work out how to get the detail right in particular scenes.

The first note here reads:

Voices in heads. Has Apollo Smintheus made Adam go to the church? Now he's Ariel's sort-of guardian, he'll be doing everything he can to help her. Does he even tell her that Adam's trustworthy? This stuff is interesting because of the questions it poses about free will, determinism, omniscience etc.

It seems that here I'm trying to work out a plot problem (I need to get Adam into the church) by considering the objectives of different characters (Adam does not want to go into the church; Apollo Smintheus wants to help Ariel). I'm also considering how the philosophical aspects of this action affect the novel. You won't necessarily need to do this in the same amount of detail but it is worth thinking what different decisions 'mean' philosophically or morally. In my example before, what are the different political impli-cations of Abby teaching Eliot to play cricket, and the reverse? One might seem a bit colonial and reminiscent of the film *Lagaan*, but a good writer could have fun with it, especially if the characters found it absurd or humorous. The other is potentially a bit gendered, but more realistic and also potentially funny. Humour will rescue a lot of awkward scenes, and as long as you're writing literary fiction for adults, not issues-drama for children, you can take some risks here. But you do need to think about what your book is implicitly endorsing. If you create a character who wears short skirts and too much lipstick and then gets raped, you'd need to be very careful indeed that you are not suggesting she deserved it.

After you have been notebooking and thinking for a while, your idea will begin to take shape. You'll have some sense of the ending and the beginning of your novel. You'll hopefully have some characters in mind, and some locations and the beginnings of some scenes. You can spend as much or as little time as you like on this initial planning stage. The more you plan, the better the resulting novel is likely to be. Sometimes my poor students only have a few weeks before they have to begin writing. I like to have about a year. With a first novel you can usually get away with a little less planning, as you will in some way have been thinking about it all your life. But however long you have, it will help you a great deal if you can work out three main things before you begin writing. You'll need one each of these:

- Narrative question (you'll actually need several of these, but one main one)
- Thematic question
- Seed word

Narrative questions will intrigue your reader and keep him or her reading. Will Cinderella go to the ball? Will Hamlet kill Claudius? Will Odysseus get home? Will Dorothy get home? Will E.T. get home? Will Eiji in *number9dream* ever find his father? A question like this will usually be the main reason we start engaging with a piece of fiction. We want to find out not simply 'what happens' (after all, things happen randomly all the time), but whether a particular question is answered and whether a particular character gets what they want or not. We came across this idea in the first part of this book, when we discovered that good plots are based on the concept of the single action. A novel will usually contain lots of small narrative questions but there will always be one main big one. *Great Expectations* opens with us wondering who Pip is, and then whether he will escape from Magwitch, and then whether he will be beaten by Mrs Joe, and so on. Lots of little questions eventually take us to the big questions. Will Pip become a gentleman? Will he discover the identity of his benefactor? And of course the main narrative question: will he win the affections of Estella? *Middlemarch* begins with us asking who is Dorothea? Why is she so plainly dressed? What tensions will arise from her being more clever than her sister? And then the big question of the whole novel, asked on the second page: whom will she marry?

While a novel usually has one main narrative question, each major character usually has one of their own. In *Middlemarch* we wonder whether Bulstrode will get found out, and, before that, why Raffles is able to blackmail him. We wonder whether Lydgate will fall for Rosamund, and whether this will lead to happiness or not. *Great Expectations*, being a first-person narrative, is more focused on Pip's questions. But we still wonder whether Herbert will be OK, and whether Joe will remarry. There is no exact science to this apart from realising that you need at least one main narrative question, and that this, or some smaller narrative question, must be asked on the first page of your novel. Take your five favourite novels and look at their first pages. How many questions are asked, implicitly or explicitly? See if you can find a novel or another book with no narrative question on its opening page (this will be quite difficult to do). How engaging do you find it?

After its famous opening statement,[288] which itself asks a question (although a thematic one, which we will come to in a moment), *Anna Karenina* begins like this:

All was confusion in the Oblonskys' house. The wife had found out that the husband was having an affair with their former French governess, and had announced to the husband that she could not live in the same house with him. This situation had continued for three days now, and was painfully felt by the couple themselves, as well as by all the members of the family and household.[289]

Although the situation in the Oblonsky house is not to be the major narrative focus of the novel, we are immediately drawn in, wondering what will happen to these two. There are a lot of questions suggested by this paragraph. Will the couple separate or not? What has actually happened over the last three days? Will 'the husband' continue his affair with the former French governess? What will become of this unhappy family?

The concept of the unhappy family – or, more accurately, the unhappy marriage – does not just lead to narrative questions; it leads to questions about the nature of human relationships, particularly romantic relationships. Throughout any good novel we should realise that we are not being asked merely to think of what happens and to whom, but *why it matters*. We should realise that in reading about Anna's doomed affair and Levin's journey through life we are, on some level, reading about ourselves. Are you more like Anna or more like Levin? What's the difference between them in the end? One is passionate and the other attempts to be rational. Therefore we may say that the thematic questions in this novel are around passion and reason. Should we give in to our desires and attempt to lead a life of pleasure (which always anyway ends in pain)? Or should we assume some sort of moral responsibility, even though this may be painful in the short term? Is the point of life sensual pleasure, or something else?

Your thematic question is an important question that you will never answer. It is important how you frame this; it should be a universal, open question ('What is power?') rather than a personal, limited question ('Should I be kind to my horse?'). That's not to say that a novel about power won't be concerned with smaller questions, such as whether a character should be kind to her horse. But if there are smaller questions then these must all relate to the larger thematic question (what Stanislavski would call the super-objective of the plot). Your thematic question will be the main point of your novel. Your novel will show not just what happens but why it matters: why it is *important*.

It is worth quoting Chekhov at length here. He is writing to his friend, the publisher Alexey Suvorin, in 1888.

Only somebody who has never written or had anything to do with images could say that there are no questions in his realm, that there is nothing but answers. The artist observes, chooses, guesses, compounds – these actions in themselves already presuppose a question at the origin; if the artist did not pose a question to himself at the beginning then there was nothing to guess or choose [. . .] You are right in demanding that an artist approach his work consciously, but you are confusing two concepts: the solution of a problem and the correct formulation of a problem. Only the second is required of the artist. Not a single problem is solved in *Anna Karenina* or *Onegin*, but they satisfy you completely only because all the problems in them are formulated correctly.[290]

You already have all sorts of interesting questions in your mind. You must do, or you would not want to write a novel. I used to tell people off for wanting to write novels simply to make money (very difficult) or for the sake of vanity (futile). I also used to give slightly haughty lectures about the novel being an *art form*, not a place to show off for the sake of it, or string a lot of clichés together for a few quid. Then I realised that if the people sitting in front of me wanted to make money above all else, they'd be doing business studies, not creative writing. Almost every way of obtaining money is easier than being a novelist. I believe it would make more financial sense for most novelists (apart from J.K. Rowling and a few others) to knit for a living instead. I realised that everyone who has even the slightest interest in writing therefore has thematic questions somewhere in their mind already. They have something they want to explore. Look on your matrix. Look at the question-and-answer section. There are some things you're interested in. Perhaps even some of the main things. Also look at your list of obsessions. There's probably something good there, too.

Formulating a thematic question can be easy or it can be hard, depending on what you are interested in at the moment, how much you have thought about it, how ambitious you want to be, and how 'big' you want your novel to be. When I wrote my novel *Bright Young Things*, I knew

I wanted it to be about young people and the sort of entertainment-based culture in which everyone is defined by the TV programmes they watch and the music they listen to. I'd put my characters on a deserted island and so the narrative question was 'Will they escape?' The thematic question then became something like 'What *is* escape?' For these characters, who are obsessed with popular culture and their fast-paced urban lifestyles, could being trapped on an island actually be a kind of escape itself? A simple question like this can be very profound and doesn't necessarily need to be made over-complex within the narrative. Good framing of a thematic question often includes giving the reader the space in which to consider it. By the time I wrote *Our Tragic Universe* I was thinking in a much more complex way about theme – and having lots of connected ideas about metafiction – and the novel reflects this.[291]

It can help a great deal to try to condense the main essence of your thematic concern into one word: what I call a *seed word* (because everything in the novel is somehow contained in it, and will grow from it). Every term I have a session where I get students to bring in dictionaries and thesauruses and then find the one word through which they can focus their novel. When they do find the right word the effect is electrifying. You could try this too. The first step – although it's very difficult – is to practise on novels you know well. Make a list of everything the novel appears to be 'about' and then see if you can find the common theme, or the word that contains all the others. Use your dictionary all the way through this exercise. It is great fun looking up even quite familiar words and seeing their full range of meanings.

Jane Austen's *Emma* is about responsibility, love, society, sincerity and authority. It is about someone being very wrong about the world around her. It is about someone who tries to take control of people's lives. What links all these things? I would suggest it is 'respectability'. The concept 'respectable' contains both the idea that someone is estimable, worthy of respect and important in some way and the idea of respectability as being inherently to do with a polite society. The central crisis in the novel, where Emma insults Miss Bates on Box Hill, turns on the characters' understanding of respect and respectability. Emma does not respect Miss Bates and thus loses some of her own respectability. Emma is also too concerned with making Harriet Smith respectable, and again loses respect because of it. It seems as if the novel is a fragile economy of respect given and lost. It asks us, *Who is respectable? Who has the right to respect? What actions are respectable?*

The novel *number9dream* by David Mitchell is about a young man trying to find his father in Tokyo while having all kinds of masculine fantasies about how this might happen. Is the novel about family? Or is it about masculinity? Or is it about fantasy? These three things, while contained in the novel, don't quite contain each other. Is there another word that does contain these three ideas somehow? Maybe agency, with its associations of being a free agent, a secret agent and an agent of your own fortune. Or maybe mastery – because a master is a young man as well as someone in control of everything. But in fact I would argue that *heroism* covers it best – the sense of being a hero (as in a – usually male – main character in a fantasy or even a family) as well as an action hero. The thematic question of *number9dream* could be formulated as *What is heroic?* Or even *What is a hero?* Suddenly, all the seemingly disparate elements of the novel come together. We have the 'hero' of a quest narrative, the Goat Writer; we have the crew-member of a nuclear submarine writing his last diary; we even have Suga, the computer hacker, attempting to be another kind of hero by hacking into the Pentagon. And all this on top of Eiji's central fantasies about himself-as-hero. This is not a reductive way to approach reading or writing; I think it's quite the reverse. It opens up rather than closes down. This novel suddenly becomes a place in which we can think about heroism in the deepest possible way. And heroism, like all themes worth writing about, is vast.

Why do you need a seed word if you already have a thematic question? The two are closely connected, after all. Well, when you find the correct seed word for your project it will make the hairs on the back of your neck stand up. While constructing a thematic question gives you focus and purpose, finding the correct seed word is quite magical. Although I never thought of one word to focus on when writing *Bright Young Things*, I see now that I would have liked to have chosen 'escapism'. What a lovely word, and so much bigger than just 'escape' (which it contains anyway). Here we find that the narrative question, thematic question and seed word are all focused on escape. But the seed word fully makes me realise that what I am really interested in in this novel is *escapism* and everything that is a part of that word, from real, practical escape to the whole of consumer culture. The 'ism' bit is important. Do we escape *into* culture or should we be aiming to escape *from* it? What does it mean when escape becomes escapism?

How do you find your word? Start looking things up in your dictionary and your thesaurus.[292] Let's take *PopCo* as an example, and pretend I am just beginning it, having made my list of subjects I want to cover (see page 193). I know I want to write about capitalism, but I also want to write about crosswords and toys and being a teenager. Is the novel about economics in some way, in the sense that there is money and mathematics and a consideration of the worth and cost of things? I look up the word *economy* in my dictionary and find that while it's a fascinating word with real depth of meaning, it is all about management of resources, which does not really fit with what I want to write in *PopCo*. What about *treasure*? Is that what the novel is really going to be about? Again, it's an interesting word with two meanings, one noun and one verb, but it's too limited. The thesaurus takes me from *equation* to *equality* to *adequacy*, none of which are right. *Innovation* is a lovely possibility, especially as an obsolete meaning recorded in the *OED* is 'A political revolution; a rebellion or insurrection'. But the meaning is so obsolete as to be unusable.

Is the novel going to be about *balance*: balancing books, balance in living and so on? Still not quite there. But how about the concept of *code*? Yes, this is much closer. This is going to be a novel about codes in the sense of 'codes and conventions' of fashion, teenage girls and so on, but also in the sense of the secret code. Using my dictionary and thesaurus I get from *code* to *cryptanalysis*, which is a step in the wrong direction. *Cryptanalysis* is too specific. You want the 'biggest' word you can get (in depth, not in length). Going in another direction again I get to *decryption*. This fits an awful lot of the novel, from the crosswords and the Voynich Manuscript to the problem of marketing to teenage girls. It also hints at something to do with close reading: working out what has been hidden in, say, marketing of animal products. There's also a sense of coming-of-age about it: Alice must decrypt or decipher everything around her. The word *decryption* initially looks too limiting, referring as it does only to the solving of cryptograms. But when I look up the definition of a cryptogram I find it means 'anything written in code'. So I get to keep all the meanings connected with *code* as well.

Make sure your word is an abstract noun, as these work best. When you have it, get a big sheet of paper and write your word in the centre of it. Now, using whatever method you like best (lists, mind maps, flow charts, whatever), brainstorm every meaning and association this word has for you. You're not using the dictionary and thesaurus any more. This is all about the relationship you have with the word, and what it means to you. Write down imagery, memories, objects and associations. One of the first things I'd write near the word *decryption* would be my memory of books I had as a child: *How to be a Spy* and *How to be a Detective*. And at the beginning of *PopCo* Alice is working on similar titles. I'd also write something about the codes that children use with one another to decide who is popular. Alice will worry about not having the right school skirt, for example, because it contains so much meaning. When you've finished, look at what you've done. Remind yourself of the power an abstract word has, and everything it contains, and vow to always treat these words with respect in future. This is not some throwaway part of a sentence or a cliché. This is what you are going to be obsessed with for the next few months or even years. Make sure you love your word. Make sure it feels special for you.

Once you think you have a seed word, imagine yourself standing at a noisy party talking to someone you admire. 'What's your novel about?' he or she asks you. At this point a common response is as follows: 'Uh, gosh, well, I don't really know how to answer that. It's all so complicated. I'm not sure I can say what it's about. OK, well, there's this guy whose sister disappeared and went to live in a cult. That's part of it. But there's also all this stuff about electricity, like the history of electricity, you know? And there might be some First World War stuff in there too, although I haven't really decided yet. But basically this woman, Grace, right, who's always on a diet . . . Well, oh, and did I mention this is taking place around 1915, maybe in Newcastle? Oh yeah, and miners, there'll be some miners . . .' If you do this in public you'll sound deranged, like Kaufman with his mini tape-recorder. When asked what your novel is about, either say nothing or say in a dignified way, 'I hope it's going to be about power', or 'I suppose I want it to be about energy'. Then if the person wants to know more you can reveal your thematic question. 'Well, I really want to ask about the extent to which power moves around. You know, electricity moves around but political influence doesn't seem to. I'm really interested in that.' If pressed further, you can move on to your narrative question. 'The main story is about this guy whose sister was kidnapped by a religious cult that said it could store divine power in these weird batteries . . .'

At some point in this process you will probably become desperate to start writing. This is the moment to begin, even if you don't feel quite as prepared as you should. Indeed, it is possible to over-prepare. Remember that no matter how much planning you do beforehand, it is in the writing itself that you work out character, theme and plot. You can sit and think as much as you like and even have a complete chapter worked out in your notebook, but it's quite likely that when you sit down to write, something else will happen. The characters will start talking to each other and then begin doing things 'of their own accord'. This isn't at all mystical or wacky. It just means that you only really see what's going to happen as it's happening. I recently sent two characters off to have afternoon tea together. Only when they sat down and looked at the menus did I realise that they couldn't possibly eat in each other's company. That's fine – they decided to have drinks instead. But I didn't know that until they sat down; I couldn't have planned it. There is an awful lot that can't be planned in a novel, and so at some point you just have to sit down and start writing it.

How do you actually do that? It's all very well talking about writing 2,000 words a day but when you are faced with a blank screen the very idea can seem impossible. What has happened to that easy flow you have when writing an email to a friend or an entry in your journal? This relaxed, conversational voice is the one you want to use for your writing, certainly for the first draft. If you can't be natural on your own, imagine you are writing the words to someone – someone relaxed and interested in you, a bit like the person who most enjoys your funny emails or your scathing blogs. If it helps, imagine your 'perfect reader' sitting in front of you in a sort of cosmic armchair. Briefly imagine what he or she looks like and what kind of person he or she is. Try not to make your perfect reader too much like one of your parents: he or she is going to be close to your own age. This is someone you want to impress, and you are thrilled that he or she has turned up to hear your story. He or she is hungry for great narrative, wonderful imagery, moving characters. You are eager to please him or her. You want to give him or her a really good time.

So what's your first line? How does your novel begin? You need someone, somewhere, doing or saying something. What kind of tone will you adopt? How is your perfect reader going to respond? Do you want him or her to laugh? Cry? Think? Keep your perfect reader in mind as you write. Now is not the time to pretend to be someone you're not. The perfect reader has turned up to hear *you*. Don't become shy and embarrassed about this. Don't turn into a parody of someone else. Now is not the time to do an impression of your favourite writer, or go all formal and wordy. Your perfect reader does not want to hear a business report or a long-winded explanation. He or she wants drama, and beauty, and understanding. *Your* version. Many writers claim not to write for an audience. Indeed, I was once the only one of seven writers on a panel who admitted that I do write for readers and not just for 'myself'. I still don't understand this concept of writing for oneself. Surely if you wanted to construct a sentence and it was only for yourself then you would simply think it? Isn't that what thinking is for? Writing implies communication and communication needs a receiver as well as a sender. Recording a thought means that you intend it to be read. You may as well be honest about that.

So there you are sitting at your desk, with your perfect reader somewhere in your mind. You may have even written your first sentence. Perhaps you've already deleted your first sentence and written a new one. But how do you write the whole novel? Perhaps one of the most important pieces of advice a writer can ever receive is this: no one ever sits down to write the whole novel. If they did, no one would ever complete one. It's far too daunting. You need to break it down. Earlier on I talked about breaking down 1,000 words into blocks of 250 words and thinking of it that way. This can help you as you begin aiming for a word-count, but it's not the most useful way to break up a novel. Not that much is going to happen in 250 words. In the first 250 words of *Great Expectations* we learn Pip's name, and that he is an orphan whose sister 'married the blacksmith'. Another 250 words tells of his brothers' graves. Then there is a 250-word section about the marsh country. Then Magwitch turns up and there is about 2,500 words of dialogue in which Magwitch commands Pip to get him a file and some food: '"You bring 'em both to me." He tilted me again. "Or I'll have your heart and liver out."'[293] Together these elements make a *scene* in which Pip meets Magwitch for the first time. And writing on the level of the scene is,

I believe, the best way to get control over your work.

The scene is the basic unit of fiction. Why the scene, rather than the chapter, paragraph, 250-word block or sentence? Because the scene is where *change* occurs. The scene is where drama takes place. The scene is where things happen. These can be big things or small things or, more commonly, both. You need to always be asking yourself, *What needs to change for my character(s) to move from this point where they are now, to the point I want them to be?* And also, *What is my objective in writing this scene?* In *The End of Mr. Y*, I wanted my protagonist, Ariel, to go from not having a cursed book to having one. So in Chapter One, she finds a cursed book in a second-hand bookshop. But in order for this to happen I had to get her in the shop in the first place. I had to have a reason for her to go there. Since she wouldn't normally go in that shop, something needed to change to make her go there. Here are the distinct scenes that make up the chapter:

- Ariel is in her office when the floor begins to shake.
- She follows people leaving buildings and observes a university building collapsing.
- She goes to the car park but it's been sealed off and she has to walk home.
- As she walks she gets cold and lost.
- She therefore enters a second-hand bookshop, where she finds the rare book, *The End of Mr. Y*.

Notice how these scenes are joined by cause and effect: the first causes the next to happen and so on. Also notice the way in which these scenes join together to produce one main action: obtaining the book. Here we have five scenes that amount to less than half a day of narrative time. Five scenes of Tolstoy or George Eliot might cover several weeks or months. Nowadays I think I prefer working more intensively on one longer scene than moving the action along with one short punchy scene after another. But both methods are valid.

Scenes are not always structured as linearly as these. Another way of organising this material would be to begin with Ariel in the bookshop and have her, say, telling the shop assistant why she is there (the university building collapsing and what happened next). This would reduce five scenes into one. If I was telling two main stories in the novel, and Ariel's was just one strand, then I could insert scenes from the other story (say Saul Burlem's narrative) between the scenes I have here. There are always a lot of choices when writing fiction. You will probably need to try things out in different ways before you find the one that works best.

If you decide on a non-linear structure, or a structure that weaves in different narratives, then you won't find an exact chain of cause and effect from scene to scene, and one scene won't necessarily cause the next to happen. But you should always be able to cut out your scenes and arrange them in such a way that there is one (or more) chronological story that works according to the rules of cause and effect, as we saw in the earlier chapters on structure. Also note the way that each scene is driven by a character's desire. In the first chapter of *The End of Mr. Y*,

Ariel *wants* to get out of the building; she *wants* to find out what's going on; she *wants* to get home; she *wants* to be warm; she *wants* the book.

While you are writing your novel, you will have to make decisions about which parts of the action you are going to expand into a scene, and which parts of the action you may just refer to. A long action can be suggested in as little as a sentence ('I spent the day in bed crying'), or a short action can be extended and dramatised over half a page, several pages – or even a whole chapter. You need to decide which action or change will be the focus of this scene. Perhaps the narrator is talking to a friend and says that she spent the day in bed crying on Wednesday, but then on Thursday she got an important letter, which she describes in detail. Incidentally, when something like this happens in a plot – your character gets an important letter – you need to decide whether you are going to directly show them getting the letter, or whether we are going to learn about it afterwards. Who is going to tell us about it, and how much do they know? There are always lots of ways to do something.

Scenes are the exciting or interesting parts of life. When you write, you should usually leave out the bits of the story that don't tell you anything about the character, themes or plot. So you wouldn't, for example, have your character going to the toilet, unless they are going to do so in a revealing way, or if some key part of the plot is going to happen there, like in *Pulp Fiction* or *Trainspotting*. Notice, therefore, how whole novels can take place without any of the characters going to the toilet at all, or having breakfast, or brushing their hair. If you were going to tell your friend about the big argument you'd just had with your mother, you wouldn't begin by saying what you had for breakfast, unless it was relevant. It's a good rule of thumb to enter the action in a scene as late as possible, and leave as early as possible (this holds for every part of the novel, incidentally, including, often, the whole novel itself). A good scene should usually both begin and end with a narrative question. It should certainly begin with you wanting to read it, and end with you wanting to read the next one.

Scenes are the episodes that, taken together (and built up using cause and effect), eventually make a whole story happen. But the good thing about scenes is that, used properly, they *show* us what the story is, and what's important about it. If you use scenes properly, you will never have to *tell* your reader what's going on in your novel. They will see for themselves, by experiencing the scenes playing out. If you are prone to long explanations of where everyone is going and how they are feeling and why they are acting, you will find it very liberating to start writing on the level of the scene instead. Just show what happens. The reader can do the interpretation. One of the biggest problems for beginning writers is this need to over-explain. Don't do it.

If you want to get an immediate sense for how scenes work, read a play or screenplay, or watch a film or a sitcom. You will notice that the most usual way to spot a change of scene in a film, play or novel is because the location changes. The time will also change. The next scene might be a flashback, but more usually it will happen some time after the last scene – *but not immediately after*. There'll be

a time lapse, usually, when the characters might travel to
the location for the next scene, powder their noses, go to
the loo, check their email, whatever. A scene will often feel
like a self-contained unit, and it will be clear where one
stops and the next begins. In a TV programme there might
be a little piece of music – along with a clear change in
time and location – to show movement from one scene to
another (as in *Friends*, *Frasier* and many others). In writing
we often have the line break, which is one step bigger than
a paragraph break and leaves a line of white space between
the end of one scene and the beginning of the next.
Sometimes people use a symbol or an asterisk to show this
change.

   Not everybody writes using a neat scene structure, but
I would suggest that you try to do so when working on
your first piece of fiction. It makes your material so much
easier to manage, and means you can experiment with linear
and non-linear structures more easily. Start studying the
way scenes work in books you read. Are there any classic
scenes that you find particularly interesting or powerful? If
so, study how they are put together? The scene in *Great
Expectations* where Pip visits Satis House for the first time;
the scene where Dorothea and Casaubon argue for the first
time in *Middlemarch*; the scene in *Anna Karenina* where
Sergei does not propose to Varenka in the woods: these are
favourites of mine and certainly worth examining not just
for the depth they contain but for their structure. All three
are very complex. But for a more contemporary way of
looking at scenes, the structures of David Mitchell's
number9dream and George Saunders's short story 'Sea Oak'

are very easily grasped. Both are excellent examples of the kind of scene structure I am talking about.

I like to have several scenes planned in advance (sometimes a plan for a scene can be just a sentence or two, for example 'Meg and Christopher argue while the roof leaks') so that I always have something to write next. But how does a plan actually turn into a scene when you are sitting at your desk writing it? It will probably be some combination of splurging, deleting, outlining, filling-in and refining. Splurging is where you type so fast you bruise the tips of your fingers (or write so fast your pen gives you blisters). This is almost like automatic writing, but with the benefit (hopefully) of some kind of plan. This can work very well for a fast-paced first-person narration or for dialogue. Try to keep some control, but don't worry that a lot of the material you produce in this way isn't very good. Let's say that on Monday you sat down to begin your novel and you splurged 2,200 words (you find when splurging that you often go over your word-target for the day). On Tuesday, then, your first task is to delete as many of these words as possible. Don't get attached to your word-count if you are a real splurger, because you're going to spend a lot of time deleting. It's all right, though, because deleting is a real joy once you get used to it. It makes your sentences all crisp and lovely and puts a beautiful frame around your scenes.

So on Tuesday you begin the day by deleting everything you don't like that you wrote on Monday. You're now left with something of an outline. You've got characters in a location, saying and doing things. But the scene needs more of something. Perhaps some imagery or some better-focused dialogue. Maybe you've left yourself some kind of a note like '[Describe the teapot here]'. So you begin slowly filling in and refining what you've got. I would usually suggest spending the first half of your writing time going over what you did yesterday, and the second half writing something new. It may be that you're not much of a splurger, which is fine. I'm not any more (although I used to be). In that case it may be that you begin with an outline which you then slowly fill in. After that you may delete a bit, or you may delete as you go. But however careful you are about putting your words down on Monday, you will still be able to go back over what you've done and make significant changes on Tuesday. Working in this way means you never have to face a blank page first thing in the morning, which is no more than one should expect from life.

Where should you work? Basically, anywhere. I have lost count of the times I've been asked in interviews about my writing habits, as if these contained some magic in themselves. Do I start at the same time every morning? Do I have a special desk? Do I have a special pen or type of paper I like to use? The less precious you can be about this type of thing the better. I confess that all my biros and ink pens are blue. But apart from that? I don't care where, when or under what circumstances I write. In fact, I do my very best writing when I have something to do in an hour's time. Say I have a seminar at 4 p.m. and I've decided to sneak in some writing between 3 p.m. and 4 p.m. Perhaps I should really be doing admin. It may take me five minutes or so to get going, but I can produce more in the remainder of that hour than I sometimes do in five hours. If I had nothing to do until 6 p.m., I would not be writing so fluently at 3.45 p.m. Why is this? Perhaps knowing you have to stop is psychologically more useful than knowing you have to continue. It takes the pressure off, somehow, and turns every minute you use into a virtue, where it feels good to be writing rather than bad to be not writing.

So if you only have a spare hour, or even only a spare fifteen minutes, don't think that this won't be productive time on your book. I know someone who wrote her whole first novel in these strange gaps between looking after two young children, running a household and doing a full-time academic job. You don't need perfect peace and quiet, a clear desk and a free schedule to write a novel. In fact, for me, that would be counterproductive. I've written at my parents' kitchen table, on trains, in public libraries and between seminars. Of course you do need to be able to focus and concentrate, and most of the time I don't write on the train because I prefer reading and looking out of the window. And I have to be at a particular point in a novel to be able to, say, write in a room where everyone else is watching *Titanic* (but I have done this). You'll need to find your own limits here. But I suppose what I'm saying is that you don't need to book a three-week retreat to get on with your writing. In fact, it may hinder rather than help you. A retreat for thinking, yes. But for writing, probably not.

I don't think it is possible to concentrate well on a novel for more than about four hours a day, and so it's counterproductive to try to do much more. It's just not true that a real writer is someone who is at their desk from nine to five every day. One of the worst things you can do is force yourself to sit at your desk for long periods feeling depressed, inadequate and a failure. You'll help your writing far more if you go for a walk, do some exercise, watch a film, go to an art exhibition or even do some laundry than if you force yourself to keep looking at the screen. To paraphrase Nietzsche, if you look long enough into the screen, the screen begins to look back through you. You don't want that. Writing is a thinking job, not a typing job. So go out and think.

When I first started writing I used to save things onto floppy disks. Ah, those innocent days when you virtually had to have a degree in computer science even to switch a computer on, and you never really knew whether you were replacing an old file with a new file or the reverse. When floppy disks became obsolete virtually overnight there was suddenly no easy way to access your old files. You could buy a new computer if you liked, but it wouldn't have a floppy disk drive. It was also possible to lose floppy disks, squash them and accidentally set fire to them. People left them on buses all the time. I can't remember what came between floppy disks and USB sticks, but in any case, at the time of writing, USB sticks are the best way of turning your files into what Mr Wemmick in *Great Expectations* would call 'portable property'. And you still get the systolic thrill of not really knowing whether you're moving the file from the stick to the computer or the reverse.

Perhaps for this reason I hardly ever use them, except occasionally to dump the whole contents of my hard drive on one. At the end of every day I simply email my novel to myself and then leave the email on the university's server until the next time I work on it, at which point I email myself the updated file and move the old one into a folder called 'backup' (if I wasn't such a hoarder I would delete it). Trust me: this method takes the fewest clicks. It is basically DIY cloud computing: the very safest way I can think of to back up your files.[294] It means that I can get access to the latest version of my novel anywhere in the world where I can get email. But, however you do it, you must have a version of your novel saved somewhere outside your house. You can have your file on a USB stick, printed out and on your laptop but if your house burns down while you are at an art exhibition then you will lose all versions of your book. If this kind of thing keeps you awake at night, you could also carry a copy of your novel around your neck on a USB stick, like my friend does.

Another practical thing I wish someone had told me when I began is about how to name your files. When I wrote my first novel I did something stupid like call it 'My Novel', and then saved it to the desktop. At some point perhaps I thought I should have a folder called 'My Novel' as well (as if I'd never write any others). When it came to editing the book I probably took the sensible step of using 'Save As . . .', and therefore keeping a copy of 'My Novel' alongside the new file, which by that stage I probably called 'Dog and Clowns edit' or something like that. The next time I significantly worked on the file I probably called it something like 'Dog and Clowns the final edit'. The next file would perhaps have been 'Dog and Clowns the real final edit', then 'Dog and Clowns really final final edit' and so on, with the file names getting longer and longer each time, with no way of telling which one actually was the most recent. Don't do this. When you begin a novel, make yourself a new folder with the same title (or working title) that you are using for the novel. You can always change this later. Then simply title your first file 'First draft' and your next file 'Second draft' and so on. It doesn't matter if you eventually get to 'Twentieth draft' or 'Fiftieth draft': at least you always know where you are.

It's worth asking yourself at every stage how much you do care if your novel is lost in a fire, or a computing accident. I always ask my students the following question: *If the only copy of your novel was stuck at the top of a mountain, would you go up and rescue it?* I tell them that if the answer is 'no' then they need to re-think what they are doing. If the mountain example makes no practical sense to you then make up your own scenario in which it would be possible, but very, very difficult, to get your novel back. How far would you go to rescue it? If you did somehow manage to leave the only copy of it on a bus, how devastated would you really be? The answers to these questions tell you how important the novel is to you, and therefore how important it is likely to be to other people.

When you've finished a first draft, what do you do next? The best thing is to leave it a few weeks (six is ideal) and then print it out and read it through thoroughly with a pencil in your hand, crossing out words, adding words and noting in the margins any new ideas or substantial changes you'd like to make. There will be a lot. At this stage you will think one of two things. If you have left it long enough, revisiting your work might make you feel like a genius, or at least quite good about yourself. *Yes, I managed to do all this and I think it really works!* But a much more common feeling is: *This is fucking rubbish and I hate myself for writing it.* There's not much that you can do about this apart from hold your nerve and realise that everyone feels like this about their own work at some point. It's normal. For me, it's usually when I get to the final proof-checking stage. By that point I'll have done numerous drafts, plus the main edit and the copy edit, and at that stage would gladly take my own manuscript to the top of a mountain and leave it there. But for you this moment might come at any stage. And it will come.

One thing that can help is getting someone else to read your draft and give you a response that is both honest and kind. This is where you find the real-life equivalent of your cosmic reader and see what they actually think. The idea is that because this person is not as close to the material as you are, they'll be able to enjoy it more and see its strengths and faults more clearly. In fact, having a good response from a reader at this moment can be really very uplifting, and can give you the strength you need to get on with the next draft. But you need to choose the person very carefully. Most of the time it will be your partner. It probably shouldn't be a parent, for lots of complicated reasons. It may well be a close friend. It should ideally be someone who loves you. But if this is not possible or practical, then at the very least they must love the novel: not your novel necessarily, but novels in general. They must read a lot of contemporary fiction. Choosing one excellent reader is far better than choosing three readers who don't understand what you're trying to do and will all tell you different things.

What about writing groups? Unless you value them for social reasons, or unless you are lucky enough to have access to one in which people are working at an extremely high level, and are completely sympathetic to what you're doing, I would avoid them. All too often the writing group can become more like a focus group in which a product is tested rather than a work of art produced. I have come across people who feel that they can't make any decision about their novel at all without first running it past their writing group. But groups can behave in very mysterious ways. I have witnessed a lot of writing workshops in my time, and there are two particular experiences that haunt me. The first was when a young woman read out a scene that was probably the best thing I've ever seen a student write. It was delicate, subtle and, well, it was art. Immediately the other students started questioning it. Someone didn't understand the way the scene ended. Someone else thought it should take place in a different location. Someone else said they found the dialogue stilted.[295] Barely anyone said they liked it. When I said it was excellent, a little wave of resentment went around the room. It took hours of tutorials to convince the student that the others were mistaken, and that the scene should remain exactly as she'd written it.

The other experience was quite the reverse. The weakest student in the room put up a piece of writing that she had obviously struggled with a great deal. There were many errors in spelling and grammar, partly because English was not her first language. As well as this, the writing was abstract, long-winded and boring. It would have failed, had it been handed in for assessment. The responses from the other students? 'That's brilliant,' they all said. 'Wow! I really want to read more.' No one had anything bad to say about it at all. So I started pointing out the numerous errors as kindly as I could. I was very worried that this poor student would go off thinking that her writing was a complete success when it was in fact the reverse. What happened then? The other students began defending the work, as if I was being very mean about it. I was so confused by this that I immediately went and asked a colleague whether anything similar had ever happened to her. 'Oh yes,' she said. 'Isn't it weird?' This colleague and I have often since pondered what makes a group act like this, and all we can come up with is that they are trying to be kind and protect the weakest student from 'getting into trouble', but we don't really know. Another interesting theory is that beginners in a subject often believe that anything they can't understand must be of high quality and anything they find easy to comprehend must be of low quality.

Somehow, you will get to the end of writing and then reading a first draft, which is where many people would say the work of beginning a novel properly starts. And writing a second draft can be highly enjoyable because this is where you really craft your sentences and produce 'good writing', rather than just say what happened. I started this chapter by suggesting that writing a novel is easy. That isn't really true. If it was easy, everyone would be doing it. But if you can make it through a book like this, and follow some of its advice, then you will have made it a great deal more achievable. Writing a novel, like running a marathon, is both absurdly easy and absurdly hard. On one level it's just putting words on a page or putting one foot in front of the other. It's doable. It's even somehow natural. But it requires great strength and determination to keep going, especially when it gets tough. All I can say is remember to breathe and keep calm and, if it helps, just think of yourself as writing 250 words (the length of a typical email) for now. Once you've done this enough times, you will have a novel. Work on one scene at a time; don't freak yourself out by sitting down to write 'a whole novel'. And try to enjoy it: if you don't, it's unlikely anyone else will. Here is a final checklist that may be useful:

- Do I have a narrative question to start with?
- Does the narrative make sense and 'function in accordance with probability'?
- Do I have a thematic question?
- Does it matter to me and will it matter to other people?
- Am I respecting my reader?
- Do my characters have superobjectives and are they the right ones?
- Do I have imagery that supports my themes/characters?
- Have I read my work out loud to myself and corrected the bits that sound wrong?
- Is the voice consistent, and authentic?
- Am I being honest?
- Have I avoided cliché?
- Have I rejected at least 20 bad ideas?

- If the only copy of my novel was stranded on the top of a mountain, would I go up to rescue it?

APPENDIX ONE: BLANK MATRIX

This can also be downloaded from my website www.scarlettthomas.co.uk.

NOVEL MATRIX

See overleaf.

Character names	4 locations you know well	Jobs you have done (or identities you have had)	Problems you have faced	Skills/ knowledge you have	What do you worry about?	List your 4 favourite novels and one reason you like each of them	What are your current obsessions?

FURTHER QUESTIONS

- Where do you stand on religion?
- What do you think about relationships?
- What is our place in the universe?
- What do you think about postmodernism?
- Is the world getting better or worse?
- Name one philosophical theory or idea that has particularly interested you.
- Complete this sentence: 'Most people wouldn't guess that I . . .'

Instructions: Fill in all sections of the matrix and answer all the questions above.

Note: It helps if you fill in the matrix as honestly as possible.

APPENDIX TWO: COMPLETED MATRIXES

NOVEL MATRIX: SCARLETT THOMAS, 1991

See overleaf.

Character names	4 Locations you know well	Jobs you have done (or identities you have had)	Problems you have faced	Skills/ knowledge you have
Eliot	Chelmsford, Essex	Waitress	Abortion that went wrong	Creating dreadlocks
Pepper		Architectural assistant	Finding out my father was someone else when I was 12	I know a lot about hip-hop, house music, and dancehall reggae
Abby	Cambridge, UK	Had a market stall selling clothes	Depression of someone close to me	I am mixed-class – I grew up on a council estate in East London and then ended up at a private boarding school aged 14
Charlie		Worked at cricket club	Family conflict	Good memory for numbers
Josh	Barking, East London	Student	German grandmother wants me to be something I am not	Speaking French
Clare		Member of Labour Party, Young Socialists and CND	Being expelled from school	Political knowledge
Kaia	Islington, London	Worked in video shop	Confusion over sexuality	Supporting people
Bob		Girlfriend	Loving someone who did not love me	I'm good at videogames

What do you worry about?	List your 4 favourite novels and one reason you like each of them	What are your current obsessions?
Racism	*The Temple of My Familiar* by Alice Walker. This is my very favourite book. I love the politics in it and the sense of definite identity. It also has feminism, humour and depth.	The war in Iraq. – I am against it, and a bit scared.
I want to impress people and know the right answers		Watching films, especially with farcical humour.
I want to be authentic	*Runaway* by Lucy Irvine. I love the gritty realism of this. My friends and I passed it around and discussed the rape scene in great detail.	Rastafarianism
My friend whose mother is dying		Dancing, especially at the reggae club
Will I be a success?	*Lucky* by Jackie Collins. I love the rollercoaster plot in this novel. It is set in a world I have no experience of. People have loads of money and sex. Good people do well and bad people get their come-uppance which is a bit cheesy but I love the explicit details.	Cooking – especially with lots of chillis.
How can I be a success academically when I'm so busy trying to be popular?		My friend's sister is so beautiful I want to be her.
A friend plans to smuggle drugs to Jamaica	Choose your own adventure books!	My family
Being unpopular or unloved		Kiss FM

FURTHER QUESTIONS

Where do you stand on religion? I am some weird cross between an atheist and a Rasta. I believe there is something out there but I don't know what. I believe a bit in the *Bill and Ted* philosophy of everyone simply being 'excellent to one another'.

What do you think about relationships? I've had my heart broken badly and so I find it very hard to commit to a relationship. Now I act like a romantic, but really I love myself best.

What is our place in the universe? I believe we are here for a purpose but I'm not sure what that is. I quite like not knowing.

What do you think about postmodernism? I'm not sure I know what this is. If it's being experimental, then I like it.

Is the world getting better or worse? Worse. America has too much power. Nuclear weapons are the worst thing ever invented.

Name one philosophical theory or idea that has particularly interested you. Existentialism. I like the idea of meaninglessness.

Complete this sentence: 'Most people wouldn't guess that I . . .' secretly love mathematics.

Name three objects, animals or images you find interesting: The concept of a perfect circle. Hedgehog. Rainbow.

NOVEL MATRIX: SCARLETT THOMAS, 2011

See overleaf.

Character names	4 locations you know well	Jobs you have done (or identities you have had)	Problems you have faced	Skills/ knowledge you have
Ione	London	Writer	Death of a close family member	Writing and storytelling
Naomi		University lecturer	Giving up smoking	I'm pretty good with technology
Virginia	Canterbury	Journalist	Breakdown of major relationship	Health and nutrition, especially alternative ideas like homeopathy
Fabien		Fruit-picker	Anxiety and panic attacks	Cooking
Mark	Deal	Care assistant	Disorganisation	A lot of sporting knowledge, particularly cricket and rugby. I play cricket, tennis and badminton.
Dorothy		Waitress	Working too hard	I know a bit about wine.
Gladwin	Sandwich	Charity shop assistant	Being labelled, or fearing that I am being labelled	I can do cryptic crosswords
Forrest		Bar worker in nightclub	Keeping friendships going	Philosophy

What do you worry about?	List your 4 favourite novels and one reason you like each of them	What are your current obsessions?
Am I too ambitious?	*Anna Karenina* by Leo Tolstoy. The contrast between reason and passion is fascinating and I'm not sure that reason wins in the end.	Plants
I'm not sure I can cope with any more death		Feeding the birds in the garden
What is the meaning of life?	*Great Expectations* by Charles Dickens. Loveable characters. Wonderful use of rags-to-riches plot. Unrequited love. A big novel that asks big questions.	Running
Aging		Paganism/pantheism
Money: do I have too much or too little? What should I do with it? What about when it runs out?	*Middlemarch* by George Eliot. Extremely thoughtful and absorbing novel that asks what it means to live a good life.	Helping my students be as ambitious as they can be
The fishing game.		Wine
My health. Every lump must be cancer.	*The Bell Jar* by Sylvia Plath. Great use of first person. Her voice is compelling and very funny. Her experience seems authentic. Her writing is beautifully specific.	Fashion
Being lonely		Jazz

FURTHER QUESTIONS

Where do you stand on religion? I used to describe myself as a Buddhist, and I practised meditation every day, but found it ultimately depressing (I'm pretty sure I was doing it 'wrong'). I want there to be something out there, but I am afraid of it being somehow disappointing. My current religious beliefs are Pagan/pantheist. I believe in respecting all life. I also practise yoga. But if you saw me walking down the street you'd probably think I was just another *Guardian*-reading atheist.

What do you think about relationships? Relationships get more complicated as you get older, but they are also more fulfilling. Being in a relationship teaches you a lot about yourself. You can never change someone else, but you can change yourself.

What is our place in the universe? We are both more important and less important then we think we are. I think a lot is hidden.

What do you think about postmodernism? It depends if it's 'good' postmodernism or 'bad' postmodernism! Art must have depth, and must enable us to think deeply about life. But we can't pretend the last eighty years have not happened.

Is the world getting better or worse? Better in some ways. A hundred years ago my ancestors were in the workhouse. Now my books are read around the world. But not everyone has the chance to make it, or to live a full life. Environmental issues, neo-liberalism, war and famine worry me a lot.

Name one philosophical theory or idea that has particularly interested you. Evolution.

Complete this sentence: 'Most people wouldn't guess that I . . .' used to speak French fluently.

Name three objects, animals or images you find interesting: Orchids. Feathers. Pumpkins.

APPENDIX THREE: TECHNICAL MATRIX

This is the story of Robert, a 10-year-old genius, who builds a rocket and flies to the moon with his talking rabbit (Martin) and his friend Olive. See overleaf.

Grammatical person	Tense	Narrator	Perspective	Time-frame	Style	Structure
First person (I)	Present	Unknown	Free indirect style	24 hours	Diary	Linear, forwards
Second person (You)	Past	Robert	Robert	2 weeks	Letters	Linear, backwards
Third person (He/she)	Future	Olive	Martin	3 months	Confession	A/B/A/B (repeat matrix for each)
First person plural (We)	Mixture	Martin	Olive	1 year	Fairy tale	Three parts
Multiple narrators (in which case choose three from the Narrator column)	Different for each chapter	Martin's mother	Mixture	A lifetime	Neutral	Circular (ends at beginning)

Note: There are many other values that could be entered in these columns. These are just for demonstration purposes. Try creating your own . . .

APPENDIX FOUR: BANK OF WORDS EXAMPLES

Here are some examples of passages of around 100 words to be 'costed' in the Bank of Words exercise in the chapter 'Writing a Good Sentence'.

The crisp April air whipped through the open window of the Citroën ZX as it skimmed south past the Opera House and crossed Place Vendôme. In the passenger seat, Robert Langdon felt the city tear past him as he tried to clear his thoughts. His quick shower and shave had left him looking reasonably presentable but had done little to ease his anxiety. The frightening image of the curator's body remained locked in his mind.

Jacques Saunière is dead.

Langdon could not help but feel a deep sense of loss at the curator's death. Despite Saunière's reputation for being reclusive, his recognition for dedication to the arts made him an easy man to revere.

(Dan Brown, *The Da Vinci Code*)

114 words

I reached for the book the people from *Ladies' Day* had sent.

When I opened it a card fell out. The front of the card showed a poodle in a flowered bedjacket sitting in a poodle basket with a sad face, and the inside of the card showed the poodle lying down in the basket with a little smile, sound asleep under an embroidered sampler that said, 'You'll get well best with lots and lots of rest'. At the bottom of the card somebody had written, 'Get well quick! From all of your good friends at *Ladies' Day*' in lavender ink.

(Sylvia Plath, *The Bell Jar*)

101 words

But halfway down the stairs, he is *gone* – my hand is blank on every side. The caterpillar must have let go and dropped. I can't see him. The stairwell is dim and the stairs are painted dark brown. I could get a flashlight and search for this tiny thing, in order to save his life. But I will not go that far – he will have to do the best he can. Yet how can he make his way down to the back door and out into the garden?

I go on about my business. I think I've forgotten him, but I haven't. Every time I go upstairs or down, I avoid his side of the stairs. I am sure he is there trying to get down.

(Lydia Davis, 'The Caterpillar')

126 words

Fran nudged me and nodded in the direction of the TV. 'Look up on top,' she whispered. 'Do you see what I see?' I looked at where she was looking. There was a slender red vase into which somebody had stuck a few garden daisies. Next to the vase, on the doily, sat a plaster-of-Paris cast of the most crooked, jaggedy teeth in the world. There were no lips to the awful-looking thing, and no jaw either, just these old plaster teeth packed into something that resembled thick yellow gums.

(Raymond Carver, 'Feathers')

99 words

Not that his whole year at Hogwarts had been fun. At the very end of last term, Harry had come face to face with none other than Lord Voldemort himself. Voldemort might be a ruin of his former self, but he was still terrifying, still cunning, still determined to regain power. Harry had slipped through Voldemort's clutches for a second time, but it had been a narrow escape, and even now, weeks later, Harry kept waking in the night, drenched in cold sweat, wondering where Voldemort was now, remembering his livid face, his wide, mad eyes . . .

Harry suddenly sat bolt upright on the garden bench. He had been staring absent-mindedly into the hedge – *and the hedge was staring back.*

(J.K. Rowling, *Harry Potter and the Chamber of Secrets*)

119 words

At Sea Oak there's no sea and no oak, just a hundred subsidized apartments and a rear view of FedEx. Min and Jade are feeding their babies while watching *How My Child Died Violently*. Min's my sister. Jade's our cousin. *How My Child Died Violently* is hosted by Matt Merton, a six-foot-five blond who's always giving the parents shoulder rubs and telling them they've been sainted by pain. Today's show features a ten-year-old who killed a five-year-old for refusing to join his gang. The ten-year-old strangled the five-year-old with a jump rope, filled his mouth with baseball cards, then locked himself in the bathroom and wouldn't come out until his parents agreed to take him to FunTimeZone, where he confessed, then dove screaming into a mesh cage full of plastic balls.

(George Saunders 'Sea Oak')

131 words

I light a cigarette – Kool, the brand chosen by a biker ahead of me in the queue – and watch the traffic and passers-by on the intersection between Omekaido Avenue and Kita Street. Pin-striped drones, a lip-pierced hairdresser, midday drunks, child-laden housewives. Not a single person is standing still. Rivers, snowstorms, traffic, bytes, generations, a thousand faces per minute. Yakushima is a thousand minutes per face. All of these people with their boxes of memories labelled 'Parents'. Good shots, bad shots, frightening figures, tender pictures, fuzzy angles, scratched negatives – it doesn't matter, they know who ushered them to Earth.

(David Mitchell, *number9dream*)

98 words

NOTES

1 In a letter to A.S. Suvorin. In *Anton Chekhov's Short Stories* (1979: 275)
2 1995: 286
3 2004: 62
4 Gourevitch (ed.), *Paris Review Interviews* (2007: 194)
5 'The Art of Poetry', in Murray and Dorsch (eds), *Classical Literary Criticism* (2004: 101)
6 377a (2003: 68)
7 In *Aspects of the Novel*, E.M. Forster maintains that an unplotted story will have no causality. His famous example is this: '"The king died and then the queen died" is a story. "The king died and then the queen died of grief" is a plot.' (2000: 87). Forster's book provides a very interesting and engaging way of looking at the novel. However, on this point I agree more readily with Aristotle and the Russian formalists, who all, as we will see later, define plot as the arrangement of events that are already connected with one another. The key thing to remember here is that there is a difference between what is told and how it is told.
8 'Thematics', in Lemon and Reis (eds), *Russian Formalist Criticism* (1965: 67)
9 There are, of course, elements in a story that cause things to happen later, but are not caused by anything themselves. This usually applies to the beginning of any chronological story. For example, we don't know what caused the first prophecy

in *Oedipus the King,* but it is this prophecy that causes every-thing else to happen. Many stories will have environmental factors that cause things to happen without being caused by anything themselves, and these may occur at any place in the story (like the snow in our made-up example). However, beware of having too much of your plot turn on these random environmental factors. The storm that forces everybody into the haunted house, for example, is just a cliché.

10 1977: 111

11 'The Art of Poetry' (2004: 102)

12 Although Socrates was a real historical figure, whom Plato only semi-fictionalises, it is worth making it clear that in *The Republic* he does function as a character, in a very interesting dramatic set-up. Although a common reading of *The Republic* is that it details what Plato and Socrates wanted to see in an ideal state, it seems rather that the dialogue is a thought experiment that asks what you would need in a society that demands luxury, 'that will want couches and tables and other furniture, and a variety of delicacies, scents, perfumes, call-girls and confec-tionary', and must therefore be funded by war. Plato is a much more satirical writer than many people realise. For me, *The Republic* is a mockery of a particular kind of 'civilisation', not an argument in favour of it. It is also a great book about plotting.

13 This discussion takes place in Part III of *The Republic*, entitled 'Education: the First Stage'. Socrates describes to Adeimantus what a child's education should include, and the dialogue begins with them discussing what kinds of stories a child should be exposed to. Socrates suggests starting young children off with fiction (as distinct from 'true stories'), although he says these will (and must) contain truth (377a). He goes on to demand a sort of realism not reflected in much of the literature of the time, suggesting that 'The greater part of the stories current today we shall have to reject' (377c).

14 378c–d (2003: 70)

15 378a (2003: 70). This idea of controlling fiction persists today, and I'm sure we are all familiar with age-classifications on films, video games and even music. Perhaps we don't try to put children off certain narratives by making them sacrifice an animal that is 'large and difficult to get' but we do hide them away on the top shelf of newsagents, behind pin numbers on Sky Box Office and in all sorts of other places. Children's fiction is expected to be more 'educational' than adult fiction, and has a noticeably different moral structure. It's not just that there's no swearing and violence (in fact, many children's stories are quite violent). But no one would take drugs and have a good time in a children's story. People might take drugs, but they would be punished for it, and realise that taking drugs is a bad thing to do. While this can also be a basic adult story (which Christopher Booker would call 'rebirth'), there are plenty of adult fictions in which people take drugs or drink too heavily and don't necessarily get punished for it. A good example of this is *Mad Men*, where peripheral characters have downfalls due to their drinking but central characters like Peggy and Don are able to indulge in sometimes excessive drinking and drug-taking with no effect to their storylines. At the time of writing, Season 5 is not yet complete, so presumably anything could happen. But long series like *Mad Men* work with complex story cycles, and Peggy and Don have each completed several of these without any narrative punishment for their indulgences.

16 386 b–c (2003: 77)

17 Socrates gives plenty of examples of courage-curdling passages that should be cut from existing literature, mainly from Homer's *Odyssey* and *Iliad*. Here are the last three:

> His disembodied soul took wing for the House of Hades,
> bewailing its lot and the youth and manhood that it left
> (386b)

The spirit vanished like a wisp of smoke and went gibbering under the ground (387a)

Gibbering like bats that squeak and flutter in the depths of some mysterious cave when one of them has fallen from the rocky roof, losing his hold on his clustered friends, with shrill discord the company set out (387a)

Socrates also argues for the removal of 'all those horrifying and frightening names in the underworld – the Rivers of Wailing and Gloom, and the ghosts and the corpses . . . ' (387c) and for poets to cut out 'pitiful laments by famous men' (387d). Citizens in the Republic must bear loss and disappointment calmly, since they are going to become very familiar with them, and must therefore be given heroes who do the same. Socrates says:

We shall therefore again request Homer and the poets not to describe Achilles, the son of a goddess, as 'sometimes lying on his side, sometimes on his back, and then again on his face', and then standing up and 'wandering distraught along the shore of the unharvested sea', or 'picking up the dark dust in both hands and pouring it on his head', with all the weeping and lamenting the poet describes. (388a-b)

If we accept that *The Republic* is satirical, then these passages are almost certainly intended to be funny.
18 *Mimêsis*, more usefully translated as 'imitation'.
19 As we have already seen, Plato demands that both 'true' and 'fictional' stories include a representation or *mimêsis* of reality.
20 We have already seen how children can be prepared for battle by stories, and persuaded by them to not fear the afterlife; we have also seen the way children are encouraged not to wail

and lament. All Plato's work is written in the form of fictional dialogues and myths, and his fictions have themselves been very persuasive (especially as many people would argue that the whole of Western philosophy is founded on his works).

21 Again, this is something that can be seen in Plato's own fictions. Many of them work in a similar way to thought experiments, where an idea can be taken to its logical conclusion in narrative, or a hypothesis tested, with the implication that this will mirror its outcome in reality. In many cases, in Plato's work and beyond, the hypothesis being tested will be thematic, and the text will be left open. A text like this is obviously something we would call art, but art has many definitions and functions and it seems clearer to call this function philosophy even though many people believe fictional texts to be somehow outside the non-fictional *logos* with which we usually associate philosophy. Perhaps this is because they represent *logos* with no end; no conclusion, only intertextuality.

22 '. . . we don't know the truth about the past but we can invent a fiction as like it as may be.' (382d)

23 This is connected with Aristotle's 'pity and fear', which we will look at later. Narrative seems to have a complex relationship with emotions, at times making us feel fear and sadness but *always* in the end making us happy – either in cathartic Aristotelian resolution, Nietzschian destructiveness, Joycean epiphany, or even perhaps via the experience of Barthesian *jouissance* in a lack of final closure.

24 Of course, the most pleasurable stories are those that include the most extreme states of happiness and sadness, or disequilibrium and equilibrium, and these are, for the reasons Plato outlines, not welcome in the Republic. Of 'Homer and the other poets', Socrates says:

> It is not to say they are bad poetry or are not popular; indeed the better they are as poetry the more unsuitable

they are for the ears of children or men who are to be free and fear slavery more than death. (387b)

25 *The Republic* Part VII: 'The Philosopher Ruler', Book VII, *The Simile of the Cave.*

26 Stories about machines taking over the world and enslaving humans have been around as long as machines have been around, as demonstrated in the writings of the nineteenth-century novelist Samuel Butler.

27 Jean Baudrillard, the first philosopher to theorise hyperreality, was cited by the Wachowski brothers as a big influence on their films, and keen viewers will notice that his book *Simulacra and Simulation* even appears in one frame of the *Matrix*. However, Baudrillard has been quite scathing about the film, saying that '*The Matrix* is the kind of film about the Matrix that the Matrix itself could have produced' (2005: 202). The 'Platonic treatment' of the idea of simulation is, for Baudrillard, a 'serious flaw' (2005: 201).

28 *Poetics* 6, 50a (1996: 11)

29 Kaufman and Kaufman (2002: 68–69)

30 There is a very readable book by Michael Tierno called *Aristotle's Poetics for Screenwriters* that develops each one of Aristotle's main points into practical screenwriting advice. It is a bit over-enthusiastic in places, but it does shed light on some of Aristotle's more tricky concepts and has lots of good examples.

31 3, 48a (1996: 5)

32 9, 51a–b (1996: 16)

33 4, 48b (1996: 6)

34 6, 50a (1996: 11)

35 6, 50a (1996: 11)

36 6, 49b (1996: 10), my emphasis.

37 7, 50b (1996: 13)

38 8, 51a (1996: 15)

39 7, 50b (1996: 14)

40 7, 51a (1996: 14)

41 8, 51a (1996: 15)

42 Of course, along the way we get Billy Pilgrim's life story as well as his account of the Dresden bombings, but this is not given chronologically. Instead, Billy 'time travels' through his own life and beyond, to the planet Tralfamadore, whose inhabitants see everything in four dimensions and therefore know everyone's life story as soon as they meet them. Note also the determinate structure of this plot device: *because* Billy believes he is able to travel through time, we are able to travel with him and learn about his past, present and future.

43 6, 48b (1996: 10)

44 Francine Prose, in *Reading Like a Writer,* makes this point very well with reference to the opening of the Alice Munro story 'Dulse'. Prose says, 'There are many occasions in literature in which telling is far more effective than showing. A lot of time would have been wasted had Alice Munro believed she could not begin her story until she had *shown* us Lydia working as an editor, writing poetry, breaking up with her lover, dealing with her children, getting divorced, growing older, and taking all the steps that led up to the moment at which the story rightly begins.' (2007: 25) Others may argue that this type of information does not have to become an introduction, but can be revealed later, perhaps in dialogue ('Do you have any children?'). But done badly, clunky expositionary dialogue is much worse than simple telling. Different writers do different things, though. Hemingway, with his principle of the iceberg, would never have included that kind of information at all. He says, 'If a writer stops observing he is finished . . . If it is any use to know it, I always try to write on the principle of the iceberg. There is seven-tenths of it underwater for every part that shows. Anything you know you can eliminate and it only strengthens your iceberg. It is the

part that doesn't show. If a writer omits something because he does not know it then there is a hole in the story.' Gourevitch (ed.), *Paris Review Interviews* (2007: 57)

45 6, 49b (1996: 10), my emphasis.

46 The film opens with Molly and Terence performing. They have a baby, then one more, then one more. They incorporate the children into their act, although it becomes clear that it is not good for them to live such a transient show-business life. So the children are sent to boarding school. Although we don't see the children in action at school (except a short episode where they try to run away), we are told that Steve is a strange boy and Tim will make a good leader one day. The children finish their schooling and come back to their home in New Jersey. But in the meantime their parents have had to work through the Depression, taking whatever jobs they can find. Soon the whole family is back in show business, although Steve soon declares that he wants to become a priest, and we follow him as he studies for this and is eventually successful. Tim has become a heavy drinker by this stage, staying out late with different women. When he meets Vicky, he falls in love with her. She appears uninterested, but then for no clear reason they become an item, and she later asks Tim and his sister Katy to join her more successful show. Katy gets married, and soon afterwards becomes pregnant.

Vicky's success starts to bother Tim. After she is late meeting him for dinner (because of negotiations about a dress she will wear) he explodes in anger at her, becoming almost violent. Soon after this he crashes a car while drunk and ends up in hospital. His father visits him and they fight. Then Tim disappears. There follows a long period where Tim is missing, and his family tries to find him. Meanwhile, the show goes on, with Molly (Tim's mother) as Tim's replacement, although Molly is frosty with Vicky because she blames her for Tim's disappearance. Later, at a charity concert where Molly is performing, the family is reunited because Tim turns up quite randomly. Everyone now loves him, including Vicky. All the characters then do the number 'There's No Business Like Show Business', which tells us that everything about this life is 'appealing', when in fact we have just seen that it isn't.

47 An adaptation of the film *Dangerous Liaisons* (Stephen Frears, 1988), which is itself an adaptation of the 1782 novel *Les Liaisons Dangereuses* by Pierre Ambroise François Choderlos de Laclos. The book is an incredibly intricately plotted tragedy, and it's very much better than either film. I chose *Cruel Intentions* to discuss here because I knew many of my undergraduate students would have seen it, and for the benefit of those that hadn't seen it I showed the trailer on YouTube. But the novel really is wonderful. I chose it as my 'Book of a Lifetime' in *The Independent*. Here is what I wrote:

> It's almost impossible to come to this book without already knowing the story. But that's never been a problem for me. I knew the stories of *Oedipus*, *Hamlet* and *Anna Karenina* before I read them, too, and it didn't make any difference. Perhaps it especially doesn't matter with great tragedies. Great tragedies are always philosophical puzzles that can be retold a thousand times without being solved. It doesn't matter how well you know the story, because there is always more story to know.
>
> *Les Liaisons Dangereuses* is certainly a great tragedy in this sense. People often talk about it as a seduction manual, and it probably could help you get laid if that was all you wanted from it. But if that's all it was it couldn't be the book of a lifetime. The power of this novel lies in its exploration of what happens if we try to control love, to impose reason on it and make it do tricks for us. Of course, the passion-versus-reason plot is

familiar, especially in this period (late eighteenth century). But this absolutely isn't a novel about two people who passionately desire one another, give in to that desire and then pay the price for it. It's so much more complicated than that, partly because this is a tragedy not of loving too much, but of not loving enough.

The two protagonists, the Marquise de Merteuil and the Vicomte de Valmont, are transgressive characters who deliberately flout romantic convention and set out to seduce (and ruin) anyone to whom they take a fancy. Of course, the widowed, independently wealthy Merteuil is the more transgressive of the two. While Valmont is positioned in the familiar tradition of the libertine, she is a rather more politicised figure who, at a crucial point in the novel, presents a manifesto in which she declares (to Valmont) that she was 'born to avenge my sex and subjugate yours'. In order to do this, she has perfected acting techniques, read literature and philosophy and seems to have found a way of indulging her passions without repercussions.

But this novel shows us that while it is possible to have sex without repercussions, love is quite different. It is clear that Merteuil and Valmont love, or have loved one another. They certainly have a past. However, Merteuil is too engaged in a revenge plot to really pay him much attention, until he pledges to seduce and ruin the innocent Madame de Tourvel. Merteuil promises herself to him as a prize if he succeeds (and gets him knotted into her plot, too). But when Valmont falls in love with de Tourvel, the knot becomes undoable. Merteuil, finally refusing Valmont his prize, tells him, 'I may well have laid claim to be able to replace a whole harem on my own but I've never felt the slightest inclination to form part of one.' She loves him but she knows there is no future for them, not least because he loves someone else, or perhaps cannot truly love at all. And because of the power of love, or the limitations of transgression, or the failure of reason, everything is destroyed.

48 9, 52a (1996: 17)
49 III, I, 121
50 III, I, 138–140
51 10, 52a (1996: 18)
52 11, 52a (1996: 18)
53 11, 52a (1996: 18)
54 11, 52a (1996: 18)
55 2003: 762–63
56 These are outlined in Chapter 16 of *Poetics*, 54b–55a (1996: 26–27)
57 Often 'false' recognitions, or misrecognitions, are based on tokens, for example the handkerchief in *Othello*.
58 Act V, Scene ii, lines 213–218
59 We know, of course, that this isn't true, and that reality TV is as plotted as any piece of fiction. Contestants on *Big Brother* frequently complain about the way their 'scenes' have been edited, and the ways in which the producers are able to create tension and drama. In the example of Jade Goody, we can be sure that no one made her be racist and no one scripted her Diary Room scene. But the production team did 'cast' the 'characters'. And the recognition scene, when it comes, is shown in full and treated structurally like a tragic recognition.
60 13, 53a (1996: 21)
61 2003: 80
62 2003: 35
63 2003: 39
64 2003: 105
65 My novel *The End of Mr. Y* is a tragedy. Once someone has spent their food money on a cursed book, and learned from

it something that no one should ever know, the result must be tragic. I have never killed a central character before. Ariel ends up not just dead in the 'real' world, but eternally trapped in a parallel world of language, where all knowledge is available, but no real understanding or truth. This is therefore a double tragedy, or perhaps even an ironic tragedy where escape into oblivion is never made possible, even through death. The book is very flawed in places, but it was the most exciting novel I've written, partly because of the Dionysiac spirit that seemed to take it over as I was writing it.

66 1998: 259

67 One useful way of distinguishing 'plot' from 'narrative' is in recognising that one narrative (e.g. *Middlemarch*) can have several connected plots or storylines. So the love story (or 'romantic comedy') involving Dorothea and Will has its own shape that is distinct from the shape of Lydgate's descent into mediocrity, or Bulstrode's tragedy. We will see later that much of the work of a novelist can be in combining and interweaving different plots, especially in a long or complex novel.

68 This is the writing manual that features in the Charlie Kaufman film *Adaptation*, which will be discussed in the next chapter.

69 William Gibson's novels often follow this kind of structure. Although the last line of *Neuromancer* is 'He never saw Molly again', the end of the main plot ends with Case and Molly united. Later novels, such as *Zero History*, leave the romantic leads in a more permanent state of union.

70 In reality, the process does not have to happen in this order. Someone who dreams of a cabin in the woods may well imagine what life would be like there before drawing up the plans. Similarly, a novel will usually not begin with someone saying, 'Well, I want to write a tragedy with a secondary coming-of-age narrative.' Ideas for novels come from all sorts of places, and it is usually only after we have had the idea that we look

for the structure. We use structure *for* something, to hold something up, or to keep it together.

71 This book was first translated into English in 1958. It influenced, among others, Roland Barthes, Claude Lévi-Strauss and Umberto Eco, who analysed Bond novels in a similar fashion.

72 His study is based on Aleksander Afanas'ev's collection of Russian fairy tales. As different translations of this kind of work use different terminology, I will use the expressions 'folk tale' and 'fairy tale' interchangeably.

73 Working with these variables is a crucial skill to have when plotting – realising that many of your elements are in fact *variable*, and that the first thing you thought of (man has problem; problem is alcoholism) may not be the best one. This is particularly important for literary writers, because it helps us move away from cliché and stereotype. That thing your protagonist breaks at her mother's house? It could be a vase, an ornament or a glass – those things are obvious. But it could equally be a favourite DVD, a bottle of brandy, a knitting needle, the clasp on a handbag, a cat-flap, a mobile phone or anything at all. If the point of the action is *something breaks*, which leads to an argument, which leads to some sort of change – then an experienced writer will realise that it is the nebulous 'something' that breaks that is both the most important and least important part of the scene. It doesn't matter to the plot what breaks, as long as something does. But what breaks matters on a much deeper level. This is the best way of beginning to work with imagery. We will come to this later on in the book, but for now, take something you've written and circle all the variables. Now choose one of these, and write down twenty other possibilities. Was your first choice the best one?

74 Sweet peas are in the family Fabaceae. A rose by any other name might smell as sweet, but by any other name we wouldn't be able to locate it in its family, Rosaceae, and note the common

features with other plants in this family: the apple, the pear, the blackberry and so on. A rose is a rose because it has characteristics: five petals, five sepals and (usually) a superior ovary, among other things. Propp reminds us that this kind of classification gives us a way of talking about something that we wouldn't otherwise have. It would be impossible, he says, to talk about the development of language if we didn't have terms for its grammatical elements; if we hadn't classified certain words as nouns, verbs and so on. We should not get confused here, however, and imagine that Propp is working on the same scale as Linnaeus. While Linnaeus created a whole taxonomic system, Propp is really writing the equivalent of a profile of one genus within the family 'narrative' (or should that be narrativaceae . . . ?).

75 2008: 6

76 2008: 13

77 Clearly it does not have the same effect in terms of theme and character, but that is not what we are looking at here. Indeed, variable elements are where you build theme and character.

78 2008: 61

79 2008: 61

80 From *OED* entry for 'McGuffin'. The definition is: 'In a film (now also in a novel or other form of narrative fiction): a particular event, object, factor, etc., initially presented as being of great significance to the story, but often having little actual importance for the plot as it develops.'

81 In the American sitcom *Frasier*, the central action focused not on the lead character Frasier Crane, but on the romance of two secondary characters, Frasier's brother Niles Crane and his father's physiotherapist Daphne Moon. The obstacles keeping these two apart mostly concerned other relationships. At the beginning of the narrative Niles is married. Once he is separated there is a further obstacle in the fact that Daphne

won't consider someone who is still married. Then she has various relationships, and so does Niles. Each is never free when the other is. Finally, Daphne becomes engaged to Donny, the lawyer who has arranged Niles's divorce, and it is only after much confusion that Niles and Daphne confess their love for one another on the eve of Daphne's wedding. It is clear that, in this narrative, illness, travel or other obstacles could stand in the way of the relationship and it would not make too much difference. In *Middlemarch*, however, Dorothea's marriage to Casaubon may structurally be there to keep her from Will Ladislaw, but it is thematically so important that it could not be simply replaced with a long period of illness, for example. It is only through Dorothea's marriage to Casaubon that we learn of her true character. Her marriage to Casaubon is also what enables her to get to know Ladislaw in the first place, so here we have an action that is structurally both enabling and disabling.

82 This is a good example of a narrative with variables. Notice that each person has a secret (except little Charlotte). It's often useful when plotting to turn specifics back to abstractions in order to turn them into better (or different) specifics. So here, if we turn the narrative back to abstractions, we have a mother who secretly gains wealth and power. Both her daughters have secrets to do with loving forbidden people, but if we look more closely, we see that Virginia's secret is something that is only taboo in the most reactionary elements of society, and is something of which her mother will approve when she finds out. Sarah's secret, however, is a source of real shame, as is her father's. If we change the specifics, Alison could be a secret princess, could have inherited from a long-lost relative, could have masterminded a bank robbery (although this would not be as 'acceptable', culturally, but could be almost acceptable depending on its treatment), could simply have got an amazing promotion at work, could have won *The X-Factor* (hard to

keep secret) or could have invented some amazing product in her spare time. Virginia could be a spy (although she'd never tell her parents this) or could be a secret genius, perhaps. She could be in love with a much older man, or may have secretly married. (It's interesting how difficult it is to come up with alternatives for Virginia, when what you want is a secret that is almost culturally acceptable, but still shocking.) There are many possibilities for Sarah and David, however. Sarah could have been humiliated at school in any number of different ways – it isn't important that she loved her drama teacher. She could have been bullied, could have failed a test (or done so well that it was embarrassing), could have started crying in a sex education lesson. The possibilities here are endless. David could be having an affair with anyone, it doesn't have to be his secretary. But he could have a completely different sort of secret. Perhaps he killed someone accidentally. Perhaps he has found out that he was adopted and his father was a murderer. Perhaps he is an alcoholic, or addicted to gambling. Note how these alternatives are much darker than an affair with a secretary, and would entirely change the tone of the narrative. They would also be slightly wrong, because the key is that he must betray Alison not just by having a secret but in what he actually does in secret. Most of the things we first reach for when looking for variables are clichés. It's worth spending time trying to be really inventive. What if David and Alison were vegans, and he was secretly eating beefburgers? What if they spent time opposing the building of a new supermarket, but David had secretly invested in the company? What if they have a joint savings account that David is secretly using to fund his online gambling addiction? When you work with variables, choose the things that you know well.

83 2008: 21

84 Headings taken from Propp, 2008: 26–63. Propp gives each of these functions a code letter ('designation') and one or more

keywords ('definitions'). For example XXI, 'The Hero is pursued', has the definitions 'pursuit' and 'chase' and the designation 'Pr'.

85 This function, 'The hero is tested, interrogated, attacked etc., which prepares the way for his receiving either a magical agent or helper', is given the designation 'D', and the variables within it are represented as D^1, D^2, D^3 and so on. 'The donor tests the hero' is D^1 and 'The hero is approached with a request for mercy' is D^5. Within each variable Propp gives several examples from fairy tales. Under D^1, examples include 'A witch gives a girl household chores' and 'The hero must listen to the playing of the gusla without falling asleep'. Although Propp's scheme sounds confusing, it is actually quite easy to follow in his book.

86 2008: 79

87 2008: 110

88 If basic plots can be so subverted, does that mean that they do not exist at all? How do we tell the difference between something that is a mistake, and something that is an interesting subversion? As we have already seen in previous chapters, narrative does have patterns that we recognise. A romantic comedy may feature animals, robots or even toys, but its focus will be the overcoming of confusion, and the happy union of two or more characters. The wedding at the end may be of any sort, as we have seen. But no one is going to die. The key to working out what basic plots exist and how they are structured is in being able to look for patterns that may, in some cases, even be quite disguised.

89 Campbell argues that archetypal characters and situations forming this 'basic, magic ring of myth' (1973: 3) are there in our unconscious from the moment we are born. Citing Freud, Jung, Nietzsche and the anthropologist Franz Boas, he asserts the existence of a 'primal psychic character' based on a set of symbols that we all share and that are fundamental to our consciousness.

90 1973: 30, Campbell's italics.

91 This basic structure is what Northrop Frye goes on to identify as the 'Romance' plot, and what Christopher Booker calls
the 'Quest', as we shall see shortly.

92 Although he is broadly in favour of comedy. 'The happy
ending of the fairy tale, the myth and the divine comedy of
the soul, is to be read, not as a contradiction but as a transcendence of the universal tragedy of man.' (1973: 28)

93 He suggests the possibility of finding a single formula that
would represent every myth. However, in order to come up
with the actual formula, he argues, much more funding and
resources would be needed from the French government.
Among other things, these resources would need to include a
'spacious workshop, a commodity particularly unavailable in
Western Europe nowadays' (1963: 229) and 'IBM equipment'.
It seems once you've collected all possible myths and chopped
them up, you need somewhere large to keep all the pieces.

94 The Greek word meaning 'stories' or 'plots', which Frye
defines as 'a structural organising principle of literary form'.
(2000: 341)

95 2000: 210

96 2004: 227

97 2004: 227

98 Having said this, however, we need to be careful with psychoanalytic theory, particularly the Jungian concept of the arche-
type, when reading and – especially – when writing. Focusing
too much on the self overcoming the ego can become, well, a
very egotistical thing to do. There are of course some unconscious aspects of texts that will always reveal deep archetypal
dramas between the hero and his/her parents, and overcoming
some kind of shadow and so on. But reading (and writing)
only in this way – unless we are able to do it in a highly
sophisticated fashion – closes us to many other deep structures
that may be interesting, for example the ideological, the

political and the aesthetic. While psychoanalytic theory is a well-established way of reading dreams, analysing relationships and understanding life-stages, it can send us in the wrong direction as writers and readers. *Oedipus the King* has undoubtedly served psychoanalysis well by providing the plot of the 'Oedipus Complex'. But knowing about the Oedipus Complex does not help us read the play. If we do read the play as an expression of Oedipus's unconscious will to kill his father and sleep with his mother, we lose both the tragedy-of-knowledge and the mystery story – which are much richer. We also lose all sense of Oedipus having any conscious motivation. The point (and tragic pleasure) of the plot is that he *does not know*, consciously or unconsciously, the identity of his parents until it is too late. And if Oedipus did somehow set out to murder his father and sleep with his mother, the plot becomes a ridiculous mess of coincidence and elements that don't make sense. We will also have major problems if we try to consciously write the unconscious. Archetypes can very easily become stereotypes, after all. Better to let this level of your writing happen on its own.

99 Or even misreads them in order that they do. Booker's analysis of the end of *Great Expectations* is that '. . . we see the mature Pip coming together with the mature, still beautiful Estella in the garden of Miss Havisham's ruined house, and "I saw no shadow of another parting from her."' (2004: 289)

100 How can we be so confident about what is dark and what is light? Can I be sure, for example, that I am a hero and not someone else's dark shadow? Is there a way of classifying narrative that retains its mystery somehow? I tried to explore these ideas in my novel *Our Tragic Universe*.

101 2004: 169

102 Act V, Scene i, lines 58–59

103 2010: 129–130

104 This is rather different from Northrop Frye's 'irony' mythos.

I am using irony as an overlay here; a veil that comes down over a plot and changes or tints it somehow. My students and I also discussed the novel as an ironic quest, in which these three heroes set off on a long complicated journey, pass a few tests (they manage to get the gas fire going in the caravan) and eventually make it to the 'great citadel' of the Hall brothers' factory. But here the quest ends. These three heroes never wanted anything like immortality or a magic ring: all they wanted was enough money to go down the pub every night. Their quest has failed. Quests are supposed to be for something very important, and usually they succeed. Here, we see a kind of anti-quest: a quest set against the very idea of a quest.

105 Is *The Matrix* a rags-to-riches plot or actually a quest? This is debatable. Neo does have to fight dark forces and save the world, which fits more with a quest plot than it does with rags to riches. However, if we take the first film on its own, what we see is Neo receiving an invitation, being told that he is 'The One' and then gaining skills and knowledge as if they were 'riches'. The climax of the film sees him finally understand that he is indeed The One, and has special powers that enable him to fight the agents in a way no one has ever seen before. As the film focuses on the gaining of these powers, and as it has as its context a whole civilisation reduced to a state of rags at the expense of the riches of the machines, I think I would probably place it in this category.

106 In a similar way to *The Matrix*, the plot of the first Harry Potter novel can probably be classified as rags to riches, but the whole series taken as one narrative is closer to a quest.

107 When I use the term 'hero' I usually mean a central protagonist who may be male or female unless I make it clear (or it is clear from the context) that I specifically mean a male hero.

108 Ultimately, of course, we hear more about – and from – the bourgeois author. But as a news story, the 'bus driver shortlisted for the Booker Prize' works so well because the perceived

distance between the rags and the riches is so great. In the end it turned out that Magnus Mills wasn't exactly a conventional bus driver. He certainly drove buses for a while, but had also worked as a journalist. Note the way in which basic plots can start to work facts into a more fictional shape.

109 Pretty much every con out there relies on its participants (unconsciously or otherwise) believing themselves to be the hero in a rags-to-riches plot. *After all, if it happens to all these fictional characters, then why can't it happen to me . . . ?* Our intrinsic knowledge of the rags-to-riches plot means that with a few triggers we can easily see ourselves as the recipients of a great fortune. Even supermarkets take advantage of this with their buy-one-get-one-free offers. There is no such thing as 'free' in a supermarket – otherwise how would they make any money? – but something in us wants to believe it is true. 140 Nectar points when you spend over £70? What a gift! If my shopping comes to only £65, I might rush over and get another bottle of wine to ensure I can collect my 'free' points. But the points are only worth 70p, far less than the mark-up on the wine. Gambling, pyramid schemes and those spam emails from 'African businessmen' also all rely on a rags-to-riches plot.

110 We learn that Yvonne is a waitress because her ex-husband took all her money and left her with debts. When she and Charlie lose all their fortune, the people of New York send them money in the form of 'tips' – but not enough for them to be rich, only enough to balance everything up.

111 The only flaw in this plot is that the oppressive 'authority' figures are the spouses of the central characters. While this certainly gives the film a contemporary feel, it is not quite right in plot terms. It leaves the by then ex-spouses unable to have happy endings of their own. It would fit the basic plot better if Charlie had an oppressive mother, for example, who wants him declared insane when he gives the money to Yvonne and embarks on all his philanthropic schemes. Another

possibility is to read this as a stranger-comes-to-town plot. As we will see later, the stranger shakes up a community and is then sacrificed. Is this not what happens to the money here?

112 The coming-of-age novel is usually called a *Bildungsroman*. The German term means literally 'foundation novel'. Dating from the eighteenth century, these are novels that focus specifically on the education and development of one young character. There is a sub-category of this known as the *Künstlerroman* that focuses specifically on the development of a (usually) young artist. However, here we are focusing on the basic plot rather than type of novel, so the term 'coming of age' will be used.

113 2005: 80. We also learn that Esther remembers Buddy Willard 'saying in a sinister, knowing way that after I had children I would feel differently, I wouldn't want to write poems any more. So I began to think maybe it was true that when you were married and had children it was like being brainwashed, and afterwards you went about numb as a slave in some private, totalitarian state.' (2005: 81)

114 2005: 72

115 On the other hand, they may do. My early novel *Bright Young Things* shows how, over the course of not much more than a week, six young characters decide (more or less) not to try to escape from the island on which they've been stranded. This is an ironic coming-of-age plot, in which what is learned is both unexpected and against the normal grain of society.

116 This is similar to, but in some respects different from, the Joycean epiphany that we frequently find in modern-realist short fiction. It is less subtle, on the whole, and shows a less complicated form of enlightenment. A coming-of-age epiphany is more complete and certain than the Joycean epiphany. It has the power to genuinely change someone's life on a material and spiritual level.

117 2007: 423

118 2002: 224

119 The Bath Abbey Diptychs by Sue Symons tell the story of Christ in a particularly powerful way, via needlework and calligraphy. There are 70 panels altogether, each representing a scene from Christ's life, death or resurrection. In the sequence, Christ is represented as a white circle, stitched into various figurative scenes. The white circle is a powerful image, showing both Christ's separation from the world, but also his immersion in it.

120 Isaiah 53: 2–3

121 2006: 97

122 2000: 113

123 1978: 26

124 1978: 27

125 1978: 30

126 As we have seen briefly above, deduction is when you have an idea or a theory that you form into a hypothesis and then you set out to investigate it. Induction is when you investigate first and build up a theory from details. In practice Holmes uses both methods, but when he succeeds where Lestrade and Gregson fail he has usually used inductive methods (and they have used deduction).

127 1978: 30

128 1978: 81

129 2011: 17

130 Fredric Jameson (1984) criticises postmodern culture for, among other things, being nostalgic and depthless. *One Day* is certainly nostalgic. For people who were young adults in the late eighties and early nineties, it does offer an irresistible 'blast from the past'. Is it this particularly vivid concoction of nostalgia and simulated grief that makes it so potent? In the end, this one remains a mystery to me.

131 Kaufman and Kaufman (2002: 68)

132 2002: 174

133 2002: 177

134 2002: 178

135 This means 'set menu'.

136 2002: 185

137 A representative sample from the offerings on the Wikipedia page for 'Bliss: short story': 'Bertha possibly has homoerotic feelings towards Pearl, as she reckons that it is Pearl who seems to inspire the bliss within her, and also the newfound sexual desire towards her own husband. These thoughts induce the reader to ponder on the implications of being homosexual in the early 20th century.' (Accessed 28 November 2011)

138 2006: 97

139 2002: 181

140 My favourite David Lynch film is *The Straight Story*. It has a clearer narrative than many of his other films, but is still a good example of modern realism. In it, Alvin, an aging man, sets off on his lawnmower to visit his seriously ill brother with whom he has fallen out some time ago. The film mostly concerns the problems that Alvin faces as he undertakes his long, complicated journey. When he arrives, we imagine that he and his brother will be reconciled, especially after the long hard journey that Alvin has made, but we do not know for sure. And there the film ends. It would be possible to argue that this is an ironic quest. After all, it is undertaken on a lawnmower. But I would argue that this makes it unconventional rather than ironic. As it has no resolution, this must be an example of modern realism.

141 The reviewer had, I presumed, learned this from press releases and interviews, not from the film itself.

142 'From Work to Text', in *Image, Music, Text* (1977: 159)

143 2001: 49

144 Although I would not class Gothic romance as a basic plot now, it may well have been on my list if I'd been writing in the eighteenth century.

145 2003: 15

146 2003: 18

147 2003: 150

148 It is arguable that all metafiction is satire, because all meta-fiction ultimately holds fiction itself up to ridicule. When B.S. Johnson tells us he is leaving out a description of the protag-onist's mother in *Christie Malry's Own Double Entry* this is ridicule by omission, which I'm not sure counts. And *If On A Winter's Night A Traveller* is rather gentle in its criticism of the predictability of fiction. This is not ridicule as much as it is defamiliarisation. But Jane Austen's account of Gothic romance in *Northanger Abbey* is, I think, more classically satirical. The features of the genre are exaggerated for comic effect, as we will see.

149 'It is now expedient to give some description of Mrs. Allen, that the reader may be able to judge, in what manner her actions will hereafter tend to promote the general distress of the work, and how she will, probably, contribute to reduce poor Catherine to all the desperate wretchedness of which a last volume is capable – whether by her imprudence, vulgarity, or jealousy – whether by intercepting her letters, ruining her character, or turning her out of doors.' (2003: 21) Here the narrator does not just address the reader, but also 'breaks the frame'; in other words, there is an acknowledgement that what is being narrated is *fiction*, rather than reality, and that fiction has conventions. For more on the conventions of metafiction, see Patricia Waugh's book, *Metafiction*.

150 There are various instances of this, but a particularly nice one is on the penultimate page, where the narrator admits that she is 'aware that the rules of composition forbid the introduc-tion of a character not connected with my fable'. (2003: 234)

151 Kaufman and Kaufman (2002: 5)

152 2002: 70

153 2002: 5. Like Jane Austen, Kaufman tells us which plot type

he wants us to know about, and gives us some of its details in order that we can understand the way he works with it metafictionally.

154 2002: 42

155 2002: 56

156 2002: 74

157 2002: 5–6

158 2002: ix

159 Is Willoughby evil? Or Wickham? No. They are misguided, selfish libertines, but they are hardly from the dark side. It's clear that Willoughby really loves Marianne, but has to make a more economically useful match. He has made some big mistakes, of course, but these are through his desire for pleasure, rather than his desire to cause anyone else pain.

160 2002: 280

161 According to the Nobel Prize-winning psychologist Daniel Kahneman, our minds are predisposed to make sense of the world through narrative rather than logic. In a feature in *The Guardian*, Oliver Burkeman gives the following example: 'Take the famous "Linda question": Linda is a single 31-year-old, who is very bright and deeply concerned with issues of social justice. Which of the following statements is more probable: a) that Linda works in a bank, or b) that Linda works in a bank and is active in the feminist movement? The over-whelming majority of respondents go for b), even though that's logically impossible. (It can't be more likely that both things are true than that just one of them is.) This is the "conjunctive fallacy", whereby our judgment is warped by the persuasive combination of plausible details. We are much better storytellers than we are logicians.' (Oliver Burkeman, *The Guardian*, G2, 14 November 2011)

162 CBC News website. http://www.cbc.ca/news/world/story/2009/05/19/f-vp-handler.html. (Accessed 13 November 2011)

163 In a letter to A.S. Suvorin, 1888. (1979: 271–2) This whole

letter is wonderful. Not only does Chekhov outline within it his belief that great writing should be the formulation of a question rather than its answer, he also has much to say about writing to deadlines, and what must be left out if one is to meet deadlines and therefore be paid.

164 *The Guardian*, 17 October 2011

165 These were crime novels all featuring my amateur sleuth Lily Pascale. I am now quite embarrassed by these novels. It's not just that they're crime novels, but also that I made so many mistakes in them. Probably the thing I hate most about them is their inauthenticity. But I don't want to completely disown them (although I did once). I learned a lot about plotting while writing them. And it was exciting, dreaming of being a novelist and then becoming one – even though I then had to work much harder to un-become a 'crime novelist' and be accepted as a literary writer.

166 When I say 'well-fictionalised autobiographical material' I don't mean that I've written versions of people from real life and changed their names and colour of their hair and so on. I've never done that. What I mean is that I've taken experiences of my own and the feelings that they inspired in me and given them to characters in a novel. I'll say more about fictionalisation later in this book.

167 I have sometimes told people, probably wrongly, that there's no point in writing at all if you don't feel that there's something you absolutely have to explore. The idea that someone may want 'to be a writer' but have no idea of what to write is quite paradoxical, in one way. After all, why write things down if you don't have a burning desire to communicate something? But actually, most people who want to write do have things to communicate, they just don't necessarily know what they are yet. I have themes and ideas in my mind constantly, as do many other people. I care about things in the world and I want to express this somehow. Part of becoming a writer is working

out which of all the strange thoughts you have in a given day are worth exploring further.

168 2004: 111–12

169 2004: 112–13

170 Chekhov claimed not to have a 'world-view'. In an 1888 letter to Dmitry Grigorovich, Chekhov describes a novel that he had planned but not yet written. He then says: 'I do not yet aspire to a coherent political, religious and philosophical world view; my opinions change every month, and therefore I must confine myself to describing how my characters love, get married, have children, die, and how they speak.' (2004: 155) Of course Chekhov does present a world-view that is consistent throughout his work and letters. One key feature of Chekhov's world-view seems to be authenticity. Another is the presentation of objective truth. As he says: 'the writer is surely not a confectioner or a beautician or an entertainer. The writer is a man bound by contract to his duty and to his conscience. In for a penny, in for a pound; however degrading he may find it, he has no choice but to overcome his squeamishness and soil his imagination with the filth of life . . . ' (2004: 77)

171 This is the first time I have referred to agents in this book. While I don't believe that anyone should write something simply because they believe agents will like it (and if you do it that way, they won't), and this means they will get published and become millionaires etc., it is true that literary agents have very good taste and, on the whole, choose to represent very good books. Why wouldn't they? They do this for a living. They have read thousands of contemporary novels. They know what is new, what is exciting and above all they know *story*. If twenty agents have turned down your material, and not one of them has sent an encouraging note with their rejection, this does not mean that they are idiots. It means your idea is not exciting enough. Do something about it.

172 1985: 434

173 He enjoyed *The End of Mr. Y* very much, but had some
     reservations about my use of present tense, likening it to
     someone breathlessly recording their thoughts into a tape-
     recorder. He thought this particularly ineffective in the scene
     in which Ariel is having bad sex in a Little Chef toilet. In
     return I queried an unquestioning use of a 'comfortable' past
     tense that lets us assume that the narrator survives the narra-
     tive and is sitting in an armchair somewhere beyond it, with
     us on his or her lap as we are told a story. In practice, of
     course, both tenses have their strengths and weaknesses.

174 You have also chosen to begin a narrative with someone
     waking up suddenly, which is a cliché not just in itself but in
     what it implies about narrative time (stories begin when people
     wake up, rather than when some drama happens).

175 A 'grammatical person' is simply the formal way of talking
     about 'first person', 'third person' and so on. It relates to the
     way you put someone in a sentence, and specifies that there
     are three different types of person who can exist in the English
     language: me, you and a 'third person' (basically, everyone
     else). If you think about it, there are no other possibilities. Apart
     from me and you, every other being in the known universe can
     be covered by him, her, them, it or some equivalent. Here is a
     list of grammatical persons – three singular; three plural:

     First person (I . . . Me . . .)
     Second person (You . . .)
     Third person (He, She, It . . .)
     First person plural (We . . .)
     Second person plural (You . . .)
     Third person plural (They . . .)

176 There are plenty of novels that are addressed to 'you', a notable
     recent example being *A Concise Chinese–English Dictionary for*

Lovers by Xiaolu Guo (2008). This is a confessional technique, not a use of the second person as such. Full second person implies that the reader of the book is carrying out the actions described in the book, which as you can imagine is quite hard to write convincingly. Here's how Italo Calvino does it: 'You are about to begin reading Italo Calvino's new novel, *If on a Winter's Night a Traveller*. Relax. Concentrate. Dispel every other thought. Let the world around you fade. Best to close the door; the TV is always on in the next room.' (1998: 3)

177 1985: 312

178 Although it is ideally a feature of omniscient narration that characters are observed rather than judged, in practice the omniscient point of view is always mixed up with characters' points of view and therefore with characters' judgements of one another. And because of the proximity of the point of view of the novel and Dorothea's point of view, Casaubon is judged in a way that other characters are not.

179 In a sense, the true point of view is close to the superobjective, which we will be exploring in the chapter 'Characterisation'.

180 The narrative time covered in the novel is more than twenty years, but it is not a lifetime. In fact, the narrative time of the novel is framed by Pip's relationship with Estella. It begins, more or less, with the circumstances of their meeting, and ends with a sort-of resolution (or, in fact, two, as Dickens wrote two endings).

181 2002: 63

182 2004: 3

183 2003: 160

184 Of course, if we were writing metafiction we might decide to break the frame in this way. But notice that even metafiction rarely dramatises movement from one dimension to the other – from fiction to reality or the reverse. More often it highlights the fictionality of fiction without completely shattering the illusion.

185 2009: 23

186 2002: 274

187 2004: 59

188 2004: 82

189 2004: 56

190 A limited third-person narration is when some rules are imposed by the author on the method of narration that limits or restricts it in some way. For example, in 'Marriage à la Mode' we can enter the consciousnesses of William and Isabel, but not Moira, or anyone else in the story. In my novel *Going Out*, the third-person narration alternates between Julie's consciousness and Luke's. We never enter the consciousnesses of any of the other characters in the novel.

191 1979: 269

192 2003: 81

193 2006: 138

194 Any present-tense narration that is not complete and imme-diate stream-of-consciousness must really be a disguised past-tense narration. Even with stream-of-consciousness there must be a time lag between the events happening and the narrator writing them down (or, as Philip Pullman had it, reciting them breathlessly into a tape recorder). In fact, *The End of Mr. Y* has a disguised past-tense narration. It begins with the words that lead us into other consciousnesses throughout the novel: 'You now have one choice. You . . .' While what is 'experienced' next is in the present tense, it is clear it took place in the narrative past: the plot tells us as much; it is a memory, wrought in language and stored in the Troposphere. Most readers realise, albeit perhaps unconsciously, that present-tense narration concerns the past, not the present. If I begin an anecdote with 'So there I am sitting at my desk, minding my own business when my boss comes over and . . .', the listener is aware that I have chosen to narrate something from the past in present tense for effect, not to convince them that

this scene with my boss is actually happening now. Next time you read a present-tense narration, see if you can spot all the different ways in which it acknowledges that this is the past.

195　2003: 48

196　2003: 198

197　In an interview in *The Paris Review*, Mitchell says that 'I felt a bit cheated that Calvino hadn't followed through with what he'd begun – which was, of course, the whole point of the book. But a voice said this: What would it actually look like if a mirror were placed at the end of the book, and you continued into a second half that took you back to the beginning?' Available at www.theparisreview.org/interviews (accessed 18 March 2012).

198　The masters of this are the French group Oulipo (Ouvroir de Littérature Potentielle, or Workshop of Potential Literature), who create works of literature on the basis of rather strict rules and limitations, often derived from mathematics. Georges Perec famously wrote a novel in which he did not use the letter 'e' (translated in English as *A Void*). Perec also wrote *Life: A User's Manual*, a novel based on the mathematical problem of the 'Knight's tour' in which, given a chessboard of n × m squares, a knight must be moved so it visits each square only once. The novel is set in a fictional Parisian apartment block. Perec describes his thinking as follows: 'It would have been tedious to describe the building floor by floor and apartment by apartment; but that was no reason to leave the chapter sequence to chance. So I decided to use a principle derived from an old problem well known to chess enthusiasts as the Knight's tour; it requires moving a knight around the 64 squares of a chess-board without its ever landing more than once on the same square . . . For the special case of *Life: A User's Manual*, a solution for a 10 × 10 chess-board had to be found . . . The division of the book into six parts was derived from the same principle: each time the knight has finished touching all four sides of the square, a new section begins.' In Mathews, Brotchie and Queneau (eds), *Oulipo Compendium* (1998: 172)

199 Available at www.theparisreview.org/interviews (accessed 18 March 2012)

200 17, 55a (1996: 28)

201 In a letter to Alexey Peshkov, 1899. (2004: 407)

202 2008a: 31

203 This is a very crude and gendered example that assumes that men like sport and women like soap operas. Of course, this is not always true. But sometimes crude examples are needed to make points that are both simple and rather complicated. Here we see that just because someone is doing something does not mean he likes it or would not rather be doing something else. In fact, as we will see later, an action as simple as 'watching a soap opera' can be almost infinitely complex if we look at it in enough detail. Old comedies might show us a rough portrait of a man who is so 'under the thumb' of 'the wife' that he emasculates himself by watching her favourite programme with her. This kind of characterisation is trivial and pointless. No one is that one-dimensional. Perhaps the man who does this action feels contrite over last week's row. Perhaps his wife watched the rugby with him yesterday. Perhaps he wants to have sex tonight. Perhaps he feels guilty because he just had sex with someone else. Even these deeper motivations are somewhat 'obvious', but they are a start. Choice based on motivation can be very complex and, as we will see, only gets more complex once you keep asking 'why' of every part of it.

204 They are designed (insofar as they are designed) to show the character of the *host* of the party, not the guest, because all they show is what the host has set up, not what a real character would do *within* this set-up. If this is the effect you want, then fine. But now you need to know all about

the host. What cheese did he buy? Where did he buy it? Did he pay with change, a note or a credit card? Why? You don't need to put all this detail in the text. But you need to know it.

205 An interesting exercise is to go into a shop for no reason and try to stay there for ten minutes. See how difficult it is to do anything naturally when you have no motivation. Waiting for a train at St Pancras recently I went to 'browse' in Boots, the big chemist. I didn't want to buy anything and had no reason to be there apart from to kill time. Immediately I felt like a character written into a scene with no focus. I drifted around looking at random things but without any real sense of purpose or desire. It took about two minutes of this before the store detective realised I was acting strangely and started following me so closely I had to leave.

206 2008b: 26–27

207 The Moscow Art Theatre, co-founded by Stanislavski, put on all Chekhov's plays. Chekhov met his future wife, the actress Olga Knipper, at a rehearsal of his play *The Seagull* (she played Arkadina). Knipper was one of 39 original members of the Moscow Art Theatre.

208 2008a: 273

209 In her translator's note at the beginning of *An Actor Prepares*, Elizabeth Reynolds Hapgood explains that Stanislavski decided to fictionalise his book of instruction partly because he wanted to address the faults of actors without naming his actual players. She also reminds us: 'That he himself appears under the name of Tortsov can scarcely escape the astute reader, nor is it difficult to see that the enthusiastic student who keeps the record of the lessons is the Stanislavski of half a century ago who was feeling his way toward the methods best suited to mirror the modern world.' (2008a: vi)

210 2008b: 31

211 Although here the word 'old', if it is used by the author and

not as part of free indirect discourse, is lazy. By using the abstract word I am asking you, the reader, to supply all the details of 'old' even though I have (when you think about it) promised you that I would do it (because in this case I am the author and you are the reader). I am also assuming that there is some consensus version of 'old' that we can all just fall back on without having to examine it in more detail. Art requires more effort than this.

212 Stanislavski (as Tortsov) reminds his actors of 'the sedimen-tation of salts and [. . .] the hardening of muscles' (2008b: 31) and various other objective realities of aging. He urges his actors to use their knowledge of these *objective* realities to create a character's action, rather than just vague assumptions about what old age is like.

213 Perhaps another unit in this scene actually belongs to the dog-walker, who is, say, my best friend's husband. His unit may well be all about wanting to get home in time to watch a rugby match. He is therefore walking the dog as quickly as possible, and in this case part of his unit would be avoiding me. So perhaps we each cross the road to avoid the other: I am in a hurry to post my letter and he is in a hurry to get home and watch the rugby. There would be more conflict in this scene if he was avoiding going home for some reason and actually wanted to stop and chat. If I know that he knows I am having an affair, and could easily tell my husband, then how does this affect my behaviour, and my unit? Suddenly there is both internal conflict (do I make small-talk to appease him or hurry to catch the last post?) as well as the tension and conflict between the two characters and their objectives.

214 2008a: 123

215 2011: 76

216 1999: 385

217 Stanislavski (or at least his translator or editor) hyphenates this as 'super-objective'. I have created a compound word not

just for ease of understanding but also to highlight the fact that my understanding and use of the term is not necessarily always the same as Stanislavski's (although all my ideas on the subject have been inspired by his).

218 And certainly isn't what Stanislavski encourages us to do. My ideas about the 'main theme' of the individual are informed more by homeopathy and Zen Buddhism, both of which show the self caught up in one *particular* drama, whether this is about looking for control or needing to be loved. In homeopathy the work of Rajan Sankaran is particularly interesting here.

219 2008a: 272

220 I have made these superobjectives static, which to some extent moves away from Stanislavski, who says all objectives should be active. I agree that all *minor* objectives should be active. But I imagine characters struggling for something final that is quite still and complete (and actually does not, and cannot ever really exist). Here the superobjective almost begins to function as a seed word for character, and that can be a valid way to approach this, as long as you remember that the word must represent a desire.

221 2003: 411

222 2008a: 279

223 2008a: 279

224 2008a: 125

225 2004: 70

226 Levitt and Dubner (2006: 19–20)

227 We learn from *Freakonomics* that people will steal only if they can convince themselves it isn't really stealing. The 'nuanced social calculus of theft' (2006: 48) means that people cheat the honesty-box system for their office bagels but do not steal the box itself. Indeed, we learn from *Freakonomics* that most people do not steal even if they are not being watched and there are no obvious incentives to be honest. Clearly people

like to feel good about themselves.

228 We also learn from *Freakonomics* that estate agents work much harder selling their own houses than their clients' houses because the percentage of the profit they get is much greater (and presumably also because they want to move house!). (2006: 8–9)

229 'Paperback Writer' column, *The Guardian*, 19 March 2005

230 In a letter to Maxim Gorky, 1899. (1979: 275)

231 1960: 32

232 1960: 11

233 1990: 344

234 I wrote to him to tell him this. I said something like, 'I want to write sentences like yours and I want to smoke on TV like you do', and asked him to read my first novel. He very graciously agreed to do so. Of course, I never heard from him again. My publisher was horrified that I'd written to him at all. After all, I was writing mass-market crime fiction and a quote for the jacket from Martin Amis would be completely idiotic, like getting J.K. Rowling to quote on the latest literary sensation to come out of New York. It doesn't matter how famous the person is, a cover quote from them means nothing unless you potentially share a readership. I'm sure the readers my publisher had in mind for my crime novels had never even heard of Martin Amis.

235 *Dead Clever* (1999 [1998]: 52)

236 'Paperback Writer' column (2005)

237 2009: 22

238 1998: 211

239 2005: 172

240 2004: 61

241 2004: 173

242 2001: 101

243 *How to be Topp* [1954]. In Willans and Searle, *The Complete Molesworth* (2000: 160)

244 'It was a queer, sultry summer, the summer they electrocuted
the Rosenbergs, and I didn't know what I was doing in New
York.' (2005: 1)

245 'Paperback Writer' column (2005)

246 2000: 93

247 2000: 92

248 1979: 269. I have also seen 'small details' translated as 'little
particulars', which is also a very good way of expressing this
idea of specificity.

249 2004: 37

250 2004: 93

251 *The Bell Jar* (2005: 6)

252 For example, instead of naming the TV shows that Luke
watches, I describe them as 'programmes full of shiny white
American malls, clean beaches, best buddies, teen angst, high
schools with cheerleaders, soccer pitches, geeks, girls with
suntans and blonde highlights, long corridors with lockers and
feuds, and perfect stories'. (2003: 2)

253 Artists are often criticised for putting ordinary objects in an
art gallery in the same way that writers can be criticised for
writing '501s' instead of 'jeans' or even 'trousers'. But, of
course, putting an ordinary object in a gallery (or in a sentence)
and treating it as 'special', when most people think it isn't, is
a wonderful way to get us to look not just at the object anew,
but also at ourselves and all the things we take for granted. In
1917, Marcel Duchamp signed the name *R Mutt* on a urinal
and displayed it in an exhibition. Much controversy followed,
although this 'readymade' (or found object) is now often cited
as the most influential piece of art in the twentieth century.
Why? Perhaps because it challenged us to consider what art
is, and how we should look at it. In this case, it was not exactly
urinals being defamiliarised, but art itself. Andy Warhol is
famous for, among other things, creating works of art consisting
of screen prints of Marilyn Monroe, and reconstructions of

Brillo Pad boxes. By placing these objects – not readymades, but painstakingly created works that only seem cheap, kitschy and popular – in the space reserved for serious art, Warhol makes us look at them in ways that we might not if they were just images on a TV screen or pictures in a magazine. Popular culture, he appears to be saying, is important. We spend much more time looking at it than we spend looking at art. So what happens then if we look at it as if it *is* art? People are, of course, used to looking for 'deep' or 'symbolic' meanings in art; not so in popular culture, or urinals. Clearly there are more or less artistic ways of writing pop culture.

254 1995: 9

255 A haiku is a form of Japanese free verse. The idea is usually to represent or imply one particular aspect of nature, or one clear natural scene in a particular season, although contemporary and western haiku can be about any subject. A haiku is made of seventeen syllables, arranged in three lines of five, seven and five syllables. So I could write: Outside my window. The birds are on the feeder. Goldfinches again.

256 In fact, for a long time I toyed with the idea of having a writer character in *Our Tragic Universe* who was obsessed with cutting, but in the end all I kept was this line: 'I'd invented a writer character from New York who deletes a whole book until it's a haiku and then deletes that, but then I deleted him, too.' (2010: 35)

257 From 'Bliss' (2002: 180)

258 *Five Miles from Outer Hope* (2001: 61)

259 21, 57b. (1996: 34)

260 21, 57b. (1996: 34)

261 1985: 557

262 2002: 174

263 2005: 114

264 2004: 105

265 2004: 110

266 1985: 408

267 2002: 142

268 This idea has been most famously expressed by T.S. Eliot in his essay 'Hamlet and his Problems' in his book *The Sacred Wood*. Eliot says:

> The only way of expressing emotion in the form of art is by finding an 'objective correlative'; in other words, a set of objects, a situation, a chain of events, which shall be the formula of that *particular* emotion; such that when the external facts, which must terminate in sensory experience, are given, the emotion is immediately evoked. (1997: 85–86)

The objective correlative therefore works very much like metaphor, where one thing 'stands for' something else. But Eliot is clear that the objective correlative must be a collection of things (objects, actions, moments in time) that evoke in the reader the state of mind of the character. Eliot complained that *Hamlet* is a failure because Shakespeare wasn't able to find an objective correlative to express Hamlet's state of mind.

269 All the following Shklovsky quotations are in Rivkin and Ryan (eds), *Literary Theory: An Anthology* (1998: 18)

270 1998: 18

271 1998: 18

272 1998: 19

273 2005: 51

274 1960: 11

275 Amis. *London Fields* (1990: 1)

276 Interview with George Plimpton, *Paris Review*, No. 101 (1986, online).

277 2002: 183

278 This includes not just my first three crime novels but also *Dog and Clowns*, the unpublished novel I wrote in 1997.

279 If this takes the pressure off, then good. But if you think,

Well, what's the point if I don't write something amazing first time round? then be reassured. People do write amazing things on a first attempt too, and I guess are more likely to do so after they've had some instruction.

280 This paragraph (in the main text) is around 250 words long, and took me around fifteen minutes to write. All you have to do, then, to complete 1,000 words, is write 250 words four times, which should take you around an hour. It's like sending four emails. I often find that my first 1,000 words in a day are a bit stilted. They're kind of warm-up words. I find the next 1,000 much easier. My ideal number of words to write in a day is 3,000, but I often delete the first 1,000 of these.

281 It is, in fact, 59,046 words long. But it is a short novel and usually you will be aiming for something closer to 80,000–90,000 words at least. But first drafts can often be around 60,000–70,000 words long.

282 This of course means a 60,000-word novel can be written in a month at a rate of 2,000 words a day. And this is exactly how I decided to proceed after I'd done my calculations. What an idiot! The book was a complete mess and needed total re-writing. But maybe it wasn't too disastrous because I sent it off after precisely 31 days and picked up both an agent and an editor. Then again maybe it *was* disastrous, as I ended up more or less signing a contract in blood to write commercial fiction for ever. But however much I complain about how hard it was to make the transition from commercial to literary fiction, it probably was easier to do it from the inside, now I look back. So it all worked out OK. At the time I thought writing a novel in a month was rather impressive and I bragged about it a lot until I realised that people respect you in proportion to the amount of time you spend writing a novel, not in *inverse* proportion to the amount of time you spend writing a novel. One of the reviews I got (in a fanzine) said something like

'Apparently this novel only took a month to write and I must say it reads like it.' Ouch.

283 Here are the lengths of the final manuscript versions of my most recent novels: *Our Tragic Universe* is 128,515 words long. *The End of Mr. Y* is 141,549 words long. *PopCo* is 177,958 words long. *Going Out* is 94,248. I don't have the computer file for *Bright Young Things* any more, but I remember it also being around 90,000 words.

284 After a long day at work one Tuesday I was watching *America's Next Top Model*. At the time I was trying to find a way of explaining to some new students why literary fiction gets marked so much more highly than genre fiction on our courses. Tyra Banks was explaining to one of the girls on the show: 'You don't want to become too commercial. You are more than just a catalogue girl. You need to be more edgy.' I suddenly thought, 'Gosh. I see. So even fashion modelling has its commercial and artistic versions . . .' From this I realised that every art form has a commercial, industrial version of itself. Poetry has greetings cards ('Roses are red, and violets are blue . . . '). Architecture has Wimpey homes. Cuisine has fast-food joints. What we know about these commercial, generic forms is that they are safe, predictable, quick and easy. They are quick and easy to create, and quick and easy to consume. I suddenly had a way of explaining this to the students, all because I'd put on a very undemanding TV show.

285 Kaufman and Kaufman (2002: 49)

286 If you use this way of conceptualising writing a novel then it's good to remember that you can actually go where you bloody well want – as long as the reader is willing to go with you. If it suddenly makes sense to go to Edinburgh from London via Wales, then do it. Just make sure the reader understands what you're doing – or at least trusts that they will understand later.

287 Before I wrote my first crime novel I went to the Harbour

Bookshop in Dartmouth and bought myself six recent crime paperbacks. I studied things like length (I was obsessed with length in those days), not just of the whole book, but of paragraphs, sentences and so on. I noted point of view, tense and other stylistic factors. I even taught myself to format dialogue from 'copying' the style in published books. For beginning writers, just opening any published novel and analysing the layout and content of one page is an incredibly useful activity.

288 'All happy families are alike; each unhappy family is unhappy in its own way.' (2003: 1)

289 2003:1

290 *Anton Chekhov's Short Stories: A Norton Critical Edition* (1979: 272). I have quoted from this very important letter elsewhere in this book. It's such a shame it is not included in *A Life in Letters*. In it, Chekhov discusses many important aspects of his writing philosophy, the central one being that the writer is the person who is required to objectively present the case, like a judge, and the reader is the member of the jury who must decide what he or she thinks 'according to his own taste'. (1979: 272)

291 Here is an excerpt from a talk I gave about the novel at the Swedenborg Society, London, on 19 May 2010. This should give some idea of the ways in which I was thinking about theme when I wrote the novel, and how complex theme can become.

I knew I wanted to continue the ideas I'd begun to explore in *The End of Mr. Y* in *Our Tragic Universe*, and I decided to look more closely at narrative – the patterns made from language – to see if the 'way out' lay there. I don't know why I am obsessed with 'ways out', but I am. Something has always seemed wrong to me about this world we're in – as if there's something everyone is missing. I think it was Chuang Tzu who talked about the

fish that doesn't know it is in water . . . At first, when I
began researching *Our Tragic Universe* I wanted to make
it a great tragedy, even though I knew I probably didn't
have it in me yet, because I'd been reading Nietzsche,
and I thought he offered a way out of the rational finite
world through suffering and compassion and primal
Oneness. Nietzsche says that the rationalist world of sense
must inevitably be less infinite and wonderful than a
destructive non-sense world of doom, uncertainty and
unknowability. He talks about the 'mystery doctrine of
tragedy' (2003: 52), which includes: 'The basic understanding of the unity of things, individuation seen as the
primal source of evil, art as the joyful hope that the spell
of individuation can be broken, as a presentiment of a
restored oneness' (2003: 52). I was – as many people are
– very taken with this. I was re-reading *Hamlet* and *Anna
Karenina* and preparing first-year lectures about them,
and I knew that in my novel I wanted to capture something of the passion of non-sense, and go beyond the
individual stuck in his or her little ball of ego, waiting
patiently for death.

One of the obvious problems I found, of course, is
that the novel – even if it is a tragedy – cannot be a
world of non-sense: the novel, with its three-act structure
and its character arcs and its reversals, recognitions and
changes of fortune, must be a world of sense and structure. Once I realised this I wanted to work with it too
– I wanted to write a novel on non-sense concealed within
a novel of sense . . . Sort of. I at least wanted to examine
narrative structures and think about whether they free
or trap us. Whether narrative takes the infinite and tries
to make it finite, or whether it can be the other way
around. Whether it creates a heaven or a hell. I also
believed that there was something beyond narrative and

the worlds it creates that one could maybe glimpse through narrative.

Not long after I'd started thinking all of this, I came upon the ideas of Frank Tipler, which for a while shattered all my hopes of the great salmon-leap of humanity – the fish realising that there is a whole other world beyond the water; the human consciousness returning to the void. Tipler suggests that at the end of this universe there will be enough power to run a new universe – a simulation. When I first read about Frank Tipler's theory – that the purpose of the human species is to create our own infinite afterlife, it gave me the heebie-jeebies. That's not strong enough – it gave me something close to a spiritual crisis. It made me think of hell. This has happened to me twice in my life before: once when I read an article in *New Scientist* about the universe being some superior intelligence's experiment in an extra-dimensional lab somewhere; and the other time when I watched *The Matrix*. Both these narratives bothered me a great deal because they suggested the existence not of an unfathomable, unknowable infinity – or God – but of a rational, rationalist and understandable creator that is not at all loving. Let me be clear – I have never been religious. My explorations of spirituality have so far really been through Zen and the Tao – which are similar but different. I have contemplated the void, sort of, and I certainly prefer the idea of the unknowable and mysterious void to the idea that some knowable entity has us stuck in a test-tube, or wired up like so many batteries.

Tipler's theory, when I thought about it, seemed worse. For humanity to create, and control, its own infinity was so disturbing to me . . . It seemed to imply a profound lack of trust in the universe; a lack, if you like, of *faith*. But I was still very interested in the idea of a man-made, materialist heaven and afterlife, because it seemed compellingly incongruous in the context of current debates about science and religion. In Tipler's schema, science would be the thing that created God: and the afterlife and immortality would be rational, explainable things. The great debates of the early twenty-first century would become a grey sludge, and no one would be wrong ever again, all through infinity. It wasn't so much that I agreed with Tipler and decided that religion and science were, or should be, powered by the same engine, striving for the same destination. But it got me thinking about how science and religion *are* different, and how each can't necessarily contain the other. Perhaps, I thought, a society that can't distinguish between science and religion, or that thought that you only needed one of them, would also end up in a kind of hell of its own.

Therefore, in the novel I don't set science against religion. I am not 'against' either one of them, and I think it's probably false to set them against one another. I like the way science keeps asking questions that lead to answers that lead to more questions about the universe and our place in it. Many scientists – and especially mathematicians – appreciate that there is a point – or there are points – where the questions become unanswerable: *What came before the beginning?*, and *What will come after the end?* Science sends out its questions, and every so often the answer comes back: 'We don't know.' For me, this is the place of religion – not to answer these questions in a pseudo-rational way, but to provide the space to meditate on them (or something). Science can't deal with unanswerable questions: religion can, in its own way. But once religion, or spirituality, tries to explain itself scientifically, big problems begin. For me, all the 'sense' of religion is a problem. How that differs from being a teenager and moaning about 'institutionalised religion', I'm not sure. Maybe it doesn't.

Our Tragic Universe isn't an argument between two 'sides' but rather a triangular conversation between science, 'rational spirituality' and faith (as distinct from religion). I surprised myself when I was writing the novel not because I didn't know the answers but because it took me the whole novel to formulate the question. This shouldn't have been a surprise – after all, one of my favourite Chekhov quotations is about art being the proper formulation of questions – but yet it *was* a surprise, because it was the first time I had written a novel that genuinely was about formulating a question, and I really didn't know what it was until I got to the end. What is better: sense or non-sense? What gives meaning: the author, the reader or the text itself? And, in the end, is meaning always preferable to non-meaning? Is it better to try to know the infinite, or just to let it go for now? The novel lets you, the reader, try it out at least two different ways, to see if you prefer sense or non-sense in the end. Ultimately I'm not sure, but for me narrative is at its most bland when it adopts a middle position of telling 'what happened' as if there was never any question of the sense of something, or the idea of sense and finite ideas being all there is in our world. Narrative should either tell so little that the world remains mysterious, and becomes a tiny porthole onto the void, or tell so much – every little connection and detail – that it becomes mysterious in a different way, as life-as-it-is-lived is mysterious. In *The End of Mr. Y* – The End of Mystery – I wanted to consider ways in which mystery can be obliterated by language. *Our Tragic Universe* is a continuation of that project in the sense that it tries to dramatise different kinds of heaven and hell in narrative, and asks, in the end, which – heaven or hell – is best described, and served, by narrative. Of course, there are no answers.

292 If you are part of an institution like a university, you will probably have access to the *Oxford English Dictionary* (*OED*) online for free. This is a wonderful resource with a connected thesaurus. Otherwise, try your local library (if such a thing still exists by the time this book is published). It will either have online access to the *OED* or it will have large multi-volume dictionaries for you to use. While it is nice to be able to use the *OED* for this task, a large home dictionary and thesaurus are usually enough.

293 2003: 5

294 An even more lo-fi version of this was when I used to email a copy of my novel to my mother for safe-keeping on her hard drive. In fact, sending your files to a friend or relative who lives somewhere else is a good method of backing up as long as they remember to save the file properly. But you might annoy them if you do it every day, and they might not be reliable. Why not just set up a Gmail or Hotmail account purely for backing up your novel? You could even get a new account for each novel you write.

295 It's interesting that students also often talk about published books in this way. It may well be that this is a particularly British problem, this desire to defend the underdog but attack anything too successful, risky, ambitious or extravagant. But groups in other cultures will have their own forms of madness and it's worth being aware of what these are likely to be. I was once so frustrated with the way a group of students were talking about two particular contemporary novels that I got them to mark the novels using our assessment criteria. They gave one of these novels, which I think had been shortlisted for a prize, a 58, which in a grade system would translate to a C+! You wouldn't want a group like this 'helping' with your novel.

BIBLIOGRAPHY

Note: where it seems interesting enough to mention, the date of first publication (or approximate time of writing) has been given in square brackets.

BOOKS

Afanas'ev, Aleksander. 1975 [1864]. *Russian Fairy Tales*. New York: Pantheon

Amis, Martin. 1984. *Money*. London: Jonathan Cape

Amis, Martin. 1990 [1989]. *London Fields*. London: Penguin

Aristotle. 1996 [3rd century BCE]. *Poetics* Tr. Malcolm Heath. London: Penguin

Austen, Jane. 2002 [1813]. *Pride and Prejudice*. London: Penguin Classics

Austen, Jane. 2007 [1815]. *Emma*. London: Vintage Classics

Austen, Jane. 2003 [1818]. *Northanger Abbey*. London: Penguin Classics

Barker, Nicola. 2001. *Five Miles from Outer Hope*. London: Faber

Barker, Nicola. 2005. *Clear* New York: Ecco Press

Barnes, Julian. 2011. *The Sense of an Ending*. London: Jonathan Cape

Barthes, Roland. 1977. *Image, Music, Text*. London: Fontana

Baudrillard, Jean. 1994. *Simulacra and Simulation*. Tr. Sheila

Faria Glaser. Michigan: University of Michigan Press

Baudrillard, Jean. 2005. *The Conspiracy of Art*. New York: Semiotext(e)

Beckett, Samuel. 1990 [1948]. *Waiting for Godot*. London: Faber

Blyton, Enid. 1971 [1939]. *The Enchanted Wood*. London: Dean

Blyton, Enid. 1971 [1943]. *The Magic Faraway Tree*. London: Dean

Booker, Christopher. 2004. *The Seven Basic Plots*. London: Continuum

Brown, Dan. 2004. *The Da Vinci Code*. London: Transworld

Calvino, Italo. 1998. *If On A Winter's Night A Traveller*. London: Vintage

Campbell, Joseph. 1973 [1949]. *The Hero With a Thousand Faces*. Princeton: Princeton University Press

Camus, Albert. 2000 [1961]. *The Outsider*. London: Penguin Modern Classics

Carroll, Lewis. 2007 [1865]. *Alice in Wonderland*. London: Macmillan

Carver, Raymond. 1983. *Cathedral*. New York: Knopf

Carver, Raymond. 2000. *Call If You Need Me*. London: Harvill

Carver, Raymond. 1995. *Where I'm Calling From*. London: Harvill

Ch'êng-ên, Wu. 1961 [16th century]. *Monkey*. London: Penguin Classics

Chaucer, Geoffrey. 2003 [14th century]. *The Canterbury Tales*. London: Penguin Classics

Chekhov, Anton. 1979. *Anton Chekhov's Short Stories*. New York: Norton Critical Edition

Chekhov, Anton. 2002. *The Lady with the Little Dog and Other Stories, 1896–1904*. London: Penguin

Chekhov, Anton. 2004. *A Life in Letters*. Tr. Rosamund Bartlett and Anthony Phillips. London: Penguin Classics

Choderlos de Laclos, Pierre Ambroise François. 2008 [1782]. *Les Liaisons Dangereuses*. Tr. Douglas Parmeé. Oxford: Oxford World Classics

Christie, Agatha. 2007 [1934]. *Murder On The Orient Express*. London: Harper

Collins, Jackie. 1995. *Lucky*. London: Pan

Coupland, Douglas. 2003. *Hey Nostradamus!* London: Flamingo

Davis, Lydia. 2007. *Varieties of Disturbance*. New York: Farrar, Straus and Giroux

Davis, Lydia. 2011. *The Collected Stories of Lydia Davis*. London: Penguin

Dickens, Charles. 2003 [1860]. *Great Expectations*. London: Penguin Classics

Docherty, Thomas (ed). 1993. *Postmodernism: A Reader*. Hertfordshire: Harvester Wheatsheaf

Doctorow, E.L. 1986. Interview with George Plimpton. *Paris Review*, No. 101. Available online at www.theparisreview.org/interviews (accessed 18 March 2012).

Donovan, Anne. 2004. *Buddha Da*. Edinburgh: Canongate

Doyle, Conan Arthur. 1978 [1887]. *A Study in Scarlet*. London: Pan

Doyle, Conan Arthur. 2003 [1902]. *The Hound of the Baskervilles*. London: Penguin Classics

Eco, Umberto. 2001. *Foucault's Pendulum*. London: Vintage

Edge, Lucy. 2006. *Yoga School Dropout*. London: Ebury

Eliot, George. 1985 [1871–72]. *Middlemarch*. London: Penguin

Eliot, T.S. 1997 [1920]. *The Sacred Wood: Essays on Poetry and Criticism*. London: Faber

Ellis, Brett Easton. 1991. *American Psycho*. London: Picador

Ellis, Brett Easton. 2005. *Lunar Park*. London: Picador

Faber, Michel. 2008. *The Fire Gospel*. Edinburgh: Canongate

Fielding, Helen. 1996. *Bridget Jones's Diary*. London: Picador

Fitzgerald, F. Scott. 2000 [1926]. *The Great Gatsby*. London: Penguin Modern Classics

Forster, E.M. 2000 [1927]. *Aspects of the Novel*. London: Penguin

Frye, Northrop. 2000 [1957]. *Anatomy of Criticism*. Princeton: Princeton University Press

Gibson, William. 1995 [1984]. *Neuromancer*. London: Voyager

Gibson, William. 2010. *Zero History*. London: Penguin

Gourevitch, Philip (ed). 2007. *The Paris Review Interviews: Volume 1*. Edinburgh: Canongate

Griffiths, Niall. 2002. *Kelly and Victor*. London: Jonathan Cape Original

Guo, Xiaolu. 2008. *A Concise Chinese–English Dictionary for Lovers*. London: Vintage

Haddon, Mark. 2004. *The Curious Incident of the Dog in the Night Time*. London: Vintage

Heller, Zoe. 2004. *Notes On A Scandal*. London: Penguin

Hemingway, Ernest. 1998. *The Complete Short Stories of Ernest Hemingway*. New York: Scribner

Hemingway, Ernest. 2009 [1964]. *A Moveable Feast: The Restored Edition*. New York: Scribner

Homer. 2003. *The Odyssey*. Tr. E.V. Rieu. London: Penguin Classics

Horace. 2004. 'The Art of Poetry' in *Classical Literary Criticism*. Tr. Penelope Murray and T.S. Dorsch. London: Penguin Classics

Irvine, Lucy. 1987. *Runaway*. London: Penguin New Edition

Jameson, Fredric. 1984. 'Postmodernism: or the Cultural Logic of Late Capitalism' in *New Left Review*, 146: 53–92. Reprinted in Docherty (ed.), *Postmodernism*, 62–92.

Johnson, B.S. 2009 [1973]. *Christie Malry's Own Double Entry*. London: William Collins

Kahneman, Daniel. 2011. *Thinking, Fast and Slow*. London: Penguin

Kaufman, Charles and Donald Kaufman. 2002. *Adaptation: The Shooting Script*. New York: Newmarket Press

King, Stephen. 2000. *On Writing*. London: Hodder & Stoughton

Lasdun, James. 2003. *The Horned Man*. London: Vintage

Lévi-Strauss, Claude. 1963 [1958]. *Structural Anthropology*. Tr. Claire Jacobson and Brooke Shoeff. New York: Basic Books

Levitt, Steven D. and Stephen J. Dubner. 2006. *Freakonomics*. London: Penguin

Mansfield, Katherine. 2002 [1920]. *Katherine Mansfield Selected Stories*. Oxford: Oxford World Classics

Mathews, Harry, Alastair Brotchie and Raymond Queneau. 1998. *Oulipo Compendium*. London: Atlas

McCarthy, Tom. 2011. *C*. London: Methuen

McKee, Robert. 1999. *Story*. London: Methuen

Melville, Herman. 2003 [1815]. *Moby Dick*. London: Penguin Classics

Miller, Arthur. 1989 [1949]. *Death of a Salesman*. London: Penguin 20th Century Classics

Mills, Magnus. 2010. *The Restraint of Beasts*. London: Harper Perennial

Mitchell, David. 2002. *number9dream*. London: Sceptre

Mitchell, David. 2004. *Cloud Atlas*. London: Sceptre

Nabakov, Vladimir. 1960 [1955]. *Lolita*. London: Penguin

Nicholls, David. 2010. *One Day*. London: Hodder Paperbacks

Nietzsche, Friedrich. 2003 [1872]. *The Birth of Tragedy*. London: Penguin

Orlean, Susan. 2000. *The Orchid Thief*. London: Vintage

Ostrom, Elinor. 2003 [1990]. *Governing the Commons*. Cambridge: Cambridge University Press

Perec, Georges. 2008 [1969]. *A Void*. London: Vintage

Perec, Georges. 2008 [1978]. *Life: A User's Manual*. London: Vintage Classics

Plath, Sylvia. 2005 [1963]. *The Bell Jar*. London: Faber

Plato. 2003 [4th3rd century BCE]. *The Republic*. Tr. Desmond Lee. London: Penguin (first published in this translation: 1955)

Pound, Ezra. 1960 [1934]. *The ABC of Reading*. New York: New Directions

Propp, Vladimir. 2008 [1928]. *The Morphology of the Folktale*. Texas: University of Texas Press

Prose, Francine. 2007. *Reading Like a Writer*. New York: HarperCollins

Rivkin, Julie and Michael Ryan. 1998. *Literary Theory: An Anthology*. Oxford: Blackwell

Robinson, Marilynne. 2005 [1980]. *Housekeeping*. London: Faber

Rowling, J.K. 1997. *Harry Potter and the Philosopher's Stone*. London: Bloomsbury

Rowling, J.K. 1999. *Harry Potter and the Chamber of Secrets*. London: Bloomsbury

Roy, Arundhati. 2004. *The God of Small Things*. London: Harper Perennial

Saunders, George. 2000. *Pastoralia*. New York: Riverhead

Saunders, George. 2005. 'Paperback Writer'. *The Guardian*, 19 March 2005

Shakespeare, William. 2007. *The RSC Shakespeare: The Complete Works*. London: Palgrave Macmillan

Shelley, Mary. 2003 [1818]. *Frankenstein*. London: Penguin Classics

Shklovsky, Viktor. 1998 [1925]. *Theory of Prose*. Illinois: Dalkey Archive Press

Smith, Ali. 2006. *The Accidental*. London: Hamish Hamilton

Smith, Zadie. 2001. *White Teeth*. London: Penguin

Sophocles. 2003. *Oedipus Tyrannus*. Tr. Judith Affleck and Ian McAuslan. Cambridge: Cambridge University Press

Stanislavski, Constantin. 2008a [1936]. *An Actor Prepares*. New York: Routledge

Stanislavski, Constantin. 2008b [1949]. *Building a Character*. New York: Routledge

Stilson, Kenneth L., Charles McGaw and Larry Clark. 2011. *Acting is Believing*. Boston: Wadsworth

Stoker, Bram. 2004 [1897]. *Dracula*. London: Penguin Classics

Stoppard, Tom. 1968. *The Real Inspector Hound*. London: Samuel French

Symons, Sue. 2007. *One Man's Journey: The Bath Abbey Diptychs*. Hampshire: Eagle

Thackeray, William Makepeace. 2001 [1847]. *Vanity Fair*. Hertfordshire: Wordsworth Classics

Thomas, Scarlett. 1999 [1998]. *Dead Clever*. London: Hodder & Stoughton

Thomas, Scarlett. 1999. *In Your Face*. London: Hodder & Stoughton

Thomas, Scarlett. 1999. *Seaside*. London: Hodder & Stoughton

Thomas, Scarlett. 2001. *Bright Young Things*. London: Hodder & Stoughton

Thomas, Scarlett. 2002. *Going Out*. London: Fourth Estate

Thomas, Scarlett. 2004. *PopCo*. London: Fourth Estate

Thomas, Scarlett. 2007. *The End of Mr.Y*. Edinburgh: Canongate

Thomas, Scarlett. 2010. *Our Tragic Universe*. Edinburgh: Canongate

Tierno, Michael. 2002. *Aristotle's Poetics for Screenwriters*. New York: Hyperion

Todorov, Tzvetan. 1977. *The Poetics of Prose*. Ithaca: Cornell University Press

Tolkien, J.R.R. 2007 [1954]. *Lord of the Rings*. London: HarperCollins

Tolstoy, Leo. 2003 [1877]. *Anna Karenina*. Tr. Richard Pevear and Larissa Volokhonsky. London: Penguin Classics

Tomashevsky, Boris. 1965. 'Thematics' in Lemon, Lee T. and Marion J. Reis (ed., trans. and introduced), *Russian Formalist Criticism*. Lincoln: University of Nebraska Press

Truss, Lynne. 2005. *Eats, Shoots and Leaves*. London: Profile

Vonnegut, Kurt. 2008 [1969]. *Slaughterhouse-5*. London: Vintage Classics

Walker, Alice. 1989. *The Temple of My Familiar*. London: The Women's Press

Warner, Sylvia Townsend. 2000 [1927]. *Mr. Fortune's Maggot* London: Virago Modern Classics

Waugh, Patricia. 1984. *Metafiction*. London: Methuen

Welsh, Irvine. 1993. *Trainspotting*. London: Vintage

Winterson, Jeanette. 1995. *Oranges Are Not the Only Fruit*. London: Pandora

Wood, James. 2009. *How Fiction Works*. London: Vintage
Willans, Geoffrey and Ronald Searle. 2000. *The Complete Molesworth*. London: Penguin Modern Classics

FILM

10 Things I Hate AboutYou. 1999. Gil Junger (director); Touchstone Pictures, Mad Chance, et al (producer)

Adaptation. 2002. Spike Jonze (director); Beverley Detroit, et al (producer)

Cruel Intentions. 1999. Roger Kumble (director); Columbia Pictures (producer)

Dangerous Liaisons. 1988. Stephen Frears (director); Warner Bros Pictures, et al (producer)

E. T. 1982. Steven Spielberg (director); Universal Pictures, Amblin Entertainment, et al (producer)

Eraserhead. 1977. David Lynch (director); American Film Institute, Libra Films, et al (producer)

Eternal Sunshine of the Spotless Mind. 2004. Michel Gondry (director); Focus Features, Anonymous Content, et al (producer)

Gentlemen Prefer Blondes. 1953. Howard Hawks (director); 20th Century Fox (producer)

Get Over It. 2001. Tommy O'Haver (director); Miramax International, Ignite Entertainment, et al (producer)

High Society. 1956. Charles Walters (director); Metro-Goldwyn-Mayer (producer)

It Could Happen toYou. 1994. Andrew Bergman (director); TriStar Pictures (producer)

Lagaan: Once Upon a Time in India. 2001. Ashutosh Gowariker (director); Aamir Khan Productions (India) (producer)

Le Quattro Volte. 2010. Michelangelo Frammartino (director); Invisible Film, Ventura Film, et al (producer)

Lourdes. 2009. Jessica Hausner (director); ARTE, Canal+, et al (producer)

Memento. 2000. Christopher Nolan (director); Newmarket Capital Group, Team Todd, et al (producer)

One Hundred and One Dalmatians. 1961. Clyde Geronimi, Hamilton Luske, Wolfgang Reitherman (directors); Walt Disney Productions (producer)

Pulp Fiction. 1994. Quentin Tarantino (director); Miramax Films, et al (producer)

She's the Man. 2006. Andy Fickman (director); Dreamworks SKG, Lakeshore Entertainment, et al (producer)

Star Wars. 1977. George Lucas (director); Lucas Film, 20th Century Fox, et al (producer)

Taxi Driver. 1976. Martin Scorsese (director); Columbia Pictures, Bill/Phillips, et al (producer)

The Matrix. 1999. Andy Wachowski (director), Larry Wachowski (director); Warner Bros (producer)

The Straight Story. 1999. David Lynch (director); Asymmetrical Productions, Canal+, et al (producer)

The Truman Show. 1998. Peter Weir (director); Paramount Pictures (producer)

The Wizard of Oz. 1939. Victor Fleming, Mervyn LeRoy, King Vidor (directors); Metro-Goldwyn-Mayer (producer)

There's No Business Like Show Business. 1954. Walter Lang (director); 20th Century Fox (producer)

Toy Story. 1995. John Lasseter (director); Pixar Animation Studios (producer)

Withnail & I. 1987. Bruce Robinson (director); The Cannon Group (producer)

TELEVISION

At Home with the Braithwaites ITV: 2000–2003

Buffy the Vampire Slayer The Wb: 1997–2001 UPN: 2001–2003
Celebrity Big Brother Channel 4: 2000–2010
Columbo NBC: 1968–1978 ABC: 1989–2003
DIY SOS BBC: 1999–present
Frasier NBC: 1993–2004
Friends NBC: 1994–2004
Goodness Gracious Me BBC Two: 1998–2001
Home and Away Seven Network: 1987–present
Mad Men AMC: 2007–present
Sex and The City HBO: 1998–2004
Supernanny Channel 4: 2004–present
The Office BBC Two: 2001–2003
The Young Ones BBC Two: 1982–1984

RADIO

The Archers BBC Radio 4: 1951–present

VIDEOGAME

Final Fantasy VII Square: 1997

OTHER

Blaine, David. 2003. 'Above the Below' stunt. London.